Smart Growth and Climate Change

Smart Growth and Climate Change

Regional Development, Infrastructure and Adaptation

Edited by

Matthias Ruth

University of Maryland, College Park, Maryland, USA

Edward Elgar

Cheltenham, UK • Northampton, MA, USA

Published by
Edward Elgar Publishing Limited
Glensanda House
Montpellier Parade
Cheltenham
Glos GL50 1UA
UK

Edward Elgar Publishing, Inc.
136 West Street
Suite 202
Northampton
Massachusetts 01060
USA

A catalogue record for this book
is available from the British Library

ISBN-13: 978 1 84542 509 8
ISBN-10: 1 84542 509 X

Printed and bound in Great Britain by MPG Books Ltd, Bodmin, Cornwall

Contents

PART I: SMART GROWTH, CLIMATE ADAPTATION AND MITIGATION

PART II: STAKEHOLDER INVOLVEMENT: NEEDS, EXPERIENCES AND CHALLENGES

PART III: MODELING, INDICATOR DEVELOPMENT AND DECISION SUPPORT

PART IV: METHODS AND CASES

List of Figures

List of Tables

List of Contributors

Anthony Amato is an environmental analyst at Eastern Research Group (ERG) with more than six years of experience in the field of energy and environmental policy analysis. At ERG, Dr Amato's work focuses on renewable energy and energy efficiency issues. Dr Amato holds a masters in Energy and Environmental Analysis from the Center for Energy and Environmental Studies at Boston University and a PhD in Public Policy, with a specialization in energy policy, from the University of Maryland.

Steven J. Burian is currently an assistant professor of Civil and Environmental Engineering at the University of Utah, where he has taught courses in hydraulics, GIS and stormwater management and design since August 2003. He earned a BS degree in Civil Engineering from the University of Notre Dame in 1993, a MSE degree in Environmental Engineering in 1995 and his PhD in Civil Engineering in 1999 from the University of Alabama. Dr Burian's research involves the interdisciplinary study of hydrologic systems and fluid mechanics in the urban environment. Specific research focus areas include urbanization effect on the hydrologic cycle and climate, urban hydrology and stormwater management, modeling of urban water systems, urban terrain analysis and informatics, and urban water infrastructure history. Reporting on these various topics, Dr Burian has authored or co-authored more than 20 peer-reviewed publications and more than 50 conference papers and project reports. Dr Burian is a member of ASCE, AWRA, AGU, WEF, IAHS and ASEE.

Carolina V. Burnier is a PhD student in the Urban Studies and Planning Program at the University of Maryland. She has recently completed her masters degree in the Transportation Program at the University of Maryland's Department of Civil and Environmental Engineering. Her research focuses on the relationship between land use and travel behavior, with special interest in the policy implications of this topic. Before beginning her graduate studies, Ms Burnier worked as a transportation engineer for the Maryland State Highway Administration.

Kelly J. Clifton is an assistant professor in the Urban Studies and Planning Program and a research scholar in the National Center for Smart Growth Research and Education at the University of Maryland. Dr Clifton's research focuses on the influence of the built environment on travel choices, which include the following areas: the relationship between transportation and land use, planning for non-motorized transportation, and the mobility needs of low-income populations. She received her PhD from the University of Texas at Austin in Community and Regional Planning in 2001. She is a member of the Transportation Research Board Committee on Traveler Behavior and Values and the Travel Survey Methods Committee.

Brian Deal is a research professor of Urban and Regional Planning at the University of Illinois, the Director of the LEAM Modeling Systems Laboratory, and the Director of Research at UI's Robert Allerton Park. His current research includes the study of sustainability and urban land use transformation. Central to this research is the Land Use Evolution and impact Assessment Model (LEAM) Laboratory, an interdisciplinary laboratory dedicated to the study of the spatio-temporal dynamics of land use change and their social, economic and environmental consequences. The work has been supported by the National Science Foundation, the Department of Defense, and the States of Illinois and Missouri.

Paul R. Epstein, MD, MPH is Associate Director of the Center for Health and the Global Environment at Harvard Medical School and is a medical doctor trained in tropical public health. Dr Epstein has worked in medical, teaching and research capacities in Africa, Asia and Latin America and, in 1993, coordinated an eight-part series on Health and Climate Change for the British medical journal, *Lancet*. He has worked with the Intergovernmental Panel on Climate Change (IPCC), the National Academy of Sciences, the National Oceanic and Atmospheric Administration (NOAA) and the National Aeronautics and Space Administration (NASA) to assess the health impacts of climate change and develop health applications of climate forecasting and remote sensing. He is currently coordinating an international project *Climate Change Futures: Health, Ecological and Economic Dimensions*, in coordination with the Swiss Reinsurance Company and the United Nations Development Program. This project involves scientists, UN agencies, NGOs and corporate/financial sector leaders in the assessment of the new risks and opportunities presented by a changing climate.

Vicky E. Forgie is an ecological economist and focuses her research on the economic drivers of local economies to better understand the links between economic activity and the environment. Her research interests also encompass

New Zealand local government and public participation. Vicky teaches in the resource and environmental planning program at Massey University.

Nancy E. Golubiewski is a research ecologist at NZCEE. Her research interests center on anthropogenic perturbations of the environment, especially the ecological consequences of land use/land cover change. To address these issues, she works at multiple scales and uses a variety of approaches, incorporating field/laboratory measurements and analyses of satellite imagery.

Nigel A. Jollands is the Principal Ecological Economist at NZCEE. His career spans 13 years in the energy, resource management and environmental indicators fields. Nigel's particular interests are eco-efficiency analysis, sustainability indicator development and the policy-science interface. Past clients include APEC, the Taiwanese Government on sustainability indicators, Fonterra on Lifecycle Assessment, the Energy Efficiency and Conservation Authority and the Ministry for the Environment.

Paul Kirshen is a research professor in the Civil and Environmental Engineering Department and the Fletcher School of Law and Diplomacy, directs and co-chairs the Tufts interdisciplinary Water: Systems, Science, and Society (WSSS) research and graduate education program. He also serves on the Provost Interdisciplinary Programs Council and on the Tufts Mystic Watershed Collaborative. He conducts research in developed and developing countries on integrated water resources management, climate change impacts and adaptation, water resources operations, decision support systems, and hydrology, and teaches courses in water resources engineering, and planning/policy. He has produced numerous publications and presentations on these topics. Presently he is co-editing books on integrated impacts of climate change and transboundary waters. He joined Tufts in 1996 after many years in consulting. He received his ScB degree from Brown University and his MS and PhD degrees from the Massachusetts Institute of Technology.

Ai-Chen Lin is a masters candidate in Public Policy and expects to get her degree from the University of Maryland in May 2005. Her studies at UMD mainly focus on international security and economic policy.

Jerry McBeath holds BA and MA degrees in international relations from the University of Chicago, and a PhD in political science from the University of California, Berkeley. He is professor of political science at the University of Alaska Fairbanks, where he has taught since 1976. Dr McBeath's publications include books and articles on Alaska state and local government, the Alaska Constitution, Alaska Native politics, political development of circumpolar northern nations, rural Alaska education, the Chinese living abroad, the domestic politics and foreign relations of Taiwan and mainland China, and environmental politics.

Garry W. McDonald is Director of Market Economics Ltd and a research associate of NZCEE. Garry has particular research interests in urban metabolism, industrial ecology and integrated economic-environmental modeling. Garry's career spans 11 years as an economic consultant to government and private sector clients. Recent research projects include ecological footprinting of New Zealand regions and the construction of a physical input-output table for New Zealand.

Alexander A. Olsthoorn (Xander) – a chemical engineer by training – is a senior research fellow with the Institute for Environmental Studies of the Vrije Universiteit Amsterdam. His research interests vary from air quality impact assessment, technical change and environment, to the origins and impacts of climate change, all in the context of policy analysis. He was co-editor of 'Climate, change and risk' (Routledge 1999) and of 'Sciences for industrial transformation: views from different disciplines' (Kluwer 2005).

Murray G. Patterson is Director of the New Zealand Center for Ecological Economics at Massey University. He is widely published in a number of fields including ecological economics, energy analysis, environmental valuation, environmental policy and policy modeling. Much of this research is of an applied and interdisciplinary nature, working at the interface of policy and sustainability concerns. In recent years he has lectured in the resource and environmental planning program at Massey University in policy analysis and evaluation.

Fang Rong is a PhD student in the School of Public Policy at the University of Maryland with a major in Environmental Policy. Her current research interests focus on integrated studies on energy consumption and urban land use. She holds a masters degree in Management Science and Engineering from Tsinghua University, Beijing, China.

Jan Rotmans is one of the founders of Integrated Assessment (IA), and has outstanding experience in IA modeling, scenario-building, uncertainty management and transition management. During the past twenty years he has led a diversity of innovative projects in the field of climate change, global change, sustainable development and transitions and system innovations. From 1992 to 2004 he held a professorship on 'Integrated Assessment' at Maastricht University in the Netherlands. He is founder and Director of the

International Center for Integrative Studies (ICIS) (1998) at Maastricht University. He has been a full professor in Transitions and Transition Management at Erasmus University Rotterdam in the Netherlands since 2004, where he founded the DRIFT-institute: Dutch Research Institute For Transitions. He is vice-chairman of the European Forum on Integrated Environmental Assessment (EFIEA), vice-president of The Integrated Assessment Society (TIAS), and founder and Director of the Dutch Knowledge Network on System Innovations: Transitions towards a sustainable society (KSI), which received a 10 million euro grant in 2004 for interdisciplinary research into transitions and system innovations.

Matthias Ruth is Roy F. Weston Chair in Natural Economics, professor and Director of the Environmental Policy Program at the School of Public Policy, and Co-Director of the Engineering and Public Policy Program at the University of Maryland. His research focuses on dynamic modeling of natural resource use, industrial and infrastructure systems analysis, and environmental economics and policy. His theoretical work heavily draws on concepts from engineering, economics and ecology, while his applied research utilizes methods of non-linear dynamic modeling as well as adaptive and anticipatory management. In the last decade, Professor Ruth has published six books and over 100 papers and book chapters in the scientific literature. He collaborates extensively with scientists and policy makers in the US, Canada, Europe, Asia and Africa.

Brian Stone, Jr is an assistant professor in the City and Regional Planning Program at the Georgia Institute of Technology, where he teaches in the areas of land use, transportation, and environmental planning. His research program is focused on the spatial determinants of a range of urban environmental issues, including air quality, climate change, and stormwater management. Stone holds a master of Environmental Management degree from Duke University and a PhD in Urban Planning from the Georgia Institute of Technology.

Zhanli Sun is a post-doctoral research associate in the Department of Urban and Regional Planning at the University of Illinois at Urbana-Champaign. He receoved his PhD (Geographic Information System and Cartography) from Institute of Geography, Chinese Academy of Sciences in 1999. He has broad research interests in spatial information theory and technology, including spatial modeling, spatial data handling and system development. He has recently focused his research interests upon the Decision Support System (DSS) for urban planning by employing the System Dynamic (DS) concept and Cellular Automata.

Richard S.J. Tol is the Michael Otto Professor of Sustainability and Global Change at the Center for Marine and Climate Research, Hamburg University; a Principal Researcher at the Institute for Environmental Studies, Vrije Universiteit, Amsterdam; and an Adjunct Professor at the Center for Integrated Study of the Human Dimensions of Global Change, Carnegie Mellon University, Pittsburgh. An economist and statistician, his work focuses on climate change, particularly detection and attribution, impact and adaptation, integrated assessment modeling, and decision and policy analysis. He is an editor of *Energy Economics* and *Environmental and Resource Economics*.

Nicolien M. van der Grijp is a senior researcher at the Institute for Environmental Studies of the Vrije Universiteit in Amsterdam. Her research interests are related to Dutch environmental law and policy, the implementation of European environmental policy and international environmental agreements. In her present work, she focuses on global legal pluralism, and more specifically on public and private mechanisms that influence environmental and social performance within international product chains.

Peter E. van der Werff is an anthropologist who has specialized in the fields of environmental management, poverty and development since 1977. He is with the Institute for Environmental Studies of the Vrije Universiteit Amsterdam and conducts scientific and applied research among different groups of stakeholders. He facilitates the local application of interactive stakeholder methodologies to reinforce project cycles, using future scenario structuring, multi-criteria analysis and cost-benefit accounting. He has long experience in liaison with donor agencies, local governments, and non-governmental organisations and civil society, as well as scientific counterparts.

Thomas J. Wilbanks is a Corporate Research Fellow at the Oak Ridge National Laboratory and leads the Laboratory's Global Change and Developing Country Programs. He conducts research and publishes extensively on such issues as sustainable development, energy and environmental policy, responses to global climate change, and the role of geographical scale in all of these regards. He has recently played roles in the first US National Assessment of Possible Consequences of Climate Variability and Change (1997–2000); a four-year Association of American Geographers project on Global Change in Local Places, 1996–2000; the IPCC Working Group II (Impacts, Adaptation, and Vulnerability) Third Assessment Report; and aspects of the UNEP et al. Millennium Ecosystem Assessment related to issues of geographic scale. He is also a Coordinating Lead Author for the IPCC's Fourth Assessment Report Working Group II chapter on 'industry, settlement, and society.' He is a member of the Board on Earth Sciences and Resources of the US National Research Council (NRC), Chair of NRC's Committee on Human Dimensions of Global Change, and member of NRC's Panel on Public Participation in Environmental Assessment and Decision making.

Mick Womersley, originally from Sheffield, England, has been studying and teaching ecology and economics in the US since 1989. He earned his MS degree in resource conservation from the University of Montana Forestry School and his PhD from the University of Maryland School of Public Affairs. Now a professor at Unity College, Mick teaches courses on human ecology, resource and land use planning, geography, and the politics and ethics of environmental policy. In addition, he is the Chair of the Unity College Campus Sustainability Committee, a group formed to discuss on-campus issues of ecological sustainability.

List of Acronyms

AAG	Association of American Geographers
ACIA	Arctic Climate Impact Assessment
ADFG	Alaska Department of Fish and Game
AFN	Alaska Federation of Natives
ANCSA	Alaska Native Claims Settlement Act
ANILCA	Alaska National Interest Conservation Act
ANWR	Arctic National Wildlife Refuge
APA	American Planning Association
APHIS	Animal and Plant Health Inspection Service
APSC	Alyeska Pipeline Service Company
AQI	Air quality index
ARCO	Atlantic Richfield Corporation
ASCE	American Society of Civil Engineers
BLM	Bureau of Land Management
BLS	Bureau of Labor Statistics
BP	British Petroleum
BTS	Bureau of Transportation Statistics
CA	Cellular Automata
CCN	Closed condensation nuclei
CDD	Cooling degree-days
CFCs	Chlorofluorocarbons
CLIMB	Climate's Long-term Impacts on Metro Boston
CMSA	Consolidated Metropolitan Statistical Area
COG	Citizens oversight group
CSO	Combined sewer overflow
CUSAT	Cochin University for Science and Technology
DEIS	Draft Environmental Impact Statement
DNR	Department of Natural Resources
DOD	Department of Defense
DOE	Department of Energy
DOT	Department of Transportation
DR&R	Dismantling, removal and restoration
DRIFT	Dutch Research Institute For Transitions
DSS	Decision Support System

EFIEA	European Forum on Integrated Environmental Assessment
EIS	Environmental Impact Statement
EIS	Energy Information Administration
EMS	Earthquake Monitoring Systems
ENSO	El Niño-Southern Oscillation
EPA	Environmental Protection Agency
ERG	Eastern Research Group
EU	European Union
FEIS	Final Environmental Impact Statement
FEMA	Federal Emergency Management Agency
GCLP	Global Change in Local Places
GCM	Global circulation model
GDP	Gross Domestic Product
GEA	Global Environmental Assessment
GHGs	Greenhouse gases
GIS	Geographic Information System
GPI	Genuine Progress Indicator
GUI	Graphic User Interface
HADCM2	Hadley Center Climate Model
HDD	Heating degree-days
HUD	Department of Housing and Urban Development
IA	Integrated Assessment
ICIS	International Center for Integrative Studies
ICT	Information and Communication Technology
IFRC	International Federation of Red Cross
IHDP	International Human Dimensions Program on Global Environmental Change
IPCC	Intergovernmental Panel on Climate Change
IPO	The Association of Provinces
IRA	Indian Reorganization Act
IRC	International Rhine Committee
ISTEA	Intermodal Surface Transportation Efficiency Act
ITE	Institute of Transportation Engineers
JPO	Joint Pipeline Office
KSI	Dutch Knowledge Network on System Innovations
LBNL	Lawrence Berkeley National Labortory
LEAM	Landuse Evolution and impact Assessment Model
LID	Low-impact development
LNV	Ministry of Agriculture, Nature Management and Fisheries (the Netherlands)
LUC	Landuse change
LUTRAQ	Land Use, Transportation and Air Quality
MALPF	Maryland Agricultral Land Preservation Foundation

MAPC	Metropolitan Area Planning Council
MDP	Maryland Department of Planning
MET	Maryland Environmental Trust
MHW	Maatgevend HoogWater
MPO	Metropolitan planning organization
MWCOG	Metropolitan Washington Council of Governments
NAAQs	National Ambient Air Quality Standards
NACC	National Assessment of Possible Consequences of Climate Variability and Change
NAO	North Atlantic Oscillation
NAS	National Academy of Sciences
NASA	National Aeronautics and Space Administration
NCDC	National Climate Data Center
NCEDR	National Center for Environmental Decision making Research
NCSG	National Center for Smart Growth Research and Education
NEPA	National Environmental Policy Act
NGO	Non-governmental organization
NIMBY	Not-in-my-backyard
NIWAR	National Institutue of Water and Atmospheric Research
NLCD	National Land Cover Dataset
NMA	Dutch anti-trust authority
NMP4	Fourth National Environmental Policy plan of the Netherlands
NOAA	National Oceanic and Atmospheric Administration
NPR-A	National Petroleum Reserve-Alaska
NRC	National Research Council
NRDC	National Resources Defence Council
NW3	Third Strategic Water Policy Plan
NW4	Fourth Strategic Water Policy Plan
NWS	National Weather Service
NZCEE	New Zealand Center for Ecological Economics
OCS	Outer-Continental Shelf
OMIRD	Office of the Minister for Industry and Regional Development
ORNL	Oak Ridge National Laboratory
PAN	Peroxyacetyl nitrate
PDF	Purchase of Development Rights
PM	Particulate matter
PR	Precipitation Radar
PSDI	Palmer Severity Drought Index
PSS	Planning support system
RCAC	Regional Citizens Advisory Council
RCM	Reliability-centered maintenance
RCS	Red Crescent Societies
RLG	Raad voor het Landelijk Gebied

ROW	Right-of-way
RS	Remote sensing
SCS	Soil Conservation Service
SERVS	Ship Escort/Response Vessel System
SIP	State Implementation Plan
SIRCH	Societal and Institutional Responses to Climate Change and Climatic Hazards
SLE	St Louis encephalitis
SME	Spatial Modeling Environment
SPC	State pipeline coordinator
SST	Sea surface temperature
SWMM	Storm Water Management Model
TAPAA	Trans-Alaska Pipeline Authorization Act
TAPS	Trans-Alaska Pipeline System
TAW	Technical Advisory Committee for Water (*Technische Adviescommissie Water*)
TCPA	Town and Country Planning Act
TDR	Transfer of Development Rights
TEA-21	Transportation Efficiency Act for the twenty-first Century
TIAS	The Integrated Assessment Society
TMINs	Minimum temperatures
TOD	Transit-oriented development
TRMM	Tropical Rainfall Measuring Mission
UA	Urban area
UCR	Upwind control region
UHI	Urban Heat Island
UIR	Urban-impacted region
UNDP	United Nations Development Program
UNEP	United Nations Environment Program
USAID	United States Agency for International Development
USFS	United States Forest Service
USFWS	United States Fish and Wildlife Service
USGCRP	US Global Change Research Program
USGS	United States Geological Survey
UTPS	Urban Transportation Planning System
UvW	Association of Water Boards (the Netherlands)
V&W	Ministry of Transport, Public Works and Water Management (the Netherlands)
VMT	Vehicle Miles Traveled
VNG	The Association of Dutch Municipalities
VOCs	Volatile organic compounds
VROM	Ministry of Housing, Spatial Planning and the Environment (the Netherlands)

VSM	Vertical support member
WMO	World Meteorological Organization
WNV	West Nile Virus
WSSS	Water: Systems, Science, and Society

Acknowledgement

This volume is the product of truly collaborative efforts by its many contributors, their colleagues and friends. Special recognition goes to Dana Coelho at the University of Maryland's School of Public Policy for her expediency in bringing the various chapters into shape, and Tara Gorvine at Edward Elgar's Massachusetts office, who kept her keen eye on both the big picture and fine details. Last but not least, my personal thanks and appreciation go to my wife, Rachel Franklin, for her love and patience throughout the years.

PART I

Smart Growth, Climate Adaptation and
Mitigation

1 Introduction

Matthias Ruth

MERGING RESEARCH AGENDAS

This book brings together two strands of applied research that to date have been carried out separately–so-called 'smart growth' research, and research into adaptation to climate variability and change. Both entail similar concerns, draw on complementary modeling tools and are concerned with bridging the gaps that may exist among science and engineering, stakeholder interests and policy implementation. This book strives to bridge that gap, create synergies between the two research strands, reconcile differences and provide insights for decision makers at national and local scales.

Smart growth research focuses on changes in land use and transportation in order to improve the quality of life of local populations within the broader contexts of social, economic and environmental change (United Nations Development Programme 2001). From this research are emerging planning and policy tools as well as recommendations to guide decisions on infrastructure systems and services. Smart growth researchers and practitioners frequently make reference to the larger environmental benefits that individual investment and policy decisions may bring (Ausubel 1988). For example, changes in land use that lead to reduced demand for automobile transportation not only improve (*ceteribus paribus*) land values, housing prices, noise conditions and public health, but also lead to reductions of harmful emissions into the atmosphere. As a consequence, smart growth at the local scale can make valuable contributions to environmental conditions at regional and global scales.

The second strand of research has traditionally concerned itself with global environmental challenges, most notably global climate change (IPCC 2001). To date, much of this research has tried to identify investment and policy decisions that reduce carbon emissions or increase carbon sequestration in order to stabilize climate. Collectively, such strategies are referred to as mitigation strategies. Information about global processes has been used to offer general guidelines for mitigation action at national scales. Only recently

3

has the field moved on to identify specific local mitigation strategies, and only a few researchers have begun to explore strategies that promote adaptation to climate change–the necessary steps that must be taken to prepare for more frequent occurrence of severe weather events (droughts, ice storms, tornadoes, downpours and so on), as well as overall hotter summers and warmer winters, that will inevitably arise over the next century even if mitigation is carried out to its fullest possible extent (Ruth and Kirshen 2001). Various scenarios suggest that climate change will imperil existing energy and water infrastructure systems. More severe thunderstorms may down power lines or overwhelm combined sewer overflows (CSOs). Research on local adaptation responses to climate change is identifying how existing systems can be changed to reduce vulnerabilities. Furthermore, electricity systems may be decentralized (as through the use of combined heat and power or 'green energy' from solar cells or small- to medium-scale wind farms) instead of being based on large-scale power generation that requires long distance transmission and distribution. Similarly, development of local infiltration systems and wetlands may deal with water runoff instead of the ever more sophisticated, large-scale water treatment and supply systems.

Many of the strategies for smart growth are perfectly consistent with strategies to adapt to a variable and changing climate, but some are not. For example, decentralizing energy supply to the point where individual households generate their own electricity or, through a sophisticated system of collection, purification and conservation, no longer require access to public water systems, may make them able to locate anywhere. Dispersed development may increase transportation demand and otherwise undermine smart growth goals.

OBJECTIVES AND STRUCTURE OF THIS BOOK

This book provides the first systematic merger of regional development and smart growth with climate adaptation research. The following chapter–divided into three main sections–addresses the key issues in climate change and smart growth research. Authors Matthias Ruth and Fang Rong give special attention to the overlap of research in the two areas and the implications for water use, energy use, transportation and urban heat island effects, as well as the health of species. All of these issues are themes of later chapters where authors of different backgrounds share research on smart growth, regional development and infrastructure impacts and adaptation in light of climate change.

The third chapter in Part I concentrates on the American experience of smart growth policies, their misconceptions and shortcomings. Mick Womersley argues that efforts to reduce greenhouse gas emissions and improve environmental quality through smart growth have largely been overwhelmed by regional economic growth, expansion of transportation infrastructure and increased affluence and consumption.

In the fourth and final chapter of Part I, Murray Patterson and colleagues present a regional analysis of development and sustainability issues in New Zealand, where conflicts between agricultural resource use, regional development and ecosystem health are escalating in response to development pressures on the fringes of urban areas and potential climate impacts on increasingly stressed ecosystems and infrastructures. Chapter 4 presents results from dynamic input-output models that connect regional economic activity with environmental impacts for business-as-usual and climate change scenarios.

Part II addresses stakeholder involvement in the context of regional and climate change investment and policy making. In Chapter 5 Thomas Wilbanks presents a detailed discussion of the need to involve stakeholders in the research and decision making, the challenges encountered when involving stakeholders, and the lessons that have been learned so far from the limited stakeholder-based climate impact and adaptation research at the regional scale. From these lessons, the chapter develops guidelines to help improve future stakeholder-based research and action.

Chapter 6 adds a case study component to the discussion of stakeholder involvement. Jerry McBeath illustrates several of the key points and lessons for oil transportation infrastructure development in Alaska. Federal, state and local interests and conflicts coalesce and intersect in many ways with the interests and rights of indigenous peoples, raising a host of strategic resource development and global climate change issues. Not only does oil provide the major source of income for the state of Alaska, but its use contributes to climate change, which in turn feeds back to affect the security of the oil pipeline infrastructure system–through thawing of permafrost and impacts on pipes. The Alaskan case study is a rich experiment in stakeholder-based conflict resolution, spanning the spectrum of local, regional and global ramifications, and simultaneously affecting ecosystems and people in remote Alaskan communities as well as the rural, suburban and urban communities in the continental United States.

The issue of stakeholder involvement is taken up again in Part III, where, in Chapter 7, Jan Rotmans argues for the need to address social, economic, institutional and environmental change from a complex systems perspective, developing and using sophisticated modeling and planning tools to address the agendas of stakeholders and to promote the sustainability of cities. In the remainder of Part III Brian Deal and Zhanli Sun provide an example of such a modeling tool, which combines Geographic Information Systems (GIS) and Remote Sensing capabilities in a dynamic modeling context. Their modeling tool is illustrated for the North American metropolitan area of St Louis,

Missouri, paying specific attention to the fact that the urban area and its environmental systems are part of regional and global networks.

Part IV, 'Methods and Cases,' turns to the analysis of specific environmental challenges faced by urban areas. In Chapter 9, Steven Burian addresses the interplay of global climate change with more localized changes in urban temperature and water regimes. His chapter provides additional evidence that urban-induced rainfall modifications are real and that they will need to be addressed in planning and policy to avoid or reduce adverse impacts on stormwater drainage systems. The insights are illustrated with a case study analysis of drainage designs, design techniques and rainfall information specific to Houston, Texas, located in the southwestern US.

While Chapter 9 concentrates on meteorological, biophysical and engineering issues surrounding urban rainfall and drainage, the next chapter, co-authored by Nicolien M. van der Grijp and colleagues, addresses the institutional changes that have occurred to advance flood risk management in the Netherlands. Here, as before, the need to include stakeholders in the assessment and management process is highlighted and the need is emphasized for institutional structures to continuously evolve in order to effectively manage the complex environmental, social, economic and technological interactions that govern flood risk in urban areas.

In Chapter 11 Kelly Clifton and Carolina V. Burnier return to the connections among local land use, transportation and emissions already alluded to in Part I. The results of empirical investigations discussed in the chapter suggest that the ability of land use strategies to curb automobile travel is mixed. Based on these findings alone, the use of smart growth strategies as a means to abate vehicular emissions and improve air quality does not seem promising. However, Clifton and Burnier make the case that for smart growth strategies to reach their full potential, they must be applied in a comprehensive, regional context and allowed to promote change across the entire continuum of a metropolitan area–a condition rarely met in current analyses and policy approaches.

Fossil fuel combustion in automobiles and electricity generation are among the chief anthropogenic contributors of greenhouse gas emissions. While much of the past research attempted to quantify the impacts on these emissions on climate, little research has been carried out on the potential climate impacts on fuel use. In Chapter 12, Matthias Ruth and Ai-Chen Lin describe a methodology used to assess potential impacts of climate variability and change on regional energy consumption in the residential and commercial sectors. They illustrate their methodology with an empirical application in the State of Maryland, US, draw conclusions for investment and policy and place their findings into the context of other regional and national assessments of climate-induced changes in energy demand.

The themes of global climate-induced changes in urban temperature regimes, urban form, transportation and energy demand, which were the focus of the preceding three chapters, are taken up by Brian Stone's treatment of urban heat island effects in Chapter 13. His discussion focuses on the causes and processes of urban heat islands, their potential impacts for public health, as well as planning and management strategies that may help reduce adverse effects.

Chapter 14 focuses on the topic of health impacts of climate change, where first Paul Epstein presents a review of the current literature about the relationships between climate change and health–ranging from direct temperature-related effects on cold- and heat-related morbidity and mortality to indirect effects associated with changes in air quality or the spread of water-, vector- and food-borne diseases. On the basis of his review, Epstein points towards a set of systems-based management approaches that can help reduce vulnerabilities. In the final chapter of Part IV, Matthias Ruth and colleagues present a case study of temperature-related mortality in metropolitan Boston, US. Their findings suggest that the declines in temperature-related mortality in the region may persist if current trends in health care improvements, early warning systems and proliferation of air conditioning in the region can be sustained. However, these trends may experience decreasing returns over the simulated time frame and thus the results presented represent best-case scenarios. The authors argue that to sustain declining temperature-related mortality will require increasingly aggressive proliferation of health monitoring, warning and service technologies as well as adaptive management of urban space.

The book closes in Chapter 16 with a brief summary of the synergies and conflicts that may exist between smart growth research and policies on the one hand, and climate change research, mitigation and adaptation strategies at the regional level on the other. Chapter 16 draws on the insights generated by the reviews, methods, tools and case studies presented by the contributors from Europe, North America and Australasia, and points towards further research on the smart growth and climate change nexus.

REFERENCES

Ausubel, J.H. and R. Herman (eds) (1988), *Cities and their Vital Systems: Infrastructure–Past, Present and Future*, Washington, DC: National Academy Press.

IPCC (2001), *Third Assessment Report, Climate Change 2001*, Intergovernmental Panel on Climate Change, Cambridge: Cambridge University Press.

Ruth, M. and P. Kirshen (2001), 'Integrated Impacts of Climate Change upon Infrastructure Systems and Services in the Boston Metropolitan Area', *World Resources Review*, **13**(1): 106–122.

United Nations Development Programme (2001), *Human Development Report*, Oxford: Oxford University Press.

2 Research Themes and Challenges

Matthias Ruth and Fang Rong

INTRODUCTION

This chapter brings together two strands of applied research that to date have been carried out separately, yet each has generated mutually relevant insights into environmental planning and management. One of these is research into urban development and smart growth, which focuses on changes in land use and transportation in order to improve the quality of life of local populations within the broader context of social, economic and environmental change (UNDP 2001). The second strand of research has traditionally concerned itself with global environmental challenges, most notably global climate change (IPCC 2001). To date, much of this research has tried to identify investment and policy decisions that reduce carbon emissions or increase carbon sequestration in order to stabilize climate. Only recently has adaptation to climate change received notable attention, and little of that attention, in turn, has been given to the vulnerabilities of urban areas and the adaptation strategies that may be employed. While the urban development and smart growth debate has pointed to strategies at the local level that may be beneficial at larger regional or global scales, climate change research is moving from identification of global processes to the identification of responses at local scales.

By reviewing the literature on urban development and smart growth on the one hand, and climate change on the other, this chapter provides a starting point for explorations into the overlap of the two. Specifically, we explore strategies suggested by each field of research to address urban sprawl and climate impacts respectively, and identify synergies and conflicts that exist among these strategies.

The following two sections provide brief primers on climate change and urban development, as well as associated response strategies. The next discusses urban infrastructure needs, vulnerabilities and dynamics, and provides the background against which urban development, smart growth, and climate mitigation and adaptation strategies may be judged. The remaining sections provide specific insights into the planning and management of water, transportation, energy, urban heat islands, and the health of humans and other species. The chapter closes with a set of challenges for research, education and decision making.

CLIMATE CHANGE AND URBAN AREAS

A Primer on Climate Change

Earth's climate is regulated, in part, by the presence of gases and particles in the atmosphere which are penetrated by short-wave radiation from the sun and which trap the longer wave radiation that is reflecting back from Earth. Collectively, those gases are referred to as greenhouse gases (GHGs) because they can trap radiation on Earth in a manner analogous to that of the glass of a greenhouse and have a warming effect on the globe. The main GHG is water, which affects the overall energy budget of the globe and–working like a steam heating system–funnels energy through the hydrological cycle across regions. Among the other most notable GHGs are carbon dioxide (CO_2), methane (CH_4), nitrous oxide (N_2O) and chlorofluorocarbons (CFCs). Their sources include fossil fuel combustion, agriculture (for example, the releasing of carbon from soils or methane from rice paddies and livestock) and industrial processes.

Each GHG has a different atmospheric concentration, mean residence time in the atmosphere, and different chemical and physical properties. As a consequence, each GHG has a different ability to upset the balance between incoming solar radiation and outgoing long-wave radiation. This ability to influence Earth's radiative budget is known as climate forcing. While some constituents of the atmosphere tend to reflect outgoing radiation back to Earth, the presence of aerosols in the atmosphere–released, for example, from coal-burning power plants–leads to reflection of incoming radiation and thus has a cooling effect that may partly offset the warming effect of greenhouse gases (Wigley 1999).

Climate forcing varies across chemical species in the atmosphere. Spatial patterns of radiative forcing are relatively uniform for CO_2, CH_4, N_2O and CFCs because these gases are relatively long-lived and as a consequence become more evenly distributed in the atmosphere. In contrast, patterns of spatial radiative forcing of short-lived constituents, such as aerosols and ozone, are closely aligned with their sources of emissions (Wigley 1999).

Steep increases in atmospheric GHG and aerosol concentrations have occurred since the industrial revolution. Those increases are unprecedented in Earth's history. As a result of higher GHG concentrations, global average surface temperature has risen by about 0.6°C over the twntieth century, with the 1990s as likely the warmest decade and 1998 likely the warmest year in the instrumental record since 1861 (IPCC 2001). These average global changes mask larger regional variations. For example, higher latitudes have warmed more than the equatorial regions (OSTP 1997).

A change in average temperatures may serve as a useful indicator of changes in climate, but it is only one of many ramifications of higher GHG concentrations. Since disruption of Earth's energy balance is neither seasonally nor geographically uniform, effects of climate disruption vary across space as well as time. For example, there has been a widespread retreat of mountain glaciers during the twentieth century. Scientific evidence also suggests that there has been a 40 percent decrease in Arctic sea ice thickness during late summer to early autumn in recent decades and considerably slower decline in winter sea ice thickness. The extent of Northern Hemisphere spring and summer ice sheets has decreased by about 10 to 15 per cent since the 1950s (IPCC 2001).

The net loss of snow and ice cover, combined with an increase in ocean temperatures and thermal expansion of the water mass in oceans, has resulted in a rise of global average sea level between 0.1 and 0.2 meters during the twentieth century, which is considerably higher than the average rate during the last several millennia (Barnett 1984; Douglas 2001; IPCC 2001). However, the rate and extent of sea level rise vary across the globe, with some areas losing heights relative to the sea, such as England and western France; others, such as Scandinavia and Scotland, are emerging (Doornkamp 1998). In some cases anthropogenic land subsidence–from mining, natural gas or groundwater extraction–significantly speeds up the potential effects of climate change-induced relative sea level rise (Gambolati, et al. 1999).

Changes in heat fluxes through the atmosphere and oceans, combined with changes in reflectivity of the earth's surface and an altered composition of GHGs and particulates in the atmosphere, may result in altered frequency and severity of climate extremes around the globe (Easterling, et al. 2000; Mehl, et al. 2000). For example, it is likely that there has been a 2 to 4 per cent increase in the frequency of heavy precipitation events in the mid and high latitudes of the Northern Hemisphere over the latter half of the twentieth century, while in some regions, such as Asia and Africa, the frequency and intensity of droughts have increased in recent decades (IPCC 2001). Furthermore, the timing and magnitude of snowfall and snowmelt may be significantly affected (Frederick and Gleick 1999), influencing among other things, erosion, water quality and agricultural productivity. And since evaporation increases exponentially with water temperature, global climate change-induced sea surface temperature increases are likely to result in increased frequency and intensity of hurricanes and increased size of the regions affected.

Large-scale efforts are under way to explore the complex causal relationships between human activities and climate change, to put the various pieces of the climate change puzzle together on computers, and to explore likely future climate conditions under alternative assumptions about biogeochemical mechanisms and human activities (IPCC 2001). A range of projections has emerged from these computer models which indicate that global averaged surface temperature is likely to increase by 1.4 to 5.8°C between 1990 and 2100, making the projected rate of warming much greater than the observed changes during the twentieth century and very likely larger than rates of warming for at least the last 10 000 years, as indicated by data derived from the paleoclimate record (Wigley 1999; IPCC 2001). Relative to any fixed threshold, the frequency of daily, seasonal and annual warm temperature extremes will likely increase and the frequency of daily, seasonal and annual cold temperature extremes will likely decrease. As in the recent past, changes in temperature could be accompanied by larger year-to-year variations in precipitation, regionally distinct rates of snow and ice cover changes, and changes in sea level (Klein and Nicholls 1999; IPCC 2001).

Climate change models increasingly show climate responses that are consistent across differently specified models, and with recent observations. These models, combined with long-term historical analyses and field experiments, indicate that humanity has indeed embarked on a real-world climate change experiment of monumental proportions. Although increasingly sophisticated, the climate models on which predictions are based continue to suffer from uncertainties in many underlying biogeochemical processes and our fundamental inability to adequately anticipate future human responses to climate change. Moreover, the models' specifications make it difficult to reflect potential discontinuities of climate processes and instead often portray only gradual changes (Schelling 1992; Kay and Schneider 1994). Examples of discontinuities include rapid changes in the direction of ocean currents that funnel significant amounts of energy among continents and fundamentally affect regional temperature, sea levels and precipitation patterns. A gradual increase in temperature may result in local climate conditions that are unfavorable to some local species, triggering a change in species composition. Changes in species composition may affect diverse ecosystem features such as soil properties, pollination of fruit trees and crop species, local food supply and livelihoods, water regimes and the spread of disease. It also may trigger changes in society and the economy. Since climate change is expected to continue and many thresholds have not yet been reached, current and future generations must expect difficult surprises.

If unprecedented climate changes occur, how vulnerable will humans–their societies, economies and infrastructures–be? We will turn to this question below after briefly reviewing recent research into, and practices of, smart growth strategies for urban and suburban areas, as well as outlining a set of general responses to climate change.

A Primer on Urban Development and Smart Growth Research

Economic development is frequently accompanied by increased urbanization. Yet, recent trends in now industrialized countries show a reversal of the historic pattern–people and jobs are leaving denser inner-city cores in favor of outlying areas. These trends are perhaps most pronounced in the United States where, in 1950, 84 million people lived in 168 metropolitan areas, 60 per cent of which lived within city centers. By 1990, the population in the same metropolitan areas had nearly doubled, while the proportion of those living in the center of the cities fell to about one-third their original size (Rusk 1998).

The new land use pattern of 'sprawl development' has been facilitated by many interrelated factors, such as significantly cheaper land and construction costs outside the city, lower property taxes and increasing job opportunities in the suburbs (Snyder and Bird 1998). Although sprawl is difficult to define and quantify (Klysik and Fortuniak 1999; Talen 2002), it is usually expressed by proliferation of single-family houses; significant spatial separation of places in which people live, work, shop and engage in leisure activities; elaborate road networks to serve auto and truck travel; shopping malls, office parks, arterial commercial strips, and residential subdivisions (Daniels 2001).

Though sprawl is associated with lower population densities and is perceived to separate newly developing communities from issues of poverty, crime and other 'societal ills' that afflict inner cities, sprawl has its own costs (Snyder and Bird 1998). Not only are changes in the quality of life outside the city closely related to urban issues, which may ripple back to affect suburban and exurban life, but sprawl may also accelerate the loss of natural areas and farmlands, require greater reliance on vehicles, lead to higher resource consumption (Cobb 1998), and necessitate greater infrastructure and service costs (Longman 1998; Anderson and Santore 2002; Burchell, et al. 2002).

Case studies comparing infrastructure requirements for sprawl with compact infill development consistently point towards significant cost savings associated with the latter (see, for example, Bragado, et al. 1995). Since these costs typically are borne by society at large while benefits are not, sprawl can affect different segments of the population differently. For example, higher costs for the collection and treatment of wastewater from sprawling communities may require increased fees charged to all households in a region. As a consequence, customers in denser neighborhoods (usually lower income households) are continuing to subsidize customers (usually higher income households) living in less dense areas (Pendall, et al. 2002).

Recognition of sprawl's growing social, environmental and economic cost has led to calls for smart growth strategies. Such strategies may involve one or more of the following: placing limits on the outward extensions of further growth (Alexander and Tomalty 2002; ITE 2003); reducing dependence on private automotive vehicles, especially single-occupancy automotive travels (Straka 2002); increasing reliance on locally available renewable energy resources such as solar, wind, geothermal and tidal (Benfield, et al. 2002); promoting compact, mixed-used development; creating more affordable housing in outlying new growth areas (Bucher 2002); redeveloping inner-city areas and infill areas (Calthorpe and Fulton 2001); removing barriers to urban design innovation in both cities and new suburban areas by encouraging pedestrian-friendly communities, mixed land uses, town centers and other design elements (Snyder and Bird 1998; Rosenberg 2003); and using market-based strategies, such as impact fees, to stifle inefficient developments (Tregoning, et al. 2002).

In the US, smart growth has received heightened attention since the mid-1990s when, under the auspices of the US Environmental Protection Agency (EPA), hundreds of individuals and organizations explored how to promote smart growth strategies among local officials, planners, developers, preservationists, environmentalists and others (Pelley 1999). Nationwide, more than 17 states have completed or begun rethinking and redefining their smart growth planning models (Maryland Department of Planning 1997). The State of Maryland, for example, passed the Neighborhood Conservation and Smart Growth Act in 1997. The Act turns to fiscal policy and incentives, rather than land use regulations, to direct growth. It identifies priority growth areas both within and adjacent to existing settlements. A residential or commercial development to be built outside of the priority growth areas would not receive state funding for infrastructure. Income tax credits are also offered to business owners who create at least 25 jobs in these areas (Johnson 1999). In 1998, Maryland's Governor Glendening issued an executive order called the Smart Growth and Neighborhood Conservation Policy, requiring state agencies to focus on locating and maintaining their facilities in central business districts and revitalization areas, and to consider the impact of projects on mass transit potentials (MDP 2000). In 2000, the Maryland Legislature passed 'Smart Codes' legislation, directing the state Department of Planning to draft model guidelines for infill development and building rehabilitation (Glendening 2001) and in 2001 enacted a 'GreenPrint' program to create an integrated network of preserved forests, wetlands and greenways to enhance wildlife habitat and rural environmental quality (Tregoning, et al. 2002).

Although the actual term 'smart growth' may be uniquely North American, the ideas behind the concept are not. Outside North America smart growth strategies are subsumed under the broad banner of sustainability. For example, in 2001 the European Union reaffirmed in the 'Strategy for Sustainable Development' that sustainability lies among the Community's policy priorities. The Strategy calls for actions to address a broad range of issues related to environmental quality (such as conserving natural resources and combating climate change) as well as public health, poverty and social exclusion. By February 2002, there were 6416 local governments in 113 countries that had either made a formal commitment to the sustainability principles, or were actively undertaking the process (Taylor and Doren 2000), though many are facing difficulties in implementing the principles because of competing short-term economic interests or because negative attitudes about living in high-density environments persist (Daniels 2001).

While smart growth strategies are credited nationally and internationally for helping to revitalize urban centers and improving the quality of the environment and life in general in a region (see for example, Benfield, et al. 2002), not all the basic elements of smart growth are agreed upon and not all smart growth efforts have received acclaim. Urban growth boundaries, for example, theoretically could control sprawl. But without adequate design guidelines and strong regional cooperation, implementation of growth boundaries may lead to growth within the boundary that is no more than the usual uninspiring residential and commercial sprawl (Staley and Gilroy 2002), while growth outside the boundary continues to spread.

Urban growth boundaries might conflict with other core principles of smart growth as well, such as the provision of affordable quality housing, by restricting supply and driving up prices or degrading quality. For example, a statistical analysis of Washington State's housing prices shows that the longer a county planned under the state's Growth Management Act, the faster housing price increased during this period, even after controlling for changes in income, population, density, household size and geographic characteristics (Burby, et al. 2001). In some instances, the pressure to use remaining land within high-density areas increased pressure to develop land exposed to natural hazards that developers, prior to growth regulation, bypassed when looking for sites for residential and non-residential projects (Downs 2003).

Additional impediments to implementing smart growth strategies lie in higher transaction and development costs, as well as increased demand for management expertise in the public, private and non-profit sectors to arrive at consensus among social, economic and environmental interests. Since planning for, and administration of, smart growth occurs typically at the regional level, authority over development is shifted from local governments, which control all land issues, to state or regional bodies because of the needs of many smart growth goals, such as limiting outward expansion, reducing traffic congestion, and preserving open space. In most cases, however, this shift is strongly resisted by local governments and residents (Alexander and Tomalty 2002), thus adding to transaction cost.

Positive relationships between density and the efficiency with which land and infrastructure are used have frequently been demonstrated (Park, et al.

1989). Awareness is growing among stakeholders about relationships between local lifestyles and global environmental challenges. What local strategies are compatible with efforts to address global climate change is not *a priori* clear, though significant potentials exist for changes in urban development and promotion of smart growth strategies to have synergistic effects with climate change policies. The remainder of this section provides background on climate change, before we return to issues of urban infrastructure, resource use, and investment and policy decision making.

CLIMATE CHANGE AND RESPONSE STRATEGIES

Climate change may have many positive and negative, direct and indirect impacts on environmental, economic and social systems, and those impacts vary across space, across time, and across various segments of an economy and society. Human settlement and resource use history is in large part characterized by adaptations to local environmental conditions. However, the scale and rate at which climate is changing poses new challenges for human response. Even if climate change impacts on socioeconomic systems are, by themselves, less than the combined non-climate impacts, their marginal effect could be significant, and they could noticeably compound existing stresses on resources, infrastructures and the institutions that govern their development and use.

To date, the climate change debate has concentrated mainly on direct, negative impacts on current generations. Global response strategies have been identified to address what has been perceived, in essence, as a global problem. However, greater attention is being given recently to adaptation strategies, especially those that are beneficial even without climate change, and that lay the footprint for future development that is robust in the light of climate change. This section briefly reviews some of these strategies, concentrating on two broad categories–efforts to mitigate the greenhouse effect, and measures to adapt to climate change. Both acknowledge that humans are not passive victims of climate change, and that simply insuring against adverse effects avoids the moral dimensions of climate change while it jeopardizes the solvency of the insurance industry (Doornkamp 1998). The timing and extent of both mitigation and adaptation strategies are influenced by the tensions between the perceived needs, on the one hand, to resolve remaining uncertainties about climate change and, on the other hand, to be precautionary (Pearce 1991; Lemons and Brown 1995).

Mitigation

The United Nations Framework Convention on Climate Change, which took effect in 1994, established as its goal the stabilization of GHG concentrations in the atmosphere 'at a level that would prevent dangerous anthropogenic interference with the climate system' (FCCC 1992). Towards that goal, parties to the convention are obliged to develop national inventories of GHG sources and sinks, to promote and cooperate in the development and diffusion of technologies which can prevent GHG emissions, to promote conservation and enhancement of GHG sinks and reservoirs, to cooperate in preparing for adaptation, to share information, and to promote education, training and public awareness. In addition, industrialized countries are asked to provide developing countries with financial resources to meet their commitments under the Framework Convention. In their 1997 annual meeting in Kyoto, the parties signed a protocol laying out mechanisms to achieve the Framework Convention's goals (FCCC 1997).

Common to the various mechanisms laid out in the Framework Convention is the intent to provide incentives to countries for reducing emissions beyond their own targets and to collaborate internationally to achieve globally cost effective emissions reductions. Specific focus is given to economic incentives, such as marketable emissions permits, and to new institutions, such as the Global Environment Facility, to foster environmentally friendly development.

Promotion of technological change plays a crucial role in the climate change and development context (Edmonds, et al. 2000). On the one hand, some changes in technology help boost output and reduce cost of fossil fuels, or energy end use devices. These changes tend to increase GHG emissions. On the other hand, efficiency improvements and increases in knowledge tend to decrease GHG emissions and cost of mitigation. The issue is further complicated by the fact that efficiency improvements and increases in knowledge are often related to production rates. Higher production and sales generate revenues for investment in new technology, and more experience is often gained as cumulative production increases (Yelle 1979; Ruth 1993). Furthermore, as the relative prices of products change and development occurs, consumer preferences are likely to change. Substitution among inputs into production and among consumer goods and leisure activities–all of which are related to where people live–are key determinants of GHG emissions (Jorgenson, et al. 2000). Yet, little attention is paid in current international agreements to the indeterminacy of the net effects of technology change, technology transfer and changes in preferences for GHG emissions.

A slew of other instruments are already available in many countries to achieve specific emissions goals, or to help leverage the effectiveness of market-based climate change policies. Among these instruments are environmental labeling requirements for electricity sources, demand-side management, tax credits and accelerated depreciation schedules, planning and sitting preferences for renewable energy facilities, renewable energy portfolio standards, land reclamation and reforestation policies, trace gas collection requirements for landfills, and more. Many of these instruments were originally implemented to achieve goals such as improvements to energy security, achievements of higher ambient air quality, maintenance of ecosystem health and species diversity, or increased energy efficiency of households and firms. Coordination of their use may help further leverage GHG emission reductions (Dernbach 2000).

The Framework Convention's call for climate change mitigation has spurred a flurry of activities in government, industry and academia to identify for individual sectors of the economy how targets can be met and what the associated costs and benefits of alternative mitigation strategies are (Gwilliam 1993; Bernstein, et al. 1999; Ruth, et al. 2000). The debate quickly zeroed in on no-regrets strategies–strategies that are considered beneficial even if climate change were not an issue. Soon the debate proceeded to address how multiple policy instruments, ranging from taxes and subsidies to enhanced research and development efforts and regulatory instruments, could be applied simultaneously to more effectively improve efficiencies and reduce emissions (Ruth, et al. 2000). More recently, the debate broadened to emphasize the wider range of social and environmental costs of energy use, aside from narrowly defined economic costs of energy conversion, GHG emissions and mitigation efforts (see, for example, Berry and Jaccard 2001). Solutions are being sought that transcend narrowly defined technological fixes and place technology policy in the broader context of development of adequate local capacity and essential support systems (Ruth, et al. 2000). It is in this context that the relationships between urban development and climate change are being explored.

While social scientists and policymakers have begun to place climate change in the broader context of socioeconomic growth and development, natural scientists have begun to emphasize that non-CO_2 GHGs have caused most of the observed warming and that it may be more practical to reduce their emissions than emissions of CO_2, thus achieving climate goals more cost effectively (Hansen, et al. 2000). How the confluence of these trends may shape climate change policy in the future is explored in more detail below, following a brief overview of the role of adaptation in dealing with climate change vulnerabilities.

Adaptation

Adaptation has often been perceived as the antidote to mitigation. Mitigation places emphasis on human capabilities to revert human-induced environmental trends. Adaptation, in contrast, means adjusting to climate change in order to reduce vulnerabilities of society and ecosystems, and is frequently perceived as an admission of an inability to noticeably revert climate change in a timely manner.

While successful mitigation depends on international cooperation, successful adaptation depends on local financial, technological and human resources. By the same token, mitigation has global benefits and adaptation has local benefits. As a consequence, mitigation has frequently been promoted as the proper response to the global issue of climate change. Yet, pursuit of adaptation strategies is neither an admission that climate change cannot be reverted, nor need it be a mere treatment of symptoms instead of eradication of the cause of the problem. As we discuss in more detail below, mitigation and adaptation can go hand in hand, and spending scarce resources on appropriate policy and investment strategies may successfully advance both mitigation and adaptation. Both also are closely related to land use, urban development and associated socioeconomic and technological issues.

Adaptation strategies can range from sharing or bearing losses, to actively reducing or preventing vulnerabilities. Some adaptations may occur as reactions to specific climate events–such as installations of pumps in basements and tunnels in response to increased rainfall, or increased chlorination of drinking water to prevent the spread of diseases at higher temperatures. Others may be anticipatory, such as implementing early warning systems for extreme weather events, adjusting agriculture and forest management practices, genetically engineering crops, re-designing bridges to reduce scour during high-flow events, laying power lines underground to minimize susceptibility to wind and ice storms, or establishing migration corridors for migratory species (Frankhauser 1996).

Like some mitigation strategies, various adaptations to climate generate benefits to society even if change does not occur. Benefits are derived from reducing susceptibilities to extreme weather events (Burton 1996) and correcting economic inefficiencies (Toman and Bierbaum 1996). Examples include changes in settlement patterns along rivers and coastlines that can help maintain healthy ecosystems that provide habitat for species, contribute to water retention and act as flood controls. In some instances retreat from susceptible areas may not be possible, making protection through biological barriers, such as reforested mangrove forests, or artificial barriers, such as sea walls, all the more relevant (Al-Farouq 1996).

The complex interrelations among climate, ecosystem health and socioeconomic development seem to call for a sophisticated set of strategies to address undesired outcomes. The fact that social and economic systems change rapidly with noticeable responses by the climate and ecosystems requires special focus on those geographic areas and sectors of an economy and society that are among the key drivers behind those changes. Consequently, the following section concentrates on urban systems.

URBAN INFRASTRUCTURE NEEDS, VULNERABILITIES AND DYNAMICS

Urban areas do deserve special attention in the climate change debate. To date, most of the work on climate change impacts has been on individual sectors of a national or the global economy, emphasizing the impacts of climate change on agriculture (Schmandt and Clarkson 1992; Cohen 1996; 1997a-b; Huang, et al. 1998). However, the number of studies conducted on regional and integrated impacts of climate change is increasing. Those studies suggest that the sum of sea level, energy, water and recreation (each infrastructure-related) impacts far exceed agricultural impacts (Ruth and Kirshen 2001). If air pollution and human life impacts are also included, the exceedances are much greater. Even if low estimates of economic impacts of sea level rise hold true, the combined damages on infrastructure systems for energy, water and recreation still significantly exceed agriculture (Yohe, et al. 1996). Though these results are by no means intended to divert attention away from potential dangers to agriculture and food supply, they do highlight that the economic impacts of climate-induced disruptions of infrastructures are similar or even greater in magnitude, and potentially regionally more concentrated because the bulk of infrastructure is typically located in urban areas.

Urbanization rates around the globe are increasing. Seventeen of the world's 25 largest megalopolises are located along coastlines and are prone to suffer from sea level rise (Nicholls 1995; Timmerman and White 1997). The advantages that historically have led to the location of cities on the coast (geographical control, access to transportation, trade, access to fish as food source and so on) are eroding at the same time as their infrastructure (transportation, flood control, sewage treatment and other systems) is impacted by climatic change. Gradual sea level rise and temperature changes are likely to be accompanied by more severe weather conditions such as higher wind and snow loads on buildings and extended droughts. Disruptions of power and water supplies, transportation and communication, and loss of many other infrastructure services may result. Direct impacts of such disruptions include economic losses, human health impacts and increased susceptibility to further disruptions. For example, climate-change induced increases in precipitation in the Midwestern parts of the US will likely result in increased traffic accidents, flight delays and potential airplane accidents (Changnon 1996).

While disruptions of infrastructure systems are most felt among the inhabitants of urban areas, and especially the cities of the developing world, they will ripple through the social and economic fabric to affect systems of interconnected cities and the larger regions and hinterlands with which cities interact. The role of cities as national and international drivers of economic growth, development, innovation, financial and other management may be reduced in light of climate-induced losses of infrastructure services and reductions in quality of life.

Part of the difficulty of generalizing geographic patterns and trends of vulnerability resides in the fact that the same individuals, households, firms or entire regions may be harmed by some manifestations of climate change while they may benefit from others. For example, milder winters will reduce demands for heating oil, while higher summer temperatures will increase expenditures for cooling and air conditioning. The opening of the Northwest Passage in response to snow and ice melt will, in effect, bring the major cities on the east coast of the US closer to Asia, enhancing their national and international competitiveness in trade of agricultural and manufacturing products. Climate change will thus have far-reaching implications for the re-distribution of wealth and welfare within a generation, across regions and across time.

Socioeconomic, technological and climate changes all together exert pressures on urban areas and collectively impact the adequacy and reliability of infrastructure systems to provide services. The following sections address, respectively, the status and pressures on water supply, water quality and flood control systems, transportation infrastructure and energy systems. We then turn to implications for urban heat island effects and ultimately the health of (human and non-human) species. Subsequently, we address issues of management and decision making from a larger systems perspective, combining insights from the smart growth debate with those from climate change adaptation and mitigation research and policy making.

Water Systems

Sea level rise
The effects of climate change on the coastal zone are varied and numerous. Glaciers and sea ice are shrinking, and global rates of sea level rise in the last century averaged between one and 2.5 millimeters (mm) per year (IPCC 2001). The magnitude of the El Niño event in the early 1990s was unprecedented. Rising ocean temperatures in the Indian Ocean have already caused widespread coral bleaching, though some biological adaptation may have helped avoid reef extinction (Baker, et al. 2004). It is also possible that the earth could experience changes in coastal storm patterns that alter their frequency and intensity as well as change ocean circulation (IPCC 2001).

The impacts of these effects on the coast are broad and include displacement and loss of wetlands, inundation of low-lying property, increased erosion of the shoreline, expansion of flood zones, and salinization of surface water and groundwater. Since many large cities and their built infrastructure are located on the coast, impacts from sea level rise on urban areas and their hinterlands will be significant.

Topographic maps and remote sensing suggest that a two- to seven-foot rise in sea level would result in a 50 to 90 per cent loss of US wetlands (Kyper and Sorensen 1985). A one-foot rise in sea level would erode the shore 50 to 100 feet in New Jersey (Everts 1985) and Maryland (Kana, et al. 1984); 100 to 200 feet in South Carolina (Wilcoxen 1986); and 200 to 400 feet in California (FEMA 1991). Areas inundated by the 100-year flood are estimated to increase from approximately 19 500 square miles to 23 000 square miles for the one-foot scenario, and to 27 000 square miles for the three-foot scenario (Miller, et al. 1989). Increasingly, public moneys will need to be directed towards protection of aquifers and other public water supply systems (Nicholls, et al. 1999).

Globally, the impacts of sea level rise are expected to be most serious in Africa, south and southeast Asia (IPCC 2001). Submergence rates of 2.5 mm per year or more are not uncommon, and higher rates apply locally, such as in parts of China, Canada and Argentina. Seawater intrusion into freshwater aquifers in deltaic and non-deltaic areas has been documented in diverse environments such as the arid Israeli coast, the humid Thailand coast, the Chinese Yangtze Delta, the Vietnamese Mekong Delta, and low-lying atolls (IPCC 1996). More importantly, the capacity to adapt to sea level rise is likely more limited in developing countries than in the US. The costs of a one-meter sea level rise in Maldives, for example, could approach one third of the country's GNP (IPCC 2001).

Human responses and adaptation to costal threats generally fall broadly into three categories: retreat, accommodation and protection (Titus, et al. 1991). Each has its own advantages and disadvantages. Retreat involves no effort to protect the land from the sea and the coastal zone is abandoned. Without human interference, ecosystems could migrate landward as sea level rises and thus could remain largely intact, although the total area of wetlands would decline. However, coastal landowners and communities would suffer from loss of property, resettlement costs and the costs of rebuilding infrastructure. It is estimated that shoreline retreat from a one-meter rise in sea level would cost the US $270 to $475 billion dollars (IPCC 1990) on top of the social and economic problems that resettlement may cause (IPCC 1990).

Accommodation implies that people continue to use the land at risk but do not attempt to prevent the lands from being flooded. This option includes erecting emergency flood shelters, elevating buildings on piles, converting agriculture to fish farming, or growing flood or salt tolerant crops. Potential problems with this option include potential changes in property values, increasing damages from storms and costs for modifying infrastructure.

Protection involves both hard structures responses, such as building sea walls and dikes, and soft solutions that utilize sediments to protect the land from the sea so that existing land uses can continue. Both are in many instances only temporary, high-cost fixes of problems associate with sea level rise and may provide a false sense of security to coastal communities.

Hard structures influence banks, channels, sediment deposits and morphology of the coastal zone, leading to a loss of coastal ecosystems (Sorenson, et al. 1984; Weggel 1989; Gleick and Maurer 1990; Leatherman 1994). For example, estimates of the fixed costs for dikes or levees built to protect against a one-meter rise in sea level ranged from $150 to $800 per linear foot in 1990 dollars (ASCE 1992). Beach nourishment, one of the most popular soft protection strategies, may solve the fundamental problem of diminishing sediment resources, especially during the early onset of erosion (Yohe and Neumann 1997), but the long-term effectiveness of beach nourishment remains uncertain due to an incomplete understanding of coastal processes and their responses to future climate change (Neumann, et al. 2000; Ruth and Kirshen 2001).

Recent studies suggest that anticipatory management strategies, based on scenarios of future potential sea levels, and pro-active management strategies could cost effectively reduce susceptibilities to sea level rise. Restrictions on construction locations, stronger building codes, aggressive flood-proofing of existing structures, forward-looking flood plain management, natural hazard zoning, a moratorium on new sea walls except for major commercial areas, and emphasis on more compact development all may be key in protecting coastal communities (IPCC 2001).

Water supply and quality
Approximately 1.7 billion people, one-third of the world's population, presently live in countries that are water-stressed, using more than 20 per cent of their renewable water supply. This number is projected to increase to around five billion by 2025, depending on the rate of population growth (Lins and Stakhiv 1998). The United States, on average, is well endowed with water. However, fresh water can be a scarce resource virtually everywhere in the US at some time, especially in the urban areas of the arid and semiarid west (Alcamo, et al. 2003). Climate change will exacerbate existing and create new water shortages in already dry areas such as the Middle East, northeast Brazil, and southern Africa (IPCC 2001), while water availability may slightly increase in some parts of Africa and Asia, occasionally exacerbating susceptibilities to floods.

Detailed regional impacts of global climate change on future water supplies are notoriously uncertain (Frederick and Gleick 2000). For example, two different models, the Hadley and Canadian GCMs, both show that temperatures and potential evapotranspiration in the US will rise significantly by 2100. However, because of the uncertainties about the implications of climate change for water resources, estimates based on the Hadley model indicate flooding could increase in much of the country, while those based on the Canadian climate model indicate increased water scarcity would pervade much of the country (IPCC 2001).

Climate change will affect the demand as well as the supply of water. It may substantially affect irrigation withdrawals (Doll and Siebert 2001). Net irrigation requirements per unit irrigated area generally would decrease across much of the Middle East and northern Africa, whereas most irrigated areas in India and northern China would require more water (Boland 1997). The most sensitive areas in municipal water use to climate change are increased personal washing and increased use of water in gardens and for lawns (IPCC 2001). Industrial use for processing purposes is relatively insensitive to climate change. Demands for cooling water, in contrast, may be noticeably affected by climate change (Cruise, et al. 1999; Frederick and Gleick 2000).

Climate change is also likely to affect water quality. Potential negative implications of climate change include lower flows, higher water temperatures and increased storm surges. Lower flows in rivers will lead to increases in salinity levels to downstream water users and increase peak concentrations of metals and chemical compounds (IPCC 2001). Higher water temperatures alone would lead to increases in concentrations of some chemical species but decreases in others, and would also encourage algal blooms, which can lead to oxygen deficits in the water, and thus directly affect riverine ecosystems and indirectly the economies that depend on them (Frederick and Gleick 2000).

Increases in the number of days with more intense precipitation could increase agricultural and urban pollutants washed into streams and lakes, further reducing oxygen levels (Frederick and Gleick 2000). However, current understanding of the hydrological impacts is insufficient to determine whether climate change would improve or worsen low-flow conditions. The direction as well as the magnitude of the climate impacts on lake quality from changes in precipitation and evaporation rates is also uncertain (Frederick and Gleick 2000), and as a consequence the direct and indirect impacts on urban areas, as well as the needs for planning and investments, are uncertain as well.

Runoff and flood control
Runoff is extremely sensitive to climatic conditions and highly dependent on the spatial and temporal relations of temperatures and precipitation. Significantly higher temperatures, even with more precipitation, can lead to large reductions in regional runoff, while smaller temperature increases and large increases in precipitation can lead to much greater runoff (IPCC 2001).

While it is generally accepted that future temperatures will be higher, detailed changes in the regional distribution of precipitation are still uncertain (IPCC 2001). Nevertheless, some general conclusions about future changes in runoff have been reached. First, precipitation is expected to increase in the mid- and high-latitudes of the Northern Hemisphere, particularly in autumn and winter, and decrease in the tropics and subtropics in both hemispheres, particularly in the northern tropics of Africa (Frederick and Gleick 2000). Second, higher temperatures can lead to dramatic changes in snowfall and snowmelt dynamics in mountainous watersheds and can lead to more rapid, earlier and greater spring runoff (Gleick 1987; Jeton, et al. 1996). This effect was already identified, for example, in the 1980s for watersheds in California (Burn 1994; Lettenmaier, et al. 1994; Lins and Michaels 1994). Third, although it is difficult to determine whether river runoff is changing over time because of a lack of long records of runoff and land use changes in watersheds, empirical evidence is mounting that rivers are exhibiting runoff trends consistent with the effects of global warming, such as earlier spring runoff and significant increases in autumn and winter stream flow (Karl and Knight 1998; Groisman 1999). Last but not least, the proportion of total precipitation from heavy precipitation events has grown at the expense of moderate precipitation events (White and Howe 2002). As a result, flood magnitude and frequency tend to increase.

Flooding is one of world's most costly and destructive natural disasters. It can seriously damage the built environment, paralyze transportation, interrupt energy distribution, impair wastewater plants, disrupt safe water supplies, pose threats to the health of species, and even cause death or severe injury. For example, flooding in England during autumn 2000 caused an estimated £1 billion of damage and brought chaos to many parts of England and Wales (Zoleta-Nantes 2000). Floods in poor districts of Manila, Philippines, exposed people to respiratory infections, skin allergies and gastro-intestinal illnesses, with children most at risk (IPCC 2001).

It is now increasingly accepted that climate change is likely to cause an increase in both flood magnitude and frequency in many areas of the world, particularly in many parts of Asia, Africa and Latin America, although the increase in flooding for any given climate scenario is uncertain and impacts will vary among basins (Milly, et al. 2002). Recent evidence shows that the frequency of great floods–floods with discharges exceeding 100-year levels from basins larger than 200 000 km^2–increased substantially during the twentieth century. This increase is consistent with results from the climate model and will continue (Fox 2003).

Similar to the responses to sea level rise, flood controls fall broadly into two categories: 'structural' and 'non-structural' approaches. Structural approaches include construction of flood defenses such as river channel modifications, embankments, reservoirs and barrages. Though prominent in the history of land development, structural approaches have achieved mixed success. Many have proven costly in economic and environmental terms, and provided a false sense of security, thus encouraging unimpeded development in areas where devastating floods occur (Parker 1999; Few 2003). Failures or poor maintenance of some flood control structures have exacerbated flood hazards (Fox 2003; Hayes 2004).

Non-structural approaches refer to measures designed not to prevent floods but to reduce their short- and long-term impacts. They typically include elevating or removing structures in flood-prone areas, land use controls, building regulations to prevent intrusion of floodwaters, flood warning and evacuation systems, as well as increased public awareness and emergency preparedness. The benefits of combined structural and non-structural approaches to flood control are generally recognized (USDOT 2002) and slowly influence built infrastructures and institutions in urban areas.

Transportation

Economic growth typically is associated with increases in the movement of goods and people across space. However, the transport sector not only contributes to, but also benefits from, economic growth. For example, in 2000 the US transportation system generated 10.7 per cent of the nation's GDP, around $1.05 trillion, producing about 4.8 trillion passenger miles of travel and over 3.8 trillion ton-miles of domestic freight, and employing more than 10 million people, about 7.4 per cent of total civilian employment (USDOE 2001). As a consequence the transport sector has not only a key role to play in the regional, national and global context but also has vested interests in perpetuating growth.

Two sets of issues surrounding transportation are of particular concern in the urban development, smart growth and climate change debate–fuel use and associated emissions, as well as land use and its impacts on natural areas and human living conditions. Each is discussed here, in turn, before we address climate impacts on transportation.

Impacts of transportation on climate
In most industrialized and many developing countries, transportation is among the top five energy-consuming sectors of the economy. For example, for decades the transportation sector has accounted for between 25 and 27 per cent of total US energy consumption. From 1980 to 2000, transportation energy use in the US grew an average of 1.5 per cent annually (DeCiccoa and Mark 1998), with more than 97 per cent of total energy consumption occurring in the form of fossil fuel combustion (USDOT 2002). Only a small fraction of transportation's energy needs are met by non-petroleum sources,

such as methanol and ethanol (Greene and Schafer 2003), and many of these require significant fossil fuel use in their production and delivery.

The predominance of fossil fuel use in transportation makes the transportation sector's greenhouse gas emissions second only to those of electricity generation. The sector's expansion in the US alone meant that between 1990 and 1999, CO_2 emissions increased by nearly 15 per cent and, if projections hold, the sector's share in anthropogenic CO_2 emissions will be 36 per cent by 2020 (USDOT 2002; World Bank 2003). Globally, pollution from motor vehicles alone produces about one-fifth of the incremental carbon dioxide arising from human activities in the atmosphere, one-third of the CFCs, and one-half of all nitrogen oxides (Greene 1997; USDOT 2002).

Besides threats to climate change, other important environmental impacts include health-related air pollution (World Bank 2003) and hazardous materials and oil spills (USDOT 2002), many of which occur in urban areas. Modification or destruction of habitat by the expansion of transportation infrastructure, transformational impacts on land use (Greene 1997; NRC 2003), a series of social costs associated with congestion, noise pollution, accidents (Levinson, et al. 1996), and changes in lifestyles towards lower physical activity levels and their associated adverse health effects (Higgins and Higgins 2003) further exacerbate the situation.

Impacts of climate on transportation
Transportation not only contributes to climate change, but climate change also has several potential adverse effects on transportation. Current climate change research models and case studies show that rising sea levels and changing coastlines could, over the long-term, require the relocation of roads, rail lines or airport runways, and could have major consequences for port facilities and coastal shipping (Hill 1996; Bloomfield, et al. 1999; Burkett 2002; duVair, et al. 2002; Titus 2002). Underground tunnels for transit systems, roads and rail could be subject to more frequent or severe flooding, which may result in large economic damages and fatalities (Hill 1996; Bloomfield, et al. 1999; Titus 2002). Thawing permafrost and heat kinks because of extreme heat could damage roads, rail lines, pipelines and bridges (Smith and Levasseur 2002). Declining water levels in the Great Lakes could adversely lead to reduced draft and increased land-based transit. Reduced ice cover and duration might lead to a greatly extended navigation system (Marchand, et al. 1988). Additionally, a possible increase in the number of hurricanes, other extreme weather events, and changes in rain, snowfall and seasonal flooding patterns would have implications for emergency evacuation planning, facility maintenance, and safety management for surface transport, marine vessels and aviation (Kulesa 2002).

Since many of these developments already occur and are likely to be exacerbated over long periods of time, long-range transportation planning process should now consider the anticipated effects of climate change on the existing or new infrastructure, potentially building in more resilience to climate variability while recognizing that there will be different impacts in different areas (Ruth and Kirshen 2001).

Response strategies
Advances in technology and insights in urban planning both offer hope that the transportation systems could evolve to provide amenities at lower cost, more equity, and without accumulating environmental damage that compromises the future. Technology approaches mainly include energy efficiency improvements, low-carbon or no-carbon alternative fuels, and increased efficiency within the transportation system. Since 1970 significant improvements in energy efficiency have been achieved in the US by nearly all modes of transport. For example, from 1978 to 1990, new passenger car miles per gallon increased from 15.8 to 28.6, and new light truck miles per gallon grew from 13.7 to 21.2. Passenger-miles per gallon for commercial air travel has increased by 150 per cent since 1975, resulting in a near doubling of aircraft energy efficiency (Hellman and Heavenrich 2002). It is projected that before 2030, advanced diesel engines, gasoline or diesel hybrid vehicles and hydrogen-powered fuel cell vehicles will likely permit new car and light truck fuel economy to be increased by at least 50 to 100 per cent (Greene and Schafer 2003).

Meanwhile, despite many challenges, alternative fuels could significantly reduce GHG emissions. If methods of producing ethanol from cellulose were commercialized, renewable liquid fuels blended with petroleum fuels could reduce transportation's CO_2 emissions by 2 per cent by 2015 and 7 per cent by 2030. If a transition to a largely hydrogen-powered transportation system were achieved, hydrogen produced from renewable or nuclear energy, or from fossil resources with carbon sequestration, could eliminate most of transportation's GHG emissions sometime after 2030 (Greene and Schafer 2003). However, each of these energy supplies have their own environmental and health impacts–such as high water, fertilizer and pesticide consumption for biomass-based energy generation, or long-term radiation in the case of nuclear energy–and both are highly energy intensive to carry out and may, on net, even be energy consumers (Faiz, et al. 1990; Greene and Schafer 2003).

More promising strategies to reduce GHG emissions from the transportation sector are to improve not simply the efficiency of individual modes of transportation or their associated infrastructures, but to enhance overall system efficiency. Approaches include providing more direct routes from origins to destinations, increasing vehicle occupancy rates, shifting traffic from modes with high emission rates to modes with low emission rates, improving the in-use efficiency of vehicles through better maintenance and driving behavior (Greene and Schafer 2003), and eliminating the need for transportation altogether, for example, by promoting telecommunication, designing walk-able and bike-able communities, and emphasizing consumption of locally produced goods.

Without strong policies and corresponding market forces to overcome the grip that transportation has on local and national economic growth, changes in technologies, transportation patterns and behaviors are difficult to achieve. For example, the federal Automotive Fuel Economy Standards (CAFE Standards), one of the most significant transportation efficiency policies in the US, resulted in a doubling of new vehicle fuel efficiency over 1974 levels. However, the standards have not been increased since 1985, with the result that fuel efficiency of the total vehicle fleet has stabilized (Greene and Wegener 1997) and recently been declining, because of exemptions for trucks (which gave rise to the proliferation of minivans and sports utility vehicles), combined with increased affluence and changes in preferences of households.

Additionally, technology improvements alone–whether industry- or government-led–cannot completely solve the environmental problems of transportation, if the demand for transportation continues its past trend. For example, annual vehicle miles traveled (VMT) in the US rose by nearly 30 per cent to 2.8 trillion miles, an average annual increase of 2.5 per cent. During the same time VMT per capita rose on average 1.3 per cent per year (USDOT 2002). These growth rates by far exceed improvements in efficiency. Consequently, some initiatives attempt to reduce the demand for transport at its origin. One strategy is to increase the cost of travel to reflect the social and environmental damages of transportation, such as by implementing a fuel tax (Harrington, et al. 2003). The other is integrated transport and urban land planning to provide greater accessibility with less travel (Newman, et al. 1995; Kenworthy 1996; Newman and Kenworthy 1999; Crane 2000; Miller and Hoel 2002; Rodier, et al. 2002).

Economists argue that taxes may be used to internalize costs associated with transportation, including its impacts on land use, congestion and climate. Simulation results show that higher fuel taxes can stimulate households to replace older cars for new ones, thus increasing aggregate fuel economy or reducing the number of vehicles owned (Harrington, et al. 2003). However, some empirical evidence exists for rebound effects–households increasing their travel demand with increased efficiencies (Greene, et al. 1999; Litman 2001) and income effects–households purchasing larger, less efficient cars as incomes increase, even though purchasing and operating costs of those cars may increase (Morrison 2000). Additional undesired side-effects include larger burdens for low income households which spend a large share of their income on fuel, and to individuals who are locked into high-mileage lifestyles (Harrington, et al. 2003).

Implementing land use policies to address problems stemming from automobile ownership and use is becoming increasingly prevalent. For example, the New Urbanism movement seeks to 'reconnect transport with land use and in particular to establish transit-oriented development (TOD) where higher-density, mixed-use areas, built around high-quality transit systems, provide a focused urban structure that can help to loosen the grasp of automobile dependence' (Newman and Kenworthy 1996). Some international examples tend to support the claims of New Urbanists of the impacts of urban form on transportation. For example, compared with most big US cities, many comparable wealthy European cities, such as Stockholm, and some wealthy Asian cities, such as Hong Kong, are more transit-oriented and thus are respectively 2.5 times and 7.5 times lower in car use (Kenworthy and Laube 1999). Evidence from simulation studies also suggests that higher residential density is strongly related to higher transit use and lower car ownership levels (Pushkarev and Zupan 1977; Smith 1984; Schimek 1996; Newman and Kenworthy 1999); increased employment concentrations do have significant impacts on transit usage, in particular on walking (where feasible) and ride-sharing (Frank and Pivo 1994; Parsons Brinkerhogg Quade and Douglas Inc. 1996); improved regional accessibility to activities is important in reducing vehicular travels and is an important determinant of mode-choice (Ewing 1995; Kockelman 1997); and mixed land use and pedestrian-oriented designs reduce trip rates and encourage non-auto travel (Friedman, et al. 1994; Cevero and Kockelman 1997). However, cause-effect relationships are difficult to discern, because households self-select for neighborhood characteristics (Crane and Crepeau 1998) and feedbacks exist between environmental factors and individual behaviors (Crane 2000). As a consequence, biases exist in the data on which many of the New Urbanism studies are based. New empirical evidence suggests, for example, that income is found to be a much better predictor of differences in trip generation than urban form (Kulkarni 1996).

The controversy surrounding empirical evidence for successes of New Urbanism suggests that the main question is not whether density, urban design, socioeconomic variables or other factors are most important in explaining impacts of urban form on transportation. Rather, the question should be how to account for the interrelatedness of socioeconomic variables, urban form and transportation, a topic discussed later in this chapter.

Energy

The link between climatic variability and energy use has been widely documented and utilized to explain energy consumption and to assist energy suppliers with short-term planning (Quayle and Diaz 1979; Warren and LeDuc 1981; Downton, et al. 1988; Yan 1988; Badri 1992; Lehman 1994; Lam 1998; Morris 1999; Pardo, et al. 2002). However, to date few analyses address the longer-term implications of climate change for energy use patterns, urban development and infrastructure investment decisions. The results of the few studies that have examined the effects of climate change on the energy sector suggest, in general, noticeable impacts on energy demand, capital requirements or expenditures. For example, Linder's (1990) assessment of climate change impacts on the US electricity sector finds that between 2010 and 2055 climate change could increase capacity addition requirements by 14 to 23 per cent relative to non-climate change scenarios, requiring investments of $200 to 300 billion (1990 dollars). In a national assessment of Israel, Segal et al. (1992) estimated an increase in temperature of 4°C to be associated with a 10 per cent increase in average summer peak loads. In Greece, a 1°C temperature increase is projected to decrease energy consumption for heating by 10 per cent and increase energy used for cooling by 28 per cent, assuming a business-as-usual scenario (Cartalis, et al. 2001). A study examining potential changes in US commercial energy use due to climate change finds that a 4°C increase in average annual temperature results in a 0 to 5 percent reduction in total energy use in the commercial sector in 2030, after accounting for changes in the building stock (Belzer and Scott 1996). Rosenthal et al. (1995) estimated that a 1°C warming in the US would reduce energy expenditures by $5.5 billion and primary energy use by 0.7 per cent in 2010 relative to a non-warming scenario. In contrast, a study examining the impacts of climate change on total US energy use finds found that a 2°C increase in average temperature would increase energy expenditures by $6 billion in 2060 (Morrison and Mendelsohn 1998). The work by Amato, et al. (2005) suggests that by 2030 climate change may account for up to 40 percent of increased energy demand in Massachusetts.

Regional analyses of energy demand sensitivities to climate and climate change are particularly important because global climate change is anticipated to have geographically distinct impacts. Regional energy systems differ in terms of energy sources, efficiencies and characteristics of supply and conversion infrastructure, age of transmission and distribution systems, end use technologies, and characteristics of end users because sectoral compositions vary across regions, with different sectors typically exhibiting different energy use profiles and propensities for change.

Several empirical studies support these arguments for regional assessments of climate impacts on the energy sector. For example, in a state-level analysis of US residential and commercial electricity, Sailor observes significantly different variation in sectoral demand sensitivities between states (Sailor 2001). He finds that a temperature increase of 2°C is associated with an 11.6 per cent increase in residential per capita electricity use in Florida, but a 7.2 per cent decrease in Washington. Even in neighboring states, such as Florida and Louisiana, residential and commercial demand sensitivities are noticeably different. Similarly, Sailor and colleagues estimate the sensitivity of state-level electricity and natural gas consumption and find considerable variation (Sailor and Munoz 1997; Sailor, et al. 1998). Warren and LeDuc

(1981) statistically estimate natural gas consumption to prices and heating degree-days in a nine-region model of the US and find noticeable regional differences. Scott, et al. (1994) use a building energy simulation model to assess the impacts of climate change on commercial building energy demand in four US cities: Seattle, Minneapolis, Phoenix and Shreveport. Each city was found to have a unique demand response to climatic changes. For instance, a 7°F increase in daily temperature increases cooling energy use 36.6 per cent in Phoenix and 93.3 per cent in Seattle.

Recent statistical analysis and computer simulations by Ruth and Lin (2005) of residential and commercial energy demand in Maryland indicate that, under a range of scenarios of climate change, winter heating fuel consumption may noticeably decrease and summer electricity demands may increase. While temperature-driven average annual energy demands may not change much, the anticipated increases in demand during summer alone may prove significant enough to warrant changes in peak load capacity planning for the region. However, by using monthly information on changes in climate and energy their study may even have under-appreciated the larger increases in peak electric demand, which often occur within narrow daily or hourly time intervals. Other studies suggest similar findings. For example, an average temperature increase of 3°C (5.4°F) in Toronto was found to be associated with a 7 per cent increase in mean peak electric demand, but a 22 per cent increase in the peak electric load standard deviation (Colombo, et al. 1999). As a consequence, energy sector decision makers need to incorporate the impacts of climate change into regional energy system expansion plans to ensure adequate supply of energy, both throughout the year and during periods of peak demand.

Identifying potential impacts for individual regions now, especially for those regions that are highly urbanized, is important because the energy industry is extremely capital intensive and therefore the flexibility of policy-induced changes in energy generation and demand trajectories over the short and medium run is limited (Gröler 1990). In the long run, as the capital stock naturally turns over, building codes may be changed to calibrate the thermal attributes of the building stock to expected future climates (Camilleri, et al. 2001). However, such changes need to be implemented in the relatively near term, or the building stock will become increasingly maladapted to climate. In the near term, polices such as urban shade tree planting and installation of high albedo or green roofs can begin to modify the thermal characteristics of energy infrastructures in order to reduce space-conditioning energy use.

Urban Heat Islands

Increased affluence–whether in the developing or industrialized world–often means more cars, more refrigerators and more air conditioners, and thus lower outdoor air quality. Asphalt and concrete for roads, buildings and other structures necessary to accommodate growing populations absorb–rather than reflect–the sun's heat. The displacement of trees and shrubs eliminates the natural cooling effects of shading and evapotranspiration. Emission from energy conversion in power plants and combustion engines, especially when combined with reduced vegetation and larger areas with darker surfaces (Taha and Meier 1997) can raise air temperatures in a city by 2 to 8°F (WMO 1984) and even change local temperature and precipitation patterns. The resultant urban heat island effect is different from global warming, though it may exacerbate, and be exacerbated by, climate variability and trends. Temperature increases and precipitation changes may stimulate further increases in energy use for cooling purposes, water pumping and more (EPA 2000), and may result in increased emissions of greenhouse gases, precursors of urban smog and contributors to changes in local environmental conditions.

Changes in urban vegetation cover and albedo can be measured remotely and correlated with climatologic information from urban weather stations. Time-series analyses, comparative time trends at one or more urban stations, comparisons along urban transects or among urban, suburban and rural stations, as well as between measurements on weekdays and weekends have helped document urban heat island effects for mega-cities across the US, including the New York metropolitan area, Philadelphia, Washington DC, Pittsburg, Buffalo, Cleveland, Albany, Atlanta and Los Angeles (Bornstein and Lin 2000). Empirical evidence of urban heat island effects also exists for Turkey (Tayanc and Toros 1997), Austria (Böhm 1998), South Africa (Hughes and Balling 1996), Japan (Hadfield 2000), Singapore (Wong, et al. 2003) and elsewhere. Although the term urban heat island implies that it is solely an urban problem, research has shown urban heat islands are also becoming prevalent in small cities (Pinho and Orgaz 2000) and suburbs (Stone and Rodgers 2001).

Research into urban heat island effects suggests that urban heat island intensity decreases with increasing wind speed and increasing cloud cover (Ackerman 1985; Travis, et al. 1987; Kidder and Essenwanger 1995; Figuerola and Mazzeo 1998; Magee, et al. 1999; Morris, et al. 2001; Unger, et al. 2001). Urban heat island intensity most likely increases in the summer (Schmidlin 1989; Klysik and Fortuniak 1999; Philandras, et al. 1999; Morris, et al. 2001) and tends to increase with increasing city size and/or population (Park 1986; Yamashita, et al. 1986; Hogan and Ferrick 1998; Torok, et al. 2001). However, several challenges to these generalizations have been mounted. For example, the greatest urban-rural difference detected in Birmingham, UK, occurs in spring and autumn (Unwin 1980). Reykjavik, Iceland, shows a tendency for negative heat island intensities, with rural areas warmer than urban areas in summer and only weak development at other times of the year (Steinecke 1999). A larger rate of growth of Prague's urban heat island has been detected since the 1920s in winter and spring than in summer (Brazdil and Budikova 1999).

The urban heat island phenomena affects the environment and population in a number of ways, including through increased demand for cooling energy, degradation of air quality, threats to public health, the triggering of adverse meteorological events and by indirectly promoting urban sprawl. Increased energy demand for cooling and air conditioning are a direct result of higher ambient temperatures and decreased air quality. Increased energy demand, coupled with increasing energy prices, can result in greater costs to consumers. It is estimated that as much as 15 per cent if the electricity consumed for cooling within Los Angeles is utilized for the sole purpose of offsetting the effects of urban heat islands (Rosenfeld and Romm 1996). The annual energy cost of urban heat islands alone within the United States is estimated to be approximately $10 billion (Rosenfeld and Romm 1996).

Degradation of air quality, a result of emissions and higher ambient temperatures, may manifest itself in elevated concentrations of volatile organic compounds (VOCs), ground-level ozone and other air pollutants which may adversely affect the health of human and non-human species (Cardelino and Chameides 1990). For example, ground-level ozone negatively impacts photosynthesis, inflames lung tissues and aggravates a range of respiratory ailments such as asthma. Researchers at the Lawrence Berkeley National Laboratory (LBNL) have estimated that each 1°F rise in temperature over 70°F increases the potential for ozone formation in Los Angeles by approximately 3 per cent (USDOE 1996).

Urban heat islands may impact precipitation events either over or downwind of communities. Naturally occurring storms often intensify as they pass through cities, and moderate rainstorms may turn into full-blown thunder and lightening storms. The urban heat island in Atlanta, for example, creates thunderstorms south of the city, which could cause urban flooding (NASA 1999). Urban heat islands have also been cited as causing torrential rains that wreaked havoc in Tokyo, Japan (Hadfield 2000).

Extreme temperature episodes, poor air quality and adverse meteorological conditions combine to worsen the habitability and comfort of human settlements in urban areas and may thus push people out of cities. Yet, at the same time, complex and subtle relations among environmental conditions in urban and suburban areas may go unnoticed by decision makers. For example, complex interactions of nitrogen oxides (NO_X) and urban ozone (O_3) may help reduce the potentially negative impacts of O_3 on plant growth in urban areas, while higher cumulative O_3 exposures and associated damages may result in suburban and rural areas having lower NO_X concentrations (Gregg, et al. 2003). As a result, urban heat island effects may make the problem of sprawl more intractable.

Researchers and policy makers have long understood the primary causes of urban heat islands, but have only recently begun to investigate various strategies to effectively reverse or mitigate them. There are mainly two kinds of mitigation strategies for reducing urban heat islands. One is a technical approach which relies upon the use of reflective roofing and paving materials to enhance urban albedo, urban afforestation to both directly reduce cooling energy use in buildings and to lower ambient air temperature through evapotranspiration, and building designs to improve natural ventilation. The other approach to reducing urban heat island effects addresses changes in residential development patterns, transportation and energy use. Both have an essential role to play in reducing urban heat islands, addressing climate change issues and reducing incentives for sprawl.

It is estimated that reflective and light-colored roofing materials can reflect from 60 to 80 per cent of incoming solar radiation. For example, a LBNL simulation model shows, in Phoenix alone, $37 million in annual savings if a substantial portion of the city implemented reflective roofs (Wade 2000). Green roofs, a layer of grasses or succulents grown over a root barrier and watertight membrane, not only reduce heat absorption in summer by up to 50 per cent, but storm runoff and smog as well (Brake 2001).

The concept of reflective roofing can also be employed on the ground. Reflective paving surfaces, such as concrete, are found cause up to a 20-degree reduction in surface temperature compared to asphalt (Wade 2000). Researchers at LBNL estimate that changing the reflectivity of pavements in Los Angeles could achieve up to $90 million in energy and smog reduction benefits each year (Lyman 2002), though costs may be double those of installing traditional asphalt surfaces (Wade 2000).

Strategically planting shade trees near homes and buildings can directly shield them from the sun's rays and reduce local air temperature and cooling energy demand. In addition to their direct cooling effect, trees help reduce ambient air temperature through the cooling effects of evapotranspiration. Other environmental benefits include the ability to sequester carbon and reduce peak stormwater flows, thereby reducing urban infrastructure costs (EPA 2000), while at the same time increasing aesthetics and property values.

Using building designs that enhance ventilation can help reduce urban heat island effects, because the free flow of air through urban structures increases the potential for heat transfer between the warm surfaces and the surrounding air. While satisfying the requirement of retaining enough air movement to disperse pollutants, key wind protection strategies may be used to protect space and buildings from cold winds, prevent buildings and landscape features from generating unacceptable wind turbulence, protect space and buildings from driving rain and snow, and protect space and buildings from cold air 'drainage' at night.

Since the technical solutions to urban heat island effects are highly site-specific and narrow in focus, they often do not address the larger issues associated with land and energy use, and emissions that lie at the heart of urban heat island effects. Urban and other land use changes account for as much as half of the observed increases in the diurnal temperature range in the US (Kalnay and Cai 2003). Some research suggests that urban design may be more relevant to urban heat islands than the density of development itself, thus making it difficult to immediately implement solutions. For example, Stone and Rodgers (2001) have confirmed a clear and consistent positive relationship between the size of a residential parcel and the excess flux of radiant heat energy. Their statistical analyses indicate that lower density patterns of residential development in Atlanta contribute more excess radiant energy to surface heat island formation, on average, than do higher density patterns. Their research supports one general design strategy to battle against urban heat islands: the imposition of restrictions on the zone of urban development (an urban growth boundary), and promotion of infill development and higher-density new growth.

Although the above mitigation strategies seem promising in the battle against urban heat islands, there are still many obstacles along the road. Ongoing research and field studies have shown the success of these strategies in some big cities. However, it is less obvious whether successful strategies can be replicated elsewhere with similar outcomes, given the numerous variables particular to different regions such as climate, topography, population growth patterns, economic conditions and institutional settings.

HEALTH OF SPECIES

The connection between climate change and human health, as well as the health of other species, has recently received heightened attention. Changes in environmental conditions may favor air-borne, water-borne or vector-borne diseases, thus posing threats to plants, animals and people. Vulnerabilities to disease outbreaks are also a function of population density, land use patterns, and the advancement of early detection and warning systems, knowledge and technology for disease control, as well as reliability of medical systems and availability of drugs. Disentangling the various influences on the health of species and reducing their negative impacts is one of the chief challenges faced by humanity. This section first briefly addresses challenges to ecosystems and species diversity in urban areas and then highlights some of the better-understood impacts on human health. However, many of the climate-land use-health relationships are speculative, and are not explored in detail here, though they may be potentially significant.

Urban Ecosystems and Species Diversity

Urban areas often are rich in species diversity and contain a wide range of habitats and habitat quality–from brownfields, landfills and industrial sites to suburban residential lots and parks. Competition between socioeconomic activities and natural processes in all these places results not only in stress for the species that occupy these habitats but also in habitat fragmentation. Some of these processes may simplify ecosystems while others may open up new niches, with the result of increasing species diversity. The net effects of the counteracting forces that affect urban ecosystems and their species diversity depend on the interplay of many local and global conditions.

Sea level rise and even modest changes in the frequency, severity and distribution of tropical storms and hurricanes, for example, may have substantial impacts on coastal wetland patterns and processes, many of which are part of urban ecosystems. These impacts will combine with other human uses of wetlands, such as agriculture, harvesting of plants and animals, industry and settlement (Barth and Titus 1984; Carter 1988; Day, et al. 1993; Michener, et al. 1997). Fragmentation of landscapes, combined with changing climate conditions, may reduce diversity of indigenous species and prove an increasing challenge to the ability of natural resource managers to maintain viable habitats and species populations (Peters and Darling 1985; Peters and Lovejoy 1992). Disruptions of existing ecosystem processes may be the result, for example, of the disruption of seed dispersal, limitations on foraging ranges, infringement on species migration corridors or increased competition between native and exotic species (Fahrig and Paloheimo 1988).

Cities are often the ports of first entry for exotic species–introduced deliberately for agricultural production, ornamental use or as pets, and inadvertently introduced in ballast waters of ships, or with agricultural and other products. The conditions for longer-term establishment of populations of exotic species may be improved through climate change, in part because present ecosystems become increasingly stressed and in part because the conditions that favored their presence at their place of origin may now be found in their new destination. Since different species are likely to respond differently to climate change, changes in species composition may result (Graham 1988). Even given that disturbance in general encourages invasion of ecosystems by new species, the abundance and diversity of exotic species is expected to increase (Lodge 1993; Sweeney, et al. 1992).

Changes in precipitation and temperature regimes of urban areas can lead to increased runoff of fertilizers and pesticides from intensively managed agricultural lands, parks and lawns. Increased release of detergents and solvents from households and industry as a result of overwhelmed combined sewer overflow systems and water treatment plants, as well as runoff of oils and other petroleum products from roads, filling stations and parking lots during periods of heavy downpours may also occur. Hurricane-induced storm surges can have deleterious effects on inland freshwater and brackish wetlands and low-lying terrestrial areas because of the salt water, sediments and organic material that the surges carry inland (Blood, et al. 1991; Knott and Matore 1991). Elevated salt levels may persist for more than a year, causing significant long-term changes in plant communities (Hook, et al. 1991).

As humans protect coastal zones from sea level rise, the natural ability of coastal wetlands to migrate landward as sea level rises may be significantly compromised. In general, human alteration of wetlands and the landscapes that surround them may increase the rates of response to climate change or totally overwhelm such responses.

The literature on climate impacts on ecosystems points towards the need to establish reserves that cover large altitudinal ranges and topographic relief as well as connected corridors to enable a range of migration options to species threatened by climate change (Halpin 1997). Since little research on climate impacts is carried out regarding species diversity, ecosystem structure and function, and ecosystem health in urban areas, no analogous set of recommendations exists at the local scale that may be within the purview of regional planners. However, by extrapolation, insights from landscape-scale analyses point towards the need to establish redundant reserves, to select reserves with a high degree of habitat diversity, and to manage for landscape connectivity and habitat maintenance (see Halpin 1997 for a discussion of large landscape scales).

Human Health

Climate asserts a significant influence on human health, as is evidenced by the geographic distribution and seasonal fluctuations of many diseases and causes of mortality (Tromp 1980; Stone 1995; Martens 1998). Public health researchers have, however, only recently begun to investigate the potential impacts of climate change and to identify adaptation strategies to reduce public health vulnerabilities to climate variability and change (Longstreth 1991; Kovats, et al. 1999; Patz, et al. 2000; WHO 2000; Watson and McMicheal 2001).

Changes in temperature and precipitation regimes, as well as in the frequency of extreme weather events, will combine to affect morbidity and mortality. From a societal perspective, changes in extreme events may be an even larger concern than changes in climatic averages (Katz and Brown 1992; Changnon 2000). Recent research indicates that the frequency of extreme heat-stress events in the US may already have increased (Gaffen and Ross 1998). The recognition of likely future increases in extreme temperature events in combination with the well-established sensitivity of mortality to temperature extremes has resulted in expanded public health research to examine the effects of climate change on temperature-related mortality.

Mid-latitudinal climates exhibit strong cyclical temperature and mortality patterns (Lerchl 1998). Higher temperatures are commonly associated with lower mortality rates and, conversely, lower temperatures associated with higher mortality rates. The seasonal nature of mortality rates has been observed, for example, in heart failure-related morbidity and mortality (Steward, et al. 2002), coronary heart disease (Pell and Cobbe 1999) and incidence of stroke (Lanska and Hoffmann 1999; Oberg, et al. 2000). Some research indicates that the magnitude of the seasonal mortality oscillation may be dampening due to advances in medicine and the ability of humans to control their micro-environments (Seretakis, et al. 1997; Lerchl 1998). Other researchers, however, find no evidence of a decline in the oscillation of seasonal mortality (Van Rossum, et al. 2001).

Exposure to temperature extremes, such as those experienced during heat waves and cold spells, is associated with rapid increases in mortality (Huynen, et al. 2001). For example, more than 700 deaths in Chicago were attributed to the July 1995 heat wave (Semenza, et al. 1996). Extreme heat events increase requirements on the cardiovascular system to produce physiological cooling which, in turn, may lead to excess deaths (Kilbourne 1997). In particular, infants, the elderly, individuals with pre-existing illnesses, the poor, the overweight and individuals living in urban areas are vulnerable to heat-related morbidity and mortality (Blum, et al. 1998; Smoyer, et al. 2000; CDC 2002; NWS 2002).

Extreme cold temperature events are also associated with increases in mortality rates, controlling for influenza (Kunst, et al. 1993; Eurowinter Group 1997). Sharp increases in mortality during cold events have been identified, mainly due to thrombolic and respiratory disease (Donaldson and Keatinge 1997). Other mechanisms through which cold affects mortality include increases in blood pressure, blood viscosity and heart rate. Coronary and stroke mortality have been shown to be associated with cold temperatures in the United States (Rogot and Padgett 1976). In Russia mortality is found to increase by 1.15 per cent for each 1°C drop in temperature (Donaldson, et al. 1998). A study of the impacts of temperature and snowfall on mortality in Pennsylvania found exposure to snow and temperatures below -7°C (19°F) to be dangerous to health (Gorjanc, et al. 1999).

The effects of extreme temperature events on mortality are not solely determined by physiological variables, but also by the degree of acclimation of the local population to the regional climate regime (Kalkstein and Davies 1989; Kalkstein and Greene 1997; Smoyer 1998; Keatinge, et al. 2000; Curriero, et al. 2002). Acclimation entails the adaptation of communities to their environmental surroundings through behavioral patterns, societal fashions and customs such as dress and siestas, the thermal attributes of the local built environment, the availability of air conditioning and the health system's familiarity and ability to deal with weather-induced health conditions. In fact, research suggests that the sensitivity of mortality to extreme heat events has been decreasing over time, possibly as a result of societal adaptation (Davies, et al. 2002).

The wide range of climatic environments inhabited by humans demonstrates our enormous ability to buffer ourselves from harsh macro-environments. As an example, in Yakutsk–the coldest city in the world–no association is present between mortality rates and extremely cold temperatures (Donaldson, et al. 1998). Yet, while acclimation enables a population to become less vulnerable to the prevalent weather events, the population remains susceptible to weather events that occur relatively infrequently (events at the tails of the probability distribution). Therefore, the changes in the frequency of extreme events accompanying climate change need to be examined in order to identify adaptation strategies such that the population can adapt to the characteristics of the new climate regime.

Studies investigating the impacts of climate on human health often employ a place-based approach in consideration of the importance of local acclimation in determining a population's morbidity and mortality (Martens 1998; Smoyer 1998). Place-specific mortality responses to changes in temperature have been found to be present even after controlling for differences in meteorological, demographic and economic variables (Smoyer, et al. 2000). In general, mortality rates of populations in cool climates are more sensitive to heat events, whereas populations in warmer climates have mortality rates more sensitive to cold events (Curriero, et al. 2002). To illustrate, Keatinge (1997) finds that for every 1°C decrease in temperature below 18°C (64.4°F) mortality rates in south Finland increase by only 0.27 per cent, while in Athens, Greece mortality rates increase by 2.15 per cent. Likewise, Kalkstein and Davies (1989) evaluate temperature-related mortality rates in 48 US cities and find considerable variation in heat threshold levels with heat thresholds in Phoenix and Las Vegas equal or exceeding 109°F (43°C), whereas in Boston and Pittsburgh the thresholds are below 86°F (30°C). A city-level study examining minimum mortality temperatures in 11 large US cities finds temperature differences of up to 15°F between cities (Curriero, et al. 2002).

Elevated temperatures not only result in heat stress–most notably among the elderly and urban poor–but also exacerbate local air pollution and thus air quality-related respiratory health problems. While one portion of society may increase their demand for air conditioning, potentially contributing to local energy shortages and urban heat island effects, others may increasingly suffer.

Though the intragenerational health effects of climate change may on occasion be notable, a host of non-climate related issues do play a major, if not overwhelming, role in the health of a population (Smoyer, et al. 2000).

These non-climate related issues include changes in a population's age structure and ethnic diversity; economic prosperity; access to air conditioning, fresh water and health care; and integrity of social networks. Increased mobility may also lead to the spread of diseases irrespective of climate change. All of these issues are intimately related to land use, and particularly development of land in urban areas.

SUMMARY AND CONCLUSIONS

The global climate change debate to date has heavily focused on anthropogenic emissions of greenhouse gases and the impacts of changing atmospheric concentrations of these gases on the stability of the climate system. Improved understanding of global climate change is used to illuminate necessary mitigation strategies to avoid adverse feedbacks from climate variability and change to human living conditions and ecosystem processes. Goals for global reduction in greenhouse gas concentrations are being translated into international policies to guide national and regional development.

More recently, efforts have been increased to explore adaptation strategies that may reduce or avoid impacts of climate variability and change on local economies and ecosystems. Mechanisms to foster the implementation of adaptation strategies are being explored, and in the process of these recent developments, social science and planning-oriented analyses and modeling have expanded to complement biogeochemical models of climate change. While many of these developments are still driven by global concerns, the smart growth research and policy agenda has focused heavily on local actions to improve quality of life through improvements in economic, social and ecosystem health.

Increasingly, benefits of smart growth strategies for global climate are being pointed out, for example when reductions in the number of vehicle miles traveled leads to reduced greenhouse gas emissions, or when expansion of local electricity generation from renewable fuels improves air quality and reduces emissions of greenhouse gases. Potential global benefits of local planning and management approaches are increasingly used to justify interventions in the urban development process towards 'smart' development strategies.

As the research citied above demonstrates, causes and effects of regional and global processes, as well as their interrelations, are often insufficiently understood. On occasion, synergies in strategies to deal with global and local issues exist; sometimes the two may point in opposite directions. Promotion of more compact urban land use and higher-density developments tends to improve overall urban energy efficiency and reduce travel demand, thus reducing emissions. Yet, reductions in heat island effects in cities and the regions within which they are located significantly depend on urban morphology, a range of regional and microclimatic conditions, as well as the effects that savings in direct energy expenditures from increased efficiencies have on households' discretionary income. To the extent that standards of living increase and those increases are used to expand energy consumption, such as for leisure travel, lower indoor temperatures in hot summer months, higher indoor temperatures in winter, or expanded demand for other, energy-intensive goods and services, gains from smart growth and energy end use efficiency improvements may be lost. More compact settlements may also place more localized stress on water supply and water treatment systems, make a larger proportion of the population susceptible to local flooding events, and foster the spread of vector-borne diseases.

All too frequently, impacts on energy, transportation, heat islands, water systems and the health of species are managed separately. Limited competencies exist for integrated assessment, planning and management that explicitly take these interconnections into account. Institutions have evolved to effectively address the systems within their immediate mandate—water authorities control water supply and quality, energy authorities the generation and distribution of energy, transport authorities the movement of goods and people, and public health authorities the physical wellbeing of individuals. Similarly, there are often few incentives in place to encourage, for example, a water authority to implement measures that predominantly improve performance in the energy or transportation sector—especially if costs accrue within the water authority—even if system-wide benefits are positive. Effectively addressing the concerns of the global climate change and urban development communities will thus require not only a realization of the many substantive interrelationships across spatial scales but also development of capacity within institutions to work across institutional boundaries.

Many of the research efforts currently under way to better understand across spatial and temporal scales the human impacts on the environment have benefited from advanced computational techniques and modeling approaches. Many of these are designed with the expressed intent to support decision making in the public, private and non-profit sectors, yet few computer models find long-term application in guiding those decisions. The planning community has much to offer to those interested in addressing global climate change issues in urban areas—the field's rich history of stakeholder involvement, development of planning tools, and case studies of interventions in local decision making provide fertile ground for dialog and learning.

Last but not least, urban development issues, smart growth strategies and environmental problems are frequently evaluated with respect to their differential impacts on individual communities. Who 'wins' and who 'loses' are key questions in the political decision making process that have historically received at least as much attention as questions surrounding the cost effectiveness of alternative actions. Costs and benefits of climate impacts and of human responses to climate change will be distributed unevenly within and across cities, countries and generations (Portney and Weyant 1999). To date, no major assessment exists of the distributional effects of climate change within urban areas. In contrast, international comparisons do point towards significant differences in vulnerabilities, mitigation and adaptation potentials.

The potential for notable reductions of environmental impact per unit of economic activity by industrialized countries is relatively low in comparison to the potential that exists in the developing world. As the many 'low-hanging fruits' of efficiency improvements have already been picked in the industrialized world, costs of additional improvements are high. In contrast, efficiency of many processes in use today in the developing world can in principle be readily raised by adopting technologies already in widespread use in the developed world.

Additional possibilities for implementing advanced technology in developing countries stem from the fact that some countries have begun to rapidly replace obsolete technology and infrastructure. Unprecedented opportunities exist to significantly raise material and energy efficiencies in these countries, to reduce greenhouse gas emissions and to cut production costs through improved efficiencies (Price, et al. 1998). In contrast, major investments in technology and infrastructure have occurred in industrialized countries over the last 20 to 50 years. Many of the technologies and infrastructure systems have expected lifetimes of decades, and in some cases exceed a century (Marland and Weinberg 1988; Ausubel 1991), making a large-scale systems overhaul unlikely.

To understand temporal variability in climate change vulnerabilities requires that we simultaneously consider changes in biogeochemical processes and changes in socioeconomic institutions and infrastructure systems. Where potentials for rapid human adjustments to changes in environmental conditions exist, vulnerabilities can be reduced significantly. Whether those adjustments will actually be made depends on an ability and willingness to base current land use, investment and policy decisions not just on anticipated future socioeconomic conditions. The preceding sections addressed the relevance of climate conditions for future urban development, socioeconomic benefits and environmental quality. The challenge ahead lies in closing the gaps in knowledge of relationships between urban development and climate change, on the one hand, and between scientific knowledge and regional planning and investment decisions on the other.

REFERENCES

Ackerman, B. (1985), 'Temporal march of the Chicago heat island', *Journal of Climate and Applied Meteorology,* **24**: 547–54.

Alcamo, J., M. Marker, et al. (2003), 'Water and Climate: A Global Perspective', *The Kassel World Water Series,* Center for Environmental Systems Research, University of Kassel.

Alexander, D. and R. Tomalty (2002), 'Smart Growth and Sustainable Development: challenges, solutions and policy directions', *Local Environment,* **7**(4): 397–409.

Al-Farouq, A. (1996), 'Adaptation to climate change in the coastal resources sector of Bangladesh: Some critical issues and problems', in *Adapting to climate change,* J.B. Smith (ed.), New York: Springer-Verlag, pp. 335–342.

Amato, A., M. Ruth, et al. (2005), 'Regional Energy Demand Responses to Climate Change: Methodology and Application to the Commonwealth of Massachusetts', *Climatic Change,* **71**(1):175–201.

Anderson, G.M. and M.K. Santore (2002), *Our Built and Natural Environments: A Technical Review of the Interactions Between Landuse, Transportation, and Environmental Quality,* Collingdale: DIANE Publishing Company.

ASCE (1992), 'Effects of Sea-Level Rise on Bays and Estuaries', American Society of Civil Engineers, *Journal of Hydraulic Engineering,* **118**(1): 1–10.

Ausubel, J.H. (1991), 'Does climate still matter', *Nature,* **350**: 649–652.

Badri, M.A. (1992), 'Analysis of Demand for Electricity in the United States', *Energy and Buildings,* **17**(7): 725–733.

Baker, A.C., C.J. Stargert, T.R. McClanahan, and P.W. Glynn (2004), 'Corals' adaptive response to climate change', *Nature,* **430**:741.

Barnett, T.P. (1984), 'The estimation of "global" sea level change: a problem of uniqueness', *Journal of Geophysical Research,* **89**: 7980–7988.

Barth, M. and J. Titus (1984), *Greenhouse effect and sea level rise,* New York: Van Nostrand Reinhold.

Belzer, D.B. and M.J. Scott (1996), 'Climate Change Impacts on US Commercial Building Energy Consumption: An Analysis Using Sample Survey Data', *Energy Sources,* **18**(2): 177–201.

Benfield, F.K., N. Vorsanger, et al. (2002), *Solving Sprawl: Models of Smart Growth in Communities Across America,* New York: Natural Resources Defense Council.

Bernstein, M., P. Bromley, et al. (1999), *Developing countries and global climate change: electric power options for growth,* Washington, DC: Pew Center on Global Climate Change.

Berry, T. and M. Jaccard (2001), 'The renewable portfolio standard: design considerations and an implementation survey', *Energy Policy,* **29**: 263–277.

Blood, E.R., P. Anderson, et al. (1991), 'Effects of Hurricane Hugo on coastal soil solution chemistry in South Carolina', *Biotropica,* **23**: 348–355.

Bloomfield, J., M. Smith, et al. (1999), *Hot Nights in the City: Global Warming, Sea-Level Rise and the New York Metropolitian Region,* Environmental Defense Fund.

Blum, L.N., L.B. Bresolin, et al. (1998), 'Heat-Related Illness During Extreme Emergencies', *JAMA,* **279**(19): 1514.

Böhm, R. (1998), 'Urban Bias in Temperature Time Series–A Case Study for the City of Vienna, Austria', *Climatic Change,* 38(1): 113–128.

Boland, J.J. (1997), 'Assessing urban water use and the role of water conservation measures under climate uncertainty', *Climatic Change,* **37**: 157–176.

Bornstein, R. and Q. Lin (2000), 'Urban heat islands and summertime convective thunderstorms in Atlanta: three case studies', *Atmospheric Environment,* **34**(3): 507–516.

Bragado, N., J. Corbett and S. Sprowls (1995), *Building Livable Communities: A Policymaker's Guide to Infill Development,* Sacramento, CA: Center for Livable Communities.

Brake, A.G. (2001), 'Rooftop oasis', *Architecture,* **90**(6): 54.

Brazdil, R. and M. Budikova (1999), 'An urban bias in air temperature fluctuations at the Klementinum, Prague, the Czech Republic', *Atmospheric Environment,* **33**: 4211–4217.

Bucher, D.C. (2002), 'Case Study: Greyfields as an emerging smart growth opportunity with the potential for added synergies through a unique mix of uses', *Real Estate Issues,* **27**(2): 46–54.

Burby, R.J., A.C. Nelson, et al. (2001), 'Urban Containment Policy and Exposure to Natural Hazards: Is There a Connection?', *Journal of Environmental Planning and Management,* **44**(4).

Burchell, R.W., G. Lowenstein, et al. (2002), Costs of Sprawl–2000, Washington, DC: National Academy Press.

Burkett, V.R. (2002), *Potential Impacts of Climate Change and Variability on Transportation in the Gulf Coast / Mississippi Delta Region,* The Potential Impacts of Climate Change on Transportation, US Department of Transportation, http://www.climate.volpe.dot.gov.

Burn, D. H. (1994), 'Hydrologic Effects of Climatic Change in West-central Canada', *Journal of Hydrology,* **160**: 53–70.

Burton, I. (1996), 'The growth of adaptation capacity: practice and policy', in *Adapting to climate change,* J.B. Smith (ed.), New York: Springer-Verlag: 55–67.

Calthorpe, O. and W. Fulton (2001), *The regional city: Planning for the end of sprawl*, Washington, DC: Island Press.

Camilleri, M., R. Jaques, et al. (2001), 'Impacts of Climate Change on Building Performance in New Zealand', *Building Research and Information,* **29**(6): 440–450.

Cardelino, C.A. and W.L. Chameides (1990), 'Natural hydrocarbons, urbanization, and urban ozone', *Jounal of Geophysical Research,* **95**(D9): 13971–13979.

Cartalis, C., A. Synodinou, et al. (2001), 'Modifications in energy demand in urban areas as a result of climate changes: an assessment for the southeast Mediterranean region', *Energy Conversion and Management,* **42**: 1647–1656.

Carter, R.W.G. (1988), *Coastal Environments*, New York: Academic Press.

Centers for Disease Control and Prevention (CDC) (2002), *Extreme Heat*, Centers for Disease Control and Prevention.

Cevero, R. and K. Kockelman (1997), 'Travel demand and the 3D's: density, diversity, and design', *Transportation Research,* **D2**(3): 199–219.

Changnon, S. (2000), 'Human Factors Explain the Increased Losses from Weather and Climate Extremes', *Bulletin of the American Meteorological Society,* **81**(3): 437–442.

Changnon, S.A. (1996), 'Effects of summer precipitation on urban transportation', *Climatic Change,* **32**: 481–494.

Cobb, C. (1998), 'The Roads Aren't Free; Estimating the Full Social Costs of Driving and the Effects of Accurate Pricing, Redefining Progress', *Environmental Tax Shifting*, San Francisco: Redefining Progress.

Cohen, S.J. (1996), 'Integrated regional assessment of global climatic change: Lessons from the Mackenzie Basin Impact Study (MBIS)', *Global and Planetary Change,* **11**(4).

Cohen, S.J. (ed.) (1997a), *Mackenzie Basin Impact Study final report*, Downsview: Environment Canada.

Cohen, S.J. (1997b), 'What if and so what in northwest Canada: Could climate change make a difference to the future of the Mackenzie basin?', *Arctic,* **50**(4).

Colombo, A.F., D. Etkin, et al. (1999), 'Climate Variability and the Frequency of Extreme Temperature Events for Nine Sites Across Canada: Implications for Power Usage', *Journal of Climate,* **12**(8): 2490–2502.

Crane, R. (2000), 'The Influence of Urban Form on Travel: An Interpretive Review', *Journal of Planning Literature,* **15**(1): 3–24.

Crane, R. and R. Crepeau (1998), 'Does neighborhood design influence travel?: A behavior analysis of travel diary and GIS data', *Transportation Research Part D: Transport and Environment,* **3**: 225–238.

Cruise, J.F., A.S. Limaye, et al. (1999), 'Assessment of impacts of climate change on water quality in the southeastern United States', *Journal of the American Water Resources Association,* **35**: 1539–1550.

Curriero, F.C., K.S. Heiner, et al. (2002), 'Temperature and Mortality in 11 Cities of the Eastern United States', *American Journal of Epidemiology,* **155**(1): 80–87.

Daniels, T. (2001), 'Smart Growth: A New American Approach to Regional Planning', *Planning Practice and Research,* **16**(3/4): 271–279.

Davies, R.E., P.C. Knappenberger, et al. (2002), 'Decadal Changes in Heat-related Human Mortality in the Eastern United States', *Climate Research,* **22**(2): 175–184.

Day, J.W., W.H. Conner, et al. (1993), 'Impacts of sea level rise on coastal systems with special emphasis on the Mississippi river deltaic plain', in *Climate and sea level change: observations, projections and implications,* R.A. Warrick, E.M. Barrow, and T.M.L. Wigley (eds), Cambridge, England: Cambridge University Press.

DeCiccoa, J. and J. Mark (1998), 'Meeting the energy and climate challenge for transportation in the United States', *Energy Policy,* **26**(5): 395–412.

Dernbach, J. (2000), 'Moving the climate change debate from models to proposed legislation: lessons from state experience', *Environmental Law Reporter,* **30**: 10933–10979.

Doll, P. and S. Siebert (2001), *Global Modeling of Irrigation Water Requirement,* Kassel, Germany: University of Kassel.

Donaldson, G.C., S.P. Ermakov, et al. (1998), 'Cold related mortalities and protection against cold in Yakutsk, eastern Siberia: observation and interview study', *British Medical Journal,* **317**: 978–982.

Donaldson, G.C. and W.R. Keatinge (1997), 'Early increases in ischaemic heart disease mortality dissociated from, and later changes associated with, respiratory mortality, after cold weather in south east England', *Journal of Epidemiology and Community Health,* **51**(6).

Doornkamp, J.C. (1998), 'Coastal flooding, global warming and environmental management', *Journal of Environmental Management,* **52**: 327–333.

Douglas, B.C. (2001), 'An introduction to sea level', in *Sea level rise: history and consequences,* B.C. Douglas, M.S. Kirney, and S.P. Leatherman (eds), San Diego, CA: Academic Press, pp. 1–11.

Downs, A. (2003), *The Impacts of Smart Growth Upon the Economy,* New Brunswick, New Jersey: Landuse Institute of the New Jersey Institute for Continuing Legal Education.

Downton, M.W., T.R. Stewart, et al. (1988), 'Estimating Historical Heating and Cooling Needs: Per Capita Degree Days', *Journal of Applied Meteorology,* **27**(1): 84–90.

duVair, P., M.J. Burer, et al. (2002), *Climate Change and the Potential Implications for California's Transportation System*, The Potential Impacts of Climate Change on Transportation.

Easterling, D. R., G. A. Mehl, et al. (2000), 'Climate extemes: observations, modeling, and impacts', *Science,* **289**: 2068–2074.

Edmonds, J., J.M. Roop, et al. (2000), *Technology and the economics of climate change policy*, Washington, DC: Pew Center on Global Climate Change.

Environmental Protection Agency (EPA) (2000), *Heat Island Effects*.

Eurowinter Group (1997), 'Cold exposure and winter mortality from ischaemic heart disease, cerebrovascular disease, respiratory disease, and all causes, in warm and cold regions of Europe', *Lancet,* **349**: 1341–1346.

Everts, C.H. (1985), 'Effects of Sea Level Rise and Net Sand Volume Change on Shoreline Position at Ocean City', *Maryland Potential Impacts of Sea Level Rise on the Breach at Ocean City, Maryland*, Washington, DC, Environmental Protection Agency.

Ewing, R. (1995), *Beyond density, mode-choice, and single-purpose trips*, the 74th Annual Meeting of the Transportation Research Board, Washington, DC.

Fahrig, L. and L. Paloheimo (1988), 'Effects of spatial arrangement of habitat patches on local population size', *Ecology,* **69**: 468–475.

Faiz, A., C.S. Weaver, et al. (1990), Air Pollution from Motor Vehicles: Standards and Technologies for Controlling Emissions, Washington, DC: World Bank.

FCCC (1992), *United Nations Framework Convention on Climate Change*, New York: United Nations.

FCCC (1997), *Kyoto Protocol to the United Nations Framework Convention on Climate Change*, New York: United Nations.

FEMA (1991), *Projected Impact of Relative Sea Level Rise on the National Flood Insurance Program*, Federal Emergency Management Agency, Washington, DC.

Few, R. (2003), 'Flooding, vulnerability and coping strategies: local responses to a global threat', *Progress in Development Studies,* **3**(1): 43–58.

Figuerola, P. and N. Mazzeo (1998), 'Urban-rural temperature differences in Buenos Aires', *International Journal of Climatology,* **18**: 1709–1723.

Fox, I.B. (2003), 'Introduction to Flood Management–Getting ADB's Water Policy to Work', *The impact of floods, drought, and other water disasters on the poor*. Asian Development Bank.

Frank, L.D. and G. Pivo (1994), 'Impacts of mixed use and density on utilization of three modes of travel: single-occupant vehicle, transit, and walking', *Transportation Research Record,* **1466**: 44–52.

Frankhauser, S. (1996), 'The potential costs of climate change adaptation', in *Adapting to climate change*, J.B. Smith (ed.), New York: Springer-Verlag, pp. 80–96.

Frederick, K.D. and P.H. Gleick (1999), 'Water And Global Climate Change: Potential Impacts on US Water Resources', Washington, DC: Pew Center on Global Climate Change.

Friedman, B., S.P. Gordon, et al. (1994), 'The effect of neo-traditional neighborhood design on travel characteristics', *Transportation Research Record,* **1400**: 63–70.

Gaffen, D.J. and R.J. Ross (1998), 'Increased Summertime Heat Stress in the US', *Nature,* **396**(6711): 529–530.

Gambolati, G., P. Teatini, et al. (1999), 'Coasline regression of the Romagna region, Italy, due to natural and anthropogenic land subsidence and sea level rise', *Water Resources Research,* **35**(1): 163–184.

Gleick, P.H. (1987), 'Regional Hydrologic Consequences of Increases in Atmospheric Carbon Dioxide and Other Trace Gases', *Climatic Change,* **10**(2): 137–161.

Gleick, P.H. and E.P. Maurer (1990), 'Assessing the Costs of Adapting to Sea Level Rise: A Case Study of San Francisco Bay, Oakland, CA', Pacific Institute for Studies in Development, Environment and Security and the Stockholm Environment Institute.

Glendening, P. (2001), Press release, 2001 legislative lesson. Annapolis, MD, Office of the Governor.

Gorjanc, M.L., W.D. Flanders, et al. (1999), 'Effects of Temperature and Snowfall on Mortality in Pennsylvania', *American Journal of Epidemiology,* **149**(12): 1152–1160.

Graham, R.W. (1988), 'The role of climatic change in the design of biological reserves: the paleoecological perspective for conservation biology', *Conservation Biology,* **2**: 391–394.

Greene, D.L. (1997), 'Environmental impacts', *Journal of Transport Geography,* **5**(1): 28–29.

Greene, D.L., J. Kahn, et al. (1999), 'Fuel Economy Rebound Effect for US Household Vehicles', *Energy Journal,* **20**(3): 1–31.

Greene, D.L. and A. Schafer (2003), *Reducing Greenhouse Gas Emissions from US Transportation*, the Pew Center on Global Climate Change.

Greene, D.L. and M. Wegener (1997), 'Sustainable transport', *Journal of Transport Geography,* **5**(3): 177–190.

Gregg, J.W., C.G. Jones, et al. (2003), 'Urbanization effects on tree growth in the vicinity of New York City', *Nature,* **424**: 183–187.

Groisman, P.Y. (1999), 'Changes in the probability of heavy precipitation: important indicators of climatic change', *Climatic Change,* **42**: 243–283.

Gröler, A. (1990), *The Rise and Fall of Infrastructures*, Heidelberg, Germany: Physica-Verlag.

Gwilliam, K.M. (1993), *On reducing transport's contribution to global warming*, Paris: OECD.

Hadfield, P. (2000), 'Totally tropical Tokyo', *New Scientist,* **167**: 10.

Halpin, P.N. (1997), 'Global climate change and natural-area protection: management responses and research directions', *Ecological Applications,* **7**: 828–843.

Hansen, J., M. Sato, et al. (2000), 'Global warming in the twenty-first century: an alternative scenario', *Proceedings of the National Academy of Sciences,* **97**(18): 9875–9880.

Harrington, W., J.N. Sanchirico, et al. (2003), *Effects of Climate Change Policies on the US Household Transportation Sector*, Resources for the Future, Washington, D.C..

Hayes, B.D. (2004), 'Interdisciplinary Planning of Nonstructural Flood Hazard Mitigation', *Journal of Water Resources Planning and Management,* **130**(1).

Hellman, K.H. and R.M. Heavenrich (2002), 'Light-Duty Automotive Technology and Fuel Economy Trends: 1975 Through 2002', Ann Arbor, MI: Advanced Technology Division, Office of Transportation and Air Quality, U.S. Environmental Protection Agency.

Higgins, P.A.T. and M. Higgins (2003), 'A healthy reduction in oil consumption and carbon emissions', *Energy Policy,* in press.

Hill, D. (1996), *The baked apple? : Metropolitan New York in the greenhouse*, New York, NY: New York Academy of Sciences.

Hogan, A. and M. Ferrick (1998), 'Observations in nonurban heat islands', *Journal of Applied Meteorology,* **37**: 232–236.

Hook, D.D., M.A. Buford, et al. (1991), 'Impact of Hurricane Hugo on the South Carolina coastal plain forest', *Journal of Coastal Research,* **8**: 291–300.

Huang, G.H., S.J. Cohen, et al. (1998), 'Land resources adaptation planning under changing climate–a study for the Mackenzie Basin', *Resources Conservation and Recycling,* **24**(2): 95–119.

Hughes, W. S. and R. C. Balling (1996), 'Urban influences on South African urban temperature trends', *International Journal of Climatology,* **16**(8): 935–940.

Huynen, M., P. Martens, et al. (2001), 'The Impacts of Heat Waves and Cold Spells on Mortality in the Dutch Population', *Environmental Health Perspectives,* **109**: 463–470.

IPCC (1996), Coastal Zones and Small Islands, in *Impacts, Adaptations and Mitigation of Climate Change: Scientific–Technical Analyses*, R. Watson, M.C. Zinyowera, and R.H. Moss (eds), Intergovernmental Panel on Climate Change, Cambridge: Cambridge University Press: 289–324.

IPCC (2001), Climate Change 2001: *Working Group II: Impacts, Adaptation and Vulnerability*, Intergovernmental Panel on Climate Change, Cambridge: Cambridge University Press.

IPCC (1990), *Strategies for Adaption to Sea Level Rise*, Intergovernmental Panel on Climate Change Response Strategies Working Group, Cambridge: Cambridge University Press.

ITE (2003), 'Task Force Report Summary: A Proposed Recommended Practice: Smart Growth Transportation Guidelines', *Institute of Transportation Engineers Journal*, 73(3): 55.

Jeton, A.E., M.D. Dettinger, et al. (1996), *Potential Effects of Climate Change on Streamflow of Eastern and Western Slopes of the Sierra Nevada, California and Nevada*, Denver, CO: US Geological Survey WRI Report, 95–4260.

Johnson, D. (1999), *Planning Communities for the 21st Century*, S. Meck, R. Cobb, K. Finucan, D. Johnson, and P. Salkin (eds), Chicago, IL: American Planning Association.

Jorgenson, D.W., R.J. Goettle, et al. (2000), *The role of subsitution in understanding the cost of climate change policy*, Washington, DC: Pew Center on Global Climate Change.

Kalkstein, L.S. and R.E. Davies (1989), 'Weather and Human Mortality: An Evaluation of Demographic and Interregional Responses in the United States', *Annals of the Association of American Geographers*, 79(1): 44–64.

Kalkstein, L.S. and J.S. Greene (1997), 'An Evaluation of Climate/Mortality Relationships in Large US Cities and the Possible Impacts of a Climate Change', *Environmental Health Perspectives*, 105: 84–93.

Kalnay, E. and M. Cai. (2003), 'Impact of urbanization and landuse change on climate', *Nature*, 423: 528–531.

Kana, T.W., J. Michel, et al. (1984), 'The Physical Impact of Sea Level Rise in the Area of Charleston, South Carolina', in *Greenhouse Effect and Sea Level Rise: A Challenge for This Generation*. M.C. Barth and J. G. Titus (eds), New York: Van Nostrand Reinhold.

Karl, T.R. and R.W. Knight (1998), 'Secular Trends of Precipitation Amount, Frequency, and Intensity in the United States', *Bulletin of the American Meteorological Society*, 79(2): 231–241.

Katz, R.W. and B.G. Brown (1992), 'Extreme Events in a Changing Climate: Variability is More Important then Averages', *Climatic Change*, 21: 289–302.

Kay, J.J. and E.D. Schneider (1994), 'Embracing complexity', *Alternatives*, 20(3): 32–39.

Keatinge, W.R. (1997), 'Cold Exposure and Winter Mortality from Ischaemic Heart Disease, Cerebrovascular Disease, Respiratory Disease, and All

Causes in Warm and Cold Regions of Europe', *Lancet,* **349**(9062): 1341–1346.

Keatinge, W.R., G.C. Donaldson, et al. (2000), 'Heat Related Mortality in Warm and Cold Regions of Europe: Observational Study', *British Medical Journal,* **321**(7262): 670.

Kenworthy, J.R. (1996), 'Developing sustainable urban transport and landuse policies in Asian cities: a global review of automobile dependence with a focus on the role of rail systems', *The Asian Urban Rail Congress,* Hyatt Regency, Singapore.

Kenworthy, J.R. and F.B. Laube (1999), 'Patterns of automobile dependence in cities: an international overview of key physical and economic dimensions with some implications for urban policy', *Transportation Research Part A: Policy and Practice,* **33**(7–8): 691–723.

Kidder, S. and O. Essenwanger (1995), 'The effect of clouds and wind on the difference in nocturnal cooling rates between urban and rural areas', *Journal of Applied Meteorology,* **34**: 2440–2448.

Kilbourne, E.M. (1997), 'Heat waves and hot environments', in *The public health consequences of disasters,* E.K. Noji (ed.), Oxford, UK: Oxford University Press.

Klein, R.J.T. and R.J. Nicholls (1999), 'Assessment of coastal vulnerability to climate change', *Ambio,* **28**(2): 182–183.

Klysik, K. and K. Fortuniak (1999), 'Temporal and spatial characteristics of the urban heat island of Lodz, Poland', *Atmospheric Environment,* **33**: 3885–3895.

Knott, D.M. and R.M. Matore (1991), 'The short-term effects of Hurricane Hugo on fishes and decapod crustaceans in the Ashley River and adjacent marsh creeks, South Carolina', *Journal of Coastal Research,* **8**: 335–356.

Kockelman, K.M. (1997), 'Travel behavior as a function of accessibility, landuse mixing, and landuse balance: evidence from the San Francisco bay area', *Transportation Research Record,* **1607**: 116–125.

Kovats, R.S., A. Haines, et al. (1999), 'Climate Change and Human Health in Europe', *British Medical Journal,* **318**: 1682–1685.

Kulesa, G. (2002), *Weather and Aviation: How Does Weather Affect the Safety and Operations of Airports and Aviation, and How Does FAA Work to Manage Weather-related Effects? The Potential Impacts of Climate Change on Transportation.*

Kulkarni, A. (1996), *The influence of landuse and network structure on travel behavior,* Department of Civil and Environmental Engineering, Irvine, University of California.

Kunst, A.E., C.W. Looman, et al. (1993), 'Outdoor air temperature and mortality in The Netherlands: a time-series analysis', *American Journal of Epidemiology,* **137**(3): 331–341.

Kyper, T. and R. Sorensen (1985), *Potential Impacts of Selected Sea Level Rise Scenarios on the Beach and Coastal Works at Sea Bright, New Jersey*, Coastal Zone '85. New York, NY: American Society of Civil Engineers.

Lam, J.C. (1998), 'Climatic and Economic Influences on Residential Electricity Consumption', *Energy Conversion and Management*, **39**(7): 623–629.

Lanska, D.J. and R.G. Hoffmann (1999), 'Seasonal variation in stroke mortality rates', *Neurology*, **52**: 984.

Le Compte, D.M. and H.E. Warren (1981), 'Modeling the Impact of Summer Temperatures on National Electricity Consumption', *Journal of Applied Meteorology*, **20**: 1415–1419.

Leatherman, S. (1994), *Coastal Resource Impacts and Adaptation Assessment Methods*, University of Maryland.

Lehman, R.L. (1994), 'Projecting Monthly Natural Gas Sales for Space Heating Using a Monthly Updated Model and Degree-days from Monthly Outlooks', *Journal of Applied Meteorology*, **33**(1): 96–106.

Lemons, J. and D.A. Brown (1995), *Sustainable development: science, ethics and public policy*, Dortrecht, The Netherlands: Kluwer Academic Publishers.

Lerchl, A. (1998), 'Changes in the Seasonality of Mortality in Germany form 1946 to 1995: The Role of Temperature', *International Journal of Biometeorology*, **42**: 84–88.

Lettenmaier, D.P., E.F. Wood, et al. (1994), 'Hydro-climatological Trends in the Continental United States 1948–1988', *Journal of Climate*, **7**: 586–607.

Levinson, D.M., D. Gillen, et al. (1996), *The Social Costs of Intercity Transportation: A Review and Comparison of Air and Highway*.

Linder, K.P. (1990), 'National Impacts of Climate Change on Electric Utilities', *The Potential Effects of Global Warming on the United States*, J.B. Smith and D.A. Tirpak (eds), Washington, DC: Environmental Protection Agency.

Lins, H.F. and P.J. Michaels (1994), 'Increasing US Streamflow Linked to Greenhouse Forcing', EOS, Transactions, *American Geophysical Union*, **75**(281): 284–285.

Lins, H.F. and E.Z. Stakhiv (1998), 'Managing the nation's water in a changing climate', *Journal of the American Water Resources Association*, **34**(6): 1255–1264.

Litman, T. (2001), 'Generated Traffic; Implications for Transport Planning', *Institute of Transportation Engineers*, **71**(4): 38–47.

Lodge, D.M. (1993), 'Species invasions and deletions: community effects and responses to climate and habitat change', in *Biotic Interactions and*

Global Change, P.M. Kareiva, J. G. Kingsolver, and B. Huey (eds), Massachusetts: Sinauer Associates, pp. 367–387.

Longman, P.J. (1998), 'Who pays for sprawl? Hidden subsidies fuel the growth of the suburban fringe', *US News and World Report.* 27 April.

Longstreth, J. (1991), 'Anticipated Public Health Consequences of Global Climate Change', *Environmental Health Perspectives,* **96**: 139–144.

Lyman, F. (2002), 'Survival plan for urban heat islands', MSNBC News.

Magee, N., J. Curtis, et al. (1999), 'The urban heat island effect at Fairbanks, Alaska', *Theoretical and Applied Climatology,* **64**(1–2): 39–47.

Marchand, D., M. Sanderson, et al. (1988), 'Climatic Change and Great Lakes Levels, The impact on shipping', *Climate Change,* **12**: 107–133.

Marland, G. and A.M. Weinberg (1988), 'Longevity of infrastructure', in *Cities and their vital systems: infrastructure past, present, and future*, J.H. Ausubel and R. Herman (eds), Washington, DC: National Academy Press.

Martens, W.J.M. (1998), 'Climate Change, Thermal Stress and Mortality Changes', *Social Science and Medicine,* **46**(3): 331–344.

Maryland Department of Planning (1997), 'Smart Growth and Neighborhood Conservation Initiative', Maryland Department of Planning, Annapolis, MD.

MDP (2000), 'Smart Growth Codes 2000 Report', Annapolis, MD: Maryland Department of Planning.

Mehl, G. A., T. Karl, et al. (2000), 'An introduction to trends in extreme weather and climate events: observations, socioeconomic impacts, terrestrial ecological impacts, and model projections', *Bulletin of the American Meteorological Society,* **81**(3): 413–416.

Michener, W.K., E.R. Blood, et al. (1997), 'Climate change, hurricanes and tropical storms, and rising sea level in coastal wetlands', *Ecological Applications,* **7**: 770–801.

Miller, J.S. and L.A. Hoel (2002), 'The "smart growth" debate: best practices for urban transportation planning', *Socio-Economic Planning Sciences,* **36**(1): 1–24.

Miller, T., J.C. Walker, et al. (1989), 'Impact of global climate change on urban infrastructure', in *Potential effects of global climate change on the United States*, J.B. Smith and P.A. Tirpak (eds), Washington, DC: US Environmental Protection Agency.

Milly, P.C.D., R.T. Wetherald, et al. (2002), 'Increasing Risk of Great Floods in a Changing Climate', *Nature,* **415**(6871): 514–517.

Morris, C., I. Simmonds, et al. (2001), 'Quantification of the influences of wind and cloud on the nocturnal urban heat island of a large city', *Journal of Applied Meteorology,* **40**: 169–182.

Morris, M. (1999), 'The Impact of Temperature Trends on Short-Term Energy Demand', Washington, DC: EIA.

Morrison, W. and R. Mendelsohn (1998), 'The Impacts of Climate Change on Energy: An Aggregate Expenditure Model for the US', Washington, DC: US Department of Energy.

Morrison, W.G. (2000), *Canadians and Their Cars and Trucks*, Canada's Energy Efficiency Conference, Ottawa, Canada.

NASA (1999), 'Atlanta's Urban Heat Island', National Aeronautics and Space Administration, http://www.nasa.gov/imagewall/LandSat.

Neumann, J.E., G. Yohe, et al. (2000), *Sea-level rise and Global climate change: A Review of Impacts to US Coasts*, Washington, DC: The Pew Center on Global Climate Change.

Newman, P. and J. Kenworthy (1999), *Sustainability and Cities: Overcoming Automobile Dependence*, Washington, DC: Island Press.

Newman, P., J. Kenworthy, et al. (1995), 'Can we overcome automobile dependence? Physical planning in an age of urban cynicism', *Cities*, 12(1): 53–65.

Newman, P.W. and J.R. Kenworthy (1996), 'The landuse–transport connection: An overview', *Landuse Policy*, 13(1): 1–22.

Nicholls, R.J. (1995), 'Coastal megacities and climate change', *GeoJournal*, 37(3): 369–379.

Nicholls, R.J., F.M.J. Hoozemans, et al. (1999), 'Increasing Flood Risk and Wetland Losses due to Global Sea-Level Rise: Regional and Global Analyses and the Science of Climate Change', *Global Environmental Change*, 9: 569–587.

NRC (2003), *Cumulative Environmental Effects of Oil and Gas Activities on Alaska's North Slope*, National Research Council, Washington, DC: National Academies Press.

NWS (2002), *Heat Wave*, National Weather Service, Silver Spring, MD.

Oberg, A.L., J.A. Ferguson, et al. (2000), 'Incidence of Stroke and Season of the Year: Evidence of an Association', *American Journal of Epidemiology*, 152(6): 558–564.

OSTP (1997), *Climate change: state of knowledge*, Washington, DC: Office of Science and Technology Policy, Executive Office of the President.

Pardo, A., V. Meneu, et al. (2002), 'Temperature and Seasonality Influences on the Spanish Electricity Load', *Energy Economics*, 24(1): 55–70.

Park, H. (1986), 'Features of the heat island in Seoul and its surrounding cities', *Atmospheric Environment*, 20: 1859–1866.

Park, R.A., M.S. Trehan, et al. (1989), 'The Effects of Sea Level Rise on US Coastal Wetlands', in *Effects of Changes in Stratospheric Ozone and Global Climate*, Smith and Tirpak (eds), Washington, DC: United Nations Environment Programme and US Environmental Protection Agency.

Parker, D.J. (1999), 'Flood', *Natural disaster management*, J. Ingleton (ed.), Leicester: Tudor Rose, pp. 38–40.

Parsons Brinkerhogg Quade and Douglas, Inc. (1996), *Influence of landuse mix and neighborhood design on transit demand*, Transit Cooperative Research Program, Transportation Research Board.

Patz, J.A., D. Engelberg, et al. (2000), 'The Effects of Changing Weather on Public Health', *Annual Review of Public Health,* **21**: 271–307.

Patz, J.A., M. McGeehin, et al. (2000), 'The Potential Health Impacts of Climate Variability and Change for the United States: Executive Summary of the Report of the Health Sector of the US National Assessment', *Environmental Health Perspectives,* **108**: 367–376.

Pearce, D. (1991), 'Evaluating the socioeconomic impacts of climate change: an introduction, *Climate change: evaluating the socioeconomic impacts,* Paris: OECD, pp. 9–20.

Pell, J.P. and S.M. Cobbe (1999), 'Seasonal variations in coronary heart disease', *Quarterly Journal of Medicine,* **92**: 689–696.

Pelley, J. (1999), 'Building smart-growth communities', *Environmental Science and Technology,* **33** (1): 28A

Pendall, R., J. Martin, et al. (2002), *Holding the Line: Urban Containment in the United States,* Washington, DC: The Brookings Institution Center on Urban and Metropolitan Policy.

Peters, R.L. and J.D. Darling (1985), 'The greenhouse effect and nature reserves', *BioScience,* **35**: 707–717.

Peters, R.L. and T.E. Lovejoy (1992), *Global warming and biological diversity,* New Haven, CT: Yale University Press.

Philandras, C., D. Metaxas, et al. (1999), 'Climate variability and urbanization in Athens', *Theoretical and Applied Climatology,* **63**: 65–72.

Pinho, O. and M. Orgaz (2000), 'The urban heat island in a small city in coastal Portugal', *International Journal of Biometeorology,* **44**(4): 198–203.

Portney, P.R. and J.P. Weyant (eds) (1999), *Discounting and intergenerational equity,* Washington, DC: Resources for the Future.

Price, L., L. Michaelis, et al. (1998), 'Sectoral trends and driving forces of global energy use and greenhouse gas emissions', *Mitigation and Adaptation Options for Global Change,* **3**: 263–319.

Pushkarev, B. and J. Zupan (1977*), Public Transportation and Landuse Policy,* Bloomington, IN: Indiana University Press.

Quayle, R.G. and H.F. Diaz (1979), 'Heating Degree Day Data Applied to Residential Heating Energy Consumption', *Journal of Applied Meteorology,* **19**: 241–246.

Rodier, C.J., R.A. Johnston, et al. (2002), 'Heuristic policy analysis of regional landuse, transit, and travel pricing scenarios using two urban models', *Transportation Research Part D: Transport and Environment,* **7**(4): 243–254.

Rogot, E. and S.J. Padgett (1976), 'Associations of coronary and stroke mortality in with temperature and snowfall in selected areas of the United States, 1962–1966', *American Journal of Epidemiology*, **103**(6): 565–575.

Rosenberg, N. (2003), 'Development impact fees: is limited cost internalization actually smart growth?', *Boston College Environmental Affairs Law Review*, **30**(3): 641–688.

Rosenfeld, A.H. and J.J. Romm (1996), *Policies to reduce heat islands: magnitudes of benefits and incentives to achieve them*, Proceedings of the 1996 LBL-38679 ACEEE Summer Study on Energy Efficiency in Buildings, Pacific Grove, CA.

Rosenthal, D.H., H.K. Gruenspecht, et al. (1995), 'Effects of Global Warming on Energy Use for Space Heating and Cooling in the United States', *The Energy Journal*, **16**(2): 41–54.

Rusk, D. (1998), 'The Exploding Metropolis: Why Growth Management Makes Sense', *The Brookings Review*, **16**: 13–15.

Ruth, M. (1993), *Integrating Economics, Ecology and Thermodynamics*, Kluwer Academic.

Ruth, M., A. Amato, et al. (2000), 'Impacts of Market-based Climate Change Policy on the US Iron and Steel Industry', *Energy Sources*, **22**(3): 269–280.

Ruth, M. and P. Kirshen (2001), 'Integrated Impacts of Climate Change upon Infrastructure Systems and Services in the Boston Metropolitan Area', *World Resource Review*, **13**(1).

Ruth, M. and A. Lin. (2005), *Regional energy demand and adaptations to climate change: methodology and application to the state of Maryland*, US: College Park, MD, University of Maryland, School of Public Policy, Environmental Policy Program.

Sailor, D.J. (2001), 'Relating residential and commercial sector electricity loads to climate–evaluating state level sensitivities and vulnerabilities', *Energy and Buildings*, **26**: 645–657.

Sailor, D.J. and J.R. Munoz (1997), 'Sensitivity of electricity and natural gas consumption to climate in the US–Methodology and results for eight states', *Energy and Buildings*, **22**(10): 987–998.

Sailor, D.J., J.N. Rosen, et al. (1998), 'Natural Gas Consumption and Climate: A Comprehensive Set of Predictive State-level Models for the United States', *Energy*, **23**(2): 91–103.

Schelling, T.C. (1992), 'Some economic of global warming', *The American Economic Review*, **82**(1): 1–14.

Schimek, P. (1996), 'Household motor vehicle ownership and use: how much does residential density matter?', *Transportation Research Record*, **1552**: 120–125.

Schmandt, J. and J. Clarkson (eds) (1992), *The regions and global warming: Impacts and response strategies*, New York, NY: Oxford University Press.

Schmidlin, T. (1989), 'The urban heat island at Toledo, Ohio', *Ohio Journal of Science,* **89**: 38–41.

Scott, M.J., L.E. Wrench, et al. (1994), 'Effects of Climate Change on Commercial Building Energy Demand', *Energy Sources,* **16**: 317–332.

Segal, M., H. Shafir, et al. (1992), 'Climatic-related Evaluations of the Summer Peak-Hours' Electric Load in Israel', *Journal of Applied Meteorology,* **31**(12): 1492–1498.

Semenza, J.C., C.H. Rubin, et al. (1996), 'Heat-Related Deaths During the July 1995 Heat Wave in Chicago', *The New England Journal of Medicine,* **335**(2): 84–90.

Seretakis, D., P. Lagiou, et al. (1997), 'Changing seasonality of mortality from coronary heart disease', *JAMA,* **278**(12): 1012–1014.

Smith, O.P. and G. Levasseur (2002), 'Impacts of Climate Change on Transportation in Alaska', *The Potential Impacts of Climate Change on Transportation.*

Smith, W. (1984), 'Mass transit for high-rise, high-density living', *Journal of Transportation Engineering,* **110**(6): 521–535.

Smoyer, K.E. (1998), 'Putting Risk in its Place: Methodological Considerations for Investigating Extreme Event Health Risks', *Social Science and Medicine,* **47**(11): 1809–1924.

Smoyer, K.E., D.G.C. Rainham, et al. (2000), 'Heat-stress-related mortality in five cities in Southern Ontario: 1980–1996', *International Journal of Biometeorology,* **44**: 190–197.

Snyder, K. and L. Bird (1998), *Paying the Costs of Sprawl: Using Fair-Share Costing to Control Sprawl.*

Sorenson, R.M., R.N. Weisman, et al. (1984), 'Control of Erosion, Inundation and Salinity Intrusion Caused by Sea Level Rise', in *Greenhouse Effect and Sea Level Rise.* M.C. Barth and J.G. Titus (eds), New York, NY: Van Nostrand Reinhold Company, Inc., pp. 179–214.

Staley, S.R. and L.C. Gilroy (2002), 'Why "Smart Growth" Isn't Smart', *Consumers' Research Magazine,* **85**(1): 10–13.

Steinecke, K. (1999), 'Urban climatological studies in the Reykjavik subarctic environment, Iceland', *Atmospheric Environment,* **33**: 4157–4162.

Steward, S., M.B. McIntyre, et al. (2002), 'Heart failure in a cold climate: seasonal variation in heart failure-related morbidity and mortality', *Journal of the American College of Cardiology,* **39**(5): 760–766.

Stone, B.J. and M.O. Rodgers (2001), 'Urban form and thermal efficiency: how the design of cities influences the urban heat island effect', *Journal of the American Planning Association,* **67**(2): 186–198.

Stone, R. (1995), 'If the mercury soars, so may health hazards', *Science,* **267**(5200): 957–958.

Straka, C. (2002), 'Local Energy Policy and Smart Growth', *Local Environment,* **7**(4): 453.

Sweeney, B.J., J.K. Jackson, et al. (1992), 'Climate change and the life histories and biogeography of aquatic insects in eastern North America', in *Global Climate Change and Freshwater Ecosystems,* P. Firth and S.G. Fisher (eds), New York: Springer-Verlag, pp. 143–176.

Taha, H. and A. Meier (1997*), Mitigation of Urban Heat Islands: Meteorology, Energy, and Air Quality Impacts,* Proceedings of the International Symposium on Monitoring and Management of Urban Heat Island, Keio University, Fujisawa, Japan.

Talen, E. (2002), *Measurement Issues in Smart Growth Research,* The Smart Growth and New Urbanism Conference, College Park, MD.

Tayanc, M. and H. Toros (1997) , 'Urbanization effects on regional climate change in the case of four large cities of Turkey', *Climatic Change,* **35**: 501–524.

Taylor, J. and P. Y. Doren (2000), *Sprawl for Me, But not Thee,* Washington, DC: The Cato Institute.

Timmerman, P. and R. White (1997), 'Magahydropolic: coastal cities in the context of global environmental change', *Global Environmental Change,* **7**(3): 205–234.

Titus, J. (2002), *Does Sea Level Rise Matter to Transportation Along the Atlantic Coast? The Potential Impacts of Climate Change on Transportation.*

Titus, J., R.A. Park, et al. (1991), 'Greenhouse Effect and Sea Level Rise: The Cost of Holding Back the Sea', *Coastal Management,* **19**: 171–204.

Toman, M. and R. Bierbaum (1996), 'An overview of adaptation to climate change', in *Adapting to climate change,* J.B. Smith (ed.), New York, NY: Springer-Verlag, pp. 5–15.

Torok, S., C. Morris, et al. (2001), 'Urban heat island features of southeast Australian towns', *Australian Meteorological Magazine,* **50**(1): 1–13.

Travis, D., V. Meentemeyer, et al. (1987), 'Influence of meteorological conditions on urban/rural temperature and humidity differences for a small city', *Southeastern Geographer,* **27**: 90–100.

Tregoning, H., J. Agyeman, et al. (2002), 'Sprawl, Smart Growth and Sustainability', *Local Environment,* **7**(4): 341–347.

Tromp, S.W. (1980), *Biometeorology: The Impact of the Weather and Climate on Humans and Thier Environment (Animals and Plants),* Philadelphia, PA: Heyden and Sons Ltd.

UNDP (2001), *Human Development Report,* United Nations Development Programme, Oxford: Oxford University Press.

Unger, J., Z. Sumeghy, et al. (2001), 'Temperature cross-section features in an urban area', *Atmospheric Research,* **58**(2).

Unwin, D. (1980), 'The synoptic climatology of Birmingham's heat island', *Weather,* **35**: 43–50.

USDOE (2001), *Annual Energy Review 2000,* Washington, DC: US Department of Energy, Energy Information Administration.

USDOT (2002), *Transportation Statistics Annual Report 2001,* Washington, DC: US Department of Transportation, Bureau of Transportation Statistics.

USDOE (1996), *Working to cool urban heat islands,* Berkeley National Laboratory PUB-775, Berkeley, CA: US Department of Transportation.

Van Rossum, C.T.M., M.J. Shipley, et al. (2001), 'Seasonal variation in cause-specific mortality: Are there high-risk groups? 25-year follow-up of civil servants from the first Whitehall study', *International Journal of Epidemiology,* **30**: 1109–1116.

Wade, B. (2000), 'Putting the freeze on heat islands', *American City and County,* **115**(2): 30.

Warren, H.E. and S.K. LeDuc (1981), 'Impact of Climate on Energy Sector in Economic Analysis', *Journal of Applied Meteorology,* **20**: 1431–1439.

Watson, R.T. and A.J. McMicheal (2001), 'Global Climate Change–the latest assessment: does global warming warrant a health warning?', *Global Change and Human Health,* **2**(1): 64–75.

Weggel, J.R. (1989), 'The Cost of Defending Developed Shoreline Along Sheltered Shores', in *Potential Effects of Global Climate Change on the United States,* J.B. Smith and D. Tirpak (eds), Washington, DC: US Environmental Protection Agency.

Wheeler, S. (2002), *Smart Fill–Creating More Livable Communities in the Bay Area.*

White, I. and J. Howe (2002), 'Flooding and the Role of Planning in England and Wales: A Critical Review', *Journal of Environmental Planning and Management,* **45**(5): 735.

WHO (2000), *Climate Change and Human Health: Impact and Adaptation,* Geneva, Switzerland: World Health Organization.

Wigley, T.M.L. (1999), *The science of climate change,* Washington, DC: Pew Center on Global Climate Change.

Wilcoxen, P.J. (1986), 'Coastal Erosion and Sea Level Rise: Implications for Ocean Beach and San Francisco's Westside Transport Project', *Coastal Management,* **14**(3): 173–191.

Wong, N., S. Tay, et al. (2003), 'Life cycle cost analysis of rooftop gardens in Singapore', *Building and Environment,* **38**(3): 499–509.

World Bank (2003), *Sustainable Transport: Priorities for Policy Reform,* Washington, DC: World Bank.

WMO (1984), *Urban Climatology and its Applications with Special Regard to Tropical Areas*, Proceedings of the Technical Conference Organized by the World Meteorological Organization, Mexico.

Yamashita, S., K. Sekine, et al. (1986), 'On relationships between heat island and sky view factor in the cities of Tama River basin, Japan', *Atmospheric Environment,* **20**: 681–686.

Yan, Y.Y. (1988), 'Climate and Residential Electricity Consumption in Hong Kong', *Energy,* **23**(1): 17–20.

Yelle, L.E. (1979), 'The Learning Curve: Historical Survey and Comprehensive Survey', *Decision Sciences* **10**: 302–334.

Yohe, G., et al. (1996), 'The economic cost of greenhouse-induced sea-level rise for developed property in the United States', *Climatic Change,* **32**: 387–410.

Yohe, G. and J. Neumann (1997), 'Planning for Sea Level Rise and Shore Protection under Climate Uncertainty', *Climatic Change,* **37**: 111–140.

Zoleta-Nantes, D.B. (2000), 'Flood hazard vulnerabilities and coping strategies of residents of urban poor settlements in Metro Manila, The Philippines', in *Floods*, D.J. Parker (ed.), p. 69.

3 Smart Growth, Sprawl and Climate Change Mitigation in the United States

Mick Womersley

INTRODUCTION

The movement of urban and suburban planning ideas and policies in the United States that has become known as 'smart growth' is quite amorphous. Academics seeking to pin the term down for rigorous analysis may be frustrated, since different jurisdictions apply varied policies under its rubric. Even so, it has attracted a good deal of attention and a lively following of advocates and partisans standing for smartness in growth and against the evils of 'sprawl.' Although the term remains elusive despite efforts by both professional associations and academics to secure it, there has, we are told by partisans and critics, occurred a considerable amount of actual implementation of smart growth around the country (APA 2002; NCSG 2004; Baum 2004).[1] And further, we are told that smart growth will save us, at least in part, from the ill effects of climate change (Heart and Birringer 2000; Li 2003; Winkelman 2003).

What are we to make of this, particularly if we are concerned either with rigorous, quantitative analysis of climate change mitigation or with a rigorous urban planning debate? This chapter attempts to turn both discussions in the direction of increased conceptual rigor, primarily by comparative analysis of urban planning policy history from the United Kingdom and by analysis of the climate change promise of smart growth in quantitative terms. I do not claim that this article is a report of original research.[2] Rather, it is a conceptual work of argument or criticism, and provides reasoned dispute of the claims of smart growth advocates and the premises on which they rest.

There are four points that must be made. The first is that smart growth is not, as partisans would have it, an ideal planning policy or even a particularly effective one. It has its origins in well-meaning attempts by American political liberals to overcome the objections of American political conservatives to planning limitations placed on the use of private property (Baum 2004). It is necessarily a compromise, a fact that becomes very clear by reasoned comparison to planning policies in Europe where the sanctity of private property is far less important. Second, despite this objection, smart growth, as a whole, comprises the only politically viable methods for US jurisdictions to control growth at all. American advocates for smart growth implicitly assume that better policies are not practicable because of American values and the legal context, a proposition that remains untested. This is regrettable and irrational, although the political hurdles required to overcome this failing are admittedly large. Third, smart growth does not exist in a vacuum. Even where it has been well defined and implemented, it remains a marginal idea in American political economy, and certainly no drag on quantitative economic growth. As a few jurisdictions attempt to impose a few compromised regulations, far more welcome both sprawl and its accompanying increases in energy and materials throughput and climate change contributions. Finally, and as a partial result of the first three, smart growth is unlikely to provide useful or even measurable climate change emissions reductions on the scale required to prevent difficulties predicted by scientists and the Intergovernmental Panel on Climate Change (IPCC 2001).

THE DEVELOPMENT OF SMART GROWTH

The roots of the trend in smart growth planning regulations in the US rest primarily in the last five decades of US politics and constitutional law, and in the long-term cultural resilience of a popular American construction of private property rights. Until the early twentieth century governmental regulation of private real property in the US was limited to planning for major highways, for railroads and occasionally for civic districts of major towns, such as the national capitol, Washington, DC. Prior to World War II, a few areas of tourist or conservation significance, mostly in vacation regions of the eastern seaboard, had pioneered the use of the conservation easement, a deeded private restriction on land use usually involving a private, non-profit 'land trust.' What would later become the US system of 'zoning' was undergoing constitutional tests before the war and was the subject of a major Supreme Court case in 1926, but was not widely used until much later (Randolph 2004; Hayden 2003). As a system of enabling what most jurisdictions wanted–rapid suburban growth and the concomitant growth in tax revenue with minimum intervention in private property rights–zoning expanded rapidly during the immediate period after the war and through the 1960s and 1970s, as did the American motor suburbs that zoning prescribed. Other forms of planning control were quite rare, as were governmental interventions of any kind.

'Comprehensive planning,' involving zoning as a main feature, remains the norm in most American non-rural jurisdictions (Randolph 2004).

These facts deserve some historic interpretation. The key feature is respect for private property rights and the decline of concepts of communal or common property. The US never underwent a socialist period, as did most European nations. The New Deal of President Franklin Roosevelt responded to the Great Depression with government investment, but never nationalized industries or development rights. Cold War fears and McCarthyism in the 1950s along with the backlash against Vietnam protests and the repression of the 'New Left' in the 1960s and 1970s took care of American socialism, such as it was. Never to be ruled by a socialist party, the closest post-war America got to national institutions of planning on a European scale were the Lyndon Johnson Great Society social welfare programs, now greatly modified by both Reagan-Bush free market conservatism and Clinton pragmatism. Social democracy, the heir to European socialism, is relatively vigorous at home, but has no counterpart of comparable importance in America. In general, most Americans believe quite firmly in being able to do as they wish with their property, and in the period since World War II this construction of private property rights has risen as socialist and communist organizations have withered and died.

The development of American suburbia proceeded apace throughout the 1950s and into the new millennium. In the mid 1980s to early 1990s, the era of 'Reaganomics,' the US Supreme Court reviewed a number of cases related to powers of eminent domain, related 'takings' of private property under the fifth and tenth amendments to the US Constitution, and the 'police' powers of the state. The influence of neoclassical economic thinking such as that of Nobel laureate Milton Friedman on US policy during the 1980s and early 1990s is well documented and need not be revisited here. The Ronald Reagan-George H.W. Bush presidential years also gave rise to increasingly conservative control of the Supreme Court, the US constitutional court. The key case was that of *Lucas v. South Carolina Coastal Commission* (1992). In previous cases, the court had upheld the general legitimacy of state interest in planning regulation, even on private property. In *Lucas*, the court ruled specifically that when a regulation is intended to control 'harmful or noxious uses' of property, no compensation is owed regardless of effects on property values. To balance this substantial statement, however, the court made rather murky what was improper use. Most essentially, regulation must 'substantially advance' a clear public interest, in which case no compensation is due. In the particular case of *Lucas*, the State of South Carolina was forced to compensate the developer by purchasing the property. If the public interest is subjective or arguable and uncompensated, therefore, the regulator had better beware of lawsuits from landowners deprived of the right to some portion of the value of their property. *Lucas* and related cases on public control of private property maintain an abiding theme in design of land use planning regulations in the US; jurisdictions are extremely wary of decisions that reduce the value or use rights of real property.

Exceptions to this innate conservatism, however, are found in American cultural constructions relating to public land conservation, as found in the extremely large acreage of national and state parks and forests, official 'wildernesses,' and so on. In the case of this 'public land,' many Americans support public or common property rights and the language of 'common property' found in the European discourse on land use is extended by a peculiarly American conservation ethic of access rights for state-regulated hunting, firewood cutting and other forms of common use. Private enterprise is strictly regulated on national or state lands, and the construction of property rights that is applied is starkly different from that applied to development land outside of the various preserve jurisdictions. This government-owned land 'belongs to the American people,' and the language of the management agencies reflects this common ownership: management is centrally or commonly planned, and benefits are (or at least are intended to be) nationalized (USFS 2004; Judd 1997; Dombeck, et al. 2003).

Again, interpretation is called for. It is possible that the fact that there are very large areas of accessible public land in America allows this dichotomous construction. In Europe where most land is private and private transportation is more expensive it is often necessary to require public use of private land in order that ordinary people can have access to outdoor recreational resources. In America, recreation can be restricted in private areas and directed instead to the lavish open access public areas even though they may be at some distance from urban centers.

As a result of this bipolar approach to public interest in land management planning, when the suburban subdivisions that would eventually be labeled 'sprawl' began to appear in force in the US during the 1950s and 1960s, little thought was given to their control for the common good. After all, the new developments were on private landholdings, generally farmland, not on public land. The basic 'comprehensive planning' technique that emerged required in its most general form the nomination of separate areas for uses deemed mutually incompatible (Randolph 2004). Refinements included listing of performance standards for particular kinds of harmful or noxious use. Under typical suburban zoning regulation, 'subdivisions' of former farmland purchased for development need only be in an area zoned 'residential' for development to proceed apace. Areas could be 'rezoned' at will by local jurisdictions interested in tax benefits and local economic growth. Other areas might be zoned 'industrial,' 'commercial' or 'mixed' use. City and town centers from earlier periods in American society, generally well laid-out around a commercial downtown with important social features such as courthouses or 'main streets' central to the scheme, became quickly circumnavigated by the inevitable arterial roads leading from the new suburban and exurban subdivisions (zoned residential) to the new retail malls (zoned retail or commercial). It is usually impossible to make this journey on foot or by public transportation. Often planning was made more difficult by large minimum areas of two, five and even twenty acres for house lots, making denser, more pedestrian-friendly development illegal in many suburban jurisdictions (Randolph 2004; Hayden 2003).

Such growth restrictions as were provided by zoning were confined to concentric districts around cities and towns. American rural areas remain for the most part either completely unplanned or very lightly planned today, and often the only hurdles thrown in the way of rural house builders are high minimum acreages for the legal division of larger plots to smaller, requiring a 'subdivision ordinance,' generally a minor legislative or administrative act of the local jurisdiction (Hayden 2003). With few restrictions placed on development in rural areas, with most existing restrictions tending towards large lot sizes in both suburban and rural areas and with increased reliance on the individual automobile (by 1950 a ubiquitous fact of American life), development of low- and very low-density commuter suburbs soon ringed all major US cities, with little provision of public transportation.

By the 1980s, opposition to the rampant conversion of land from farming to low-density residential suburb began to form. The first attempts to control subdivision development appeared on the coasts, with the South Carolina and California coastal commissions as early examples. Both quickly produced takings lawsuits, including *Lucas*. Finally, during the early 1980s, in Montgomery County, Maryland–actually a suburb of Washington, DC and home to large numbers of professional people working in the capital–a comparatively enlightened jurisdiction began a program designed to reduce development pressure on farmland, not by directly limiting property rights, but by making them a tradable commodity and thus avoiding takings concerns by providing an avenue for compensation. The Montgomery County Transfer of Development Rights (TDR) program allotted a certain number of development rights (in residential units per acre) to remaining undeveloped parcels and allowed landowners to sell these rights to developers wishing to build denser properties such as flats or condominiums in the county's burgeoning suburban areas. The program was intended in part to permanently fix the final or 'build-out' density on much of the farmland acreage at a relatively low level (Fehr 1997; Randolph 2004). Other Maryland counties followed suit with similar measures aided by the State's Democratic governor at the time, Parris Glendening. By the late 1990s two further techniques were added to Maryland's laws: jurisdictions could selectively purchase development rights directly from landowners (through PDR programs) and several state-aided conservation easement programs were formed (Randolph 2004; MET 1998a-e; MALPF 1997a-b).

Outright transfer of development rights (TDR) and purchase of development rights (PDR) programs exist in Maryland at both the state and county level. They allow landowners and developers more freedom to avoid zoning limitations on land development in one part of a county when it serves some greater public good, usually farmland preservation, in another. In TDR and PDR programs, zoning density may be transferred from remote rural areas to already built-up urban and suburban sites, allowing concentration, intensification and, presumably, assisting in the retention or development of a more socially functional neighborhood scheme in place of the standard suburban sprawl (Fehr 1997). Both techniques, however, require that the jurisdiction (usually a county) can agree that a portion of its land should always be relatively rural. Landowners in the set-aside portion are effectively compensated for development rights they may now never utilize, and may never have intended to utilize (Fehr 1997).

In Maryland rural land conservation and land use control the most important programs are those that employ financial development rights transactions of one form or another such as PDR and TDR described above. Conservation easements and agricultural preservation easements also aim to permanently reserve or condemn a landowner's development rights, in return for tax benefits or cash payments. Maryland has three such easement programs run by the state. They vary in operation and philosophy. Maryland Environmental Trust (MET) runs a straightforward conservation easement program based on preservationist ideals and tax break incentives (MET 1998a; 1998b). The Maryland Agricultural Land Preservation Foundation (MALPF) offers payments up to 100 per cent of the value of development rights for choice farmland easements, based on the traditional conservationist principle of protecting high quality soils from development (MALPF 1997a; 1997b). Finally, Maryland's 'Rural Legacy' program aims to strengthen agricultural and environmental easement acquisition by providing a pool of money to rural neighborhoods and counties that can manage to work with preservation non-profit organizations such as land trusts and historic societies to come up with a 'Rural Legacy' proposal (Maryland Office of Planning 1998). A successful proposal results in large grants to purchase conservation and façade easements on historic buildings in designated areas, preventing exterior development or redevelopment. A percentage is calculated in for 'stewardship': monitoring and ongoing planning, usually involving the local land trust or historical group (Maryland Office of Planning 1998). In addition to these programs most important for land conservation, there are a wide variety of subsidies and incentives that aim to encourage various conservation-minded behaviors on the part of landowners and municipalities. These range from tree planting subsidies for 'buffering' Chesapeake Bay tributaries to tax breaks in support of historic building preservation. One list of conservation incentives and subsidies exclusively for Chesapeake Bay watershed protection included 36 separate programs (Environmental Finance Center 1998). Another state-published list of programs to encourage 'landowner stewardship' totaled 40 (Maryland Department of Natural Resources 1998). To help implement all this, there is a network of over 40 local Maryland land trust groups, legally qualified to accept tax-exempt conservation easements (Maryland Environmental Trust 1998c). More land trusts are added each year.

Development discouraged in rural areas is redirected to certain urban and suburban areas. Maryland's 'Smart Growth and Neighborhood Conservation' law (Annotated Code of Maryland 1997) aims to strengthen the rural protection movement by 'taking the subsidy out of sprawl.' Developers who build large numbers of new, single family houses or apartments in pristine, 'green field' sites now find that the state will not contribute to the necessary road and school improvements, whereas it will support such projects in designated priority funding areas, or 'PFAs.' At the same time, developments in difficult city areas such as blighted row house neighborhoods, urban 'brown fields' or 'infill' areas may attract subsidies from other programs, particularly from the federal government. Local historical societies also have a role to play, as do downtown revitalization initiatives such as Maryland Main Street, organized by the Maryland Historical Trust and the National Historical Trust (Maryland Historic Preservation Society 1998; Maryland Main Street 1998; MET 1998d). These more voluntary programs tend to rely on the added value of visitor sales as incentive for participation by downtown business owners. In at least one case I know of, the downtown revitalization program became the vehicle for citizen opposition to a new major retail development on the edge of town.

By 1996, the bare bones of Maryland 'Smart Growth' were in place. The collection of laws, regulations and techniques that will supposedly control growth in Maryland has since become formidably large and complex. The flagship state land conservation and planning programs–Smart Growth and 'Rural Legacy'–although much vaunted and highly publicized, are actually better seen as coordinating and corrective legislation that aims to supplement and organize myriad other programs and techniques, some of which have existed for many decades. While recent books and other publications designed to promote smart growth emphasize active planning ideas involving design and layout of urban and suburban developments, these ideas are intended to be employed by architects working within a development firm. Government is not seen as an active designer of development. Instead, smart growth publications advise jurisdictions to permit more 'livable,' typically denser development by changing zoning ordinances and building codes, and to discourage rural development by purchasing, condemning or otherwise transferring development rights away from those areas. If we take the Maryland example as comprehensive of most smart growth techniques, if not entirely typical, some conceptual structure can be determined. Smart growth programs in Maryland work together with existing planning and zoning regulations primarily by tinkering in various ways with landowners' 'bundles' of development rights. The basic mechanism is to provide alternative profitable expressions of those rights for landowners to choose, instead of actual development. The following is a list of the techniques used, with brief explanation:

- Purchase of Development Rights (PDR): Jurisdictions purchase development rights outright, either at market value or at reduced value.
- Transfer of Development Rights (TDR): Jurisdictions allow profitable trading of development rights from one area to another, with the intent of reducing the use of those rights in protected areas as the cost of increased density in preferred areas.
- Paid for Conservation Easements (similar to PDR): Jurisdictions and private non-profits purchase development rights from landowners, with easements inserted in the property deed prohibiting future development.
- Tax Break Conservation Easements: Landowners donate development rights to private or publicly owned charitable 'land trusts.' Givers of charitable donations in the US do not pay income taxes (and in some jurisdictions property taxes) on the value of those donations. The refunded income tax comes in the form of an annual tax refund, an attractive lump sum.
- Various subsidies and incentives to builders, developers, landowners and businesses, including historic preservation tax credits, Live Near Your Work incentives, brown field clean up, Main Street, Historic Districts and so on.
- Urban growth boundaries or 'green belts' (such as that for Portland, Oregon): These boundaries define the geographic area of the city open to development and are usually less restrictive than their European counterparts in use since the 1930s.

THE ACTUAL, RATHER THAN INTENDED, EFFECTS OF POLICIES

How does the complex range of programs called smart growth work out in reality? Does it succeed in doing what it is supposed to do? The Maryland system, even in the simplified form presented above, is unwieldy and hard to understand, and the difficult business of fathoming the regulations ensures that often only those communities where leadership is augmented by professional management have the time and the knowledge necessary to access benefits. Property developers in particular, as modern professionals, probably understand quite well how to work with TDR and PDR and other regulations, and the wealthy new residents of villages-become-suburbs are often willing members and suppliers of money for the land trust, the museums and the various historic preservation organizations that are the agents of preservation proposals. This process leads to the probability that the historic and landscape features preserved by smart growth are those preferred by the urban middle class rather than those cherished by rural working people or working class people in general. But there are also many more purely financial inequities built into the programs themselves–inequities caused predominantly by the programs' reliance on individual agency and financial interest as incentives for preservation and by their general lack of a cohesive central plan or shared public vision of what it is that should be preserved.

One landowner whose fortunes I followed over the course of an earlier study (Wasserman and Womersley 2001) purchased several farms specifically to apply easements, using the cash payments or tax breaks to help finance the purchase of other farms. This landowner would then either resell the farms or rent them. Although he had no intention of developing the properties, he was happy to take the government's payments not to develop and use it to acquire more farmland. He freely admitted that he did not expect to lose much money on his transactions over the long-term, as the value of the farms under easement remained high, despite their theoretically reduced commercial value without development rights. He also believed he was providing a public service in 'cycling' land through the conservation system, a belief not generally shared by his rural neighbors, who saw instead a kind of conspiracy to take over their neighborhood. Paying significant landowners, who are often already wealthy, to do the right thing and preserve the public good depletes the public coffers to benefit financially those who need it least.

In another portion of the earlier study, I used ethnographic interviews with fishermen, inhabitants of a rural fishing village in the path of development, to see if they had knowledge of or interest in using the tools offered by the State to prevent development. They had little knowledge of the new regulations. Developers and business people in the tourist industry, already the boosters and *de facto* leaders of another village a little further up the peninsula from the first, were highly knowledgeable of the new regulations and were using them to find state aid for their project to make the tourist village financially well-off by boosting the historic and landscape features of the village and its surroundings. When interviewed, they did not conceive that this was a form of gentrification.

Maryland's smart growth programs thus have two troubling features. First, they are regressive–they provide tax breaks and cash payments to a relatively wealthy section of the State's population because they offer significant benefits only to those with considerable property to preserve or considerable income with which to acquire preservation-worthy land, and their sheer complexity makes them difficult to utilize without legal expertise. Second, they put forward an inauthentic idea of preservation–they tend to preserve an idealized pastoral landscape rather than a working countryside. Preservation of the fishing village mentioned above will only take place after the fishermen have mostly left, to be replaced by commuters and retirees.

This combination might easily come to be seen as a matter of environmental justice. Traditionally, environmental justice has focused on the distribution of site-specific economic burdens, such as toxic waste dumps and more general burdens such as noise and pollution. But environmental justice concerns the distribution of benefits as well as burdens, and it concerns the distribution of control over decision making about burdens and benefits. If it is an environmental injustice, for instance, to allow poor neighborhoods to suffer more from industrial pollution than wealthier ones, it is also an environmental injustice to subsidize the preservation of large trophy farms and tourist havens, but not ramshackle fishing villages, and to do so by a decision making process in which poor and working class working residents play almost no role.

Smart growth planning regulation as exercised in Maryland and other US states is therefore not really regulatory at all, in the sense that it controls planning by active expression of public priorities. The actual 'smart' design of new settlements is left up to private enterprise–architects and development firms working within existing or modified zoning and building codes. What smart growth instead does is provide a series of incentives for landowners to, in the American idiom, 'do the right thing.' As a result, public priorities are given weak and unclear expression, if any expression at all. Smart growth provides weak enforcement to the existing and already weak US systems of planning and zoning. Smart growth does, however, provide jurisdictions with the feeling that they are doing something to protect open land from wasteful development, without contravening either the strong cultural expectations that Americans are free to do as they wish with their property, or the constitutional doctrine against public takings of private property. This might be the important thing.

Another troubling feature of smart growth is that it does not actively curtail economic growth. What it does is enable some forms of development to proceed more easily and at less cost than others by subsidies of various kinds, while mildly preventing development in some areas by separating development rights from property using cash payments or tax breaks to landowners, payments which necessarily come from the public coffers. Presumably, those developments that could not possibly meet smart growth standards will still take place, only outside of smart growth areas. 'Sprawl' is still expanding throughout Maryland, a fact easily demonstrated by any brief drive through the northern suburbs of Washington, DC. Overall Maryland or

US economic growth is therefore unaffected, a fact that has some significance for climate questions raised below.

THE UNITED KINGDOM'S PLANNING REGIME

For comparison, the legal situation with regard to public interest planning and property rights in the United Kingdom was made quite clear much earlier in the same five-decade period (1950–2000) through the 1947 Town and Country Planning Act. The TCPA was and is a Fabian Socialist construction in which the development rights of all property were legally appropriated by central government. [3] Property rights holders were taxed on any future development values gained, initially at 100 per cent. The Labour government of Clement Atlee (1946–1951) proceeded to reallocate the development rights thus appropriated to the public as a whole though a cascading system of regional and local jurisdictions based initially on the existing counties and parishes (but since then much modified). Political jurisdictions, made the *de facto* holders of all development rights, could then decide whether or not to allow a developer to proceed with a scheme based on statutory 'planning permission' applications, in effect, to decide whether or not to return some portion of development rights to the private landowner. The results are wide reaching and run deep in the British psyche with regard to cultural constructions about rights to the development of land. To this day in Britain, whether or not a property owner can build a modest extension to a residence, modify a business to a new use, or even put up a small shed, will generally depend on whether or not permission is obtained. The need to apply for permission is rarely challenged legally. The idea of planning permission is built into the British cultural construction of what are appropriate landowners' rights. Most other European countries have similar arrangements for planning in which the government has control over development, but the British system, for which considerable literature is available in English, and which relied on the initial purchase of private property rights under common law, is most useful to the American experience.

Of further interest in understanding the cultural construction of property rights at work in the UK is its National Park system. In the UK, as contrasted to the US, a National Park consists primarily of privately held land: farms, moorlands, marshes and forests that belong to private landowners. There are private houses, villages and even small market towns, all within the boundaries of the park system. Local counties or regions maintain the road networks and business uses of the land continue regardless of the conservation designation. The development rights, appropriated in 1947 under the TCPA, are controlled by 'Special Planning Boards' and only reassigned to property owners when the development is considered to meet the stricter requirements that apply in UK national parks. In most European nations, national parks and protected areas similarly do not exclude private ownership or private use in the way that the American system does.

Public access to private land for recreational purposes is also guaranteed by statute. The UK system differs slightly between England and Wales, and Scotland. In England and Wales, statutory access protection is given only to ancient public 'rights of way' over private land. In Scotland, access is protected on all open land; the hiker can wander at will. In all the countries of the UK, common access is jealously guarded by interest groups such as the Rambler's Association, and recent attempts have been made to extend the 'freedom to roam' concept applied in Scotland to other areas of the UK uplands.

CASE COMPARISON: THE QUESTION WHY?

In comparison, then, European ideas of planning, particularly the UK example cited in some detail, put American smart growth ideas in sharper perspective. It clearly is possible to enact a much stronger expression of public interest in private land and land development through planning regulation in a common law environment. It could be argued that the UK system and the US system are two extremes of a continuum of ideas about property rights and the public good, with the best ground being in fact somewhere in the middle: a compromise between private rights and public control. The question about the American system that remains is: Why are American planners forced to adopt such a weak posture? The answers lie in consideration of local political factors and their engagement with planning policies and in the US Constitution.

The political economy of US minor jurisdictions is not immediately transparent to international observers who have not spent a good deal of time living in the US. Minor jurisdictions also vary a good deal by state. In the south and west, counties are often the most powerful local entities. Elected commissioners, usually three, typically govern counties. In the northeast, towns have a good deal more planning power than counties and boards of largely unpaid amateurs, town selectmen and selectwomen, control planning, subject to votes of annual town meetings. Larger city governments vary from executive town councils not unlike many European models, to purely administrative city governments, where professional managers serve under ceremonial mayors. There are a small number of regional organizations, such as New York State's Adirondack State Park. In almost all states, the state legislatures have a coordinating role, and make enabling legislation that helps determine which methods of local control can be legal in that state. The federal government's role is minimal and restricted: in the case of the executive branch (Department of Housing and Urban Development), to providing incentives (grants, block grants and other funding) or setting limits on environmental pollutants (Environmental Protection Agency); in the case of the legislative branch, to making appropriations of funds to new or existing grant programs; and in the case of the federal judiciary, to deciding what is and is not legal or constitutional. There is therefore essentially no active federal government urban planning capability. The federal judicial power to deny authorities the right to control development is thus innately far stronger than the corresponding executive government ability at any level to plan development in the public interest.

In order for any planning policy to be established in American urban, suburban or rural jurisdictions three conditions of political viability must first be met. First, the policy must be a locally-led, or, at most, a state-led effort. Second, there must be a majority of elected and appointed officials in local or state jurisdictions willing to vote for and/or administratively endorse the policy. Third, there must be sufficient political acceptance on the part of the affected people and organizations, including individuals and organizations owning or using real property in the jurisdiction, and people and organizations affected by the decision resident elsewhere such as investors. Sufficient acceptance in this case probably means acceptance at a level where takings lawsuits would not be brought against the jurisdiction. National or supranational electoral politics really do not apply to urban planning as they do in the countries of the European Union and the constitution, which still effectively bans takings of private property, is a key player in the way things work out.

As a result of the conditions described above, smart growth ideas comprise the only politically viable policy for most American jurisdictions wishing to control sprawl development. Since to use sprawl development, in the sense of being able to own a large house in a suburban or semi-rural area far from working or commercial zones, is still an aspiration of many Americans; smart growth policies are intrinsically weak expressions of state planning. It is not clear that American planners understand this.

CLIMATE BENEFITS FROM SMART GROWTH?

As policy makers and politicians have become better acquainted with the threats associated with climate change, climate science has been applied to developing mitigation policies. The emerging applied field of climate emissions accounting is an intrinsically quantitative operation relying on data of human economic inputs and waste outputs. This quantitative characteristic is not, however, well understood by many environmental activists, often leading to conceptual error in their advocacy. The recent phenomenon of US smart growth advocates claiming climate benefits from their policies is subject to this error. Accounting for reductions of climate-altering emissions is a member of a general class of sustainability accounting problems that has a longer history and a broad theory of its own. The central concept of this theory is ecological carrying capacity.

During the late 1960s and 1970s the concept of human ecological sustainability, including the intrinsic understanding that there is some overall maximum human carrying capacity of planet Earth, was defined by academics such as economists Nicholas Georgescu-Reogen and Herman E. Daly. Academic discourse sparked by their work and the voices of other important commentators such as the European industrialist E.F. Schumacher or the ecologist Paul Erhlich, led to an international discourse on what was then termed sustainable development. This discourse was informed and modified during the 1980s and 1990s by emerging scientific information about the earth's climate.

The 1987 report of the UN Bruntland Commission on human ecological sustainability, *Our Common Future*, sparked a series of international diplomatic actions leading eventually to the specific climate treaty known as the Kyoto Accords. The reception of *Our Common Future* led almost directly, through UN General Assembly deliberations in December of 1989, to the UN Rio Conference, or second 'Earth Summit,' of 1992 in which the United States under then President George H.W. Bush first conspicuously signaled American reluctance to accept sustainability goals by not participating fully in the deliberations. Through its outcome in the Agenda 21 international sustainability treaty, Rio led to and authorized the Kyoto process, which produced the Kyoto Protocol, also known as the Framework Convention on Climate Change. As environmental treaties go, however, Kyoto is more easily implemented, accounted for and enforced because it concerns itself with a narrower range of measures of sustainability than Agenda 21.

The disparity in ease of implementation has its basis in an acknowledged disparity in definitions of sustainability. The Bruntland Commission (1987) defined sustainable development as 'development that meets the needs of the present without compromising the ability of future generations to meet their own needs,' a definition also invoked in Principle Three of the Rio Declaration (Robinson 1993). Herman Daly, on the other hand, offers the following more precise scheme, detailed in terms of matter and energy throughput–matter and energy flowing into and out of the human economy:

Output Rule
Waste emissions should be within the assimilative capacity of the environment to absorb without unacceptable degradation of its future waste-absorptive capacity or other important services.

Input Rules
1. Renewables: harvest rates of renewable resources should be within the regenerative capacity of the ecosystem.
2. Non-Renewables: depletion rates should be equal to the rate at which renewable substitutes can be developed and deployed. (Daly, in *Photiades*, 1998 and in course lectures, 1997).

It can easily be seen that the Daly rules, defining quantitative measures, potentially offer simpler implementation than the generalized Bruntland definition. The two could be seen as complementary: one ethical, the other operational.

Daly's rules are reflected in the Kyoto Protocol, which is also essentially a quantitative procedure. The UN sponsored Intergovernmental Panel on Climate Change (IPCC), on whose predictions the Protocol and subsequent linked agreements are based, reports that, based on the results of general circulation models, global average temperatures will rise between 1.4 and 8°C over the next one hundred years as a result of climate agent emissions such as carbon dioxide or methane, producing a range of climate effects. Among the most likely are higher maximum temperatures over most land areas, fewer cold and frost days over most land areas, greater incidence of extreme weather and greater peak precipitation in some areas. Examples of projected human impacts as a result include increased summer deaths related to heat in large cities, effects on agriculture, on floods, avalanches, mudslides and other natural catastrophes. All of these impacts mentioned here are given a high probability of occurring, some over 95 per cent; a value based on IPCC meta-analysis of the various modeling experiments involved and their individual statistical reporting. Projected impacts are quite large in scale and in potential disturbance of economic activities. Climate change is therefore a major element of overall concern for the sustainability of the global human economy in its current form. The IPCC believes that only quantifiable reductions in the output of climate agent emissions can prevent these effects, an application of the Daly rule for waste outputs.

In order to prevent climate change from occurring the international diplomatic community, using data and policy advice proffered by the IPCC, negotiated Kyoto. The key features of Kyoto are the staged reduction in greenhouse gas emissions required of participating countries. This has led, in the US, not currently an active Kyoto participant, to 'side' agreements such as that of the New England governors and eastern Canadian premiers; agreements that call for Kyoto-style staged reductions, even though the federal government is not a Kyoto participant. These agreements have resulted in the development of expertise in climate emissions accounting in some American states. Another international agreement, albeit between university and college presidents rather than heads of state, the Talliores Declaration of

1990, has resulted in development of skills in climate emissions accounting capability at US colleges and universities, where many climate scientists and ecologists work. Talliores, which predates Kyoto, originally called for the practice of 'institutional ecology,' by which was meant a wide range of 'green' or sustainable practices following the broader Bruntland idea, but the involvement of climate scientists and student activists has led to a focus on climate accounting as a proxy measure for sustainability in general.

If American smart growth planning measures were actually to aid in implementing Kyoto, they would have to result in quantifiable reductions in climate emissions outputs. It can quite easily be seen that this can never be the case. New developments planned under the smartest of smart growth measures are just that: new developments. No older housing or retail stock is retired. No emissions are reduced. Emissions are instead added. No systematic reduction in greenhouse emissions is achieved; in fact, total greenhouse agent emissions will increase as a result of smart growth. It can be argued that emissions will rise by less than they might have without smart growth, but this is not necessarily the case.

Take, for instance, the Maryland example. New housing built in Montgomery County in a planned suburban development that is the recipient of TDR development rights taken from more rural land to the west of the county is still an addition to overall housing and a component of overall economic growth in Montgomery County. There is no requirement to reduce the housing stock elsewhere. Since many of the new residents that will take up residence in the apartments and condominiums that are built are immigrants from other cities and rural areas elsewhere in the US, it is possible that their previous housing will be put to other uses, but it is unlikely to be retired or demolished. In fact, the only Maryland housing that is currently being retired and demolished in significant quantities is center city slum housing in nineteenth century center cities such as Baltimore. This housing, typically nineteenth century row housing, is characterized by small unit size (under a thousand square feet) and sixty-amp electrical supply. New housing built in Maryland is typically larger, has central heating and has 200-amp electrical supply, even when it is part of a smart growth scheme. The new housing will consume more energy and therefore be responsible for more climate agent emissions than the housing being demolished.

Most old housing will in fact not be retired or demolished, but filled with new residents since Maryland has a growing population. Their climate emissions must be added to those now occupying the new development. Emissions have therefore increased as a result of smart growth, not diminished. Likewise, even when a smart growth housing scheme provides some commuters the ability to walk or use public transportation, old patterns of commuting elsewhere are not curtailed. New people will take up the older housing left vacant by the residents of the new development. The new residents of the old housing will also take up similar commuting patterns. No energy is saved overall. No climate agent emissions are curtailed.

American smart growth planning policies do not, therefore, provide any conceivable climate benefit when a precise and quantifiable definition of climate benefit is used, such as that mandated by the Kyoto Protocol. Advocates who claim climate benefits from smart growth policies make both conceptual errors and accounting errors.

CONCLUSION

The aim of this chapter, which will no doubt seem polemic to most smart growth advocates and in fact to many American environmentalists, is to clarify both the nature of smart growth planning policies and the nature of global climate change, and to weigh the efficacy of the former in light of the imperative raised by the latter. Sprawl development and its climate effects are clearly a problem, one that should quickly be addressed for the sake of the American, and the global, environment. But it needs to be addressed with reasoned thought as well as advocacy, or advocates will make policy mistakes. Establishing current smart growth praxis as a solution to climate change is one such mistake. As the twenty-first century proceeds, the climate predictions made by the IPCC will become more and more a reality for ordinary people, as will other global sustainability problems such as oil depletion. The situation with regard to planning control over development rights will be revisited. As we did several times in the twentieth century, Americans and western people in general will develop new and different ideas about private property, the public good, housing and transportation, and map them onto the ground in the form of new kinds of residential developments.

ACKNOWLEDGEMENTS

We would like to acknowledge the contributions of David Wasserman, JD, University of Maryland School of Public Policy.

NOTES

1. Various sources were used for the history, development and definition of smart growth, but primarily the American Planning Association's (APA) Policy Guide on Smart Growth, ratified by the APA Board of Directors, 15 April 2002; the many documents published electronically by both the National Center for Smart

Growth Research and Education at the University of Maryland, College Park Maryland (http://www.smartgrowth.umd.edu) and The Smart Growth Network in conjunction with the International City/County Management Association (http://www.smartgrowth.org).

2. This chapter uses original research work reported in conference presentations and an unpublished paper 'Whose 'Rural Legacy' is it Anyway?' (see Womersley and Wasserman 2001).

3. Fabian Socialism was the particular philosophy of socialism institutionalized in the British Isles though the Labour Party and their various post-war governments (Clement Atlee, Prime Minister, 1945–1951, Harold Wilson, 1964–1970, 1974–1976, James Callaghan, 1976–1979). The government of Clement Atlee laid the foundations of the British Welfare State; Margaret Thatcher dismantled some of it (1979–1990). The current Labour government of Tony Blair campaigns under the banner 'New Labour' and attempts to distance itself in some ways from Fabianism. In its heyday, British Fabianism was ridiculed on the European continent and elsewhere for not being sufficiently revolutionary. (Alleged slogan: What do we want? Revolutionary Change! When do we want it? In due course!)

REFERENCES

APA (2002), *American Planning Association's Policy Guide on Smart Growth*, ratified by American Planning Association Board of Directors, 15 April 2002.

Baum, Howell S. (2004), 'Smart Growth and School Reform', *Journal of the American Planning Association*, **70**(1).

Corkingcale, John (2004), *Fifty Years of the Town and Country Planning Act: Time to Privatise Development Rights?* London: Institute of Economic Affairs.

Dombeck, Michael P., C.A. Wood, and J.E. Williams (2003), *From Conquest to Conservation: Our Public Lands Legacy*, Washington, DC: Island Press.

Environmental Finance Center (1998), *Funding for Water Quality: Stormwater, Nonpoint, Source Pollution, Erosion Control and Education Projects*, College Park: Environmental Finance Center, University System of Maryland.

Fehr, Stephen C. (1997), 'Montgomery's Line of Defense Against the Suburban Invasion', *Washington Post*, 25 March 1997.

Gore, Albert (1999), 'Livable Communities for the 21st Century', Vice President Gore, 11 January 1999.

Hayden, Dolores (2003), *Building Suburbia: Green Fields and Urban Growth, 1820–2000*, New York: Pantheon Books.

Heart, Bennet and Jennifer Biringer (2000), *The Smart Growth-Climate Change Connection*, by Conservation Law Foundation, 1 November 2000, http://www.clf.org/pubs/SGCCC_A_Look.html. Last accessed 16 June 2004.

IPCC (2001), *Third Assessment Report: Summary for Policymakers*, Intergovernmental Panel on Climate Change, http://www.ipcc.ch/pub/spm22-01.pdf.

Judd, Richard W. (1997), *Common Lands, Common People: The Origins of Conservation in Northern New England*, Cambridge, MA: Harvard University Press.

Maryland State Legislature (1997), 'Smart Growth and Neighborhood Conservation–Rural Legacy Program', Annotated Code of Maryland, Annapolis, MD: 1997, Chapter 757.

Land Trust Alliance (1998), 'Lands Protected by Local Land Trusts in Maryland as of 10/98', Washington, DC: Land Trust Alliance.

Li, Mike (2003), *Does Smart Growth Matter? Drawing the Link Between Smart Growth and Climate Change*, Governor's Office of Smart Growth, State of Maryland, http://yosemite.epa.gov/oar/globalwarming.nsf/ UniqueKeyLookup/ADIM5GZR2N/$File/09_Michael_Li. pdf. Last accessed 16 June 2004.

Lucas v. South Carolina Coastal Commission (1992), case in the US Supreme Court.

Main Street Maryland (2000), *Revitalizing our Neighborhood*, Crownsville, MD: Main Street Maryland.

MALPF (1997a), *Annual Report for 1997*, Annapolis, MD: Maryland Department of Agriculture, Maryland Agricultural Land Preservation Foundation.

MALPF (1997b), *Instructions for Completing the Application to Sell Easement*. Annapolis, MD: Maryland Agricultural Land Preservation Foundation.

Maryland Department of Natural Resources (1998), *A Guide for Funding and Assistance*, Annapolis: Maryland Department of Natural Resources.

MET (1998a), *Program Description and Potential Tax Benefits of Conservation Easements*, Crownsville, MD: Maryland Environmental Trust.

MET (1998b), *Easement Process Steps*, Crownsville, MD: Maryland Environmental Trust.

MET (1998c), *List of Maryland Land Trusts*, Crownsville, MD: Maryland Environmental Trust.

MET (1998d), *The Rural Historic Village Protection Program*, Crownsville, MD: Maryland Environmental Trust.

MET (1998e), *Tax Advantages of Conservation Easements*, Crownsville, MD: Maryland Environmental Trust.

Maryland Historic Trust (1997–1999), *In Context: A Newsletter of the Maryland Historic Trust*, Crownsville, MD: Maryland Historic Trust.

Maryland Office of Planning (1998), 'Key Growth Management and Preservation Tools for Successful Rural Legacy Proposals,' Crownsville, MD: Maryland Office of Planning.

Maryland Sea Grant (1997), *Environmental Protection and Watermen Communities: Assessing the Effects of New Initiatives on Old Ways of Life*, R/PO-04, Maryland Sea Grant.

NCSG (2003), *National Center for Smart Growth Research and Education at the University of Maryland 2003 Progress Report*, College Park, MD: National Center for Smart Growth Research and Education, http://www.smartgrowth.umd.edu.

The National Trust for Historic Preservation (1996), *The Community Partners Program*.

Randolph, John (2004), *Environmental Land Use Planning and Management*, Washington, DC: Island Press.

USFS (2004), *Mission Statement*, United States Forest Service, http://www.fs.fed.us/plan.

Wasserman, David and M. Womersley (1997), *Preserving the Watermen's Way of Life*, College Park, MD: Report from the Institute for Philosophy and Public Policy.

Wenz, Peter S. (1988), *Environmental Justice*, Albany, NY: State University of New York Press.

Winkelman, Steve (2003), *State Leadership on Smart Growth and Climate Change*, Washington, DC: Center for Clean Air Policy, Climate Solutions for the Northeast.

Womersley, Mick (1998), 'Thirty Years in the Highlands and Islands of Scotland', in *Globally and Locally: the Economics of Sustainable Development*, Alan McQuillan and Ashley Preston (eds), Lanham, MD: University Press of America.

Womersley, Mick and D. Wasserman (2001), 'Whose "Rural Legacy" is it Anyway?: Ethical and Cultural Problems with Maryland's Rural Preservation Programs', Society for Human Ecology XIth national meeting, Jackson Hole, WY, http://www.unity.edu/facultypages/ womersley/ whose8.htm.

Zinn, A.J. (2000), *Conserving Land Resources: Legislative Proposals in the 106th Congress*, Washington, DC: Congressional Research Services, Resources, Science and Industry Division.

4 Climate Change Impacts on Regional Development and Sustainability: An Analysis of New Zealand Regions

Murray G. Patterson, Garry W. McDonald, Nancy E. Golubiewski, Vicky E. Forgie and Nigel A. Jollands

INTRODUCTION

Connecting Climate Change and Regional Development

Regional development and climate change have recently emerged in New Zealand as major areas of policy development and implementation. For many years, regional development has been missing from the national policy agenda, as various governments (of the center-left and center-right) have pursued 'free market' economic policies. With the establishment of the Ministry of Economic Development in February 2000, industry and regional economic development programs were re-introduced in New Zealand after nearly two decades of absence. The government's Regional Development Strategy is based on three principles:

1. An approach that makes the most of what regions have rather than solely being a vehicle for transfers from prosperous to less prosperous regions;
2. Engagement with local communities that allows for and facilitates the development of local strategies to respond to local opportunities and that integrates social, environmental and economic concerns; and
3. A 'whole-of-government' response where activities of central government are integrated into regional strategies (Office of the Minister for Industry and Regional Development 2000).

With New Zealand's ratification of the Kyoto Protocol in 2002, the New Zealand Climate Change Office was established within the New Zealand Ministry for the Environment in 2003. Its goal is to 'enable New Zealand to make significant greenhouse gas reductions and to manage the risks and opportunities arising from the effects of climate change.' The Climate Change policy is being developed in conjunction with the National Energy Efficiency and Conservation Strategy, the New Zealand Transport Strategy, the New Zealand Waste Strategy, and the Growth and Innovation Strategy. The Climate Change policy is also consistent with the government's Sustainable Development Program of Action.

There appears to be little connection made, either at the political or the research levels, between regional development and climate change policy. This chapter is a first attempt at addressing the issue, by analyzing how climate change is likely to affect regional development in New Zealand. The analysis looks at not only how the regions fare economically under climate change, but also at the environmental implications. This is consistent with the government's approach, which argues that 'regional development is about applying the sustainable development approach at a regional scale' (OMIRD 2000).

How Climate is Expected to Change in New Zealand

New Zealand's climate is affected by the surrounding ocean as well as its diverse topography. The country lies between 34°S and 48°S latitude, and its climate varies from subtropical to temperate. Alpine climates can also be found in the country's more mountainous regions. Changes occurring in the twentieth century, included increasing temperatures (approx. 0.7°C), reductions in frost frequency, retreat of South Island glaciers and snowlines, reduction of alpine snow mass and rising sea level (approx. 14–17 cm) (NIWAR, et al. 2004). The decrease in frost frequency, by up to 15 days, has occurred mostly in the southeast of the South Island and the central North Island. To date, climate change has brought about warmer winters and higher overnight temperatures, resulting in a longer growing season and a pronounced decline in the diurnal temperature range. Precipitation has declined overall except in parts of the South Island, due in large part to more frequent El Niño Southern Oscillation events since 1975 (McGlone 2001). In the future a large part of lowland northern New Zealand will become subtropical, whereas novel climate regimes will exist in other areas (McGlone 2001).

Temperature
New Zealand will experience mean annual temperatures 1–4°C higher than those experienced over the last three million years. This warming trend will

lag behind global estimates due to the slow thermal response of the southern ocean. Estimates are that New Zealand will undergo a 0.7°C increase for every degree of global warming during 1990–2100. Across the North Island, temperatures could be 3°C warmer over the next 70 to 100 years, whereas temperatures in the South Island could increase by 2.5°C. As the North Island warms, most regions will become increasingly tropical. The climates of Wellington and Hawke's Bay will shift towards the subtropical. The warming projected for Otago and Southland could make these regions similar to present-day Christchurch. Based on general circulation models (GCMs), two major changes are expected: 30 fewer frost days by 2100 (or half the existing frost days), and more warm days (above 25°C) in the north and east of the North Island (McGlone 2001).

Precipitation
Changes in the precipitation regime will be patchier than temperature changes. In general, precipitation changes 10 per cent for each degree of warming, and this will exaggerate current gradients across the islands (McGlone 2001). In addition to the changes mentioned above, precipitation events will alter in several ways: annual average rainfall will increase in the west of the country but decrease in many eastern areas; heavy rainfall events will become more frequent; and risk of droughts in some eastern areas will grow (NIWAR, et al. 2004).

Extreme events
According to the Climate Change Office (2004), flooding could be four times as frequent by 2070 throughout all New Zealand regions. The Climate Change Office (2004) forecasts that 'more frequent intense winter rainfalls are expected to increase the likelihood of flooding by rivers, as well as flash flooding when urban drainage systems become overwhelmed.' Storm flooding could harm low-lying areas of Whangarei and estuaries in Otago and Southland. Flooding from the sea may add to flood problems in the Bay of Plenty and the West Coast. Landslides may exacerbate flooding where eroded soil silts up rivers.

Storm events may become more frequent, but not necessarily more severe. It is, however, widely acknowledged that more tropical cyclones may occur in Northland and in northern New Zealand. New Zealand's capital, 'Windy Wellington,' may also lose its notorious winds as they become lighter. The predicted intensification of westerly wind flow across the rest of the country will result in more severe fire episodes in the east (McGlone 2001).

CLIMATE CHANGE IMPACTS IN NEW ZEALAND

Impacts on Ecosystems

New Zealand's biota will be affected significantly by altered temperature and precipitation regimes, increased atmospheric concentrations of CO_2 and the occurrence of extreme events that create new disturbance cycles. Given these changes, species ranges may shift and ecosystem processes change.

Biodiversity
New Zealand is considered a biodiversity hotspot due to four aspects of its indigenous diversity:

1. A high degree of endemism;
2. A concentration of species belonging to ancient or unique groups;
3. Adaptation to an isolated continental island; and
4. Threat from exotic invasive species (McGlone 2001).

Few, if any, changes to biodiversity have been attributed to temperature increases during the last century. Declines in biodiversity commenced with Polynesian settlement in the twelfth century and accelerated with European settlement in the nineteenth century. Current and continuing environmental stressors including forest fragmentation and clearance, loss and fragmentation of seed sources (due to clearance and from the loss of avian dispersers), invasion of alien weed species, pest and disease outbreaks, and increased fires play a major role in biodiversity and ecosystem changes in New Zealand. Climate change would exacerbate these pressures but not serve as a primary driver.

While it is assumed that changing climatic conditions will result in both species movement and species loss, the real and net effects of climate change upon biodiversity are unclear. For example, Northland hosts a rich biota suited to warm climates that are not found further south. Some species, such as tawa, may migrate south as areas become warmer, but others, such as kauri, will not move due to physiological constraints such as day length and soil type (Basher, et al. 2001; McGlone 2001). Likewise, the widely dispersed invertebrate species may not be affected much by climate change. According to the Climate Change Office (2004), earlier springs and a longer frost-free season could affect the timing of bird egg-laying, as well as the emergence of the first flowering and leafing of plants. Climate-induced alterations in New Zealand's ecosystems are likely to be slow and progressive since, as McGlone (2001) argues, they 'tend to be dominated by long-lived perennial species, which give little scope for major ecosystem alteration.'

The effect of climate change on alpine plants remains ambiguous. Clear signals of tree line advancement into alpine areas have not yet been found (Basher, et al. 2001). A warmer regime may cause the reduction or loss of current alpine and cold-winter habitats, so that cold-adapted species become stranded in a small and shrinking climatic niche. On the other hand, many alpine communities inhabit specialized environments such as fens, where trees may not encroach.

Forest systems

Modeling studies show that forests are sensitive to climate change and predict that there will be a major modification of New Zealand forest composition. One study that examined relationships between forest composition and the biophysical environment, including climatic parameters, found warm lowland forests to be sensitive to projected temperature increases, whereas beech forests in cooler sites were unlikely to change compositionally (Ministry for the Environment 2001). Northern broadleaves and kauri might become more restricted under a warming scenario of 4°C because gains in these species' ranges to the south will not be offset by declining populations in current ranges (McGlone 2001). On the West Coast, dense rimu forest growing near sea level in south Westland forests may be killed off by salt in groundwater and increased flooding (Sinclair 2001). Due to reduced rainfall and increased drought, the Ministry for the Environment (2001) foresees that 'the fragmented native forests of drier lowland environments in Northland, Waikato, Manawatu, and in the east from East Cape to Southland are ... probably the most vulnerable.'

Water systems

The seasonality and magnitude of river and stream flows will shift as upland vegetation and precipitation regimes change. River flows are likely to be higher in winter (as snow shifts to rain) and lower in summer. The latter will raise water temperature and aggravate water quality problems. Warmer temperatures will affect lake mixing and eutrophication processes. Overall, water demand will be heightened during hot, dry summers, which will reduce soil moisture and groundwater recharge.

Altered water flows will also reduce habitat for native species (particularly at low flows), increase nutrient loadings and further the loss of wetlands and associated wildfowl populations. Higher temperatures in freshwater lakes and streams will harm some fish while encouraging exotic fish and weeds. Exotic trout could move south (to the benefit of indigenous fish in the north). A general change in ocean fish populations is predicted with an influx of subtropical reef fish.

Wetlands will experience increased risk through changes in species composition, salinization as well as increased drought conditions and subsequent increased demand for agricultural and domestic water supplies (Basher, et al. 2001; Warrick, et al. 2001). In the Waikato, swamps and wetlands could move farther inland. In the Otago/Southland region, wetlands may increase as the extensive marshlands expand. Estuaries, already under pressure, will be affected by warming temperatures, increased sedimentation and rising sea level (Basher, et al. 2001). The extent of mangroves could increase (McGlone 2001).

Soil
Soil development will be affected by the predicted increase in erosion. More landslides are predicted for most regions, particularly in those that have erosion-prone soils and in some coastal areas. Lowland soils typically are rejuvenated by erosion and loess, but with disturbance cycle changes large areas of low-lying and rolling country will slowly lose mineral nutrients through the leaching of upper soil layers (McGlone 2001). Thus, erosion will contribute to the loss of soil nutrients and increase water logging in winter.

Exotic species
Warmer weather creates conditions that favor increased competition from exotic species (by reducing the resistance of indigenous species) and the spread of disease and pests (Basher, et al. 2001). Although exotic grasses have moved southward, the same has not been documented for indigenous species.

Possibly connected with more intense El Niño fluctuations, mast-seeding (common in plants such as beeches, snow grasses and conifers) may occur more frequently after warmer than normal summers. This provides an abundant food source to rabbits, rats and mice, which could lead to an increase in stoats and cats. The resulting increase in predation on native birds may inhibit pollination of some native plants.

Impacts on Social Wellbeing

Health
Climate change is likely to induce higher incidences of many health problems currently occurring in New Zealand. As temperatures rise, summer smog will cause more respiratory problems, particularly in the Auckland region (Ministry for the Environment 2001). Woodward, et al. (2001) point out that new health problems will result from both heat waves and the colonization of mosquitoes that carry diseases such as dengue fever. Pest eradication programs are expensive and only partially successful with many people reporting health complications from spraying. Warmer winters will reduce the incidence of winter-related illnesses such as colds and flu as well as the need for open fires for heating, which contribute to air pollution. The negative health impacts of a warmer climate in New Zealand are likely to be most

pronounced in northern regions, while benefits likely will be greater in southern regions (Ministry for the Environment 2001).

Indirect health impacts are likely as a result of floods and droughts. Heavy rain disperses pathogens such as cryptosporidiosis by washing animal excreta into water supplies (Basher, et al. 2001). Drought periods will require extraction of water from poorer quality sources, resulting in increased health risks.

Built environment

In 2030, the built environment will be under more pressure from population growth and transport than from climate change. The biggest direct climatic threats to buildings are likely to be heavy rainfall and associated floods (Minnery and Smith 1996). Sea level rise and temperature increase will affect the built environment directly by damaging buildings and causing landslips at exposed sites, and indirectly by increasing utility and material costs (Camilleri 2000). Increases in temperature may damage building materials, including plastics, rubber, paint, varnish, fabric and wood.

More than 40 per cent of New Zealand's population is exposed to flood risk. As Camilleri (2000) notes, 'Flooding will result in water damage to houses, drain damage, erosion and slips, and damage to services such as roads, pipes, and cables.' Sheltered coastlines such as the Hauraki Gulf, where houses are built close to the high tide line, are expected to incur more damage than houses located on exposed coasts. Currently marginal housing areas near riverbanks and lakeshores also are likely to become more prone to floods.

Minor temperature changes can alter humidity levels with consequential impacts on mold and other allergens, which affect the comfort and health of building occupants (Isaacs 1995). Camilleri (2000) claims that heating costs for buildings may be reduced by up to 70 per cent in 2030 in the Auckland region. This, however, could be offset by increased use of air conditioning.

Land Use Changes

New Zealand's land use patterns will shift as a result of how climate change affects the viability and economics of existing farming, forestry and horticultural activities. Climate change will enable existing crops to be grown in new areas, and tropical crops also may be introduced into New Zealand.

Pasture

Pasture-based systems dominate New Zealand's primary production sector. Increases in temperature and more frequent drought conditions may affect the composition of pastures, with more drought-tolerant, and often less palatable, species becoming more dominant (Basher, et al. 2001). This is likely to lead to a reduction in the feed quality of pastures, especially in the middle to north of the North Island, and may already be happening. According to the Ministry for the Environment (2001), a 1990 study found a southward shift of 1.5 degrees latitude (roughly from mid-Waikato/East Cape to Wanganui/Cape Kidnappers) in the occurrence of the invasive subtropical grass *Paspalum dilatatum* between 1976 and 1988.

Importantly, in areas where rainfall and water availability are not limiting, annual pasture yields could increase 10 to 20 per cent by 2030 due to increases in CO_2 concentration (the carbon [C] fertilization effect) and in temperature (Ministry for the Environment 2001). The highest increases are expected in cooler, wetter areas such as the southern South Island. But, water limitation due to decreased rainfall would dominate over the C fertilization effect (Basher, et al. 2001), thus imposing a mixed climate change effect on pasture productivity.

Arable crops
Arable cropping is common in the Waikato, Bay of Plenty, Manawatu, Canterbury and Southland regions. Crops include maize, wheat, oats, barley and peas. As with pasture, productivity of these crops is expected to increase with higher temperatures and perhaps with C fertilization. This could allow a slow southward shift of some crops and even the introduction of new species, but this depends on the availability of other resources such as water for irrigation and long-term soil fertility. The climate in Canterbury is expected to become increasingly suitable for maize production from about 2030 onwards due to reduced risk of frost and warmer summer temperatures (Kenny, et al. 2000; Ministry for the Environment 2001).

Horticulture
Temperate fruit production requires cool winters to promote bud break. Warmer temperatures might not produce enough flowers to make production economically viable in northern areas of New Zealand (Kenny, et al. 2001; Ministry for the Environment 2001). Regions such as Marlborough, Canterbury and Central Otago could become increasingly suitable as a result of warmer summers and lower frost risk if sufficient irrigation is available. However, research on the two economically most important crops (apples and kiwifruit) suggests that the pip and stonefruit industries are well placed to adapt actively to the effects of warmer temperatures. Scientists expect kiwifruit to be hard hit in the Bay of Plenty region (Kenny, et al. 2001).

The wine industry seems set to benefit overall from climate change. Scientists expect accelerated exports and vintage years for the next few decades. This is due to a combination of warmer, drier weather on New Zealand's eastern coast, a larger number of microclimates and falling grape harvests elsewhere. There will be, however, regional losers–in particular, vineyards may disappear from most parts of west Auckland within a couple of decades.

Forestry

Wood production from planted forests has become an important component of New Zealand's primary industry. Similar to crops, the growth rate of trees is expected to increase due to higher temperatures and possibly from C fertilization. Studies carried out on pine seedlings confirm increases of about 20 per cent under doubled CO_2 concentrations (Ministry for the Environment 2001). Changes in rainfall patterns could have a negative impact on plantation growth rates. Radiata pine requires about 1500 mm of annual rainfall for optimal growth and therefore drier areas on the east coast of the North Island could experience reductions in growth (Ministry for the Environment 2001).

Policy Responses

Although the New Zealand research community addressed climate change issues in the 1980s (see, for example, Ericksen 1988), it did not really emerge on the central government policy agenda until 1992 when New Zealand signed the United Nations Framework Convention on Climate Change. Following 1992 considerable effort was devoted to a long-term climate change strategy. This was intended to cover both preventative and adaptive strategies (Ministry for the Environment 1993). However, in July 1994 the government announced a policy package focusing solely on preventative measures (Ministry of Commerce 1999).

Over the next five years, central government policy development was relatively low-key with only one further policy package in 1999 attempting to advance the climate change issue. This changed in late 1999, with the election of a new government that undertook two public consultation rounds and eventually confirmed its policy package on climate change in October 2002. Two months later, New Zealand ratified the Kyoto Protocol.

New Zealand's policy approach to climate change has been driven by central government with limited attention devoted to clarifying the role of local government until recently. Last year, central government passed the Resource Management (Energy and Climate Change) Amendment Act 2004. This act required regional and local government to 'plan for the effects of climate change... but not to consider the effects on climate change of discharges into air of greenhouse gases.' Also, the Ministry for the Environment published a report entitled 'Climate Change Effects and Impacts Assessment–*A Guidance Manual for Local Government in New Zealand*' (NIWAR, et al. 2004) Under the Local Government Act 2002, the Resource Management Act of 1991 and other legislation, local government is responsible for a range of functions that may be affected by climate change.

For regional councils, these functions range from management of regional water, air and land resources, to biosecurity and natural hazards management. Local authorities also own community assets that may be vulnerable to the effects of climate change.

IMPACTS OF CLIMATE CHANGE ON THE REGIONAL ECONOMIES AND THEIR SUSTAINABILITY

Methodology

Scenario generation using economic models and GIS

Dynamic input-output models were used to project levels of economic activity in the 16 New Zealand regions. These models have been developed as part of the *Eco*Link Project sponsored by the New Zealand Ministry for the Environment (Patterson and McDonald 1996; McDonald and Patterson 1999a-b). A key feature of these models is that they connect economic activity and environmental impacts (production of wastes, use of biophysical resources and ecosystem services) through to the target year of 2040, given two scenarios: business-as-usual and climate change. The business-as-usual scenario assumes a continuation of trends that have occurred in the regional economies over the past 20 to 30 years with no climate change impact. The climate change scenario also assumes a continuation of economic trends, but superimposes the effect of climate change; it assumes that by 2040 North Island temperatures will increase by 2°C and South Island temperatures will rise by 1.5°C, which is consistent with the scientific evidence (McGlone, et al. 1990; Salinger and Hicks 1990).

The business-as-usual scenario was generated using a regression-based time-series analysis to project trends in 48 sectors across the regional economies. These sectoral trends were fed into the dynamic input-output models as exogenous variables. The climate change scenario (in addition to the sectoral trends) took account of a number of changes expected as a result of climate change:

1. Land use shifts, for example, more tropical crops become viable in the North Island;
2. Yield improvements of agriculture, horticulture and forestry;
3. Impacts of extreme climate events, for example floods and droughts;
4. Impacts of changed prevalence of diseases and other climate dependent health outcomes;
5. Impacts on ecosystem services and biodiversity; and
6. Impacts on other climate sensitive sectors such as tourism.

The economic modeling approach allows for the calculation of flow-on effects of these exogenous impacts. They are often just as significant as the initial direct impact. For example, increased horticultural activity may lead to downstream food processing activities that have a greater environmental impact than the initial horticultural development.

Performance indicators

A combined economic modeling-GIS approach enabled the projection of a number of economic and sustainability outcomes for each of the sixteen regions (Tables 4.1, 4.2 and 4.3):

Economic outcomes
- Gross Domestic Product
- Sectoral Activity (48 sectors)
- Employment
- Regional Balance of Trade

Environmental impacts and pressures
- Energy use
- Water use
- Land use intensification
- Water pollution, as indicated by BOD (basic oxygen demand) and total volume of water discharge
- Carbon dioxide emissions

Ecosystem services
- Eighteen ecosystem service types (as defined by Costanza, et al. 1997 and Patterson and Cole 1999)

Impacts of Climate Change on the Metropolitan Regions

The metropolitan regions include Auckland and Wellington. Auckland's economy is based on a large manufacturing sector and, to a lesser extent, on a business services sector. Wellington is an administrative and business services center, although it has a sizeable manufacturing base. These metropolitan regions are equivalent to 'core' regions in the 'core-periphery' model of regional change (Friedmann 1973) because of the influence they have over other regions through the agencies of both business and government.

Auckland

Under the business-as-usual scenario, the economic model indicates that Auckland's economy will continue to grow at a rate that out-performs the rest of the country. The Auckland economy is expected to more than double (117 per cent increase) over the 1998–2040 period. This is consistent with an independent population projection made by Statistics New Zealand (2000).

Table 4.1   Business-as-usual versus a climate change scenario: percentage change in performance indicators (1998 to 2040) for New Zealand regions

	GDP (% change, 1998–2040)		Energy Use (% change, 1998–2040)		Water Use (% change, 1998–2040)	
	Business-As-Usual Scenario	Climate Change Scenario	Business-As-Usual Scenario	Climate Change Scenario	Business-As-Usual Scenario	Climate Change Scenario
Metropolitan Regions						
Auckland	117	115	110	108	84	86
Wellington	54	63	45	61	33	45
Heartland Regions						
Waikato	64	75	71	84	40	46
Bay of Plenty	87	96	115	131	76	89
Hawke's Bay	62	67	67	76	38	43
Taranaki	19	16	10	7	0	-1
Manawatu-Wanganui	34	36	27	30	26	30
Canterbury	93	101	85	98	89	112
Otago	54	80	42	76	32	68
Marlborough	97	212	84	223	78	194
Nelson	104	113	90	100	63	64
Peripheral Regions						
Northland	24	30	17	22	6	11
Gisborne	14	19	2	6	15	32
West Coast	28	8	17	-2	7	2
Southland	21	28	-1	4	3	11
New Zealand	80	86	74	83	37	45

Auckland's climate is projected to become more tropical, with increased humidity, higher temperatures and a greater frequency of storms. There is some evidence of greater shoreline erosion and drainage problems in low-lying areas. In addition, there are some indications of infrastructure problems emerging as a direct result of climate change, such as major drainage problems at Auckland International Airport, problems with landfills currently sited along estuaries and streams, and the possible inundation of parts of a major motorway. Under the climate change scenario, however, Auckland will be relatively unaffected in general terms since it is not as directly dependent on rural production as other regions. Overall, GDP in 2040 is expected to drop by $\$_{1998}$ 378 million (-0.55 per cent) due to the effects of climate change. The model predicts increased horticulture production and intensification of rural land use in the manufacturing (-$\$_{1998}$ 27 million) and services and tourism sectors (-$\$_{1998}$ 495 million).

Table 4.2   Business-as-usual versus a climate change scenario: percentage change in performance indicators (1998 to 2040) for New Zealand regions

	Land use Intensification (% change, 1998–2040)		Water Pollution (Biological Oxygen Demand) (% change, 1998–2040)		Air Pollution (Carbon Dioxide Emissions) (% change, 1998–2040)	
	Business-As-Usual Scenario	Climate Change Scenario	Business-As-Usual Scenario	Climate Change Scenario	Business-As-Usual Scenario	Climate Change Scenario
Metropolitan Regions						
Auckland	396	436	190	195	126	124
Wellington	213	294	39	38	52	65
Heartland Regions						
Waikato	181	224	35	36	86	99
Bay of Plenty	213	259	63	62	139	159
Hawke's Bay	181	214	46	36	85	95
Taranaki	97	93	31	23	18	14
Manawatu-Wanganui	149	166	28	28	35	39
Canterbury	272	319	81	72	94	106
Otago	188	296	43	46	49	78
Marlborough	246	471	81	85	92	203
Nelson	216	266	82	75	98	106
Peripheral Regions						
Northland	108	135	29	32	22	28
Gisborne	92	114	-5	-5	5	9
West Coast	115	119	26	-7	21	-1
Southland	111	139	17	23	7	13
New Zealand	187	229	44	43	88	97

Wellington

Like Auckland, Wellington's metropolitan economy will be relatively unaffected by climate change with the exception of the rural Wairarapa sub-region. The model projects that horticulture in the Wairarapa region (particularly apples and summer fruits) will expand from about 3000 hectares in 1998 to about 13 000 hectares in 2040. This will have positive flow-on impacts (particularly forward linkages into the manufacturing sector), as well as put increased pressures on the use of water resources, to the tune of an extra 9 172 000 m^3 of water required annually under the climate change scenario.

Impacts on the Heartland Regions

The Heartland regions are the rural regions that have traditionally driven New Zealand's resource-based export production. The economies of these regions are more mixed than the other rural regions and they are well endowed with physical resources, not the least of which is highly productive farmland.

In general, the Heartland regions are expected to gain the most economically from climate change, due to land use shifts to more productive and profitable forms of farming and horticulture. However, the negative impact on the biophysical environment in terms of increased demand for resources such as energy, water, fertilizers and soil, and the increased pressures on the natural environment from more intensive farming (for example, resulting in the eutrophication of waterways) will be most profound in these regions.

Waikato

The Waikato climate will become more subtropical, which will significantly affect agricultural land use patterns. Greater pastoral yields will lead to increased milk production as will the expansion southwards of dairy farming, but invasive weed species (such as *Paspalum dilatum*) will become more prevalent and make dairy farming less profitable (Kenny, et al. 2000). The model assumes that horticultural production, including kiwifruit growing, will increase from 16 951 ha in 1998 to 50 852 ha in 2040. Overall, the Waikato GDP is expected to increase from $_{1998}$ 8589 million to $_{1998}$ 14 001 million in 2040 mainly due to increased dairy and horticultural production and the downstream processing of these products.

The effects on the natural landscape and the biophysical environment of the Waikato will also be significant. More rainfall and frequent storms will put pressure on low-lying areas, and there is evidence of increased costs for drainage and flood protection schemes in the Waikato, particularly in the Thames Valley area.

Bay of Plenty
The strong inward migration forecast in the Statistics New Zealand's (2000) population projection indicates that this region will grow rapidly under the business-as-usual scenario. Climate change will enhance this effect as the region becomes increasingly tropical. Lychees, bananas, pineapples and other tropical fruits could replace the traditional kiwifruit. As a result, horticultural land could increase by 5328 ha (20 per cent). However, fewer dairy farms are projected under the climate change scenario due to the increased prevalence of invasive weeds. There will also be negative impacts on ecosystem processes due to climate change, such as more frequent flooding, increased eutrophication of lakes and larger oxygen deficits in lakes.

Hawke's Bay
Land use intensification of the more fertile land within Hawke's Bay is expected. Some land will move out of dairy and sheep/beef farming, and there will be more kiwifruit and red wine grapes, but no apple production except in southern Hawke's Bay. Napier and other low-lying settlements may face problems and costs in upgrading drainage and sewerage infrastructure. Overall, the region's GDP is expected to increase by a margin of $_{1998}$ 176 million (3.31 per cent) due to the effects of climate change, primarily due to increased agricultural production and its downstream processing.

Taranaki
Under the business-as-usual scenario Taranaki's economy is projected to grow slowest of all the Heartland regions. Statistics New Zealand (2000) similarly predicts that Taranaki's population growth to 2021 will be the second lowest of all regions at -21 per cent. Under the climate change scenario, Taranaki's GDP growth is expected to slow even further, falling from 19 per cent to 16 per cent over the 1998–2040 period. Even though dairy production is increasing, it will not be able to increase at the same rate as historical trends due to a less favorable climate (wetter, warmer and with more storm events) and associated problems such as the increased prevalence of subtropical weeds. Under climate change, the economic model indicates that Taranaki's growth profile will become similar to those regions currently classified as 'peripheral.'

Manawatu-Wanganui
In terms of economic production, Manawatu-Wanganui will be one of the regions least affected by climate change, with a projected 2 per cent increase in GDP. Some shifts in land use are expected, although they will be relatively insignificant compared to other regions. For example, the model predicts less production of wheat, barley and field peas and more production of soybeans, peanuts and sunflowers. However, significant impacts in the incidence of soil

erosion are expected, as reflected in the ecosystem services valuation (Table 4.3).

Canterbury

Canterbury's regional economy is expected to grow by $\$_{1998}$ 919 million (3.97 per cent) under the climate change scenario. The change is largely driven by increased rural production (horticulture and dairy farming) and its flow-on effects. The forward linkages to the food processing industries, as predicted by the economic modeling, are particularly significant. This increased production will also lead to a significant increase in water usage in Canterbury: 25 668 000 m^3 of water will be required in 2040 in a region that is already dry and expected to become 20 per cent drier. The infrastructure costs of meeting increased water demand will be significant.

Otago

Central Otago will be up to 30 per cent wetter, although 10 per cent drier in coastal and North Otago. Central Otago will also become less prone to frosts. This is projected to lead to a large expansion of horticultural activity in Otago from 10 410 ha in 1998 to 68 964 ha in 2040. Overall, with more intensive land-based production as well as flow-on effects in the economy, the regional GDP is expected to increase $\$_{1998}$ 7410 million (16.58 per cent) due to climate change impacts. The resource inputs (particularly water) and environmental impacts resulting from intensified land use will be significant (Table 4.3). Under the climate change scenario, energy use from 1998–2040 is expected to increase by 6900 TJ (33.90 per cent) and, more significantly, water use by 26 878 000 m^3 (275.57 per cent). The provision of irrigation infrastructure to meet this extra demand for water will prove costly.

Marlborough and Nelson

The business-as-usual scenario indicates that Marlborough and Nelson are expected to be the two fastest growing economies in New Zealand after Auckland, their regional GDP increasing by 97 per cent and 104 per cent, respectively. Climate change impacts are expected to accentuate these trends. Horticulture expansion in Marlborough is expected to be most significant, increasing from 13 930 ha to 48 754 ha, mainly due to climate change effects. The most critical constraint to development will be water availability. Sea temperature may become too warm for some forms of aquaculture in Marlborough and Nelson.

Table 4.3 Marginal impact (NZ $mil 1998) on the economy and on ecosystems of climate change for the year 2040

	Impacts on the Economy				Impacts on Ecosystem Services							Net Benefit
	Primary Industries	Mfg & Construction Industries	Utilities & Service Industries	Sub-total	Climate & Disturbance Regulation	Water Services	Erosion Control and Soil Formation	Bio-Control	Refugia	Other	Sub-total	Total of Economy & Ecosystem Impacts
Metropolitan Regions												
Auckland	144	-27	-495	-378	-9	-2	-3	-2	-1	0	-16	-394
Wellington	179	1,018	-79	1,118	-7	-10	-31	-3	0	-2	-53	1,065
Heartland Regions												
Waikato	550	487	-35	1,002	-126	-158	-103	-13	-4	-11	-415	587
Bay of Plenty	267	249	-40	475	-16	-19	-50	-3	0	-8	-97	378
Hawke's Bay	121	75	-20	176	-11	-15	-71	-5	0	-3	-105	71
Taranaki	-21	-71	-6	-98	-4	-1	-26	-3	0	-2	-36	-134
Wanganui	92	22	-18	96	-16	-6	-122	-10	0	-5	-160	-64
Canterbury	372	681	-134	919	-33	-277	-110	-19	-1	-17	-457	463
Otago	388	699	-33	1,054	-20	-60	-22	-7	-1	-6	-116	938
Marlborough	257	862	-7	1,113	-10	-13	-23	-3	0	-2	-52	1,061
Nelson	101	89	-21	169	-12	-6	-13	-2	0	-5	-39	129
Peripheral Regions												
Northland	132	53	-11	175	-34	-13	-54	-6	-2	-3	-111	63
Gisborne	33	17	-3	47	-9	-3	-69	-3	0	-4	-87	-40
West Coast	-96	-49	-5	-150	-87	-87	-83	-1	-2	-29	-290	-440
Southland	100	66	-8	158	-59	-92	-42	-3	4	-24	-223	-65
New Zealand	2,620	4,171	-914	5,876	-455	-762	-821	-84	-16	-121	-2,258	3,618

Impacts on Peripheral Regions

The peripheral regions include those that have been in decline for a long period, have highly specialized and vulnerable economies or face difficult physical conditions.

The peripheral regions generally have the lowest trends of projected GDP growth under the climate change scenario, along with the Heartland region of Taranaki (Tables 4.1 and 4.2). Statistics New Zealand (2000) also projects that three of the four peripheral regions will experience negative population growth until 2021.

Northland
Under projected climate change, the Northland climate will become more tropical and more susceptible to extreme events such as tropical cyclones and floods. Horticulture will include more tropical crops like lychees, bananas, pineapples and rice, to the exclusion of traditional crops like kiwifruit. Dairy farming will become more difficult due to invasive tropical grasses. Overall, under the climate change scenario, greater yields in land-based activities (and more downstream processing of these land-based products) are expected, increasing GDP by $_{1998}$ 175 million (4.91 per cent).

Gisborne
The climate change scenario predicted no dramatic shift in Gisborne's land use patterns. Rather, horticultural production is projected to become more productive (higher yields per hectare) and more dominated by tropical crops. This would boost GDP by $_{1998}$ 47 million (4.68 per cent) in 2040. However, these positive impacts on the economy are expected to be less significant than the negative environmental impacts, notably the $_{1998}$ 69 million cost of increased erosion per anum for 2040 (Table 4.3).

West Coast
The West Coast of the South Island will become much wetter under in the face of climate change. All forms of land-based production (particularly dairying and forestry) will become more difficult. This will have critical flow-on effects on the West Coast economy, which is highly dependent on such activities. Tourism may also be affected adversely by a more inhospitable climate. It is therefore projected that the West Coast GDP will decrease by $_{1998}$ 150 million (-15.0 per cent) due to climate change effects, making it the slowest growing economy in New Zealand. There will also be significant impacts on biodiversity (such as the die-off rimu forests) and increased pressure from flooding on urban settlements due to more frequent and heavier rain.

Southland

Changes in climate will make Southland more suitable for dairy farming, reinforcing the existing rate of dairy farm conversion in the region. Forestry and various forms of cropping will become more important. Climate change effects are estimated to boost the Southland economy by $\$_{1998}$ 158 million (5.62 per cent) in 2040. However, both the business-as-usual and climate change scenarios project significant depopulation of Southland.

Regional Shifts in Ecological Footprints with Climate Change

One of the patterns emerging from the modeling in the face of climate change was expansion of the ecological footprints of most regions, often in a spatially differentiated manner. The 'environmental space' appropriated by regional economies is predicted to expand with climate change: induced increases in production will use more resources (energy, water, land and fertilizers) and produce more pollutants (nutrients, air emissions and solid wastes).

The national and regional shifts in the energy, water, CO_2 water discharge and the biological oxygen demand footprints are outlined in Table 4.4. The most significant impact of climate change is the increasing size of the water footprint. At the national level, the water footprint increased by 5.67 per cent due to the effects of climate change.

The water footprint increases most dramatically with climate change in Waikato, Canterbury, Otago and Marlborough. To provide this water, extensive water supply and irrigation schemes will have to be put in place, which will have a significant impact on the regional economies in the construction phase of these projects. This particularly applies to drier regions of the country (such as Canterbury, Otago and Marlborough) where rainfall will be insufficient to meet much of the water requirements.

Other footprints (energy, CO_2 and water discharge) all record smaller, yet significant, increases at the national level under climate change effects, although there are significant regional differences. The overall energy footprint is projected to increase 4.81 per cent due to climate change. Some of the largest increases in the energy footprint are in the South Island, which will have implications for energy infrastructure provision in these regions that may not be anticipated in current planning.

The input-output analysis built a detailed picture of the ecological footprint of each region under climate change. For example, changes in the Otago water footprint with climate change can be measured (Table 4.5). The effect on Otago's water footprint of horticultural expansion, and to a lesser extent the downstream processing of horticultural products, is evident.

Table 4.4   Marginal impacts on regional ecological footprints with climate change for the year 2040

Region	Energy Footprint (TJ, Oil Equivalents)	CO_2 Footprint (tons)	Water Use Footprint (000 m^3)	Water Discharges Footprint (000 m^3)	BOD Footprint (kg)
Northland	744	46,695	3,137	2,958	5,315
Auckland	-3,432	-196,205	3,798	184	12,822
Waikato	6,788	432,714	20,850	15,894	65,525
Bay of Plenty	5,923	539,434	9,842	10,852	-13,157
Gisborne	166	8,508	1,044	16	59
Hawke's Bay	1,661	122,117	3,525	-633	-65,213
Taranaki	-802	-49,811	-3,491	-3,371	-65,521
Manawatu-Wanganui	649	47,810	1,836	931	4,576
Wellington	8,049	356,810	9,172	-510	-44,451
West Coast	-834	-54,209	-2,830	-2,173	-45,094
Canterbury	7,861	377,947	25,668	-3,182	-194,906
Otago	6,900	315,159	26,878	2,123	29,793
Southland	1,264	87,414	3,836	2,794	36,392
Nelson	1,074	45,774	532	-1,231	-24,527
Marlborough	7,333	315,125	14,830	555	4,841
New Zealand	43,343	2,395,281	118,628	25,207	-293,548
(% Increase)	4.81	4.37	5.67	1.02	-0.99

DISCUSSION AND POLICY IMPLICATIONS

Regional Development Implications

Climate change by 2040 will have uneven regional effects in New Zealand. In general, climate change effects will not alter the longstanding trends in regional development in New Zealand, but in some cases, will exaggerate and in other cases lead to slight reversals in the trends.

Overall, in the year 2040 climate change will add $5876 million to New Zealand's GDP (3.42 per cent increase). Increased agricultural, horticultural and forestry production in many regions will increase GDP by an estimated $2620 million and, more significantly, $3958 million in the processing of these land-based products. GDP will also increase due to increased expenditure in pest control, flood protection and other infrastructure services.

Table 4.5   Estimated changes in the Otago water footprint with the climate change impact, 2040

Economic Sector	Water Footprint With No Climate Change (000 m³)	Water Footprint With Climate Change (000 m³)	Change in the Size of the Footprint (000 m³)	Change in the Size of the Footprint (%)
Horticulture and fruit growing	4,900	25,924	21,023	429.0
Livestock and cropping farming	4,314	6,711	2,397	55.6
Dairy cattle farming	2,497	3,159	662	26.5
Other farming	684	787	103	15.0
Services to agriculture, hunting and trapping	66	85	19	28.5
Forestry and logging	32	37	5	15.0
Meat and meat product manufacturing	11,836	12,145	309	2.6
Dairy product manufacturing	3,942	4,988	1,045	26.5
Other food manufacturing	105	814	709	673.8
Beverage, malt and tobacco manufacturing	87	652	564	646.1
Textile and apparel manufacturing	220	231	11	4.8
Wood product manufacturing	121	138	17	14.5
Paper and paper product manufacturing	461	516	54	11.8
Retail trade	36	36	0	-1.1
Accommodation, restaurants and bars	321	295	-25	-7.9
Cultural and recreational services	712	698	-14	-2.0
Other Sectors	67,551	67,551	0	0.0
Total	97,887	124,765	26,878	27.5

The Heartland regions stand to gain the most from climate change, with the general level of economic activity increasing at a rate higher than otherwise expected. Although economic activity initially will be increased by more intensive and profitable forms of land use, the economic model indicates that there will be significant flow-on impacts (forward linkages) on the manufacturing and services sectors. Under climate change, the growth rates of some of the regional economies (Nelson, Marlborough and Canterbury) will be similar to or outperform Auckland's metropolitan economy. An enhanced inflow of migrants into these regions and, in the case of Marlborough, a reversal of the recent trend of net outward migration is expected.

Climate changes will also reinforce the already poor prospects of some regions. For example, Taranaki has the second-lowest projected GDP growth rate of any region from 1998 to 2040 with a 19 per cent projected increase.

Climate change is expected to decrease this to only 16 per cent. The Taranaki economy is built on a narrow base (dairy farming) which is vulnerable to climate change impacts. Given these revised growth projections, Taranaki can now be more appropriately classified as a peripheral region, unless it can diversify its narrow economic base.

West Coast regional development prospects also worsen under the impacts of climate change. A wetter, less hospitable climate will make all forms of land-based production less profitable, which according to the economic model will have significant flow-on effects for the regional economy. Climate change impacts will negatively affect tourism. The 1998–2040 GDP growth rate is expected to drop from 8 to 20 per cent, the lowest in the country.

The projections indicate that, under the business-as-usual scenario, peripheral regions will continue to lag behind the other regions in New Zealand in terms of GDP growth. Although climate change is projected to have a positive effect in three of these regions (Northland, Gisborne and Southland), the effect is not enough to improve their prospects to a level equal to the Heartland regions. The growth rate of all three peripheral regions still falls short of all the Heartland regions (except Taranaki).

The metropolitan (core) regions will be relatively unaffected by climate change in terms of GDP growth. Decreased tourism volumes are expected to affect Auckland, as will decreased inward migration, particularly from the Heartland regions into Auckland City. Auckland will have to deal with a number of infrastructure issues (such as storm protection, water supply and road construction) that will be prompted by climate change. None of the impacts will be enough to affect significantly the high rate of GDP growth, and Auckland will still remain the second-fastest growing economy in the country next to Marlborough.

Infrastructure Implications

Physical infrastructure provision has always been a central feature of regional development initiatives in New Zealand. Regional development patterns and growth modes can often be traced to provision of infrastructure. An active Public Works Program, which started in the 1880s with railroad schemes and continued through the 1970s with the 'Think Big' energy projects, has facilitated regional development in New Zealand.

There is a clear need for significant infrastructure provision to deal with the adverse effects of climate change, as well as to capture the regional development opportunities afforded by climate change. The economic cost of this infrastructure provision will be significant, probably approaching the size and cost of previous investments in the 'Think Big' energy projects of the 1970s or the hydro-electricity developments of the 1930s–1950s.

Flooding and drainage infrastructure
Flooding is expected to become four times as frequent, more severe and less predictable in many regions. The Waikato is one region likely to be affected significantly. The existing Thames and Waihi flood control schemes are likely to fail more frequently under climate change and swamp/wetland areas will move further inland. Low-lying urban areas throughout New Zealand, such as Greymouth, will be at greater risk of flooding. A number of flood/drainage risk problems have also been identified in Auckland as a result of more rainfall and sea level rise. The capital costs of improved flood protection infrastructure (for example, stop banks) is significant, but probably justified given the cost of major flooding events ranging from $100 to $1000 million (Ericksen 1986; Morgan as reported in Nash and Wallis 2004). Northland, Auckland, Waikato and Manawatu-Wanganui are expected to incur large investment of flood protection and drainage infrastructure.

Wastewater infrastructure
More intense rainfall will cause more inflow and infiltration into wastewater networks. Wet weather outflow events will also increase in frequency and volume with climate change. Longer dry spells will increase the likelihood of blockages and related dry weather outflows. Also in some regions, with more processing of agro-food products and with climate change-induced population growth, the capacity of private and public wastewater treatment plants will need to be increased. The BOD loading in Waikato, Otago and Southland is expected to increase significantly.

Water supply infrastructure
The demand for water is expected to increase more than 118 628 000 m^3 (a 5.67 per cent increase) due to climate change. This is particularly significant in regions such as the Waikato, Bay of Plenty, Wairarapa, Canterbury, Otago and Marlborough. This will require significant investment in irrigation schemes and other water supply infrastructure. Without this investment in water supply infrastructure, some of the expected growth in regions such as Otago and Marlborough will not eventuate. The problem of putting in place such infrastructure is often exacerbated by the dry climate of these regions and their low natural levels of water supply. In the short run, this investment in water supply infrastructure is likely to have a positive effect on many regional economies.

Energy supply network
Climate change is expected to increase energy demand by 4.81 per cent in 2040. This will require extra investment in energy supply plants, above that currently anticipated to address New Zealand's problems with electricity generation and supply network infrastructure. Much of this extra demand for

energy will be in the South Island regions such as Otago and Marlborough. This demand will require significant upgrading of the supply networks for electricity. Furthermore, under climate change, the decreased reliability of water supply in some South Island regions (such as Canterbury) may mean less reliance can be placed on traditional sources of hydro-electricity.

Roading infrastructure
Capital investment in New Zealand's road system exceeds that of all other forms of transport. More extreme rainfall and extreme weather events due to climate change will affect the road infrastructure. The cost of repairing damage to roads in areas that are prone to flooding and landslides are considerable, as exemplified in the recent storm event that hit the central North Island area (Morgan as reported in Nash and Wallis 2004).

In regions that will grow under climate change (Nelson, Marlborough and Otago) there will be a need for improved roading and transportation infrastructure to facilitate transport of the increased amount of products. On the other hand, decreased tourism volumes under climate change will decrease slightly the pressure on the nation's roading infrastructure.

Climate Change: Net Benefit or Net Cost to the Regions?

The economic benefits and positive flow of effects on New Zealand's regional economies are significant. By 2040, climate change will increase the nation's GDP by an estimated $5876 million (3.42 per cent).[1] The regions expected to benefit most are Otago and Marlborough, with the West Coast and Taranaki experiencing depressed economic growth as a result of climate change. In general, the economic flow-on effects of climate change will not be enough to affect the longstanding regional development patterns in New Zealand: the redistribution of economic activity away from the peripheral regions to the core growth regions.

Provision of infrastructure will play a critical role in realizing the economic benefits of climate change in a number of regions. The costs will be significant, and in many cases beyond the capacity of regional government providers. Arguably, there is a need for central government intervention, perhaps by the Ministry of Economic Development, to overcome funding issues relating to infrastructure provision.

The environmental cost of climate change will be significant. Increased rainfall and more intense rainfall events in the west will lead to increased soil erosion and landslides. Increased temperature, reduced rainfall and drying westerly winds in the east will lead to changes in the distribution of native forest ecosystems. There will be an increased biosecurity risk with increasing temperature and subtropical species affecting flora and fauna. Sea level rise will also affect some localities. Higher levels of economic activity in some regions will increase the ecological footprint of industries in particular regions.

We have attempted to crudely measure the negative impact on ecosystems and compare this with the economic benefit of climate change for various regions. Overall, we estimated the cost of the loss of ecosystem services to be $2258 million for 2040, with the biggest single cost being the loss of 'erosion control and soil formation' services at $821 million (refer to Table 4.4). Once these environmental costs are factored into calculations, it is clear that the peripheral regions (Gisborne, West Coast and Southland) are most adversely affected by climate change. Auckland, Taranaki and Manawatu-Wanganui also come out as 'net losers' ($environmental costs > $economic benefits) in the face of climate change. All other regions are 'net winners' ($economic benefits > $environmental costs) according to the model.

NOTE

1.   It may be useful in future research to enumerate 'economic benefits' in terms of the Genuine Progress Indicator (GPI) system of measurement—refer to Anielski and Rowe (1999). In this case, the 'economic benefits' will probably not be as great as in our current analysis, as the GPI subtracts from the GDP (rather than adds into) 'negative' economic activities such as flood control and pest eradication which result from climate change.

REFERENCES

Anielski, M. and J. Rowe (1999), *The Genuine Progress Indicator–1998 Update,* San Francisco, CA: Redefining Progress.

Basher, R.E., B. Bates, M. Finlayson, H. Gitay, and A. Woodward (2001), 'Australia and New Zealand', in *Climate Change 2001: Impacts Adaptation, and Vulnerability*, J.J. McCarthy, O.F. Canziani, N.A. Leary, D.J. Dokken, and K.S. White (eds), Cambridge: Cambridge University Press.

Camilleri, M.J. (2000), *Implications of Climate Change for the Construction Sector: Houses*, SR094, Judgeford.

Climate Change Office (2004), *How might climate change affect my region?*, Wellington, NZ: New Zealand Climate Change Office, Ministry for the Environment.

Costanza, R., R. d'Arge, R. de Groot, S. Farber, M. Grasso, B. Hannon, et. al. (1997), 'The value of the world's ecosystem services and natural capital', *Nature*, **387**: 253–260.

Ericksen, N.J. (1986), *Creating flood disasters? New Zealand's need for a new approach to urban flood hazard*, Wellington, NZ: Water and Soil Miscellaneous Publication Ministry of Works and Development.

Ericksen, N.J. (1988), 'Preface, Human Dynamics of Climate Change in New Zealand: Research Needs and Strategies', in *Proceedings of a Joint Symposium Between the SSRFC and the School of Social Sciences*, Waikato University.

Friedmann, J. (1973), *Urbanization, planning, and national development*, Beverly Hills, CA: Sage.

Isaacs, N. (1995), 'The Built Environment', in *Industry Research Priorities for Climate Change*, The Royal Society of New Zealand (ed.), Wellington, NZ: The Royal Society of New Zealand, pp. 19–21.

Kenny, G.J., R.A. Warrick, B.D. Campbell, G.C. Sims, M. Camilleri, P.D. Jamieson, et al. (2000), 'Investigating climate change impacts and thresholds: An application of the CLIMPACTS integrated assessment model for New Zealand agriculture', *Climatic Change*, **46**: 91–113.

Kenny, G.J., W. Ye, T. Flux, and R.A. Warrick (2001), 'Climate variations and New Zealand agriculture: The CLIMPACTS system and issues of spatial and temporal scale', *Environment International*, **27**: 189–194.

McDonald, G. and M.G. Patterson (1999a), *Eco*Link Overview Report, Auckland: McDermott Fairgray Group Ltd.

McDonald, G. and M.G. Patterson (1999b), *Eco*Link User Guide, Auckland: McDermott Fairgray Group Ltd.

McGlone, M.S. (2001), 'Linkages between climate change and biodiversity in New Zealand', Contract Report (for Ministry for the Environment) LC0102/014, Lincoln: Landcare Research.

McGlone, M.S., T. Clarkson, and B. Fitzharris (1990), *Unsettled outlook: New Zealand and the greenhouse effect*, Wellington, NZ: GD Books.

Ministry for the Environment (1993), *Information for the guidance of local authorities in addressing climate change*, Wellington, NZ: Ministry for the Environment.

Ministry for the Environment (2001), *Climate Change Impacts on New Zealand*, ME396, Wellington, NZ: Ministry for the Environment.

Ministry of Commerce (1999), *Climate change–what you should know*, Wellington, NZ: Ministry of Commerce.

Minnery, J.R. and D.I. Smith (1996), 'Climate change, flooding and urban infrastructure', in *Greenhouse: Coping with climate change*, W.J. Bouma, G.I. Pearman, and M.R. Manning (eds), Collingwood, Australia: CSIRO Publishing, pp. 235–247.

Nash, T. and A. Wallis (2004), '$1.26 billion GDP flood hit but economist sees growth in rebuilding', in *Manawatu Standard*, Palmerston North.

NIWAR, MWH NZ Ltd and Earthwise Consulting (2004), *Climate Change Effects and Impacts Assessment: A guidance manual for Local*

Government in New Zealand, ME 513, Wellington, NZ: New Zealand
Climate Change Office, Ministry for the Environment.

Office of the Minister for Industry and Regional Development (2000),
Regional Development Strategy, Wellington, NZ: Ministry of Economic
Development.

Patterson, M.G. and A. Cole (1999), 'Assessing the value of New Zealand's
biodiversity', *Occasional Paper 1*, School of Resource and
Environmental Planning, Massey University, Palmerston North.

Patterson, M.G. and G. McDonald (1996), 'Regional level environmental
accounting systems in New Zealand using input-output methodologies',
in *Tracking Progress: Linking environmental economy through
indicators and accounting systems,* Fenner Conference, Australian
Academy of Science, The University of New South Wales, Sydney.

Salinger, M.J. and D.M. Hicks (1990), 'The Scenarios', in *Climate change:
Impacts on New Zealand*, Wellington, NZ: Ministry for the Environment,
pp. 12–18.

Sinclair, J. (2001), 'Heavy Weather', *North and South*, pp. 66–76.

Statistics New Zealand (2000), *Sub National Population Projections (1996
base–2021)*, Wellington, NZ: Statistics New Zealand.

Warrick, R.A., G.J. Kenny, and J.J.E. Harman (2001), *The effects of climate
change and variation in New Zealand: An assessment using the
CLIMPACTS system*, Hamilton: International Global Change Institute.

Woodward, A., S. Hales, and N. de Wet (2001), *Climate change: potential
effects on human health in New Zealand, A report prepared for the
Ministry for the environment as part of the New Zealand Climate Change
Programme*, 0478240430 (pbk), *Gratis*, limited distribution, Wellington,
NZ: Ministry for the Environment.

PART II

Stakeholder Involvement: Needs, Experiences
and Challenges

5   Stakeholder Involvement in Local Smart Growth: Needs and Challenges

Thomas J. Wilbanks

INTRODUCTION

'Smart growth' includes processes that operate at a global or national level, such as economic globalization and technological change, but it also includes processes that operate at a local scale, such as democratization, local empowerment, and local innovativeness and problem solving. One of the distinctive characteristics of a local scale is that both assessments and actions at that scale can facilitate and, in fact, be based upon social processes that extend beyond organizational structures (Wilbanks 2003a). Agency at a local scale encourages and benefits from exchanges of information between promoters of activities, whether studies or decisions, and individual stakeholders–not just organizational representatives of constituencies. A local scale not only enables democracy in a fuller sense than a more global scale, but the sustainability of the actions often depends upon support from such processes.

How, then, can local participation in developing and implementing infrastructure strategies that are at the heart of smart growth be stimulated and facilitated? This chapter reviews a range of issues in assuring stakeholder involvement in urban land use and infrastructure initiatives related to such concerns as climate change, suggesting some realistic guidelines for meeting a challenge that is often viewed as a political risk and a logistical burden rather than a constructive alternative or a democratic imperative.

By 'stakeholders,' we mean parties with a stake in what happens. This term, which has no equivalent in many languages other than English, includes decision makers and experts but also extends to business people, interest groups, citizens at large, and citizens in particular categories likely to be especially impacted. The concept of 'stakeholder involvement' substantially overlaps the concept of 'public participation,' but in practice it is often more inclusive and more interactive, with components that reflect both differences in sectoral or constituency interest, such as between business and 'the public,' and differences in the geographic scale of concern, such as local or regional.

One reason that such an exercise is not simple is that it is informed by two bodies of knowledge: knowledge resulting from theory and knowledge based on practice. The two are often poorly connected, which means that drawing lessons from both cannot be done neatly. Consequently, this summary should be considered a starting point for discussion, not the final word, although the suggested guidelines are generally consistent with both bodies of knowledge.

THE CENTRAL ISSUES IN STAKEHOLDER INVOLVEMENT

The Issues in Practice

One way of viewing the central issues in stakeholder involvement is in terms of the key operational questions: why, who and how (NCEDR 1998).

The knowledge base about why stakeholder participation is important indicates that arranging effective participation depends directly on having a clear sense of the reasons for it, because the same approach is not appropriate for every purpose. Consider, for instance, the difference between involvement in an assessment versus involvement in decision making, or involvement in order to increase public awareness versus involvement to reduce political controversy. The purpose shapes one's decisions about the who and the how, and it affects stakeholder involvement and response. In many ways, the nature of participation is framed by the goals and purposes imbedded in the process, which in turn shape the way issues are identified, presented and considered. Stakeholders enter the process with their own goals and motives, which may be multiple and complex. As one example, organizers of stakeholder involvement are often targeted on a particular decision or product, when stakeholders are often more concerned about longer-term linkages and processes related to building participation and mutual trust beyond that single target. In deciding whom to invite to participate, a number of issues appear:

1. Who are the stakeholders in this activity? How can oversights be avoided that might later lead to criticism? What are possible sources of bias?
2. What constitutes involvement? Simply receiving communications does not seem to be enough. Involvement seems to involve some sort of volition: a decision to attend a meeting, respond to an inquiry and so on.
3. How much stakeholder involvement is enough, in terms of quantity and in terms of representation? For instance, how many different categories of

stakeholders and different geographic subdivisions need to be represented? To what degree can an individual from a larger group, such as a constituency interest group, be considered to be speaking for the members of the larger group? Given limited resources to support stakeholder involvement, what are the tradeoffs between quantity and quality?

Finally, given the why and the who, how should involvement be handled: the modes, the formats and the content? Alternatives include direct or indirect contact, formal or informal contact, and frequent or infrequent contact. Most of the alternatives that are rich in information content tend to be labor- and resource-intensive, and there is always an issue of the best balance between active solicitation of participation versus informing stakeholders of an activity and providing structures for them to participate by their own voluntary initiative. Clearly, for some critical stakeholder roles, face-to-face contact is essential, but electronic media such as interactive internet websites offer opportunities to avoid feelings of exclusion and to reduce dangers of unintended bias in centrally-initiated network construction.

One challenge related to smart growth is that some subject matter is rooted in scientific content, and many citizens without a technical background could have difficulty understanding the issues, risks and options. A classic example is evaluating risks associated with nuclear energy facilities, where stakeholder involvement has sometimes depended on technical experts in representative non-governmental organizations.

Another challenge is stimulating stakeholder involvement in planning that appears unrelated to a direct sense of threat. Participation is easier to assure, for instance, in cases involving 'not in my backyard' issues, such as the location of large new facilities that are perceived as risky or disruptive, from freeways to waste disposal sites. It is more difficult to stimulate among people busy in their normal lives when the implications are distant, fuzzy or generalized.

The Issues in Theory

To those who conduct research on stakeholder involvement, the issues are defined somewhat differently in terms of vocabulary, concerns and subdivisions of research fields. Related to involvement in environmental activities, a 1996 NAS/NRC report, *Understanding Risk: Informing Decisions in a Democratic Society*, developed the concept of an analytic-deliberative process that combines scientific analysis with deliberation involving a spectrum of stakeholders or their representatives. A December 2001 NRC Workshop on 'Public Participation in Environmental Assessment and Decision Making' considered issues that might be posed in following up the risk report with an NRC study on the public participation challenge, considering such issues as its audience, measuring success with public participation, and what contributes to success: for example, access to information, the quality of information, opportunities to participate, characteristics of participants, the procedures used for the participation, and sponsor characteristics related to credibility and trust.

By early 2004, such a study was under way by an NRC panel which had identified a number of knowledge bases that illuminated the challenge of effective public participation, including group processes and group dynamics, organizational behavior and learning, democratic theory and deliberative democracy, decision theory, communications theory and conflict resolution.[1] Preliminary NRC panel discussions of understandings from this literature suggest the importance of broad representation, effective leadership and facilitation, appropriate modes of interaction (small group interactions are better than large group or impersonal modes), a lack of underlying conflicts among stakeholders, the quality of information, and the quality of interpersonal relationships among the stakeholders and between them and activity leaders.

SOME BASES OF EXPERIENCE RELATED TO LOCAL EFFECTS OF CLIMATE CHANGE

Climate change is not the only challenge to smart growth or sustainable development, but in recent years it has been a catalyst for attention to broader issues (Wilbanks 2003b). One source of learning about how to make stakeholder involvement a reality for urban area smart growth is the still-emerging experience with broad participation in climate change assessments at a local or small regional scale.

Most of the attention to climate change during the 1980s and early 1990s was focused first on determining whether climate change was occurring and then, if so, why it was occurring. These were treated as questions for science and global policy making, not local debate. Relatively little attention was devoted to impacts of climate change, beyond the sense of a global threat. In fact, until late in the 1990s the ability to forecast climate change at a small regional scale was so limited that local impacts were difficult to identify.

One of the first attempts to examine what global climate change might mean at a local scale was the 'Global Change in Local Places' (GCLP) project of the Association of American Geographers (AAG) in 1996–2000, supported by NASA. This five-year study of four small regions in the United States sought to identify greenhouse gas emissions generated by each place over time, the forces driving such emissions, and potential for people who live and work in each place to reduce the emissions (AAG 2003; Kates and Wilbanks 2003; Wilbanks and Kates 1999). The research approach relied upon study teams in or near each study site, with extensive local knowledge and contact networks, and it included surveys of households and interviews of representatives of major emitters to determine local awareness and concern. It also included attention to tangible local actions related to climate change concerns and to historic analogs of local responses to environmental challenges.

One of the most successful aspects of the project was its expectation that local knowledge would inform global change studies at all scales and that institutions with a sustained commitment to local area studies and outreach would be invaluable in uncovering such local knowledge. Long-term global change studies at a local scale need to be housed within institutions maintaining such a commitment, so that they may retain continuity as key persons come and go. Based on GCLP's experience, it appears that local research on global change is heavily dependent on existing local information infrastructures. In the local case studies, the investigations could not be conducted effectively in the face of limited county-level statistical data. Local information sources were essential for framing the issues, understanding the local context, uncovering inventories and other data sources available only at a local or small regional scale, and appreciating the local meaning of numbers available from more general sources, especially over a period of two decades or more. Personal knowledge and expertise was often more instructive and insightful than routine quantitative analysis of available statistical data, and this means identifying and appreciating local information infrastructures, formal and informal.

GCLP also found that, consistent with other findings about the assessment process, eliciting local knowledge is facilitated by using local experts as 'gatekeepers.' A relatively robust recent finding in studies of environmental assessment experiences worldwide is that the results of assessments are much more likely to be put to use in local areas if they are channeled through local experts. GCLP also found the reverse to be true. Local experts are uniquely suited to assist in accessing local knowledge because they are repositories of so much of that knowledge and because their local contact networks–strengthened by the presence of former students in local institutions–usually embrace the most important of the local information infrastructures.

A grander experiment was the first United States National Assessment of Possible Consequences of Climate Variability and Change, 1997–2000 (NACC 2000). The NACC assessment began as a largely bottom-up exploration of stakeholder concerns about possible impacts of climate change, based on a commitment to interchange and mutual exploration. Sponsored by a variety of federal agencies, it included 19 regional workshops, 16 of which were followed by regional assessments; five sectoral workshops and assessments; and a synthesis team and an advisory group. The regional and sectoral assessments were to include stakeholder participation as a significant element, with one of the objectives of NACC being to report regional and sectoral stakeholder views and concerns.

This was an historic experiment with stakeholder involvement in the discussion of a major national environmental policy issue, well-intentioned and implemented in many cases through active participation by a range of stakeholders. The experience was not without difficulties, such as a dispersed approach to agency funding that led to different levels of support for the stakeholder component of different assessments, problems in supplying reliable scenarios for consistency across assessments, and some suspicions in the national political process that the advocacy of stakeholder participation in NACC was related to political agendas rather than to a learning process.

In many cases, however, stakeholder involvement was significant not only in its scope but in its relevance to regional assessments. A number of proposals were developed to assure that the NACC public participation experience would be observed, recorded and evaluated in a comprehensive manner, but no support came forward and that opportunity was missed, although key participants have shared their experiences and views in informal ways.

Perhaps the most troublesome issue, and one that continues to reverberate today, is that many of the stakeholder participants were persuaded to lend their time and legitimacy by a promise that their participation would be just the beginning of a long-term commitment and structure for involvement, linking regional and sectoral stakeholders with federal government deliberations. Within half a year, that commitment was in serious question and, despite efforts by some assessment leaders and agency representatives, there has been no follow-up, as some parties at the national level continue to view the regional component of NACC as fundamentally political rather than scientific.

One of the regional workshops and assessments was specifically selected to focus on an urbanized area, while several others included attention to urban impact vulnerabilities as well. The one pioneering urban assessment was called the Metropolitan East Coast, but in effect it was concerned with the New York City metropolitan area. Supported by the National Science Foundation (NSF), this study identified a number of possibly significant impacts, ranging from health and water supply to effects of sea level rise and storm surges on low-lying transportation infrastructures. Adaptation strategies were identified, although some of them could be expensive to implement (USGCRP 2001). The assessment included substantial interactions with local government, industry and constituency groups.

Soon afterward, a major study of Boston (CLIMB: Climate's Long-term Impacts on Metro Boston) was initiated with assistance from the Environmental Protection Agency (EPA). This study has projected impacts associated with health and energy requirements of warming and impacts on coastal property of sea level rise (Ruth and Kirshen 2002; also see Chapter 15 in this book). The CLIMB study has analyzed costs of adaptive flood-proofing under several different response scenarios, showing that costs are significantly affected by the amount of sea level rise. As in the case of the New York study, CLIMB included interactions with local government and other parties potentially concerned with impacts of climate change, such as electric utilities providers whose demands might be affected by seasonal changes in electricity demand.

Other studies have been carried out in other countries. Canada was the first country to explore climate change impacts at a regional scale in its classic Mackenzie Basin study (Cohen 1997). The Canada country study of climate impacts and adaptation (Environment Canada 1997) was the first to document the fact that variance in net impacts is a function of the geographic scale of attention. The Mackenzie Basin study, in particular, broke new ground in involving local stakeholders in impact-related discussions and in considering possible responses to reduce impacts and/or risks (Cohen 1997; 2002). The tradition continues today in the Northern Climate ExChange in Whitehorse, Yukon, which serves as a point of contact for the collection of local information and perspectives and for community participation in research and decision making.

In addition, the UK Climate Impacts Program at Oxford has commissioned a number of studies of adaptation strategies and adaptation responses for regions of the UK[2], and a study of possible climate change impacts has been conducted for London, with extensive stakeholder involvement (London Climate Change Partnership 2002).

A different kind of example is the first assessment of vulnerabilities to climate change impacts and appropriate response strategies in a developing country city. Supported by the US Agency for International Development (USAID) and carried out in Cochin, India, by the Oak Ridge National Laboratory and the Cochin University for Science and Technology, the assessment focused on the potential for climate change to exacerbate current stresses on sustainable development for the urban area and responses that address current needs as well as longer-term risks (ORNL and CUSAT 2003). Linked to a local science awareness initiative, the assessment included consultations with local experts on particular assessment topics, such as health impact issues; meetings with groups of local 'smart growth' planners and analysts; and a public meeting that was attended and widely publicized by newspaper and television media.

A comprehensive effort to derive lessons learned from a variety of experiences with environmental assessments in the United States, Europe and internationally, including their experience with stakeholder involvement, was the Global Environmental Assessment (GEA) project at Harvard University (conclusions summarized in Clark, et al. 2001). A particular challenge is subject matter with considerable scientific content, where many citizens without a technical background could have difficulty understanding the issues, risks and options. For instance, Clark, et al. (2001) note an 'issue attention cycle' as public interest is triggered by evidence of possible risks or threats, expands with growing demands for information and with increasing visibility in information media and public discussions, tends to peak in connection with major decision points, and then falls as new concerns emerge. Issues related to scientific facts and uncertainties are often serious in the second and third stages, depending on some combination of citizen representation by experts themselves and third-party translation of complex issues into understandable terms.

Finally, the National Research Council (NRC) panel effort noted above has suggested that a wide range of particular environmental assessment and decision making contexts offer information about stakeholder involvement. As of early 2004, examples being considered for case study attention included not only NACC but also the National Environmental Policy Act (NEPA) environmental assessment/statement process, Department of Energy (DOE) site-specific advisory boards, habitat conservation plans, watershed partnerships, Great Lakes restoration, and comparative risk assessment in EPA. A recent report by Resources for the Future identifies and analyzes 239 cases of public participation in environmental decisions based on available literature, limited as it often is.

LESSONS LEARNED FROM RELEVANT EXPERIENCE

Identifying lessons learned about stakeholder involvement from this body of experience is limited by the fact that most of the experience has been poorly documented and the state of the art is still formative. Even so, it is possible to suggest a number of relatively robust lessons as a basis for action. Stakeholder involvement can contribute to scoping and conducting strategy development, reviewing and refining the strategy, and assuring that the resulting strategy is implemented. The value of stakeholder involvement in scoping and reviewing is familiar and uncontroversial, but the value and appropriateness of stakeholder involvement in conducting the strategy development is less universally accepted:

- Stakeholders may lack sufficient knowledge of the topic and the science associated with it.
- Participation by 'non-experts' may be considered inconsistent with rigorous analysis.
- Stakeholders may introduce biases and agendas inconsistent with an unbiased strategy development process.

However, recent experience indicates that stakeholder involvement is often more positive than these concerns would suggest. In many cases, climate change assessment leaders report that stakeholder participation was invaluable. Specifically, involvement improved the assessment team's understanding of regional/sectoral issues and processes, opened up sources of information not previously available to analysts, and resulted in assessments that were more useful and understandable to user audiences. Other cases report that assessments were fundamentally changed as scientists recognized that stakeholder participant views of issues, priorities and impact concerns were more valid than their own.

In the regional assessments carried out by NACC, leaders reported no troublesome issues with scientific rigor or agenda-related biases, at least partly because many stakeholder participants were selected through the pre-existing contact networks of assessment leaders (a non-random sample, but with credibility and communication already established); and those who continued as a part of the assessment were those stakeholder participants in the preceding workshop who showed value-added in that first encounter. There are indications that, in some cases, sectoral assessments conducted by NACC (at a national rather than a local scale) had their results shaped by agendas of stakeholder participants, who in a few cases are reported to have intervened in higher-level political processes to try to assure assessment reports consistent with their views.

This last point introduces the question of how to determine appropriate levels and methods of stakeholder involvement. An appropriate or desirable level of involvement depends on a balance of incentives and concerns. Incentives (from the perspective of an agency conducting strategy development or implementing a strategy) include legitimization, access to information, increased likelihood that the strategy will be implemented and sustained, and the ability to reframe the policy dialogue/discourse. Concerns about assuring the technical quality of assessments, controlling the assessment process, fairness to participants (who are seldom fully compensated for the time they invest), and resource requirements/triage are equally important. Finding the right balance between incentives and concerns depends upon:

- What the sponsor of the assessment or action wants: What are the goals and who is the audience? Is the process or product more important?

- What the content of the activity is: How technical is it? How value-laden?
- Where the issue is in its evolution: In terms of public awareness? Local/regional salience? Sense of threat?
- How much the stakeholders know: What is the current knowledge base? What is the feasibility of education and outreach in the time frame involved?
- The degree to which participation can be targeted on a limited number or range of stakeholders.
- The nature and degree of uncertainties.

Strategies for Stakeholder Involvement in Issues with Scientific Complexity

Strategies for stakeholder involvement in issues with scientific complexity require specific considerations regarding the accuracy and consistency of information as well as maintaining open two-way communication between experts and community members. Specifically, stakeholder involvement must strive to:

- Involve and/or develop local sources of expertise to assist in communications between local stakeholders and representatives of the scientific knowledge base;
- Begin the interaction by listening to stakeholder concerns after local parties have been provided with understandable background information, not with tutorials on the science that intimidate local stakeholders and stifle local expression through a flood of technical information;
- Plan for a rich, sustained process of iterative two-way learning, including flexibility in responding to unanticipated issues, questions and/or resource constraints; and
- Recognize that it is as important to 'get the right science' as to 'get the science right' (NRC 1996). Scientific information that responds to stakeholder concerns, including an accurate depiction of the nature and extent of uncertainties, may represent a somewhat different set of questions than those most often asked by science.

Meanwhile, What are We Learning?

Stakeholder involvement is evolutionary, and process is a central issue, with constant learning changes in the cast and sometimes in the knowledge base. Keeping the process (and the participants) open to such change and learning is critical. While this is a lesson in itself, several others have emerged from relevant experience.

Different assessment and/or decision making stages may call for different participant roles and structures. For example, the framing/scoping stage calls for broad consultation. The conduct of the activity usually calls for a relatively small number of participants devoting a considerable amount of time. The review stage again can involve a wide range of stakeholders. And finally, implementation is more narrowly focused on parties with defined institutional roles. Adapting to the flow of the process will help facilitate effectiveness.

Not all participants with the same label are alike, whether environmentalist, industry, conservative or liberal. Stakeholder involvement works best when it moves past constituency stereotypes and establishes personal relationships among a diverse group of people. In some cases, remarkable breakthroughs in consensus development become possible as new ideas and points of view are shared in an open environment.

Leadership also has a powerful impact on the decision making process. Sponsors and patrons delivering on promises and protecting the integrity of the process facilitate trust. Activity leaders (local or issue experts) who are able to be inclusive, to listen well, and who can handle dissent get the most done.

Finally, long-term participation structures are hard to sustain unless they can be built into the roles of local institutions that maintain a commitment to the issues and the locality for the long-term.

Coming to the Bottom Line

The right balance is often more stakeholder involvement than sponsoring agencies are comfortable with, because such involvement offers access to essential information that cannot be acquired in other ways, in spite of the risks. But this balance is often less than advocates of public participation are comfortable with, because stakeholder involvement requires financial, human and managerial resources that may be limited and because such involvement demands time and effort on the part of participants, when an equitable payoff to them may be hard to assure.

GUIDELINES FOR ACTION

Even though the knowledge base about stakeholder involvement is still formative, it does not seem premature to offer a number of guidelines for thinking about such involvement and, where it is considered desirable, for doing it right (NCEDR 1998).

Guidelines Regarding the Why

Understand and communicate why stakeholder involvement is being included in the formation of smart growth policies. Have a clear sense of the reasons for the involvement and be able to articulate these reasons to participants of all sorts, from funding sources to individual citizens.

Communicate all the goals honestly. Do not pretend that the situation is simpler than it is. Do not hide the fact that the activity includes a number of goals, that stakeholder involvement is only one aspect of decision making processes, and that compromises are likely. And clarify which goal(s) have the highest priority and what this means for stakeholder involvement.

Guidelines Regarding the Who

Deciding who is to participate in stakeholder discussions is not an easy task, but the decisions do rest with some basic considerations and strategies.

Approaches to determine the roles of representative organizations and individual stakeholders reflect different philosophies of representative democracy, but both are worth considering, and stakeholder involvement can include both kinds of representation of views. For instance, incorporating the views of the poor and disenfranchised may be difficult to arrange without working through representative organizations, but a dozen organizational representatives may fail to represent many of the views of local citizens.

Use review processes to guard against unintentional biases in group composition. One of the best-documented lessons from more than thirty years of experience with stakeholder participation in the United States is that, however, an activity is organized and conducted from within, it is valuable to include a much wider range of stakeholders in reviewing the scope, nature and direction of an activity, and any articulations of it. This includes not only disseminating information and inviting comment but also defining a process for taking the comments seriously.

Assure transparency to minimize suspicion. Make it clear who is involved and in what ways, and assure that the activity process is open to those who participate. It is more difficult to imagine stakeholder involvement in activities including components that must be classified, such as homeland security strategy development; but this adds considerably to the importance of the credibility of the activity leadership. It may also be important to recognize different levels and types of participation for different stages or aspects of an activity.

Deliver on promises. If stakeholders are promised particular kinds of involvement, they should get what they are promised. It is better to indicate a positive intent but to limit one's promises than to take a chance that unanticipated resource limitations or political complexities will lead to disillusionment.

Finally, document the participation. The more important stakeholder participation is to an activity, the more important it is to record that participation. What stakeholders were involved? What do you mean by involvement? How did they participate? If a system is set up at the outset to maintain such records, this challenge is not onerous, but it is very difficult to reconstruct after the fact.

Guidelines Regarding the How

Implementation of effective stakeholder involvement requires attention to local conditions and participant dynamics, but still relies on several basic guidelines. First, it is important to use local experts as 'linch-pins' in the decision making process. As indicated above, stakeholder involvement is likely to work best if it uses technical experts at a local scale as links between local concerns and national or global knowledge bases. In some cases, this may call for some local capacity building, or at least relatively intensive information transfer and interactive discussion. However, local stakeholders should not be considered 'non-experts' in contrast to technical experts from without. They are just as expert in their own worlds. Their expertise and experience is important in designing smart growth strategies. Stakeholder involvement is a matter of mutual partnership, not one-way outreach.

Stakeholder involvement strategies must plan for iterative interaction. We know from a variety of experiences that stakeholder involvement works best when the quality of exchanges ratchet up in quality as each party learns more about the knowledge base of the other. This and other aspects of the process can be enhanced through the use of information technologies. We live in an era when more citizens every day are accessing information and exchanging messages electronically through e-mail and the internet; and this has the potential to change the nature of stakeholder involvement in many kinds of public discourse. However, we are still learning what the potential and limitations of these kinds of interactions are; in many cases, they work best when they accompany (rather than replace) direct personal interactions, and they work better for some communication objectives than others.

Test proposed approaches before committing to them. A time-honored lesson from the emerging knowledge base is that every approach to participation should be tested before it is implemented. This need not be an expensive or extensive process, because major flaws will usually turn up fairly quickly, but it is a step not to be overlooked. And build adaptability into the process. It will nearly always make sense to include in stakeholder involvement processes some flexibility to respond to what is learned and a capacity for adaptation and change. It is often useful, in fact, to include periodic self-assessments of how the involvement is working, inviting the views of stakeholders themselves.

Building the stakeholder involvement process using these guidelines and those that emerge from initial local planning stages will set the stage for effective decision making. There are, however, still realities and potential pitfalls to be concerned about.

Facing Some Realities

Participation does not necessarily lead to consensus. A frequent question about the 'how much' aspect of stakeholder involvement is how much participation is needed in order to get a consensus about the issues. The fact is that if there is not a genuine consensus among the stakeholder communities, broadening participation will decrease the likelihood of consensus; it will uncover and publicize the range of views. This is not a failure. It provides useful information. But it is important in inviting stakeholder involvement to consider how a divergence of views, if that happens, will be handled.

Stakeholders may be more concerned about the process than the product. While the organizers of an activity, such as a smart growth strategy for an urban area, are likely to be preoccupied with that one product, some stakeholders are likely to be more concerned about the nature of the relationship, agendas driving the activity, and how the activity relates to longer-term stakeholder roles. This means that such relationships between product and process need attention and thought from the beginning, because they raise issues that cannot be ignored.

Once initiated, stakeholder participation cannot be controlled entirely. One aspect of the democratic process is that once stakeholder involvement is initiated it can lead in unexpected directions. Organizers of activities need to be prepared for the possibility of unintended spin-offs from broad involvement, which are as likely to be positive for the effort as negative but which may require creative accommodation.

The Main Things to Worry About, and What to Do About Them

Any person or group inviting stakeholder participation can anticipate certain kinds of concerns on the part of interested parties. In many cases, these kinds of complications will be unavoidable and the general response should be for local activity leaders to be open, understanding, communicative and patient.

More specifically, leaders should be prepared for complaints regarding the purposes of the activity, including suspicions of agendas. This concern is likely to be expressed when the purposes of organizers and the purposes of stakeholder participants differ, and most especially when the purposes are complex and multi-dimensional and local skepticism of authorities is already an issue. The best way to reduce such risks is to be as open and honest as possible about the purposes from the outset, warts and all, and to include individuals with widespread credibility in the consultation process.

Given that it is generally impossible to include every individual who might wish to be involved, when some individuals who would wish to be involved may not be identified until late in the activity process, it is difficult to avoid accusations that the process has not been inclusive enough. The best way to avoid such problems, although there is no way to avoid them entirely, is to be very aggressive in publicizing the activity at the outset and providing mechanisms for people to express interest in being involved. An additional strategy is to make provision for some participants to be added during the course of the activity, not generally for political reasons but because the added participants bring valuable knowledge to the activity.

Stakeholders may also voice complaints about incomplete constituency, sectoral and/or geographical coverage. Clearly, the possible permutations of participants are infinite, while resources are limited. The best general strategy is to assure that the chosen strategy will meet a standard of common sense: that reasonable observers, considering the purposes of the assessment and the resources available, will agree that the representation is reasonable. Involving politically and socially sensitive stakeholders in reviews of the activity plan early in its framing reduces risks of serious criticism. Assuring that the activity can fine-tune its processes by making changes as it evolves is also helpful.

Complaints about how stakeholder inputs are handled and incorporated (or not) into the activity are most often a problem when the structures, processes and protocols are not made clear to all participants from the outset. A minimal strategy is to record all inputs and responses (ideally in a living database) and make them available to all stakeholders, in order to respond to any specific concerns. The biggest problem is not a judgment that an input, carefully and thoughtfully considered, has not been incorporated with a solid rationale for that decision, it is when the input has not been explicitly considered.

A lack of interest/support or even active criticism from constituencies involved in conceiving and implementing the activity may hinder group progress and effectiveness. Particularly frustrating is a situation where the organizers believe that a stakeholder group should be involved but no one from that group can be persuaded to be involved. In some cases, they are not convinced that the activity is important. In others, they may see participation as compromising their independence–cooption rather than inclusion. In general, the best strategy is to publicize the activity as widely as possible and let the democratic process work. In some cases, though, it will be necessary for individuals in the organizing group to use their own personal contact networks to find willing stakeholder participants, considering what incentives might be helpful in convincing essential constituencies to get involved.

Finally, when mutual trust is so important, stakeholder participation is often endangered by unavoidable changes in external conditions (time schedules and other operating conditions) that largely determine what will be possible. Frequently, the organizers of a local smart growth initiative pass on their own ideals and optimism without assuring that stakeholders are informed about the fragility of the process. It is important for organizers to be realistic and sophisticated in envisioning multiple scenarios for the course of the activity and to communicate the range of possible trajectories to stakeholders. Organizers and stakeholders may eventually share many of the same frustrations, but it is the responsibility of the organizers to assure that stakeholders are not disillusioned by a process that seems entirely inconsistent with any of the scenarios they had understood were possible when they agreed to be involved.

The preceding cautions are not reasons to choose to exclude stakeholder participation; in fact, they are unavoidable dimensions of the messy genius of participative democracy. The experience of the past decade tells us that stakeholder involvement not only contributes to the politics of decision making, it also makes the science of smart growth better by enlarging its knowledge base. Simply stated, it is a lot of trouble, but the record of experience indicates quite strongly that it is worth the trouble.

It is quite possible, in fact, that stakeholder involvement is one of the watershed issues in smart growth. Done right, it is a key to finding the right pathways and mustering support for implementing them. Done casually or half-heartedly, it is a catalyst for opposition and delays in political and legal processes. Those who believe in smart growth are well-advised to try to get stakeholder involvement right.

NOTES

1.   See http://qp.nas.edu/publicparticipation.
2.   See http://www.ukcip.org.uk for details on the UK Climate Impacts Program adaptation studies.

REFERENCES

AAG (2003), *Global Change and Local Places: Estimating, Understanding, and Reducing Greenhouse Gases*, Association of American Geographers, Cambridge: Cambridge University Press.

Clark, W.C., J. Jaeger, J. van Eijndhoven, and N. Dickson (2001), *Learning to Manage Global Environmental Risks*, 2nd edn, Cambridge: MIT Press.

Cohen, S.J. (2002), 'Challenges and Opportunities for Scientist–Stakeholder Collaboration in Integrated Assessment of Climate Change', in *Implementing Sustainable Development: Integrated Assessment and Participatory Decision Making Processes*, H. Abaza and A. Baranzini (eds), London: Edward Elgar, pp. 155–181.

Cohen, S. J. (1997), 'Scientist–Stakeholder Collaboration in Integrated Assessment of Climate Change: Lessons from a Case Study of Northwest Canada', *Environmental Modelling and Assessment*, 2(4): 281–293.

Cohen, S.J. (ed.) (1997), *Mackenzie Basin Impact Study Final Report*, Downsview, Ontario: Environment Canada.

Environment Canada (1997), *The Canada Country Study: Climate Impacts and Adaptation*. Downsview, Ontario: Adaptation and Impacts Research Group.

Kates, R., and T. Wilbanks (2003), 'Making the Global Local: Responding to Climate Change Concerns from the Bottom Up', *Environment*, 45(3): 12–23.

London Climate Change Partnership (2002), *London's Warming*. Oxford: UK Climate Impacts Program.

NACC (2000), *Climate Change Impacts on the United States: The Potential Consequences of Climate Variability and Change*, Washington: US Global Change Research Program.

NCEDR (1998), Stakeholder Participation in the US National Assessment of Possible Consequences of Climate Variability and Change: Suggested Guidelines for Doing It Right. Knoxville, TN: National Center for Environmental Decision Making Research. NCEDR Technical Report NCEDR/98–19, November 1998.

ORNL and CUSAT (2003), 'Possible Vulnerabilities of Cochin, India to Climate Change Impacts and Response Strategies to Increase Resilience', Oak Ridge National Laboratory and Cochin University of Science and Technology, August 2003.

Ruth, M. and P. Kirshen (2002), 'Dynamic Investigations into Climate Change Impacts on Urban Infrastructure: Background, Examples, and Lessons', paper presented to the Western Regional Science Association, Monterey, CA.

USGCRP (2001), *Climate Change and a Global City: An Assessment of the Metropolitan East Coast Region*, US Global Change Research Program.

Wilbanks, T.J. (2003a), 'Geographic Scaling Issues in Integrated Assessments of Climate Change', in *Scaling Issues in Integrated Assessment*, J. Rotmans and D. Rothman (eds), Lisse, the Netherlands: Swets and Zeitlinger, pp. 5–34.

Wilbanks, T.J. (2003b), 'Integrating Climate Change and Sustainable Development in a Place-Based Context', *Climate Policy*, supplement on Climate Change and Sustainable Development, November 2003, pp. 147–154.
Wilbanks, T.J. and R. Kates (1999), 'Global Change in Local Places', *Climatic Change*, **43**(3): 601–628.

6 Oil Transportation Infrastructure: The Trans-Alaska Pipeline System and the Challenge of Environmental Change

Jerry McBeath

INTRODUCTION

The Trans-Alaska Pipeline System (TAPS) transports 17 per cent of US domestic oil production and about six per cent of the nation's oil consumption. President George W. Bush's National Energy Policy calls TAPS 'the single most important crude oil pipeline in the United States' (BLM 2002a). Royalties, severance and corporate income taxes on Alaska's North Slope oil production produce about 75 per cent of the general fund revenue of the state of Alaska, which gives the state an even greater interest in the pipeline's health and efficacy than the federal government.

In the security-conscious era of post-9/11 America, attention has focused on TAPS' role in national economic and military security. However, for most of the 28-year history of the pipeline and into the future, it is the environmental security of TAPS that most prompts critical scrutiny and review. This is explained by the varied ecosystems, extreme and inclement weather, and climate conditions the pipeline encounters, as well as the complexity of the infrastructure itself.

The environment of TAPS is Alaska, America's most northern and only arctic state. In the developing national discussion of environmental change and particularly climate warming, the Alaska environment figures prominently. Changes in the world's polar regions already have been greater than in temperate and tropical regions. For example, observations from meteorological stations across the far North show increases in annual mean temperatures of about 9°F over the twentieth century, a greater increase than elsewhere (IPCC 2001).

In Alaska, glaciers are melting and ice cover of the Arctic Ocean and Bering Sea has shrunk. The greatest change to the immediate environment of TAPS is soil condition. Thawing of permafrost (soil that has remained in the frozen state for two or more years) increases subsidence and lessens the stability of soils and slopes, which cushion infrastructure. In this chapter we tell the story of the response of the private sector, non-governmental organizations and government regulators to the first signs of climate change impacts on infrastructure. It is part of the broader narrative of the creation and maintenance of America's first arctic oil pipeline.

TAPS consists of an 800-mile, 48-inch diameter warm oil pipeline, eleven pump stations, the Valdez Marine Terminal and several support facilities. Beginning at pump station #1 in the Prudhoe Bay oil field off the Arctic coast, the pipeline travels south to the nearly ice-free port of Valdez on Prince William Sound (see Figure 6.1). The pipeline crosses seven major physiographic provinces, more than 800 rivers and streams, and three mountain ranges. Nearly half of the pipeline corridor traverses ice-rich soil that becomes unstable if thawed. Some 420 miles of the pipeline are above ground to avoid exposing such soils to the warm pipe. Above-ground sections are supported by 78 000 vertical support members (VSMs). Remaining sections of the pipeline traversing stable soils are buried (IPCC 2001).

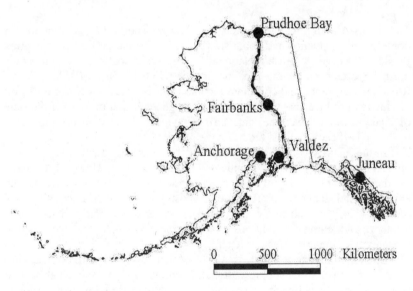

Figure 6.1   TAPS pipeline

The pipeline crosses five seismic zones and is designed and built to withstand the most severe earthquakes to be expected in each zone. Upon TAPS completion in 1977, eleven pump stations pushed Prudhoe Bay oil through the pipeline. With the noticeable decline of production by the mid-1990s, pipeline operators closed four of these stations temporarily. Pump stations include valves, pipe, tanks and control equipment to relieve excessive pressures on the pipeline when shut down. Nearly 300 roads and gravel workpads provide access for surveillance and maintenance of the pipeline. The Valdez Marine Terminal is a huge facility for storage and pipeline monitoring. Oil leaving the pipeline can be loaded directly onto tankers or stored (in tanks accommodating 9.18 million barrels of crude). Currently a fleet of 26 tankers (three with double hulls and 13 with double sides) serves the terminal, but these numbers will change because the Oil Pollution Act of 1990 requires that the fleet consist entirely of double-hulled tankers by 2014 (BLM 2002a). The Valdez port also treats ballast water from incoming tankers and other oily water. The Valdez terminal is the headquarters of surveillance and monitoring of TAPS. The current owners of TAPS are:

1. BP Pipeline (Alaska), Inc.–46.9263 per cent share
2. Phillips Trans Alaska, Inc.–26.7953 per cent share
3. ExxonMobil Pipeline Company–20.3378 per cent share
4. Williams Alaska Pipeline Co.–3.0845 per cent share
5. Amerada Hess Pipeline Corp.–1.5000 per cent share
6. Unocal Pipeline Company–1.3561 per cent share

The Alyeska Pipeline Service Company (APSC or Alyeska) operates TAPS for the owners. The federal and state governments play dual roles as owners of the land over which the pipeline passes (with a landlord–tenant relationship to Alyeska and the owner companies) and as regulators under terms of the Agreement and Grant of Right-of-Way (ROW) for the Trans-Alaska Pipeline (federal grant) and state ROW Lease (state lease), issued on 23 January 1974 and 3 May 1974 respectively.

This chapter takes a comprehensive view of TAPS. First, it considers the environmental factors influencing design and construction (from 1974 to 1977, when oil first flowed through the pipeline). Then it presents the TAPS regulatory regime, headed by the Joint Federal–State Pipeline Office (JPO). The heart of the chapter is an analysis of TAPS renewal in 2001 and 2002, with a focus on areas of concern to environmental and Native organizations. The final section of the chapter discusses how industry and government have reacted to increasing evidence of climate change in Alaska.

TAPS DESIGN AND CONSTRUCTION

Construction of TAPS was an outgrowth of exploration for and discovery of oil on the Alaska North Slope. The region's Inupiat Eskimo population knew of oil seeps long before western traders, whalers, and government bureaucrats entered the area in the early twentieth century. Alaska geologists selected North Slope lands as the first part of the federal land grant after statehood in 1959. Then, in late 1968, the Atlantic Richfield Corp. (ARCO) discovered oil on state lands it had leased at Prudhoe Bay. Initial surveys indicated that the discovery wells contained 13 billion barrels of oil (now estimated to exceed 23 billion barrels), making it the largest oil field in the western hemisphere.[1]

For a year, oil company and government planners evaluated alternate routes to move the oil to tidewater. An all-sea route seemed feasible until icebreakers encountered too much fast ice in the Arctic Ocean. A route through the Mackenzie Delta in Canada to the US Midwest attracted interest because it would direct oil to the greatest source of demand. However, the Alaska state and local governments strenuously objected to this proposal (as well as to a more feasible route paralleling the Alaska–Canada Highway), because they would not be able to tax oil pipeline property in Canada.[2] Finally, industry and governments agreed to an all-Alaska route, from Prudhoe Bay to Valdez in southcentral Alaska.

In 1969, oil industry executives proposed to build a buried warm oil pipeline, which they estimated would cost about $800 million. None of the major partners in the TAPS consortium–ARCO, British Petroleum and Humble Oil (later renamed Exxon)–had constructed pipelines in the Arctic, but they reasoned that pipelines developed in temperate zones were applicable models. Federal and state regulators instantly objected, mandating that pipeline sections traversing unstable soils must be built above-ground. Industry filed paperwork for federal and state grants of right-of-way and leases, expecting that they would be granted within a one month period (Ross 2000). These plans ran into opposition from Alaska Natives and the burgeoning environmental movement as well as from government regulators. The pattern of energy industry advocates pushing against NGO and governmental resistance seems odd in the context of the early twenty-first century. Now governments at the federal and state level attempt to spur industry to develop new oil fields and a trans-Alaska natural gas pipeline. Clearly changes in American energy security as well as the globalization of energy multi-nationals have changed the terms of discourse.

The claims of Alaska Natives to lands held from time immemorial had not been resolved by federal and state governments, and a pipeline could not cross Native-claimed lands until the issues were settled. Realizing this, the oil industry supported a congressional resolution in the Alaska Native Claims Settlement Act (ANCSA) of 1971. Once Native claims were resolved, Native organizations as landowners had different interests and became supportive of TAPS development. (In 2004, ANCSA Native corporations broadly favored development of energy resources on their lands and transport of oil/gas to market over them.) Environmental protests, however, were of a different order.

TAPS planning coincided with the birth of the American environmental movement. Following the Santa Barbara oil spill in 1969, Congress passed and President Nixon signed the National Environmental Policy Act (NEPA), with its path-breaking requirements for environmental impact review of all major federal actions. The issuance of a grant for the pipeline right-of-way most definitely would be a major federal action, and the entire environmental impact statement (EIS) process unfolded, with its mandates for public notice, public hearings, and extensive commenting opportunities for environmental and other organizations.

The oil companies formed Alyeska Pipeline Service Company in 1970, and Alyeska took charge of re-designing the pipeline system. Many of the design modifications were imposed upon Alyeska, accompanied by stringent federal stipulations drawn up to govern construction (Coates 1993). This included planning for insulating sections of unstable soils where the pipe would be buried; developing the support structure for above-ground sections of the pipeline, and providing several means to avoid melting of permafrost soils; developing stream and river crossings that would not jeopardize fish habitats and planning elevated sections to accommodate migration routes of caribou. Alyeska lost credit with the public when it prematurely ordered pipe from Japanese producers (claiming that no American firm manufactured 48-inch diameter pipe) and then left it rusting in Fairbanks while awaiting EIS approval.

Construction of the pipeline was a controversial national issue in 1973 and 1974, and has been amply covered in the professional and popular literature. At its completion in 1977, TAPS cost ten times more than projected in 1969–about $8 billion. TAPS design changes accommodated critiques by government regulators and environmental organizations; at completion and to the present, industry claims it to be an 'engineering marvel.'

MONITORING TAPS

Organizational Structure

A State Pipeline Coordinator (SPC) oversaw construction of TAPS, from January 1974 through 1977, supported by joint state/federal fish and wildlife advisory teams. The state disbanded the SPC in 1977, returning permitting activities to state resource agencies.[3] In 1979, the US Department of the Interior delegated its pipeline oversight authority to the Bureau of Land Management's (BLM) Alaska state office, in its special projects bureau. This loosely coordinated system conducted oversight in the 1980s (BLM 2002a).

Problems in the detection of corrosion in pipeline sections and then the Exxon Valdez oil spill focused public attention on TAPS oversight, which led to the formation of the Joint Federal–State Pipeline Office (JPO) in 1990. Initially, it included four agencies and under 40 employees, but by 2003 had expanded to 12 agencies and about 75 to 80 employees. The JPO oversees activity along the pipeline corridor and issues ROWs for new common carrier pipelines. Its authority is based on the federal pipeline lease and the state grant. It is jointly headed by a federal representative of the BLM and a state Department of Natural Resources (DNR) representative. JPO staff believe it is the most successful coordinating agency of the major projects review processes concerning oil and gas development in Alaska. They attribute this to its focus on the pipeline corridor, co-location of federal and state regulatory agency offices,[4] sufficiency of finance, and a long history of operation.[5]

Clearly, the close relationship between government regulators and the consortium of owner companies is unusual in the United States, where adversarial relationships between government and industry in top-down command-and-control systems tend to prevail. It could be argued that the monitoring system veers in the direction of European and Asian corporatist systems, which have been applauded for their more effective means of mitigating adverse environmental consequences.

Pipeline Security Issues

Pipeline operation for the last 28 years has occasioned concern about the integrity of the pipeline itself, localized spills, safety of tanker transport from the marine terminal and response to earthquakes. During construction of TAPS the issue was flawed welds on many pipe sections. Corrosion problems in the Atigun Pass section led to rerouting and some replacement. However, corrosion problems have been a more serious concern at Prudhoe Bay than along the pipeline route itself.[6] Hydrological changes as well as permafrost melting have affected 6000 VSMs and about 200 tilting VSMs are on a watch list.

Between 1977 and 1999, 4283 spills were recorded along the pipeline and at the Valdez marine terminal. Most of the spills were contained in a lined area or cleaned up within about a year. With the exception of a 1979 spill caused by a hairline crack due to pipe settlement in Atigun Pass, no direct spills to surface water (outside Prince William Sound) have been documented. Of the total spills, only 87 required management under Alyeska's contaminated site management program, less than 1 per cent of the total number of spills (BLM 2002a). The most recent spill happened after the 9/11 terrorist attacks on the World Trade Center and the Pentagon. A Livengood resident who had 'always wanted to shoot a hole in the pipeline' did so, releasing 285 600 gallons of oil into the environment, and causing residual contamination of groundwater.

The largest oil spill occurred in Prince William Sound. On 24 March 1989, the Exxon Valdez went off course and ran aground on Bligh Reef. Carrying over 1.25 million barrels of crude, more than 10 million gallons spilled into the Sound. Although most of the floating oil was removed by skimmers, left the coastal area, evaporated or was degraded, residues remain in bays, coastal areas and in bottom sediment.

Oil pollution legislation at the federal and the state level reacted to the Exxon Valdez catastrophe. In addition to the requirement of double-hulled tankers, significant improvements were made in spill prevention and response capability for Prince William Sound. This included the creation of Alyeska's Ship Escort/Response Vessel System (SERVS), which provides escort vessels for transit of tankers through the Valdez Narrows (BLM 2002a). Legislation and regulations also increased the amount of spill response equipment, drills and training exercises. Finally, the Oil Pollution Act of 1990 required formation of the Prince William Sound Regional Citizens Advisory Council (RCAC) to improve spill prevention and response readiness. As noted below, in 2002 critics of pipeline security urged that a similar advisory council be formed to monitor TAPS.[7]

Earthquakes have tested the stability and integrity of the pipeline too. Since TAPS was built, the three largest earthquakes that have been recorded in east or southern Alaska occurred with moment magnitudes of 7.5 (1979), 7.8 (1988) and 7.9 (1987), respectively. The epicenter of each of the three earthquakes was more than 190 miles southeast of Valdez. The quakes did no damage to the pipeline (BLM 2002b).

The most serious earthquake threat to date occurred on 3 November 2002, when an earthquake registering 7.9 on the Richter scale occurred on the Denali Fault, some 55 miles west of the pipeline. The TAPS Earthquake Monitoring Systems (EMS) performed as designed by initiating automatic shutdown of the pipeline, calculating the severity of the event, and identifying locations and features to be evaluated for damage. The pipeline was not breached and no oil was released; the line was restarted three days later (BLM 2002b).

This earthquake damaged eight above-ground VSMs near Milepost 589. Eight pipeline support shoes separated from the pipe there and five cross beams were damaged; several shoes displaced longitudinally. Also, longitudinal movement of the pipe tripped several anchor assemblies, which were installed on the pipeline specifically to adapt to such an event by absorbing energy. The Final EIS indicated the need for caution in estimating potential damage from a large quake. However, it is uncertain whether an earthquake as large and as close as the Great Alaska Earthquake of 1964 (also known as the Good Friday Earthquake, 9.1 moment magnitude) would damage the TAPS. If an earthquake-triggered landslide or ground cracking occurred in an area crossed by TAPS, the integrity of the pipeline would likely be threatened (BLM 2002b).

To the present, three types of events have threatened TAPS security: human error, large-scale environmental disruptions, and gradual, incremental environmental change. The TAPS monitoring system has handled small-scale human error reasonably well. The precautionary designs of the pipeline (such as automatic shutoff valves) and comprehensive surveillance have enabled Alyeska to mitigate spills and corrosion problems. Large-scale human error, however, displays troubling weaknesses in the system. Exxon Valdez was an eco-disaster revealing inadequate response to huge oil spills, and as we note below, the post-disaster corrective actions of Congress and the Alaska State Legislature have not satisfied critics.

The monitoring of extreme environmental events such as earthquakes has been more effective. These events are unpredictable but their probability of occurrence, if not exact time, can be factored into design equations and calculations. As we note below, climate change differs from both events. While predictable following climate models, the period of greater impact will occur past the designed life time of the pipeline, and–in the view of industry and government regulators (but not environmental NGOs)–this discounts the need to adopt precautionary measures.

TAPS Renewal in 2004

The original federal grant for the primary ROW was issued in 1974, with the state lease following shortly thereafter. Because the federal Mineral Leasing Act limits ROWs to no more than 30 years, the federal grant expired in January 2004. Owner companies requested a renewal of the ROW, and to BLM this constituted a major federal action under NEPA, requiring an EIS. In 2001, BLM conducted a scoping analysis, which indicated a range of concerns.

Foremost among the scoping comments were security issues. Commentators questioned whether TAPS could operate at design capacity for an additional 30 years and recommended that attention be paid to metal fatigue, corrosion, changes in pipeline design and construction criteria and climate change (JPO 2001a). Second were concerns about ecosystem effects from pipeline operation: air quality, wildlife and aquatic habitat, water quality, potential catastrophic incidents, noise, and impacts on cultural resources. Native employment opportunities, use of Native lands, damages to subsistence as well as more general socioeconomic effects on Native Alaskans were among the comments, as well as the Native Alaskan role in the TAPS regulatory process. A few comments addressed oversight and regulatory requirements. These concerns reflected the objectives of an EIS process, which must take a 'hard look' at the environmental and human consequences of a large-scale federal action.

BLM issued the draft environmental impact statement (DEIS) in four volumes of more than 1700 pages in July 2002. It considered three alternatives:

1. Renewal of the TAPS federal grant for 30 years;
2. Renewal for less than 30 years; and
3. Non-renewal, the 'no-action' alternative (BLM 2002a).

The agency published a notice for public comments in the *Federal Register*, defining a 45-day comment period (which all environmental and Native organizations protested as too brief).

The comments and agency responses filled four volumes of the FEIS (BLM 2002b). More than 580 individuals and organizations provided letters, oral testimony, internet-based comments, faxes, or voice message comments (including more than 100 recognized organizations) (BLM 2002b). Roughly, comments can be categorized into these five groups:

1. Environmental organizations;
2. Native corporations and non-profit organizations;
3. Federal and state agencies such as USFWS, ADFG;
4. Oil companies and affiliated industries (the Alliance, VECO); and
5. Local governments, chambers of commerce.

We give examples of comments from each of these groups below.

Environmental organizations
Three examples illustrate the approach Alaska (and national) environmental organizations took to TAPS renewal. Trustees for Alaska, the state's oldest and best-known public interest law firm, submitted comments on behalf of a large number of Alaskan and national organizations. Adopting a legalistic stance, Trustees alleged that the DEIS was insufficient under NEPA for five reasons: its purpose was too narrowly defined; it failed to consider direct, indirect, and cumulative impacts adequately; it did not consider an adequate range of reasonable alternatives; it failed to consider mitigation measures; and it failed to address incomplete information adequately.[8] The organization suggested that the DEIS probably also failed to meet requirements of the Endangered Species Act, and it lacked compliance with relevant Alaska statutes.

A second example is the joint memorandum of the Alaska Forum for Environmental Responsibility, the Alaska Center for the Environment, and the

Northern Alaska Environmental Center. Summarizing testimony of its representatives at the seven hearings on the DEIS, the memorandum questioned:

1. The pernicious effect on the safety of TAPS operations resulting from chronic cost-cutting pressure by the TAPS Owners;
2. The effectiveness of the Reliability Centered Maintenance (RCM) process, which both the state and federal monitors constituted as a major reason to assume the adequacy of the TAPS Owners' program for assuring adequate maintenance on TAPS;
3. The citation of the RCM process as a basis for finding the TAPS Owners to be in compliance with certain Grant and Lease requirements;
4. The failure of the government monitors to devote sufficient attention to risks associated with human factors and shortcomings in operating procedures;
5. Alyeska's failure to identify and abate conditions adverse to safe operations in a timely manner;
6. The failure of the government documents to deal with demonstrated inadequacies in the required TAPS mainline oil spill prevention and response program;
7. The failure of the government documents to deal adequately with Alyeska's efforts to deal with the risks associated with climate change;
8. The failure of the government documents to deal adequately with Alyeska's efforts to deal with the risks associated with seismic events; and
9. The failure to provide details as to how (or whether) Alyeska has dealt with the problem of restarting TAPS after an extended winter shutdown–a design requirement that the Joint Pipeline Office (JPO) identified in 2001 as the most significant operational compliance issue on TAPS (BLM 2002b).

Finally, environmental organizations collected signatures on a 'Petition for Conditions of TAPS Lease Renewal,' listing these seven conditions:

1. The grant lease should establish a citizens oversight group (COG) funded by the TAPS Owners through the Department of the Interior;
2. TAPS dismantling, removal and restoration (DR&R) funds should be immediately placed in an escrow account;
3. Grant and Lease renewal should be made conditional on satisfactory completion of an immediate comprehensive independent field audit, as well as an independent technical review and field audit every five years;
4. TAPS should be transferred to a single responsible managing party with no North Slope production;

5. A TAPS Employee Concerns Program should be incorporated into lease and right-of-way renewal to ensure critical problems are adequately addressed to prevent spills;
6. Stipulations attached to the original federal and state Grant and Lease agreements should be carefully reviewed to ensure that they reflect a) scientific and technological advances during the last three decades and b) experience with the operation of TAPS; and
7. The public comment period must be extended by at least 45-days to ensure ample time for meaningful input (see BLM 2002b).

BLM gave generic responses to these environmental organizations' concerns and complaints. In Section 2.5 of Volume 2, it included most as 'alternatives and issues considered but eliminated from detailed analysis,' for several reasons. First, it indicated that it did not 'require additional authority to achieve the purpose of the suggested alternative' (BLM 2002b). Thus, given the broad authority granted BLM under the Trans-Alaska Pipeline Authorization Act (TAPAA), it could establish advisory committees or conduct audits at any time. Second, referring to two Ninth Circuit decisions,[9] the agency found support for its decision to exclude from analysis alternatives 'whose effect cannot be reasonably ascertained, and whose implementation is deemed remote and speculative,' or alternatives 'that are infeasible, ineffective, or inconsistent with the basic policy objectives for the management of the area.' (BLM 2002b) Finally, BLM indicated that some recommendations, such as a transfer of TAPS ownership to another entity, exceeded its authority.

Environmental organizations were disappointed at the response to their critiques. Said Alaska's foremost critic of pipeline security, Dr Richard Fineberg:

The process was a sham ... and invalid. [The FEIS] was an edifice of paper not dealing with the real issues. [What were they?] The root problem that concerned many of us was that chronic delays in identification and correction of problems subject the environment to undue risk. Another example is the question of strategic configuration–reducing personnel in the pipeline corridor and moving the control system out of Valdez without adequate feedback. The oil spill response plan, which depends on people, is the Achilles' Heel of strategic reconfiguration.

[What were your objectives? What would have satisfied you?] To deal with these problems we wanted a citizens' oversight group similar to the one Congress created for Prince William Sound after the Exxon Valdez spill. In view of the difference between our concerns and the agencies, we wanted an independent evaluation of the condition of the pipeline, not a review based on JPO conclusions. We wanted a review of the stipulations aimed at incorporating operating experience and scientific and technological advancements. During the renewal period, we wanted an independent audit every five years to assure both stipulation compliance and that best available technology were being used. (McBeath 2004c)

Yet government regulators contend that they have made special efforts to involve not only environmental but also Native organizations. At the time of the renewal, BLM held a number of meetings and tried to establish an ongoing dialogue. JPO sends out regulatory reports to stakeholders. In the context of reviewing amendments to the oil spill response plan, JPO has sought out information from major players and invited groups to meetings (McBeath 2003b).

The TAPS reauthorization process does raise issues about stakeholder involvement that are treated comprehensively elsewhere in this volume (see Chapter 5 in this volume). BLM did invite broad participation and in one sense (public notice, equal opportunities to comment) appeared inclusive. However, BLM took a legalistic and administrative approach in evaluating comments. It gave less attention to environmental NGOs, somewhat more to Native organizations, and most credence to industry. This might be justified in terms of the relevance of industry's comments to agency mission and authority. Environmental NGOs, however, believed that economic values were superior to environmental protection concerns, which BLM treated as speculative and hypothetical.

Native organizations
Native organizations, if they represent Inuit Research Advisors (IRA) councils or other federally-recognized Indian governments, have a special status in EIS participation since the issuance of Executive Order 13175 in November 2000, an order which recognizes a government-to-government relationship. In 2001, BLM identified 19 (later increased to 21) tribes as 'directly and substantially affected' by TAPS and entitled to consultation during the NEPA process (BLM 2002b).

Nearly a dozen Native organizations made specific comments beyond these consultations, and they included the Alaska Federation of Natives (AFN), IRA councils, traditional councils, ANCSA for-profit corporations, and regional non-profit corporations. Perhaps most representative of comments were those of the state's Native federation, AFN, which made these recommendations:

1. That Alyeska and its owners negotiate with BLM an amendment to the Alaska Native Utilization Agreement to provide an enforcement mechanism if Alyeska does not meet its Native hire goals (20 per cent of workforce);
2. That the Grant contain a new stipulation requiring collection of data clearly showing trends in subsistence taking of fish and game and the impact of non-subsistence hunting and fishing on these trends, with tribal and other Native organizational involvement;

3. That BLM promulgate regulations clearly setting out the process for Natives to follow in filing claims under the Alaska National Interest Conservation Act (ANILCA) when subsistence resources are challenged;
4. That the FEIS include information on village economies emphasizing the importance of subsistence in community, economic and cultural preservation;
5. That JPO effectively involve tribal governments in TAPS oversight; and
6. That the FEIS recognize the need for additional spill response equipment along waterways crossed by TAPS and recommend training and certification of additional village crews for oil spill responses (BLM 2002b, 6:1, pp. 423–33).

BLM in general was more responsive to Native comments and complaints than to those of environmental organizations. Some ANCSA corporations are landowners in the pipeline corridor, and Alaska Natives as an aboriginal people have a special government-to-government relationship with the federal government (Case and Voluck 2002). BLM did add additional descriptions of the problems of village economies and of threats to subsistence pursuits in the Final EIS, but in the latter case suggested that the pipeline was only one of many factors pressuring fish and game resources in rural areas of the state. It acknowledged the special status of tribal organizations under Executive Order 13175, but simultaneously pointed out that attempts to elicit comments from the 21 Native communities directly affected by TAPS had come to naught. Nevertheless, JPO added a Native liaison to its office in 2002. Finally, the agency commented that Native organizations had not taken full advantage of opportunities available under the Grant and Lease (see, for example, comments in BLM 2002b, 6:1, pp. 458–66).

Federal and state agencies

Two resource agencies made extensive comments on the DEIS. The federal Fish and Wildlife Service (USFWS) noted that the pipeline was aging and that increased maintenance likely would be required to avert the probability of either a major oil spill or small, chronic leaks with a large cumulative impact. Additionally, this agency pointed to the danger in introduction of non-indigenous aquatic species from the intake of water from ports outside Alaska and released into Alaska waters through untreated ballast discharged from oil tankers (BLM 2002b, 6:2, pp. 827–31). It noted that 14 such species already had been identified as having arrived in Port Valdez (Hines and Ruiz 2000). The state Department of Fish and Game (ADFG) found TAPS in compliance with all relevant state statutes and stipulations. However, the agency expressed concerns about reclassification of state lands with a diversity of fish and wildlife species as a corridor for oil and gas transportation in the North

Slope, and it recommended incorporating buffers, easements and setbacks in to the plan (BLM 2002b, 6:2, pp. 1209–11).

The FEIS reiterated a point made in many of BLM's responses to criticism of the pipeline's age: 'Age alone does not dictate reliability or performance. Myriad factors can impact system performance' (BLM 2002b, 6:2, p. 832). It suggested that existing leak detection systems were adequate to monitor both large and small leaks. However, the agency did acknowledge the risk in introduction of non-indigenous organisms through untreated segregated tanker ballast water, and added this to its analysis of cumulative effects.

Oil companies and affiliated industries

Two large coalitions of oil field industries and oil field service workers, The Alliance and VECO, contributed highly supportive testimony at public hearings and in memoranda to the public record. The Alliance, representing 420 member companies deriving livelihoods from Alaska's oil and gas industry with 35 000 employees statewide, urged BLM to support the preferred alternative: renewal of the Grant and Lease for 30 years. It spoke against a citizen's oversight council because of the expected increase in production costs and reduction of state revenues. It forcefully recommended renewal, arguing that renewal for less than 30 years 'would disenfranchise new investment in the North Slope and increase business risk for Alaskan operators ultimately leading to downward spirals in employment, population, state product and income' (BLM 2002b, 6:2, p. 748).

All the owner companies either sent representatives to the seven public hearings (in Cordova, Valdez, Glennallen, Anchorage, Fairbanks, Minto and Barrow) or submitted memoranda for the record. For example, Phillips Alaska, Inc. made strong arguments for a 30-year renewal of the lease. A three-decade continuation 'enables the maximum commercial recovery of ANS hydrocarbon reserves to take place by establishing a favorable investment climate, leading to the realization of the optimum economic benefit of ANS production for all stakeholders' (BLM 2002b, 6:2, p. 1231). Moreover, a shorter-term of renewal would likely increase the companies' largest operational expense, marine and pipeline transit fees, which cost $5.19 per barrel presently. To renew the ROW for 30 years would 'reduce uncertainty and contribute to a pro-investment climate and continued commitment to further investment in TAPS itself' (BLM 2002b, 6:2, p. 1233).

The company also argued against any increase in the regulatory burden through addition of 'unnecessary stipulations,' specifically the establishment of a citizen oversight body the costs of which would be borne by TAPS owners. To the industry, 'TAPS has operated safely for 25 years with over 99 per cent system reliability':

Federal law does not favor the creation of formal advisory functions. Public oversight is the province of the government and, in the case of TAPS, a special purpose agency (the Joint Pipeline Office or JPO) was established to carry out just that function.... Such oversight is, in Phillips' experience, unprecedented anywhere else in its world-wide operations ... Advisory or so-called citizen oversight groups are necessarily comprised of individuals who represent much narrower and/or special interests. This compromises the objectivity and effectiveness of such groups and is another reason they are not favored under the law. (BLM 2002b, 6:2, pp. 1235–36)

The TAPS ROW Renewal office echoed this view, remarking that '[P]ublic oversight is the responsibility of the government,' and that 'The authority does not exist within the context of the right of way renewal process to establish such an advisory group or to compel the TAPS owners to provide funding' (BLM 2002b, 6:1, p. 500). BLM certainly agreed with these sentiments, as can be noted in its arguments to exclude consideration of advisory councils and other new requirements from formal consideration in the EIS.

Local governments and boosters
A final group of comments came from local governments along the pipeline corridor (for example, the cities of Cordova and Valdez) and chambers of commerce. Uniformly, these organizations referred to the tax revenues, jobs and other economic benefits flowing into their communities from TAPS. They called for a 30-year renewal of the Grant and Lease, and remarked on the safe operation of the oil transportation system.

Overall, the tenor of comments received from the broader public was critical of the continued safe operation of the TAPS, but supportive of 30-year renewal of the Grant and Lease.

Adapting to the Challenge of Climate Warming

At the time of TAPS construction, 1974–77, climate change was not in the vocabulary of the oil industry, government regulators, environmental organizations or the broader public. However, within the last decade, as scientific consensus has developed on the anthropogenic causes of increased greenhouse gas emissions, and as scientists have confirmed increasing temperatures, particularly in polar regions, impacts on transportation infrastructure have been evaluated.

As mentioned, the chief climate change impact relevant to TAPS is warming of permafrost areas, and the impact this will have on the stability and integrity of the pipeline. The zone of continuous permafrost currently poses few challenges to oil transport technology. Instead, it is the second, discontinuous permafrost zone, ranging from just north of the Yukon River to south of the Copper River Basin and mid-point in the Matanuska-Susitna Borough. This region covers most of the Alaska Interior; its intermittent patches of permafrost currently are thawing as a result of climate warming. Most lowlands of southcentral Alaska are free of permafrost.

Temperature increases such as those noted in Alaska lead to a thawing of the permafrost layer. Where this permafrost is ice-rich, thawing leads to disruptions of the ground surface, causing subsidence, which has an impact on the pipeline. In 2001–02 we studied the reaction and response of government institutions and private industry to evidence of warming along the pipeline corridor, and report a summary of our findings here (see, for example, McBeath 2003a). We followed up on these matters in a briefer study in late 2003–early 2004.

Thermal changes occur in the southern section of the TAPS,[10] and they affect both VSMs and slope stability. In 2001, the JPO and Alyeska noted tilting and jacking of VSMs in the southern region. A JPO representative stated 'Out of 78 000 VSMs, there are 200 on a watch list, [but] we don't expect to replace all of them. A suite of things create an integrity problem' (McBeath 2001b). This official referred to the tilting of one VSM at Squirrel Creek, where the surface had thawed, as perhaps related to climate change effects. Yet he maintained 'It is hard to say the reason that the ground thawed was only because of climate warming. There are other factors—work pad size, snow fall history' (Reimer 2001).

JPO is more concerned with slope stability, because of the potential for the pipeline to move, and it actively monitors stability of slopes. JPO engineers have agreed on criteria to judge slope stability, including both static and dynamic factors. 'We have investigated 58 slopes ... some are very small, some large. The whole monitoring system is risk-based. We know which are the worst ones.' The representative was unsure of the causes of slope instability, but said 'We cited some global warming stuff' (Reimer 2001).

A second JPO representative took a more skeptical view of the impact that climate changes had on the pipeline:

> It is not easy for anyone to separate out the ground effects—what percentage is created by climate change as opposed to other factors. If you disturb the permafrost, strip vegetation, there will be a heat intake more than in the natural environment, without global warming ... There is a problem attributing cause.
> [The 200 tilting VSMs?] [T]hat's not attributable to global warming. If there were no ... climate change, there would be some subsidence of soils anyway due to the presence of work pads and changes in local site conditions. The changes in VSMs, these are slow response things. (McBeath 2001a)

When questioned about pipeline stability, an integrity engineer for Alyeska commented:

> There are three major ways we do this [guarantee pipeline stability]: We monitor the pipeline by continuous optical surveys; second, we send a crew to do load tests; and third, we look at all the heat pipes using infrared cameras ... If there's a need for maintenance because of permafrost melting, we fix it. (McBeath 2002a)

He also noted that 'The same VSMs that showed up on the radar during the first five years after construction (as tilting) are the ones that have showed up now.' In other words, this was a consequence of removing the vegetative cover and other environmental impacts when the pipeline was constructed. In a later interview, this engineer indicated that pipeline security staff were trained to take measurements, tracking the changing tilt against previous measurements. Since his work for Alyeska began in 1998, he has ordered replacement of 24 VSMs (Sorenson 2004). A second Alyeska veteran, a seismic engineer, reiterated this observation:

> You could attribute it (tilting of VSMs) to climate change, but it is most likely due to local effects and changes. You can't test the hypothesis, because there is no long-term data to support or reject it. But as operators, we really don't care. We still respond the same way whatever the cause of the tilting is. (McBeath 2002b)

Like other respondents, he mentioned that a very small number of VSMs had jacked (less than 0.1 per cent), compared to the total number on the line, and that the TAPS was 'designed for permafrost.'

A more important consideration than climate change in the view of engineers in 2004 was the type of crude oil pumped through the line. 'As the crude becomes thicker, containing more asphalt, it could present a challenge.' They compared the pumpability of Prudhoe Bay crude oil with the very viscous crude that Russians pump, which restricts pipeline operations to the summer months. Nevertheless, the engineers noted that 'The system will be adapted as time goes on. The modeling techniques are well-established' (McBeath 2004a).

A publication of Alyeska scientists addresses climate change issues. It argues that 'continued warming of the air temperature will most likely also have negligible impact on TAPS operation or pipeline integrity' for the following reasons:

- Where above-ground pipe is located in areas of relatively warm permafrost, heat pipes are used to help maintain frozen conditions;
- Heat pipes can be added, if necessary, to VSMs that do not currently require them;
- In areas that are ice-rich, such as areas of high moisture content, the rate of ground temperature change will be slow, especially at depth; and

- Continued monitoring and maintenance will identify and repair any areas where settlement or heave may exceed operational standards (Norton, et al. 2002).

The authority under which TAPS operates requires inspection of any degradation that would jeopardize the foundation of the VSMs, valves and pump stations. TAPS legislation gives the JPO the opportunity to add or to modify requirements in arctic and subarctic conditions. For example, in early 2001 the JPO imposed a new geotechnical performance standard to reduce the risk of slope instability. In mid-year, JPO required Alyeska to update a corrective maintenance schedule for VSMs because of 'changing foundation conditions' (Brossia and Britt 2001). This regulatory flexibility, as well as the JPO's good working relationship with industry, provided opportunities for mitigation. However, throughput of the pipeline has declined and operations and maintenance costs have come under greater scrutiny by the owner companies. They asked Alyeska to cut its costs by 10 per cent in 2002, while critics of pipeline safety asked that it spend more, and the state Department of Environmental Conservation registered concerns about safety with the layoff of 140 employees (Cockerham 2002).

The TAPS renewal process served as an expanding register of the importance of climate change effects to environmental organizations and the general public. In the scoping process, from late July to mid October 2001, climate change factored in only two of the 20 categories of public responses to the EIS preparation. First, commentators focused on climate change as associated with the age and condition of TAPS, suggesting that it 'be considered in evaluating future TAPS operations' (JPO 2001a, p. 3). Second, several responses focused directly on climate change: 'Some commentators suggested that the contribution of TAPS to global climate change and the impact of climate change on TAPS be considered' (JPO 2001a, p. 3).

The DEIS issued by BLM in July 2002 specifically addressed climate change issues. It stated that 'The risk of earthquake-triggered liquefaction and landslides is expected to increase,' and 'Melting of permafrost along the ROW could change the number and size of thaw bulbs' (BLM 2002a). As mentioned, most environmental organizations mentioned climate change in the course of their call for tighter regulation of Alyeska and a stricter regulatory structure when making public comments on the DEIS. For example, one organization commented, 'Global warming and melting permafrost threaten to make at least one-third of the 77 000 vertical support members of the TAPS unstable with potentially catastrophic effects on the pipeline' (BLM 2002b, 6:2, p. 1039).

Climate change scientist Dr David Klein, who was a member of the Arctic Environmental Council that functioned as a citizen oversight committee during the construction phase of TAPS, criticized the incompleteness of the DEIS with respect to response to climate change:

> [The DEIS] does not adequately address the consequences of global climate change, which are accounting for global warming with greatest warming on the entire globe occurring in arctic and interior Alaska. The associated thawing of permafrost already occurring and projected to continue by all current climate models ... will require much greater scrutiny of structural security of the support members in the above-ground sections of the pipeline as temperatures of permafrost continue to increase and thawing continues. New and expensive design modifications will need to be developed to deal with this problem as is becoming the case with oil field infrastructure. This will require additional staffing of engineers with appropriate expertise to deal with this situation to insure structural integrity of the line. (BLM 2002b, 6:2, p. 58)

In fact the FEIS makes somewhat more forthright statements about the challenge of climate warming to TAPS. Selections from 'Proposed Action Alternative Analysis' state:

> General warming along the TAPS would promote increasing average temperature of the soils, melting of ground ice, release of meltwater, and lowering of the permafrost table. The resulting effects may lower the mechanical strength of frozen to non-frozen soil and promote solifluction, debris flows, rock falls, potential landslides, differential settlement, liquefaction, and alternation of local hydrology. These processes would continue to impact the integrity of the TAPS, if not carefully monitored and managed ... The integrity of the structures of the TAPS, including the VSMs, may be affected by the consequences of the warming of Alaska. However, the extent and the magnitude of the impacts vary spatially, ranging from insignificant to credible. The extent of impact depends on many factors, including the expected magnitude of the warming in the next 30 years, the thermal regime of the permafrost, the geologic material in the subsurface, groundwater conditions, topography, the engineering practices used in constructing the TAPS, and the maintenance and monitoring programs used by APSC. Changes to natural systems caused by climate changes may also magnify the adverse impacts of earthquakes were they to occur ... Most of the impacts can be mitigated through regular monitoring and maintenance. (BLM 2002b, 2:4)

Notwithstanding the greater acknowledgement of climate change effects, the response of the owner companies, Alyeska, and government regulators has been to re-emphasize its use of 'adaptive management' and 'reliability-centered maintenance (RCM).'[11] RCM is an engineering system developed by United Airlines in the 1970s, under contract with the Department of Defense. It is a process that comprehends all the parts of a complex system. For each part, it compiles statistical information on probabilities of failure, which influence decision points. The pipeline owner companies as well as JPO have adopted RCM (Moubray 1997).

In other words, no special adaptation is warranted to meet the increasing evidence of climate change in interior and arctic Alaska. When asked about tilting VSMs, one engineer commented, 'We continue to adjust as there are needs for adjustment. The economic analysis shows [that it is best to] do incremental maintenance until there is a need to replace them' (McBeath 2004b).

CONCLUSIONS

The Trans-Alaska Pipeline is the most important crude oil transportation system in the United States and a vital element in national energy security. It is far more important to the economic security of the state of Alaska, which fuels most of its general fund budget on proceeds from oil royalties, severance and oil company income taxes. Because TAPS crosses fragile ecosystems and encounters environmental conditions rare elsewhere–such as permafrost and seismic zones–its construction, maintenance and future operation attract national interest and scrutiny.

In the 28 years of operation, TAPS has functioned reliably. Two large oil spills caused by felonious action of humans and the Exxon Valdez eco-disaster caused by human and corporate negligence stain the operational record, but the pipeline system has not collapsed. This is attributable to the design of TAPS as well as monitoring and surveillance by government regulators.

At the onset of construction in 1974, no oil company had constructed a warm oil pipeline in the American Arctic. Environmental organizations used new and powerful instruments of the developing environmental movement and particularly the EIS process to require that the oil industry prepare for environmental challenges, such as permafrost and earthquakes, and mitigate environmental disturbances, such as removal of vegetative cover when burying the pipe. The TAPS design was innovative for its time and has accommodated nearly all the challenges the American subarctic and Arctic present.

After TAPS had operated thirteen years, governments created a new regulatory system to supervise its operations–the Joint Federal–State Pipeline Office, or JPO. Twelve federal and state offices co-located in downtown Anchorage offer one-stop services to oil and gas firms, including their major client, Alyeska Pipeline Services Co. Most of JPO's costs are reimbursed by Alyeska, and private industry cooperates with public agencies in what is called a 'compliance partnership' that eschews the adversarial tensions of the typical American command-and-control system of regulating resource development.

The approach of the thirtieth anniversary of the TAPS ROW federal Grant and state Lease occasioned a penetrating examination of pipeline integrity, stability and security in a full-scale EIS review. Environmental and Native organizations directed blistering critiques toward Alyeska, the owner companies, the TAPS system, and even the JPO; they also vented their frustrations at the overriding importance of economic values in the decision to renew the ROW and lease. Most cognizant Americans and Alaskans, however, saw little reason to renew for a period shorter than 30 years when North Slope oil production seems likely to last this duration, and when the pipeline itself has operated smoothly.

Climate warming presents a new environmental challenge to the Alaska oil transportation infrastructure, one not present at design and construction of the TAPS. The owner companies and Alyeska have adopted an incremental attitude toward the impact of climate change, treating it largely as an issue of routine surveillance, monitoring and maintenance.

Government regulators share this perspective, much to the dismay of environmental organizations and climate scientists. To assure timely identification and remediation of problems, they would prefer citizens' oversight, frequent audits of pipeline performance, more stringent regulations and a more comprehensive view of the impact that changing environmental conditions, such as climate change, have on pipeline operation.

NOTES

1. The current and potential oil resources of the North Slope are vast. The state of Alaska estimates that the North Slope oil reserves contain 12.8 billion barrels of oil. The federal government estimates that an additional 22.5 billion barrels of oil and 22.5 trillion cubic feet of natural gas lie in the Arctic Outer-Continental Shelf (OCS). The National Petroleum Reserve-Alaska (NPR-A) contains an estimated 2.1 billion barrels of oil and 8.5 trillion cubic feet of gas. The most controversial oil/gas province of the North Slope–the Arctic National Wildlife Refuge (ANWR)–is estimated to hold between 5.7 and 16 billion barrels of oil. (See BLM 2002a, 4.7–19; Alaska Department of Natural Resources, *Annual Report*, Division of Oil and Gas, Anchorage, Alaska, 2000; and National Energy Policy Development Group, 2001, *National Energy Policy: Report of the National Energy Policy Development Group.*)
2. The state and local governments voiced similar objections when an 'over the top' route was proposed for an Alaska natural gas pipeline. These governments insisted on an all-Alaska pipeline route.

3.   The state's authority to monitor pipeline integrity lies in AS 38.35.225, which specifies police and regulatory powers to protect lands and the public from contamination.

4.   In 2003, JPO contained six federal and six state offices. Federal agencies included the BLM, Department of Transportation's Office of Pipeline Safety, EPA, Coast Guard, Army Corps of Engineers, and Minerals Management Service. State offices included DNR, departments of Environmental Conservation, Fish and Game, Labor, Transportation/Public Facilities, and the state Fire Marshal's Office (see BLM 2002a, 4:1–2).

5.   According to Jerry Brossia, Director, JPO, federal–state cooperation on pipeline matters began in 1974 by terms of an agreement between Interior Secretary Rogers Morton and Governor Bill Egan, which provided for joint monitoring of pipeline construction and maintenance. When industry sought to construct a Northwest Alaska gas pipeline in 1978, expenditure of $80 million on government oversight without a result renewed attention to improving coordination. This experience led to nomination, through presidential executive order in 1979, of a federal inspector. During this period, permits were issued to extend TAPS to Kuparuk, Endicott, Point MacIntyre and Milne, and authorization of 1400 miles of gathering lines. The JPO today is most influenced by the Exxon Valdez disaster and aging problems of the pipeline. Governor Cowper (1986–90) sought to strengthen the office of review and improve oil spill plans and to correct massive corrosion problems on the pipeline. Providing coordination for the gas line project (then spearheaded by Yukon Pacific) was an objective as well. JPO today offers a one-stop agency to the oil and gas industry. It is financed primarily by Alyeska, representing the consortium of oil companies, which pays over $3 million annually in order to have permits issued expeditiously (Interviews, 27 January 1998; 21 July 2000; 29 December 2003).

6.   Prudhoe Bay BP workers complained about maintenance problems and violations, including pressure valves and fire-suppression systems at oil processing centers, which had not been inspected on schedule. Their complaints reached the ear of Rep. John Dingell (D-Mich) and Rep. George Miller (D-Calif) who pressured BP to investigate complaints and remedy safety and maintenance problems. (See 'Corroding Pipelines Show Prudhoe Bay's Age', *Fairbanks Daily News-Miner*, 23 April 2001; *Fairbanks Daily News-Miner*, 18 July 2001.)

7.   For example, Walter Parker and Stan Stephens, 'Oil Pipeline Oversight Needed', *Fairbanks Daily News-Miner*, 3 July 2002, and Alaska Forum for Environmental Responsibility, Alaska Center for the Environment, and Northern Alaska Environmental Center, 'Public Comment on Draft Environmental Impact Statement, Renewal of the Federal Grant for the Trans-Alaska Pipeline System Right-of-Way', in BLM 2002b, 6:1, pp. 223–229, 20 August 2002.

8.   Trustee's memorandum of 20 August 2002 makes reference to these groups: Alaska Center for the Environment, Alaska Conservation Alliance, Alaska Conservation Voters, Alaska Forum for Environmental Responsibility, Alaska Public Interest Research Group, Alaska Wilderness League, Arctic Audubon Society, Eyak Preservation Council, National Wildlife Federation, Natural Resources Defense Council, Northern Alaska Environmental Center, Sierra Club, Sierra Club Denali Chapter, and the Wilderness Society (see BLM 2002b, 6:1, pp. 186–194).

9. *Headwaters v. BLM*, 914 F.2d 1174, 1180 (1990) and *Northern Plains Resource Council v. Lujan*, 874 F.2d 661, 666 (1989).
10. The affected sections are south of the Brooks Range. Warming permafrost occurs in that region, within 1–2°F of freezing. An increase in the mean annual soil temperature of 1°F would affect this region.
11. Adaptive management is defined by BLM as 'ongoing surveillance, monitoring and testing that provides APSC and JPO with the data and information necessary to evaluate and change, if conditions warrant, the operations and maintenance of TAPS.' RCM is 'an on-going system-by-system audit that determines function, failure modes, consequence and preventative maintenance of critical systems.' BLM further stated that it is 'committed to RCM and believes that this process represents a pro-active approach to oversight and regulation of TAPS. In addition, RCM is the industry standard for reducing risk of failure to critical system components.' (BLM 2002b 6:2, p. 1171)

REFERENCES

Alaska Department of Natural Resources (2001), *Annual Report*, Anchorage, AK: Division of Oil and Gas.

Berry, M.C. (1975), *The Alaska Pipeline: The Politics of Oil and Native Land Claims*, Bloomington, IN: Indiana University Press.

Brossia, J. (Authorized Officer, BLM/OPM) and William G. Britt (State Pipeline Coordinator, ADNR/SPCO) (2001), Letter to Robert J. Shoaf (Vice President, Alyeska Pipeline Services Co.).

BLM (2002a), *Draft Environmental Impact Statement: Renewal of the Federal Grant for the Trans-Alaska Pipeline System Right of Way*, Anchorage, Alaska: Bureau of Land Management, US Department of the Interior

BLM (2002b), *Final Environmental Impact Statement: Renewal of the Federal Grant for the Trans-Alaska Pipeline System Right-of-Way*, Anchorage, AK: Bureau of Land Management, US Department of the Interior.

Case, D.S. and D.A. Voluck (2002), *Alaska Natives and American Laws*, 2nd edn, Fairbanks: University of Alaska Press.

Coates, P.A. (1993), *The Trans-Alaska Pipeline Controversy*, Fairbanks, AK: University of Alaska Press.

Cockerham, S. (2002), *Fairbanks Daily News-Miner*, 12 June and 2 July 2002.

Hines, A.H. and G.M. Ruiz (eds) (2000), *Biological Invasions of Cold-water Coastal Ecosystems: Ballast-mediated Introductions in Port Valdez/Prince William Sound, Alaska*, Final report to Regional Citizen's Advisory Council of Prince William Sound.

IPCC (2001), *Climate Change 2001: Impacts, Adaptation, and Vulnerability,* Intergovernmental Panel on Climate Change, Cambridge: Cambridge University Press.

JPO (2001a), *Summary of Public Scoping Comments: Trans-Alaska Pipeline System Right-of-Way Renewal Environmental Impact Statement,* Anchorage, AK: Joint Pipeline Office.

JPO (2001b), *The Trans-Alaska Pipeline System: A Comprehensive Monitoring Program Report Examining Grant and Lease Compliance,* Anchorage, AK: Joint Pipeline Office.

McBeath, J. (2001a), Personal interview with J. Dygas (Engineer Design and Review Specialist, JPO), Anchorage, 20 December 2001.

McBeath, J. (2001b), Personal interview with G. Reimer, Public Information Officer, JPO, Anchorage, 23 June 2001.

McBeath, Jerry (2002a), Personal interview with S. Sorenson (Integrity Engineer, Alyeska), Fairbanks, 27 June 2002.

McBeath, J. (2002b), Personal interview with Dave Norton (Seismic Engineer, Alyeska), Anchorage, 28 June 2002.

McBeath, J. (2003a) 'Institutional Responses to Climate Change: The Case of the Alaska Transportation System', *Mitigation and Adaptation Strategies for Global Change,* **8**(1): 3–28.

McBeath, J. (2003b), Personal interview with R. Dobosh, Public Information Officer, JPO, Anchorage, 30 December 2003.

McBeath, J. (2004a), Personal interview with Doug Lalla, Joe Dygas, Jerry Brossia (JPO) and Steve Sorenson (Alyeska), Anchorage, 29 January 2004.

McBeath, J. (2004b), Personal interview with Steve Sorenson (Integrity Engineer, Alyeska), Anchorage, 29 January 2004.

McBeath, J. (2004c), Personal interview with Dr Richard Fineberg, Fairbanks, 6 February 2004.

Moubray, J. (1997), *Reliability-Centered Maintenance,* New York, NY: Industrial Press.

National Assessments Synthesis Team (2000), *Climate Change Impacts on the United States,* Cambridge: Cambridge University Press.

National Energy Policy Development Group (2001), *National Energy Policy: Report of the National Energy Policy Development Group.*

Norton, J.D., B. Jokela, E. Haas and R.G. Dugan (2002), 'Environmental Impact of 25 Years of Trans-Alaska Pipeline Operations,' *Permafrost.*

Ross, Ken (2000), *Environmental Conflict in Alaska*, Boulder, CO: University Press of Colorado.

Weller, Gunter and Patricia Anderson (eds) (1998), *Implications of Global Change in Alaska and the Bering Sea Regions*, Fairbanks, AK: Center for Global Change and Arctic System Research, University of Alaska, Fairbanks.

PART III

Modeling, Indicator Development and Decision Support

7   A Complex Systems Approach for Sustainable Cities

Jan Rotmans

UNDERSTANDING THE COMPLEX DYNAMICS OF CITIES

Modern cities are undergoing unprecedented social-cultural, economic, environmental and institutional transformations as their sizes, structures, functions and roles change. These rapid transformations and transitions are still poorly understood and raise fundamental questions that cannot be answered yet. What is the future role of cities at a time when information and telecommunication technologies render distance increasingly irrelevant to business, education and culture? Are virtual communities able to replace city neighborhoods as new units of social cohesion? To what extent is globalization changing the relationship between cities and their environments? The complexity and pace of these rapid transformations has outrun city councilors' ability to understand them.

In this context, it is of crucial importance to develop new concepts that can measure the ability of a city to monitor its contribution to the sustainable development of a region. Although the term 'sustainable city' is value-loaded and bears no single interpretation, it can be characterized as a more balanced development among the social-cultural, economic and environmental domains both within and outside of the city. Because social-cultural, economic, environmental and institutional processes have become increasingly intertwined in cities, city management has become a complex undertaking (Bredenoord 1997). This is mainly due to globalization, technological development, acceleration in turnaround time of many processes, and advances in knowledge about cities and their complex dynamics. Important trends in this respect are not only the continued spatial expansion and growth of cities, the emergence of clusters of cities ('network-cities') and the reshaping of the economic potential of cities, but also growing social segregation, stagnant or increasing unemployment and declining quality of urban life. Because these processes differ in nature and operate at various scales in time and space, an integrated systems approach makes sense to analyze the complexity of the interrelated problems and developments with which today's cities are struggling.

Also, a shift in perspective on cities has taken place over the past decade. Cities used to be seen as 'problem-creating nuclei,' causing large-scale pollution, waste and congestion and as sources of poverty and crime. Nowadays cities are more often regarded as 'problem solving nuclei'–as motors for regional development, as innovative knowledge centers and as spiders in the new information and communication web. Further, cities are now viewed not only as economic stimulators, but also as social, cultural and ecological motors for sustainable development. And finally, the focus on city planning has also changed. City planning used to focus on the physical infrastructure of cities, and particularly on spatial planning, housing, transport and urban water systems. Modern city planning is focusing on the integration of the physical infrastructure, the social-cultural infrastructure, the urban economy and the environment.

The points above indicate the need for an integrative, cross-disciplinary research approach for analyzing complex urban dynamics. International research programs have recently shifted their focus onto integrated approaches for 'sustainable cities.' Examples are the EU Fifth Framework Program on the 'Cities of Tomorrow,' the US National Science Foundation Program on 'Understanding Urban Interactions' and the International Human Dimensions Program on Global Environmental Change (IHDP) on 'Cities and Industrial Transformation.' Although the latter program still focuses on physical issues including transport, water, food, waste and the carbon cycle (Rockwell 1999), the integrated approach is a focal point of research. Some examples of key issues for the future development of cities addressed from an integrated viewpoint are presented below.

Transport

Current transport systems in many European cities are facing severe problems. Questions arise about how current urban transport systems can be re-designed to minimize their negative impacts in terms of congestion, pollution, energy use and inefficiency. Re-design of transport systems in a more sustainable manner requires an integrated approach, where multiple dimensions of urban transport are taken into account (Nijkamp, et al. 1997). This means that transport, as a major stock, is not only considered from the economic perspective, but also from social-cultural, environmental, spatial and institutional perspectives. Future urban transport systems will be the result of developments within and between these highly interlinked domains. An integrated approach can estimate the consequences of modal shifts in urban transport from multiple dimensions, resulting in structural solutions that tend to be more sustainable.

Water

Current urban water systems are far from sustainable in the sense that they are highly inefficient, cause lots of pollution and dissipation and have a low level of recycling. More sustainable urban water systems should aim at closing the water cycling loop within the urban system. This can only be realized if the urban water system is approached from multiple perspectives: the economic, social-cultural, environmental and institutional (Hoekstra 1998). In economic terms water needs to be considered as an economic good and should be managed with an appropriate pricing policy. In environmental terms both the quantity and quality of water resources have to be safeguarded, which means, for example, protection of the river basin supplying the city's water. It also means protection of groundwater supplies by treating sewage and avoiding contamination from industry and agriculture. The social-cultural dimension involves the notion that water is a limited resource that cannot be consumed in an unlimited manner. Institutionally, new arrangements have to be created between industrial companies to make use of each other's water facilities. Implementing such an integrated, multi-dimensional approach would require a re-design of the urban water system.

Waste and Food

City inhabitants require productive ecosystems outside the borders of the city in order to produce the food, energy and other resources that are consumed within the city. Cities also use ecological resources (land and water) for waste disposal (Folke, et al. 1997). Cities extract nutrients from soils all over the world for the food and textiles they consume, which mostly end up in landfills or in water bodies, which may cause substantial ecological damage. However, current city planning does not take into account the usage of ecosystems by cities. In the long run the capacity of ecosystems to produce services for sustaining cities may become a limiting factor. Therefore, new concepts are needed to allow for explicit calculation of the total amount of food, waste and resources that a city consumes. The ecological footprint, pioneered by Wackernagel and Rees (1996), estimates the amount of ecosystem area appropriated by a city, region or country. However, this method is controversial because of the rather unscientific and normative way in which various processes are translated into land surface area (Van den Bergh 1999).

Information and Communication

The information and communication technology revolution that is under way will fundamentally change the infrastructure of cities. The economic urban infrastructure will profoundly change due the penetration of traditional economies by electronic commerce. In the new urban economy the notion of distance will become virtual, changing the dynamics and structure of demand and supply mechanisms. Advanced telecommunication techniques will thoroughly alter the social urban infrastructure, both in terms of accessibility of all kinds of social services and in terms of social cohesion, which may be virtually grounded. The pressure on the ecological urban structure may be alleviated through telecommunication as a substitute for transportation. And institutionally, the information revolution may change urban governance and may stimulate and facilitate civic participation by citizens. The way in which the modern information and communication technology will influence future urban infrastructure and its urban population is still poorly understood. There is, however, an urgent need for integrated approaches in order to increase our understanding of the nature and magnitude of these impacts on our cities of tomorrow.

HISTORICAL CONTEXT OF CITY PLANNING APPROACHES

During the past decades a wide range of analytical tools have been developed and used to support urban analysis and planning (Leitmann 1999). These methods include urban indicators and economic valuation techniques, multi-criteria analyses, risk assessments, rapid urban environmental assessments and Geographical Information System (GIS)-based methods. Remarkably, integrated systems analyses have not been widely applied to the field of city planning, with a few exceptions. In the 1960s, Forrester (1969) developed an integrated systems approach for cities, focusing on the relationships between the physical urban infrastructure, economic development and pollution. The urban metabolism concept (Wolman 1965) represented a holistic approach to urban planning, indicating that environmental quality improvement in urban areas rests on the careful use and removal of energy and water. This concept of urban metabolism was elaborated further by exploring the interactions among resource flows, urban transformation processes, waste streams and quality of life (Newton 1997). However, strategic urban planning systems developed over the last decades based on the urban metabolism concept mainly focused on land use, transport and energy use, and were often understood in terms of carrying capacity or ecological footprints. These urban planning tools consisted of a modeling framework linked with a set of indicators, by which the economic and environmental implications of city policies could be assessed.

So far sustainability of the city as a whole has not been a guiding principle for the development of these urban planning tools. Current knowledge of city dynamics, however, indicates that changes in the physical and economic infrastructure strongly interfere with changing social-cultural, ecological and institutional dynamics (Miller and de Roo 1999; Camagni, et al. 1998). This underlines the urgent need for real integrated systems approaches, taking account of the whole palette of both physical and less tangible changes in city dynamics. Another important element in support of an integrated systems approach for studying city dynamics is given by contemporary information and communication technology, which offers growing opportunities to study complex systems in a cross-disciplinary way. GIS, internet technology, spatial decision support systems, cellular automata models and database standards are developments that enable researchers to cut across disciplinary boundaries. Recent examples of studies where these innovative techniques were used in city planning tools are given in de Kok, et al. (2000) and Alberti and Waddell (2000). However, even the most recent urban planning tools making use of these sophisticated Information and Communication Technology (ICT) techniques still mainly focus on the physical and economic infrastructure of cities (DG–XII 1999).

In view of the urgent need for integrated approaches for city planning, it is surprising that integrated systems analyses have not often been applied to the field of city planning. This lack of application is all the more surprising because the concept of integrated systems analysis has a long history (Miser and Quade 1985) and has been applied to a range of problems, from transportation to water management, and from civil aviation to river dike improvement (Miser 1995; Walker, et al. 1994).

Process-orientation in the form of participation of a broad range of stakeholders is a key element in the proposed integrated approach. Historically, the principal objective of traditional urban planners has been the orderly development of the urban environment, where the proximate goals of a city plan are derived from standards that supposedly measure desirable arrangements (Branch 1981). In the past decade, however, the conviction has grown that the traditional way of planning has to be changed more to a 'process route,' exploring the communicative dimensions of collectively debating and deciding on matters of collective concern (Bredenoord 1997). Such a process route is nowadays characterized as a participatory process, which is an umbrella term describing approaches in which a variety of stakeholders (such as policy people, business people, NGO people and citizens) play an active role.

With regard to tools for city planning, a plethora of planning tools has been developed (Rotmans and van Asselt 2000). Unfortunately, most urban planning instruments developed over the last decades have not been used by city councilors or urban planners. If used at all, they were mainly used in an indirect and non-interactive manner in the urban policy process. This means that urban planning exercises are being undertaken by the tool developers, who are advising their clients indirectly by presenting the outcomes and the resulting insights from these exercises. A variety of reasons may account for this mismatch between the supply and demand of urban planning instruments.

A common objection to formal urban planning tools is that they are too complex but still incomplete and unrealistic, requiring streams of data that do not exist. It is therefore important to strive for a balance between simplicity and realism, not aiming at building a complex tool that is data-intensive, but developing a relatively simple instrument which can also handle qualitative data. Also, the city planning tool should not be developed for but with representatives of the city in question, as part of a participatory process with a variety of stakeholders. These stakeholders then become co-developers of the tool, which means specifying the tool's inputs and outputs, the temporal and spatial scale considered, the level of aggregation (detail) needed for developing policy strategies, themes and processes to be included or left out, and presentation of the model set-up and model results in terms of transparency. This culminates in a 'user model,' which helps tailor the model to the user's needs (Rotmans 1998).

Often, city planners show some timorousness towards decision support planning tools. This is mainly due to misconceptions with regard to what such a city planning tool cannot do. A planning instrument is not meant to replace the city policy process, because city policy making has its own rationality that cannot be captured instrumentally. Another misconception is that a planning instrument would be able to make choices. This is not true at all, because we are not dealing with rational optimality, but with uncertainty and subjectivity (Rotmans and van Asselt 2001). What a city planning instrument can do, however, is estimate the consequences of specific choices that might be made. Also, the notion that the city planning instrument takes over work of city planners is groundless, because the instrument is a means rather than a goal in the city planning process. And finally, integration itself is an intricate process that has to become internalized within an organization. In such an integration process, the planning instrument can only play a facilitating role.

An example of an integrated city planning tool is that which has been developed for the city of Maastricht (Rotmans and van Asselt 2000). An intense participatory assessment involving many relevant stakeholders, and an integrated stock and flow analysis, has enabled the city of Maastricht to gain insights into its strengths and weaknesses in a systemic way. Based upon this qualitative assessment, a quantitative prototype of the Maastricht stock and flow model has been developed (Yang 2002). For example, the prototype is filled with stocks such as housing, population structure, economic structure, labor force, and land use; and relations (flows) between these stocks including migration rates, labor participation and unemployment rates. This prototype can be used in an envisioning process as a policy support tool, to analyze the impacts and consistency of various scenarios that could lead to a sustainable Maastricht by 2030.

A COMPLEX, ADAPTIVE SYSTEMS APPROACH FOR SUSTAINABLE CITIES

Within the context of our previous integrated assessment research, we used to consider cities as dynamic, integrated systems of stocks and flows, describing the sustainability of a city in terms of the dynamic interaction of three sorts of highly interrelated capital forms: economic capital, ecological capital and social-cultural capital (Rotmans and van Asselt 2000). In our most recent research, we go one step further, viewing cities as complex, adaptive systems. So here we advocate a complex, adaptive systems approach as a basis for managing cities towards sustainable development. We explain the rationale for this complex and adaptive systems approach below.

Current cities are highly complex systems, as illustrated by a number of properties:

1. There are non-linear cause and effect relationships between the components;
2. There are feedback loops in the system which may be negative (damping effect) or positive (amplifying effect);
3. The system is open so that energy and information are constantly being imported and exported across system boundaries;
4. The system's structure is diverse and contains a variety of interacting components;
5. The system has multiple attractors–preferred system states–where the system is moving towards a specific attractor;
6. The components of the system are themselves complex systems (subsystems) creating an overall nested structure; and
7. Patterns emerge as a result of relationships between components.

Further, we speak of complex adaptive systems if the individual components are able to respond to changes in their environment, which implies that the system as a whole is able to adapt to changes in its environment. The environment of complex adaptive systems, however, is also made up of other complex adaptive systems, all competing for resources. This means that a complex adaptive system is co-evolving with its environment, where both competition and cooperation are at work. So the key characteristics of complex adaptive systems are emergence and co-evolution, which has the intriguing consequence that these systems have the ability to self-organize–ordered patterns emerge simply as a result of the relations and interactions among the constituent components, without any external control. When a complex system is at the edge of chaos, these changes may occur easily and spontaneously (Holland 1995; Kauffman 1995). The occurrence of crises (or catastrophes) is an important characteristic in the behavior of complex adaptive systems. Crises are small periods during which relatively big changes occur. Although there are small and big crises, they always have a profound impact on the structure of the system in question, either favorable or unfavorable.

With regard to the dynamics of a complex, adaptive system, the following pattern can be discerned. A complex adaptive system continually changes and is never at a standstill. A dynamic equilibrium means a constant process of reconfiguration, modification, revision and re-ordering. Relatively long periods of equilibrium are alternated with relatively short periods of radical change, which we call punctuated equilibrium (Gersick 1991). This is in contrast with the traditional, pervasive paradigm of incremental, cumulative change that has been strongly influenced by Darwin's theory of evolution as a slow stream of small mutations, gradually shaped by environmental variation and selection into new forms. Punctuated equilibria are not smooth trajectories towards pre-defined goals, but whimsical trajectories with high levels of unpredictability. Complex systems do not evolve gradually from one state to the next and do not necessarily evolve from a worse to a better state, through a generic sequence of stages.

In order to generate fundamental and radical change the deep structure of the system must be dismantled, leaving it temporarily disorganized. This is quite difficult, because the equilibrium period offers advantages to a complex system during a specific, limited period of time and because a paradigm shift is needed to make such a change happen. By 'paradigm' we mean the whole of shared starting points, conceptions and interpretations through which people perceive the functioning of a system. Finally, many actors are dependent upon and committed to the current equilibrium state and its constant provision of resources. This explains why incremental change will not fundamentally alter the whole system and why only great forces can bring the system far out of equilibrium, over the threshold of instability.

Based on the aforementioned ideas, a cyclical mechanism unfolds: first, the system in question evolves in the direction of a certain attractor, using resources from a preceding phase; then the system settles with a dominant regime that uses the majority of the available resources and there is a stable system state within the influence area of one attractor; third, the internal structure of the system changes as well as the environment of the system, causing tensions between the system and its environment, leading the system to a critical point: a crisis appears, a highly instable and chaotic but relatively short period; the system then re-organizes itself, resulting in a fundamentally different structure and a new regime with new resources, heading for a different or adjusted attractor, where the overall complexity has increased, or alternatively, the system is not able to recover from the radical internal and external changes and dies out.

How can we break the existing deep structure (inertia) of a complex system? Among the most widely mentioned mechanisms is that of newcomers attacking and breaking the old deep structure and establishing a new one. Unlike established experts, revolutionary newcomers have not yet been infected by the virus of the current equilibrium and are not yet committed to its rules, practices, agreements and resource allocations. In order to disperse this radical change through the system, these newcomers need protection in the form of a 'nucleus.' No single change can break an entire system instantaneously. Therefore, the change must become established within a protected environment, the nucleus. So overall, in order to break the traditional, dominant deep structure of a system the following conditions are needed: internal and external perturbations (events, interventions and surprises), enough anomalies to indicate an upcoming crisis, enough newcomers with fresh ideas, a protected environment in the form of a nucleus and an adequate timing of events and interventions.

What insights can we derive for cities as entities of complex, adaptive systems? In brief, we can draw the following lessons:

• A city is never finished and faces continuous change. Spontaneous, unplanned change occurs as a result of the interactions among the constituent components of a city: the social, physical, economic and ecological pillars. This implies that total control of a city is impossible.
• City goals need to be flexible and adaptable. The complexity of a city is at odds with fixed goals. Because of the structural uncertainty and intrinsic unpredictability of city dynamics we need flexible and often non-quantitative goals that can be adjusted in a goal-seeking process. Goals must evolve during the process, based on insights from experiments to deal with complexity and uncertainty in a more advanced manner.
• Cities need to be viewed from multiple scales. The properties of a city cannot be recognized from only one viewpoint. Some properties are hidden at broader scales, but emerge at lower scales. We call them emergent properties. We therefore need, at minimum, two scale levels to manage the complexity adequately.

- The state of a city guides its management. Managing the complex dynamic landscape of a city means discovering common and diverse places as well as places with fast and slow dynamics. If the city is dominated by fast dynamics–if a period in between two different equilibria is characterized by a certain level of chaos, disorder and rapid change–the conditions favor radical change.
- Only a great force or effort can bring a city far out of equilibrium. In order to cross the instability threshold, a city needs to be forced out of equilibrium, which means that the deep structure of city must be dismantled, against which there will be major resistance. Incremental force will not help to break down the deep structure of a city.

MANAGING CITIES AS COMPLEX, ADAPTIVE SYSTEMS

Steering in the most general sense means influencing an environment and the actors involved. More specifically, in terms of complex systems, steering means bringing (transforming) a system from one state (attractor) to another one (attractor). Adaptive steering then means steering while the system's structure is changing. Overcoming resistance is an important aspect of steering complex adaptive systems. Resistance is needed to maintain the stability of the system: too little resistance may cause instability, while too much resistance may cause a system's structure to be too rigid. Resilience is a measure of the level of perturbation needed to create a change in the structure of a system. Or, resilience is a measure for the resistance against an attractor change. The more a system is settled in an attractor area, the higher the resilience. An example is the traffic system in a city; when a catastrophe happens, people adjust their behavior, by taking the train, and the dominant attractor of the car loses strength. However a structural change will not occur, because the resilience of the car-using system is too big.

Insights from complex adaptive systems theory inform the steering or managing of these systems (see, for example, Rotmans 2003; Rotmans and Rothman 2003; Geldof 2002; and Kickert 1991). It is a misconception to think that the principles underlying the complex systems theory will lead to deterministic management rules. On the contrary, the nature of complex systems theory is not deterministic at all. Determinism cannot go along with the strong non-linear character of the dynamics of a complex adaptive system. Determinism fits with a linear orientation. That is not to say, however, that complexity leads to probabilistic rules. It does lead, however, to insights into the limitations of managing complex systems on the one hand, and possibilities and conditions under which managing complexity is possible, on the other hand. The following insights into steering have been derived from complexity science:

- Steering a city at the level of networks is important. In addition to social networks, one must also consider networks determined by physical, economic and ecological processes. The interaction between social, physical, economic and ecological processes is crucial. The more dynamics these interfering networks show, the higher the potential for radical change.
- Uncertainty offers a chance for influencing a city in a sustainable direction. Uncertainty is often regarded as a problem, or something that should be avoided and neglected. However, uncertainty is an intrinsic part of a city that is unavoidable. If processes are certain, there is little space for influencing them. However, the more uncertain processes are, the higher the potential for change and influence will be.
- Timing of the interventions is important. The closer to a critical point (the borderline of two attractor areas), the more effective an intervention will be. Crises are also system states where direct and effective intervention is possible. However, the more stable a city is, the more difficult it is to influence a city's behavior, because in stable states the city's adaptive capacity is big enough to set off external changes.
- Only newcomers within a protected environment can break the regime of a city. Only newcomers have enough degrees of freedom to maneuver within the context of the current inertia, while still being able to attack the current regime and break it down. But because this takes time, a protected environment (nucleus) is needed to establish this new radical change in such a way that it can withstand the pressure of the current structure.
- Managing a city is not maintaining equilibrium but using disequilibria in order to innovate. In a city equilibrium means stagnation and impedes innovation. Disequibrium means instability and chaos; it is a source for structural change towards a new order. So, in management terms, instability, chaos and disequilibria are opportunities for bringing a city into a more sustainable state.
- Managing a city by avoiding crisis can result in instability. In other words, managing a city with the goal of maintaining the existing equilibrium will most likely lead to a crisis and therefore instability. Managing the crisis, rather than trying to avoid it, offers opportunities for innovation of the system.
- Crossing the instability threshold means self-steering. If a city is far from equilibrium and crosses the instability threshold, a new order is created. This new order organizes itself. Self-organization is a specific form of self-steering at a meta-level of the structure of a city.

So overall, complexity and uncertainty are not difficulties that need to be controlled, but are motors for innovation and the emergence of a new order and structure. Creation of the new order and structure depends on having enough newcomers with deviant ideas, a protected environment in the form of a nucleus, an adequate timing of interventions and enough external pressure on the city in question. However, creating the right conditions does not guarantee a breakthrough resulting in a transition. Achieving transition depends on internal perturbations, enough anomalies to indicate an upcoming crisis and the modulation of autonomous trends.

TRANSITION MANAGEMENT AS A NEW CONCEPT FOR SUSTAINABLE CITY PLANNING

Obviously transitions toward sustainability cannot be managed in the traditional sense–they are too complex and uncertain. What one can do, however, is influence the direction and speed of a transition through various types of steering and coordination. Thus, transitions defy control but they can be influenced. In this section we offer a conceptual as well as a practical model for managing transitions to sustainability. The conceptual model has been developed and used for the Fourth National Environmental Policy plan of the Netherlands (NMP4).

Transition management consists of deliberate attempts to stimulate transition towards a more sustainable future. The basic steering philosophy underlying transition management is that of anticipation and adaptation, starting from a macro-vision on sustainability, building upon bottom-up (micro) initiatives, while in the meantime influencing the mesoregime. Goals are chosen (often implicitly through debates and opinions) by society, and the systems designed to fulfill these goals are created through a bottom-up approach using adaptive policies. The policies designed to further the goals are not set into stone, but constantly assessed and periodically adjusted in development rounds (Teisman 2000). Existing and possible policy actions are evaluated against two criteria: first, the immediate contribution to policy goals (for example, in terms of kilotons of CO_2 reduction and reduced vulnerability through climate change adaptation measures); second, the contribution of the policies to the overall transition process. A schematic view of transition management is given in Figure 7.1 on the following page.

Transition management is based on a two-pronged strategy. It is oriented towards both system improvement (improvement of an existing trajectory) and system innovation (representing a new trajectory of development or transformation). The role of government varies per transition phase.

Transition management breaks with the old planning-and-implementation model aimed at achieving particular outcomes. It is based on a different, more process-oriented and goal-seeking philosophy which helps to deal with complexity and uncertainty in a constructive way. As such, transition management also breaks with the famous Dutch consensus-based or polder-model by opting for consensus on long-term sustainability goals, while at the same time allowing for diversity and informed dissent in the short-term. Key elements of transition management are:

- Complex systems-thinking in terms of more than one domain and different actors at different scale levels (multi-level). This means analyzing how developments in one domain or level gel with developments in other domains or levels, and trying to change the strategic orientation of regime actors;
- Long-term thinking (at least 25 years) as a framework for shaping short-term policy;
- Back- and fore-casting: the setting of short-term and longer-term goals based on long-term sustainability visions, scenario-studies, trend-analyses and short-term possibilities;
- A focus on learning and the use of the philosophies of learning-by-doing and doing-by-learning;
- An orientation towards system innovation and experimentation;
- Learning about a variety of options (which requires a wide playing field); and
- Participation of and interaction between stakeholders.

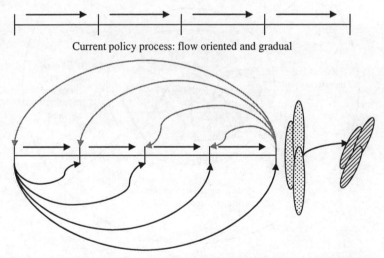

Current policy process: flow oriented and gradual

Transition management: oriented towards long-term sustainability goals (plurifocal)

Figure 7.1   Current policy process versus transition management process

The Transition Management Cycle

Transition management conceptually can be described as a cyclical and iterative process. To make the conceptual model of transition management outlined above operational, transition management could be organized in so-called development rounds. In this section we will present a model to make transition management operational, which is being tested at various (governmental) levels.[1] One round consists of four main activities: establishing and further developing a transition arena for a specific transition theme; the development of a long-term vision for sustainable development and a common transition agenda; the initiation and execution of transition experiments; and the monitoring and evaluation of the transition process. Those four activities are (cyclically) represented in Figure 7.2. Based on the experiences now available, one transition cycle is estimated to take about two to five years, depending on the practical context within which one has to operate.

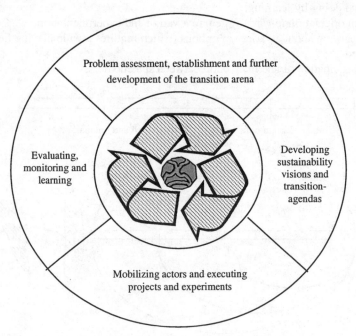

Figure 7.2   Activity clusters in transition management

The Establishment, Organization and Development of a Transition Arena

The establishment and organization of a transition arena forms the basis of the transition management process. The selection of participants for the transition arena is of vital importance since they need to reflect the complexity of the transition at hand. Participants need to have some basic qualities at their disposal: they need to be visionaries, forerunners, able to look beyond their own domain or working area and be open-minded. They must function quite autonomously within their organization but also have the ability to convey the new vision(s) and develop it (them) within their respective organizations. Apart from this, they need to be willing to invest a substantial amount of time and energy playing an active role in the transition arena process. It is important to specify explicitly the criteria with which the participants of the transition arena are selected, and to document these criteria.

Also important is the facilitation of the transition arena, not only in terms of process but also in terms of substance. A continuous process of feeding the participants in the arena with background information and detailed knowledge on a particular topic is necessary to enable a process of co-production of knowledge among the participants. This is of vital importance because arena experiences show that in most cases participants have insufficient time, lack specific knowledge or do not have enough perspective with which to deepen their understanding of the complex problems that arise.

There is an important role here for the transition manager, who brings together the various parties, is responsible for the overall communication in the transition arena, acts as intermediary in discordant situations and has an overview of all the activities in the arena. The transition manager should also ensure a balanced representation of participants from business, governments, non-governmental organizations, knowledge institutions and end users (consumers). As conditions evolve, arena participants may be replaced by new participants with other competencies and practical orientations.

The Development of Sustainability Visions and a Transition Agenda

Organizing an envisioning process for sustainable development is a difficult and cumbersome task. It requires questioning one's own paradigm and leaving aside the everyday noise. It also requires insight and imagination to look ahead one or two generations (or more). Last, but not least, it requires reaching agreement among often diverging opinions on what sustainability means for a specific transition theme. Many sustainability visions are still imposed by the government upon other parties in a top-down manner, or originate from a select group of experts who are far from representative of the broader social setting.

Long-term visions of sustainability can function as guides for formulating programs and policies and setting short-term and long-term objectives. These visions must be as appealing and imaginative as to be supported by a broad range of actors. Inspiring final visions are useful for mobilizing social actors, although they should also be realistic about innovation levels within the functional subsystem in question.

The inspiring, imaginative and innovative transition visions are represented by transition images. Rather than considering transition images as optimal societal blueprints, we consider transition images as integral target images that evolve over time and depend on new insights and learning effects. The transition images embrace transition goals, which are multi-dimensional and qualitative rather than quantitative. The goals should not be defined in a narrowly technological sense, but should represent the three dimensions of sustainability: economic, ecological and social-cultural.

Participants generate multiple transition visions, represented by multiple transition images, creating a basket of images as represented in Figure 7.3. The fact that sustainability is an essentially contested notion is thus addressed by allowing for diversity in the short-term while trying to achieve consensus on long-term ambitions.

Various transition pathways lead to a particular transition image, and from various transition images a particular transition pathway may be derived. The transition images can be adjusted as a result of what has been learned by the players in the various transition experiments. The participatory transition process is thus a goal-seeking process where the transition visions and images, as well as the underlying goals, change over time. This process differs from so-called 'blueprint' thinking, which operates from a fixed notion of final goals and corresponding visions.

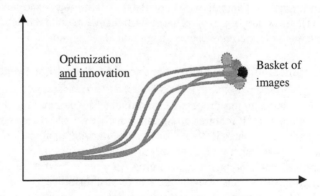

Figure 7.3   Transition process as a goal-seeking process

Based on a process of variation and selection, new visions and images emerge, others die out and existing ones are adjusted. Only during the course of the transition process will the most innovative, promising and feasible transition visions and images be chosen. This evolutionary goal-seeking process means a radical break with current practice in environmental policy, where quantitative standards are set on the basis of studies of social risk, and adjusted for political expediency. Figure 7.3 shows the similarities and differences between current policy making and transition management. In each case, interim objectives are used. However, in transition management these are derived from long-term objectives (through 'back-casting') and contain qualitative as well as semi-quantitative goals and measures. In other words, the interim transition objectives contain content objectives, process objectives (speed and quality of the transition process) and learning objectives (what has been learned from the experiments, what is blocking progress and identification of things that we want to know).

Based on the common problem perception and the shared vision(s) of sustainability, a joint transition agenda can be designed. This is important because all arena participants take their own agendas into the transition arena, whereas a joint transition agenda contains common problem perceptions, goals, action points, projects and instruments. A transition agenda is actually a joint action program for initiating and furthering transitions. It is important to set down which party is responsible for which type of activity, project or instrument to be developed or applied. The transition agenda forms the compass, which the transition arena participants can follow during their transition journey.

The Initiation and Execution of Transition Experiments

From the transition visions and images, transition experiments are derived. The transition experiments are supposed to contribute to the sustainability goals at the system level and should fit within the transition pathways. It is important to formulate sound criteria for the selection of experiments and to make the experiments mutually coherent. The crucial point is to measure to what extent the experiments and projects contribute to the overall system sustainability goals, and to measure in what way a particular experiment reinforces another. Are there specific niches for experiments that can be identified? What is the attitude of the current regime towards these niche experiments? The aim is to create a portfolio of transition experiments that reinforce each other and contribute to the sustainability objectives in significant and measurable ways. Preferably, these experiments should link up with ongoing innovation projects and experiments in a way such that they complement each other. Often, many experiments exist, but are not set up and executed in a systematic manner, resulting in a lack of cohesion. Because transition experiments are often costly and time-consuming, the existing infrastructure for innovation experiments should be used as much as possible. A lack of cohesion puts constraints on the feasibility and running time of experiments. Experiments should be executed using the existing networks of arena participants to ensure the direct involvement of forerunners within participating organizations.

Transition processes are beset with uncertainties of different kinds. It is therefore important to keep a number of options open and to explore the nature of uncertainties in the transition experiments in order to determine which are structural and which ones can be reduced. Uncertainties can be the result of a lack of knowledge and may thus be reduced, but they can also be caused by the variability of the system, and so are structural and irreducible by nature. In the transition management cycle uncertainties need to be explored and mapped in a systematic manner. Through learning with transition experiences the estimation of uncertainties changes over the course of the transition process. This in turn may lead to adjustment of the transition visions, images and goals. In this search and learning process, scenarios play an important role, in particular explorative scenarios, which look to future possibilities without very many decision making constraints (Van Notten, et al. 2003).

Monitoring and Evaluating the Transition Process

Continuous monitoring is a vital part of the search and learning processes of transition. We distinguish between two different processes to be monitored: the transition processes itself, and transition management. Monitoring the transition process has to take place at different levels in terms of monitoring the slowly changing macro-developments, the sharply fluctuating niche developments, as well as the individual and collective actors at the regime level. This provides the 'enriched context' for transition management. First, the actors within the transition arena must be monitored with regard to their behavior, networking activities, alliance forming and responsibilities and also as to their activities, projects and instruments. Next, the transition agenda must be monitored with regards to the actions, goals, projects and instruments that have been agreed upon. Finally, the transition process itself must be monitored with regards to the rate of progress, the barriers and points to be improved and so on. In this way, transition management can be seen as the meta-environment in which various processes take place and are monitored.

The philosophies of learning-by-doing and doing-by-learning are the essence of transition management. Learning-by-doing concerns the development of theoretical knowledge from practice, whereas doing-by-learning is the development of practical knowledge from theory. Monitoring these learning processes, however, is easier said than done. Experience with monitoring and documenting these kinds of learning processes is rare. The phenomenon of 'social learning' is in large part still an abstract notion that cannot easily be translated into components for monitoring. It is therefore important to formulate explicit learning goals for transition experiments, which can be monitored.

The evaluation of the above learning processes is in itself a learning process, and may lead to adjustment of the developed transition visions, agenda and management process within the transition arena. The set of interim objectives are evaluated to see whether they have been achieved; if not, they are analyzed to see why not. Have there been any unexpected social developments or external factors that were not taken into account? Have the actors involved not complied with the agreements that were made? Once these questions have been answered, a new transition management cycle starts, which takes another few years. In the second round of this innovation network the proliferation of acquired knowledge and insights is central. This requires a specific strategy for initiating a broad learning process.

Because transition management cycles take several years within a long-term context of 25 to 50 years the creation and maintenance of public support is a continuous concern. When quick results do not materialize and setbacks are encountered it is important to keep the transition process going in order to avoid a backlash. One way to achieve this is through participatory decision making. Societal support can also be created in a bottom-up manner, by bringing in experiences with technologies in areas in which there is local support. The experience may remove broader fears and prepare proponents to move forward. With time, solutions may be found for the problems that limit wider application.

TRANSITION MANAGEMENT IN URBAN REGIONS IN PRACTICE

A practical example of an urban region where the concept of transition management has been applied over the past couple of years is the region 'Parkstad Limburg.' This region is located in the southeastern part of the Netherlands, consists of seven municipalities, and was a mining district during the late sixties and mid-1970s. At that period the Dutch government decided to close down the coalmines in order to transform the mining district into a modern industrial area. Billions of euros were pumped into the former mining area, governmental bodies were established and new industries and employment were tempted to settle in the Parkstad Limburg area. In spite of this immense investment effort, several decades later the overall conclusion is that the intended transition of the mining area has only been partly realized.

On the one hand the transformation was successful, in the sense that the Parkstad Limburg area showed a remarkable resilience after the closure of the coalmines. Remarkably quickly the area recovered from this shock, and initiatives taken by many individuals, networks, institutes and organizations demonstrated the willingness to contribute to the resurrection of the area. Nevertheless, the transition stagnated: after several decades the former mining area still has no alternative, clear-cut, sound profile and social problems are pressing. The unemployment level is high; higher educated youth are leaving the area; the regional income is low; there are too few starting enterprises; there is a fast graying in the area, where the overall population is declining; and finally the seven municipalities do not form a coherent political and administrative unit.

Against this background and context there was a need to initiate a transition management process with the overall aim to further and stimulate the development of a sustainable Parkstad Limburg. To this end, two transition managers were appointed, representatives of the two largest municipalities in Parkstad Limburg, Heerlen and Kerkrade. Together with the transition researchers involved, these two managers selected the stakeholders for the transition arena, based on the following criteria:

1. No politicians or administrators from the current political regime of Parkstad;
2. Balanced representation from private sector, NGOs and knowledge institutions;
3. Individuals who can act autonomously rather than representing established interests;
4. People who can think 'out of the box';
5. People who can listen to others and can work with others;
6. No people from the 'old boys networks';
7. No 'solution-driven' people, but open-minded people, the so-called front runners;
8. No dominating big egos who disturb the group process;
9. People who are willing to invest substantive time and energy in the process; and
10. No more than 15 people in the arena.

After a careful selection process about 15 people were selected from a range of sectors: from education to health care, from banking and finance to culture, from religious to tourism and from the labor union to retail. A chairman was appointed, and, structured as a social learning process, a biweekly series of learning sessions was organized. During the first phase the problem perception was explored, which turned out to be quite cumbersome and difficult: the sense of urgency was not shared by everyone in the arena.

The researchers supplied the arena process with integrated assessments, exploring short-, medium- and long-term trends in mutual coherence, in order to inform the arena participants as adequately as possible. After a sequence of divergence and convergence, a shared and joint problem perception was formulated that expressed a high sense of urgency on behalf of a cross section of the social midfield, a process that took about half a year. Based on this joint arena perception, a transition agenda was formulated with shared responsibilities, duties and tasks to be fulfilled.

Then a process of envisioning was started, aiming to develop sustainability visions for the Parkstad Limburg region. In order to structure this envisioning process the triangular model as described in Rotmans, et al. (1999) was used, where important stocks and flows from the three forms of capital of the region (social-cultural, economic and ecological) needed to be equally distributed over the three capital forms by the arena participants. Long-term future goals (qualitative rather than quantitative) were formulated by the arena participants around which transition images were devised, which in turn yielded diverse visions for a future Parkstad Limburg. Because we consider sustainability as intrinsically normative, subjective and ambiguous, the arena stakeholders ultimately needed to agree on what they perceived as sustainable or not. Out of these visionary transition pictures, common building blocks and drivers were picked in order to arrive at a shared overall vision. Although this is not favored by transition management–multiple visions are what maintain diversity in the process–there was a strong need within the transition arena to converge to one vision.[2]

In the latter phase all kinds of initiatives, niche-experiments, both ongoing and novel, were discussed in light of the created sustainability vision. The transition management process was monitored and evaluated, and the designed vision was promoted and communicated with people of many different segments of the Parkstad Limburg region, creating broad public support for the sustainability vision. The vision itself was broadly supported and warmly received by many, acting as mobilizing and catalyzing factor, where the process of envisioning was at least as important as the vision itself. In the history of the region, this was the very first vision that was developed by the social midfield rather than by policy makers, politicians or consultancies. The whole process, which covers one cyclic round in the transition management cycle (see Figure 7.2), took about three years, from originating the idea to nailing down the sustainability vision. In the next round of the transition management cycle the transition experiments need to be performed, the actual phase of the transition process needs to be investigated, the sustainability vision needs to be adjusted, the setting of the arena needs to be evaluated, other sub-arenas need to be established (at the tactical and operational level), the transition agenda needs to be checked and possibly reformulated, the transition pathways need to be validated, and the social learning process needs to be documented. The whole process is documented in detail and will appear as a major case study in the forthcoming PhD dissertation of Derk Loorbach.

In quite a few other regional and urban settings in the Netherlands transition management processes and concomitant transition experiments are taking place. At the national level five ministries are experimenting with transition policies, and at the provincial level governments are doing the same. At the regional/urban level a floating city is being trialed, adapting and mitigating the effects of upcoming anthropogenic climate change and its impacts in terms of sea level rise and changing river discharges, in combination with a drop in land level, in the Netherlands.

CONCLUSIONS

In view of the growing complexity of managing rapidly evolving cities, there is a definite need for integrative approaches to assist city planners and councilors in their striving to achieve a sustainable city and hence a higher quality of urban life. Regarding the instrumental aspect of this complex city planning process, sophisticated planning instruments are needed. These instruments no longer focus on the physical and economic infrastructure of cities, in particular on spatial planning, housing and transport, but also on the integration of the physical infrastructure, the social-cultural infrastructure and the city economy and labor market. Such an integrated planning tool can be helpful in decisions regarding tradeoffs between investments in stocks and in the monitoring of current and future developments in relation to its sustainability targets. In order to develop and use such an integrated city planning tool in an effective and efficient way, it needs to be developed in a participatory manner, taking into account the needs, knowledge and expertise of the diverse stakeholders.

A recent development is to develop city planning tools that are grounded on complex systems theory on the one hand and new forms of governance (management) on the other hand. Analytically, this means that cities can be considered as complex, adaptive systems. This means that cities co-evolve with their environment, that they contain emergent behavior and that they have the (self-organizing) ability to adjust to changes in their environment (external conditions). Process-wise, this means that managing complexity involves starting from uncertainty and complexity, rather than going around them. It practically means that one attempts to steer a complex system, while realizing the limitations and boundaries of the steering possibilities, but also realizing the possibilities for steering complexity. Managing complexity then means subtly influencing in an evolutionary way rather than command-and-control steering. This falls into the category of reflexive governance (management), with anticipatory, participatory and adaptive components.

The concept of transition management is an example of a form of reflexive governance rooted in complex systems theory. While many cities all over the world show symptoms of non-sustainability, such as pollution, congestion, ecological footprint, overpopulation, criminality, etc., they are increasingly seen as motors for the sustainable development of global regions. This requires a transition, a radical pattern of change from a non-sustainable to a sustainable city development pathway. Managing a city into a more sustainable direction then implies furthering and stimulating a transition process over a period of decades. The concept of transition management could be an interesting tool to further/stimulate such a city transition process. Although the transition management theory is still in its inception stage, it has a great potential–because of the generic underlying principles that could be applied to any kind of city or urban region, because its logics and the sound rationale behind it, and because its ability to test the validity of the steering principles in so-called experimental gardens or testing grounds. The concept of transition management needs to be empirically validated much more thoroughly in these testing grounds. That is also the reason why many of these transition experiments are going on in the Netherlands, and to an increasing extent also in other European countries. Notwithstanding the profound empirical testing work that still needs to be done, the very first results of transition management projects and concomitant transition experiments look quite promising.

NOTES

1. In the Netherlands, the model has been adopted by five different ministries who are trying to implement it (http://www.energietransitie.nl).
2. The overall sustainability vision is available on the website: http://www.ophetekolen.nl (in Dutch).

REFERENCES

Alberti, M. and P. Waddell (2000), 'An Integrated Urban Development and Ecological Simulation Model', *Integrated Assessment*. **1**(3): 215–227.
Branch, M.C. (1981), *Continuous City Planning: Integrating Municipal Management and City Planning*, New York, NY: John Wiley and Sons.
Bredenoord, J. (1997), *Planning and managing the city of the future* (in Dutch), Delft, the Netherlands: Technical University of Delft.

Camagni, R., R. Capello, and P. Nijkamp (1998), 'Towards Sustainable City Policy: an Economy–Environment Technology Nexus', *Ecological Economics* **24**: 103–118.

Deelstra, T. and D. Boyd (eds) (1998), *Indicators for Sustainable Urban Development*, Delft, the Netherlands: The International Institute for the Urban Environment.

DG–XII (1999), *Spartacus: System for Planning and Research in Towns and Cities for Urban Sustainability*, Helsinki, Finland: Environment and Climate Research Programme, Human Dimensions of Environmental Change.

Folke, C., A. Jansson, J. Larsson and R. Costanza (1997), 'Ecosystem Appropriation by Cities', *Ambio*, **26**(3): 167–172.

Forrester, J.W. (1969), *Urban Dynamics*, Portland, OR: Productivity Press.

Geldof, G.D. (2002), *Dealing with Complexity in Integrated Water Management*, Deventer, the Netherlands: Tauw BV.

Gersick, C.J.G. (1991), 'Revolutionary Change theories: A multilevel Exploration of the Punctuated Equilibrium Paradigm', *The Academy of Management Review*, **16**(1): 10–36.

Hoekstra, A. (1998), *Perspectives on Water: An Integrated, Model-based Exploration of the Future*, the Netherlands: International Books.

Holland, J. (1995), *Hidden order: how adaptation builds complexity*, US: Perseus Books.

Kauffman, S. (1995), *At home in the universe: the search for laws of complexity*, Oxford, UK: Oxford University Press.

Kemp, R. and J. Rotmans (2004), 'Managing the transition to sustainable mobility', in *System Innovation and the Transition to Sustainability: theory, evidence and policy*, B. Elzen, et al. (eds), Cheltenham, UK: Edward Elgar Publishing.

Kickert, W.J.M. (1991), *Complexity, Self-Steering and Dynamics*, Samson H.D., Erasmus University Rotterdam, 12 September 1991, Rotterdam, the Netherlands: Tjeenk Willink Alphen aan den Rijn.

Kocelkorn, G., M.B.A. van Asselt and J. Rotmans (1999), *Future on course: city vision and planning instrument for Maastricht on the way to 2030* (in Dutch), International Centre for Integrative Studies, Feasibility Study commissioned by the City of Maastricht, Maastricht, the Netherlands.

de Kok, J.L., M. Titus and H.G. Wind (2000), 'Incorporation of social science concepts in integrated assessment models: application to the urbanization of Ujun Pandang, Indonesia', *Integrated Assessment*, **1**(3): 177–188.

Leitmann, J. (1999), *Sustaining Cities: Environmental Planning and Management in Urban Design*, New York, US: McGraw-Hill.

Miller, D. and G. de Roo (eds) (1999), *Integrating City Planning and Environmental Improvement: practicable strategies for sustainable urban development*, Aldershot, UK: Ashgate Publishers.

Miser, H.J. and E.S. Quade (eds) (1985), *Handbook of Systems Analysis: Overview of Uses, Procedures, Applications and Practice*, New York, NY: Elsevier Science Publishing.

Miser, H.J. (ed.) (1995), *Handbook of Systems Analysis: Cases*, Chicester: John Wiley and Sons.

Newton, P. (1997), *Reshaping cities for a more sustainable future: exploring the link between urban form, air quality, energy and greenhouse gas emissions*, Report of the Australian Academy of Technological Sciences and Engineering, Melbourne, Australia.

Nijkamp, P., H. Ouwersloot, and S.A. Rienstra (1997), 'Sustainable Urban Transport Systems: an Expert-based Strategic Scenario Approach', *Urban Studies*, **34**(4): 693–712.

Rijkens-Klomp, N., M. van de Lindt, M.B.A. van Asselt, et al. (2003), 'Integrative policymaking for the improvement of the quality of urban life', in *The human sustainable city: challenges and perspectives from the Habitat agenda*, L.F. Girard, B. Forte, M. Cerreta, et al. (eds), England: Ashgate Publishing Limited.

Rockwell, R. (1999), *Cities and Industrial Information: framework for a core theme of the International Human Dimensions Programme–Industrial Transformation Science Project*.

Rotmans, J. (1998), 'Methods for Integrated Assessment: the challenges and opportunities ahead', *Environmental Modeling and Assessment*, **3**(3): 155–181.

Rotmans, J. (2003), *Transition management: key to a sustainable society*, Assen, the Netherlands: van Gorcum Publishers.

Rotmans, J. and D. Rothman (eds) (2003), *Scaling Issues in Integrated Assessment*, Lisse, the Netherlands: Swets and Zeitlinger.

Rotmans, J. and M.B.A. van Asselt (2000), 'Towards an Integrated Approach for Sustainable City Planning', *Journal on Multi-Criteria Decision Analysis*, **9**: 110–124.

Rotmans, J. and M.B.A. van Asselt (2001), 'Uncertainty Management in Integrated Assessment Modelling: towards a pluralistic approach', *Environmental Monitoring and Assessment*, **69**(2): 101–130.

Rotmans, J., R. Kemp, and M.B.A. van Asselt (2001), 'More evolution than revolution: transition management in public policy', *Foresight* **3**(1): 15–32.

Rotmans, J., M.B.A. van Asselt, and N. Rijkens (1999), *The Think Model for the Province of Limburg*, ICIS–Working Paper I99-D004, Maastricht, the Netherlands.

Teisman, G. (2000), 'Models for research into decision making processes: on processes, phases and decision making rounds', *Public Administration* **78**(4): 937–956.

Thompson, M., R. Ellis, et al. (1990), *Cultural Theory*, Boulder, CO: Westview Press.

van Asselt, M.B.A. and J. Rotmans (1996), 'Uncertainty in Perspective', *Global Environmental Change*, **6**(2): 121–157.

Van den Bergh, J. (1999), 'Ecological Footprint: a Critical Evaluation', *Ecological Economics*, May 1999.

Van Notten, P., J. Rotmans, M.B.A. van Asselt, et al. (2003), 'An updated scenario typology', *Futures*, **35**(5): 423–445.

Wackernagel, M. and W. Rees (1996), *Our Ecological Footprint: Reducing Human Impact on the Earth*, Gabriola Island, BC, Canada: New Society Publishers.

Walker, W.E., A. Abrahamse, J. Bolten, et al. (1994), 'A Policy Analysis of Dutch River Dike Improvements: Trading off Safety, Cost and Environmental Impacts', *Operations Research,* **42**(5): 823–836.

Wolman, A. (1965), 'The metabolism of cities', *Scientific American,* September: 179–188.

Yang, Kang-Hun (2002), *System dynamics modeling: case of the city of Maastricht*, Delft, the Netherlands: Technical University Delft.

8 A Spatially Explicit Urban Simulation Model: Land Use Evolution and Impact Assessment Model (LEAM)

Brian Deal and Zhanli Sun

INTRODUCTION

Urban growth and the resultant sprawling patterns of development are causing social, economic and environmental strain on US communities (Schmidt 1998). According to the Sierra Club, undesirable urban growth, also known as urban sprawl, has become one of the costliest problems in America. Related to these costs are the connections between climate change and urban land use dynamics. Urbanization pressures at the local (Chung, et al. 2004; Jauregui and Romales 1996) and continental scales (Bonan 1997) are being implicated in both micro and macroclimate change patterns. Conversely, changes in climate patterns can have profound impacts on urban systems, including transportation, utility infrastructure, air quality, water quality, energy and the general quality of life of urban residents (Patz, et al. 2001; Rosenzweig and Solecki 2001; Wilbanks 2003; Agrawala 2004; Duerden 2004). With growing concerns about the negative impacts of land use change, public agencies and policy officials are seeking principles and tools designed to manage land use change under the flag of 'smart growth' or 'sustainable growth.'

During the last two decades, spatial analysis tools, Geographic Information System (GIS) and Remote Sensing (RS) technologies have been widely deployed to monitor, analyze and visualize urban growth phenomena. Maps and satellite images, however, are limited to static displays of past and current data sets. They portray the current state of the system, with neither the reasons why things appear as they do, nor possible future states. Although GIS-based tools provide useful analysis and have been widely used to assist urban planners, the static mapping concepts on which they are built are clearly insufficient to study the dynamics of urban growth (Hopkins 1999). The causal mechanisms associated with land use change remain relatively poorly understood, in part due to the complexity of urban systems. Consequently, policy makers and planners are often faced with the difficult task of making land use decisions without sufficient analysis or vision.

Computer-based urban system simulation models are now being employed to forecast and evaluate land use change (Batty and Xie 1994; Birkin 1994; Landis 1994; Engelen, et al. 1995; Wu and Webster 2000; Waddell 2002). These models represent a spatial and dynamic approach that enables planners to view and analyze the future outcomes of current decisions and policies before they are put into action. These models have the ability to help improve our fundamental understanding of the dynamics of land use transformation and the complex interactions between urban change and sustainable systems (Deal 2001). These spatial dynamic modeling techniques are becoming essential elements in the Planning Support System (PSS) literature (Hopkins 1999; Kammeier 1999).

To date spatial dynamic urban modeling is considered to be in its infancy. Few models have been developed that are able to represent the complex dynamics of urban land use change that are consistent with observable data (Almeida 2003). As a result few such models are operational and used to assist in professional urban planning practices.

In this paper we present a comprehensive dynamic spatial urban simulation model, the Land use Evolution and impact Assessment Model (LEAM). LEAM was originally developed as a research project by an interdisciplinary team of researchers at the University of Illinois with support from the National Science Foundation. After a successful full-scale pilot application in Peoria, IL, LEAM has been selected to assist planning practices in the St Louis metro area as part of the Department of Defense (DOD) encroachment analysis and as part of the Smart Growth initiative introduced by the State of Illinois. Described here is a bi-state application of LEAM consisting of the five counties in southwestern Illinois, and the five counties in east central Missouri that make up the St Louis metropolitan region. In the following sections, the conceptual framework and relevant features of the LEAM simulation environment are described followed by the results of the St Louis metropolitan area application.

LEAM DESIGN

LEAM is a new modeling environment designed to support regional planning practices. Understanding the interactions between subsystems in complex urban environments will enable policy makers and planners to make better land use management decisions. However, interacting systems behave in complex and dynamic ways, and can be understood best using spatial dynamic models. The LEAM research team, which brings together expertise in the social sciences, economics, geography, urban planning, ecology, visualization and high-performance computing, has been designing and developing an operational planning support tool for the past five years.

To design a planning support tool that is focused on land use change, we incorporated recent progress in complex systems analysis techniques, ecological modeling concepts, geographic spatial analysis and cellular automata modeling into the LEAM design. Compared with other planning support tools and models with similar foci, like CommunityViz® (Sipes 2003), Quest®, What if® (Klosterman 1999), Index® (Brail 2001), CUF (Landis 1994) and CUFII (Landis and Zhang 1998), LEAM is quite unique. At the same time, LEAM shares some features and approaches with other modeling environments. The key features described below illustrate the principles of the LEAM approach.

An Ecological Approach

LEAM builds on a body of work on large-scale ecosystem models that have seen a recent resurgence (Deal 2001). The theoretical underpinnings of LEAM are based on integrated, multi-disciplinary, ecological and engineering approaches to modeling spatial dynamics.

Applying ecological concepts and methods to urban research has roots that trace back to the 1920s when R.E. Park and E.W. Burgess developed a concentric, static urban structural model based on ecological equilibrium theory. In the 1960s Forrester further advanced urban ecology ideas by adding a dynamic component. This was manifested in his urban dynamics model based on concepts of 'industrial dynamics' and 'industrial ecology' (Forrester 1961, 1970). However, the ecological approach has not been applied systematically to urban problems until very recently, when urban ecology began to emerge as a new branch of environment science, which studies urban ecosystems.

Urban ecology broadens the concept of traditional ecology to consider human systems as major actors in ecosystem analysis. Its goal is to promote a sustainable urban environment through the study of the interactions between human and environmental systems. Urbanization impacts studied include feedbacks on human society as well as on the natural environment. LEAM models not only the drivers of urbanization, including biophysical factors and socioeconomic factors, but also the impacts and feedbacks that urbanization has upon itself and on other systems.

New theory, tools and research methods in ecological systems have the potential to improve the dynamics of change in urban environments. A variety of sophisticated computational and theoretical tools exist for characterizing urban systems at a conceptual level and for visualizing and understanding these characterizations. An integrated platform for a high-performance spatial modeling ecosystem, the Spatial Modeling Environment (SME) developed at the University of Maryland (Maxwell and Costanza 1997), is utilized in LEAM. This modeling environment, which transparently links icon-based modeling tools, like STELLA®, enables us to develop LEAM models in a user-friendly, graphical environment, requiring very little knowledge of computer programming. Therefore, the combined use of SME and STELLA® allows us to build LEAM collaboratively in an open architecture form.

Collaborative, Distributed and Open Architecture Design

To build a comprehensive urban simulation model involves collaboration of scientists from multiple disciplines. Traditional approaches to complex multi-disciplinary modeling require one or more programmers to 'translate' substantive contextual models developed by others into computer code. The programmers separate the modelers from the actual model implementation and they are often the only ones that understand the inter-relationships and nuances of the entire model. To further complicate the situation, the black-box nature of these implementations leaves the substantive experts unable to assess whether their expertise has been adequately and accurately captured. In this traditional approach, the processes of model formulating, calibrating, coding and integration are time consuming, error-prone and very difficult. The entire model ends up as a black-box system to users, even to model developers. It is extremely hard to use and maintain.

With these problems in mind, LEAM was developed using an alternative strategy. This strategy can be characterized by two key differences from the current set of approaches: first, an open model-building environment rather than a black-box; second, dis-aggregated and distributed model-building in which various subject experts can contribute directly and collaboratively to the model-building process rather than working through a single programmer as translator. An open model-building environment would allow model parameters and drivers (the local rule set) to be easily inspected and evaluated. Dis-aggregated and distributed model-building would ensure that groups of experts could work directly on parts of the model with which they are most familiar.

Such an alternative is available in the combined use of STELLA® for constructing the cellular models which are local rules that define cell behavior, and SME for assembling and linking the cellular models spatially across the lattice. STELLA® is a graphically based dynamic simulation software package based on Jay Forrester's System Dynamics language that uses icons and symbols to communicate a model's structure (Forrester 1961). STELLA® has a good mix of simplicity in manipulating model components and power of model expression. Icons include reservoirs representing stocks of resources as well as 'pipes' and 'valves' representing flows and controls between those reservoirs, each with an associated user-defined equation (Hannon 1994).

Variables of interest can be scaled and plotted in different formats to help visualize model behavior. The effects of changes made can be viewed immediately in a user-friendly, graphical environment, requiring no knowledge of computer programming. Using iconographic modeling techniques greatly increases the ease with which the model can be changed and calibrated, allowing the user to concentrate on modeling instead of computational details (Maxwell and Costanza 1997).

SME spatializes the single cell STELLA® models, applying them to a geographic area (represented in this case as a matrix of cells), and simulating the changes that take place in the state of each cell over multiple time-steps. SME automatically converts the STELLA® models into computer C++ code that can be run on multiple processors (and multiple computers) in parallel. The spatial simulations are, as a result, processed in a distributed high-performance fashion that is transparent to users. Results can be displayed in a number of ways, including a built-in mapping and animation tool when running SME with Graphic User Interface (GUI); results can also be exported to images and GIS format files, and then visualized and analyzed in image processing or GIS software. Other representations such as map movies, animations that show change over space and time, summary tables and summary maps can be easily generated.

SME imposes constraints of modularity and hierarchy in model design, and supports archiving of reusable model components (Maxwell and Costanza 1997). In these ways this approach eliminates black-box complexities and advances an open, dis-aggregated approach to spatial modeling. By applying this collaborative spatial modeling approach, LEAM is developed in an open, modular approach that promotes collaboration.

Cellular Automata Based Model

Under the framework of SME, a spatial region is broken down into cells, which are analogous to GIS grid cells. The behavior of each cell object, also called local rules, is described by the STELLA® model. A set of intercellular links can also be defined, representing spatial contiguity and local spatial interactions. Typically, any two cells are linked if they share a boundary, but more flexible and general linkages are possible (Costanza 2004). Essentially, SME provides a perfect platform for Cellular Automata (CA) modeling, which emerges as a microscopic simulation approach to model urban dynamics.

Cellular Automata are discrete dynamical systems whose behavior is completely specified in terms of a local relation. In a typical two dimension cellular automaton, a uniform grid represents space, with each cell holding a discrete value as its state. The cell state changes in discrete steps, and its new state is computed based on the configuration of its neighbor cells. The concept was originally conceived by John Von Neumann (1966), who is known as the 'father of the modern computer,' and introduced to the public by another mathematician, Stanislaw Ulam, in the 1950s. In the 1970s, Conway's 'Game of Life' raised a lot of attention and interest in CA research. CA has been widely applied to chemistry, physics, computer graphics and so on. CA has established itself as an important tool used to study complex systems. In his new book *A New Kind of* Science, Stephen Wolfram (2002) even defined CA as a revolutionary model tool that changes how we look at and simulate the world.

CA is embedded with a spatial dynamic feature, which makes it a natural tool for spatial modeling. CA application in geographic modeling dates back to the spatial diffusion model developed by Hagerstrand (1967), which is essentially a stochastic CA, although he did not use the term CA. Tobler (1979) first defined CA as geographical models although he believed some CA are too simple to be usefully applied. Later on, the implication of CA to geographic modeling, including advantages and theoretical obstacles of its application to geographic modeling, was explored theoretically (Couclelis 1985, 1987, 1997; Batty, et al. 1997). CA is very appealing to geographic modelers because:

1. The CA-based model is simple and intuitive, yet able to simulate self-organizing complex systems;
2. The natural born spatial dynamic feature enables modeling of spatial dynamic systems in extreme spatial detail;
3. The cellular structure of CA has a natural affinity with raster data format of RS images and GIS grid maps, and can be easily integrated with GIS through generalization of map algebra (Takeyama and Couclelis 1997);
4. The bottom-up approach of CA provides a new strategy of geographic modeling; and
5. CA is a computational model running in parallel, which fits with high-performance geo-computation.

Subsequently, CA application in geography has been experiencing exponential growth, especially on urban land use simulation. Batty was one of the earliest geographers to sketch the general framework of CA-based urban models (Batty and Xie 1994). An integrated platform, named DUEM, was designed by Batty and his group for geographic CA exploration (Batty, et al. 1999). Engelen, et al. (1995) used CA to model urban land use dynamics to forecast climate change on a small island setting. Wu and Webster (1998) presented a model that also included user decisions to determine model outcomes. White's St Lucia model (White and Engelen 1997) is an example of high-resolution CA modeling of urban land use dynamics and an attempt to use the standard non-spatial models of regional economics and demographics, as well as a simple model of environmental change for predicting the demand for future agricultural, residential and commercial/industrial land uses. An urban growth model of the San Francisco Bay Area by Clarke and Gaydos (1998) is another example of using relatively simple rules in the CA environment to simulate urban growth patterns. Li and Yeh (2002) integrated neural-networks and CA in a GIS platform and successfully applied it to urban land use change simulation in Guangdong, China.

Although dozens of models have been proposed and built over the last twenty years, CA-based on a land use modeling technique is still far from mature. Despite the flexibility of the CA approach, limitations remain (Torrens and O'Sullivan 2001). The hypothetical urban forms emerging from CA models with surprisingly simple local transition rules are certainly plausible. However, in reality, an urban system evolves in a much more complex way. The current CA-based urban models are just too simple to capture the richness of urban systems. Consequently, most CA models are still developed as research projects, and applications are conducted more like experiments to test models. To date, few CA-based models are operational as productive tools to support regional planning practice.

To build useful operational models, modelers are trying to extend the concept of CA by loosening its strictness and integrating a diversity of models, such as traditional regional socioeconomic models (White and Engelen 1997; Wu and Martin 2002). In LEAM, cells evolve in a constrained surface defined by biophysical factors, such as hydrology, soil, geology and land form and socioeconomic factors, such as administrative boundary and census district, instead of the homogeneous space used in a traditional CA model. The probability of each cell change is not only decided by the local interactions of neighbor cells, but also by global information. Therefore, cells in LEAM are intelligent agents, which not only can capture local information, but also can sense the regional or global information, like social environment and economic trends. Also, LEAM has a hierarchical structure with multiple scale models incorporated. These models are loosely coupled in a modular framework where the information can be exchanged on the fly through aggregation or dis-aggregation approaches. By adapting such a strategy, LEAM can integrate cellular micro models and regionalized macro socioeconomic models into a single model framework.

LEAM FRAMEWORK

The LEAM framework consists of two major parts (Figure 8.1): a land use change (LUC) model, and urbanization impact models. The LUC model is the core of LEAM and answers the question: how does land use change under certain assumptions and policies? The second part, consisting of the urbanization impact models, is a further interpretation and analysis of urban land use change, and answers the questions: what does the resultant land use change pattern mean? How does it affect water quality, air quality, traffic patterns, property values and so on? Besides these two parts, a hidden part involving dialogue with planners and policy makers completes the workflow in a circle as feedback. Feedback is very import to LEAM as a planning support tool, asking planners questions such as: Are you happy with the land use change pattern? If not, how should policies or decisions be revised? What are the alternatives? These answers from planners can be used as the feedback input for running another scenario of the LUC model.

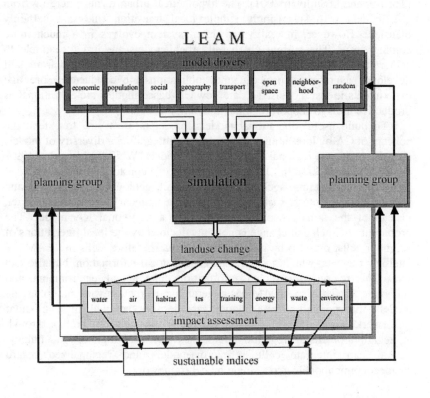

Figure 8.1   LEAM framework

In the first LUC model part, LEAM evaluates land use transformation potential by explicitly quantifying the forces that contribute to land use change. Model drivers represent the dynamic interactions between the urban system and the surrounding landscape. Each of these forces (also known as 'drivers') is developed as a contextually independent sub-model that allows for calibration before being run simultaneously in the LEAM model. Vacant lands, or developable lands, can be transformed to three categories of urban cells, residential, commercial/industrial and urban open space. Driver sub-models currently address urban dynamics influenced by regional economics, social factors, transportation infrastructure, proximity to city centers, facility infrastructure, neighboring land uses (where the CA model is adapted), geographic factors and spontaneous growth. The open architecture and modular design facilitates incorporation of extra local drivers into LEAM.

LEAM is a cell-based model, running on 30 m × 30 m GIS raster maps. An initial land use map based on the USGS National Land Cover Dataset (NLCD) is adapted to represent the current land use conditions in the region of interest. The model then uses the same resolution to simulate the socioeconomic parcel-by-parcel decision making that influences urban growth patterns (Deal 2001). Each of the drivers contributes to the calculation of the development probability of each grid cell. Each driver is developed as a sub-model; definitions are completed and run independent of the larger LEAM organization. Each cell's land use is changed based on the collective influence of each of the sub-models that represent actual forces present in the landscape. The influence of these changing forces is different for each study area. Consequently, each driver sub-model can be weighted so as to provide the appropriate local influence.

This modeling process determines the overall growth potential of each land cell. This potential, also called score, defines the relative preference among cells, but it is not exactly a probability. A regional input-output econometric model coupled with cellular micro models provides regional population change and economic trends over time. The results can be used in allocation models to deduce residential, commercial/industrial and open space regional demands. Based on these demands, the development potential of each cell can be adjusted to real probability to meet regional demand. At last, a Monte Carlo stochastic simulation is conducted on the probability surface to select developable cells for urban growth. Compared to the approach which selects the top cells with the highest probabilities, as in Engelen and White's model (Engelen, et al. 1995; White and Engelen 1997), the Monte Carlo approach gives a more visually realistic pattern, avoids the unfairness in selecting due to the spatial order, and enables the running of the simulation in parallel mode.

Environmental, economic and social system impacts of alternative scenarios such as different land use policies, growth trends and unexpected events can be modeled and tested in the LEAM modeling environment. LEAM's visual representation of each scenario's outcome provides an intuitive means of understanding the potential of decisions and acts as a catalyst for discussion and communal decision making.

CASE STUDY: ST LOUIS PLANNING SUPPORT SYSTEM

Like most other older metropolitan areas, St Louis faces the great challenge of sustainable growth. With relatively slow population growth, even negative growth in the urban core, the city continues to sprawl. According to Census data, the urban population had a very modest 7 per cent growth over the past three decades (1970–2000). However, new urbanized land mushroomed 125 per cent. That means people are leaving city neighborhoods for suburban ones. Consequently, open space and valuable farmland are lost; there is under-investment in the city core; the tax base and property values decline; and racial segregation and economic disparities become more severe, exacerbating socioeconomic problems. Traffic congestion and air pollution are also symptoms of urban sprawl. The East-West Gateway Coordinating Council (EWGateway), the metropolitan planning organization and council of governments for the St Louis region, forecasts continuing slow population growth for the region as a whole during the next 20 years, with some level of continuing decline in the core and expansion in the outlying counties.

Can we afford to let growth happen in this way? What will be the physical, fiscal and governmental infrastructure needed to support future growth? What are the potential economic, social and environmental impacts of a planning project or policy? How should we encourage economic development opportunities to maintain and build attractive, high quality, healthy communities that provide good jobs and a sustainable future for today's workers and for our children and grandchildren? These are some of the questions that come before the policy makers and planners of metropolitan St Louis. Unfortunately, answering these questions is not a trivial task. To attain smart growth, smarter tools need to be deployed. Compared to other urban modeling tools, LEAM has an open architecture, which makes it easier to incorporate multiple models and build a localized urban model. LEAM is also more open to inspection and, because it runs on supercomputers, can handle large regions at a very fine resolution. In 2003, EWGateway began to work with the LEAM research group and to use LEAM as a planning tool to assist communities in making decisions that affect the economic efficiency, health and viability of both the local community and the region as a whole. LEAM also provides a framework for public officials and citizens to enter into dialogue with planners and to evaluate public investments through scenario exploration. This is also the second full-scale application project, after the Peoria Tri-County project.

Spanning parts of the states of Missouri and Illinois on both sides of the Mississippi River, the study region includes ten counties, five in Illinois (Clinton, Jersey, Madison, Monroe and St Clair) and five in Missouri (City of St Louis, St Louis, St Charles, Jefferson and Franklin) (Figure 8.2). This area stretches about 120 miles from east to west and about 90 miles from north to south. It accounts for a little more than 30 million grid cells at 30 m × 30 m spatial resolution.

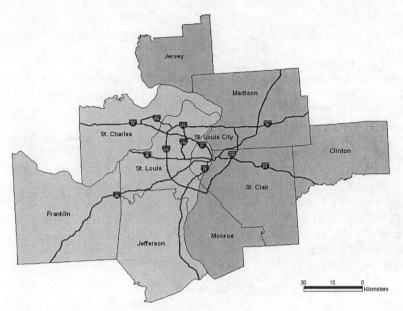

Figure 8.2   Study area: larger metropolitan St Louis

As the first step the team conducted a generic LEAM run for the region. In the generic application, the land use simulations were generated using a limited set of drivers, those for which national data sets could be used. The model parameters are either empirical or based on national averages. It is certainly not the best prediction; it can, however, serve as the basis for public discussion of regional drivers of land use change and scenarios of interest in public workshops.

Figure 8.3 is a map showing the outcome of one generic LEAM simulation; new areas of development in the year 2025 appear darker, and the larger dark areas towards the center represent existing development. Based on input from local planners and residents, the next step is to build a tailor-made LEAM model for the St Louis metro region. To develop a localized LEAM model a significant amount of work needs to be done collecting data and building models.

First, successful model runs require substantial accurate data be acquired and processed. It is impossible to get reliable results without accurate data input. Up-to-date and accurate land use is especially important to LEAM simulation. Multiple data sets from various sources have been used to produce a land use map for the year 2000, the start year of the LEAM model.

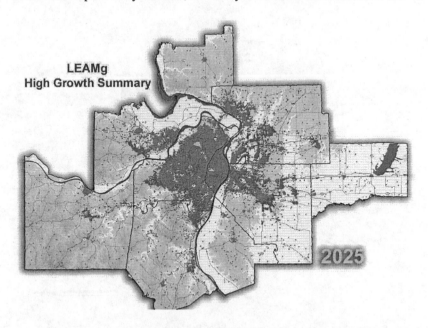

Figure 8.3   A generic LEAM simulation of 2025 land use change (The dark areas represent new growth in the region. Lighter central areas are existing development.)

Second, each sub-model needs to be refined and calibrated based on local data. For example, the input-output econometric model for projecting population and jobs has to be localized by using local data sets and the transportation model needs to be calibrated to emulate traffic congestion caused by bridges on the Mississippi River to plot out the local traffic pattern.

Third, a number of new sub-models need to be developed. The additional driver models are designed to capture the local urban growth pattern; impacts models are built to address the problems in this region. For instance, the generic LEAM simulations used proximity to city centers as a driver of land use change. Public review of these simulations suggested that land use change in this region is likely to be driven by proximity to other centers such as employment, shopping, health and cultural amenities. A spatial interaction model, also called a gravity model, is developed based on proximity (travel time) to these centers. Besides adding these attractors models, a social model was developed. The social model acts as a repelling driver, which discourages growth based on vacancy rate, rental rate, income level and other socioeconomic factors.

Finally, sub-models need to be integrated, tested and calibrated in the LEAM framework. This localized model is called a blueprint LEAM model. It is more powerful, capable and accurate than the generic model. When compared to the generic LEAM application (Figures 8.4 and 8.5), growth is shifted from the Illinois to the Missouri side, and much less growth happens in the urban core. More detailed quantitative analysis and validation further proves that this model produces a more realistic urban growth pattern in this region.

Armed with this blueprint model, the next step is to explore scenarios based on planning projects, policies or 'what if' assumptions. Here we will present two scenarios: one is the new bridge scenario showing how a transportation project affects the land use change pattern; the other is fiscal analysis showing what urban growth means to a city's fiscal status.

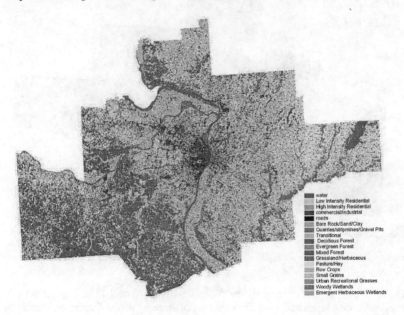

water
Low Intensity Residential
High Intensity Residential
commercial/industrial
roads
Bare Rock/Sand/Clay
Quarries/stripmines/Gravel Pits
Transitional
Decidious Forest
Evergreen Forest
Mixed Forest
Grassland/Herbaceous
Pasture/Hay
Row Crops
Small Grains
Urban Recreational Grasses
Woody Wetlands
Emergent Herbaceous Wetlands

Figure 8.4   A blueprint LEAM simulation of land use in 2025

New Bridge Scenario

Changes and enhancements to the road network in the region are likely to impact land use patterns. In this scenario, we assume that the new bridge on the Mississippi River planned in the first phase of the St Louis Long-range Transportation Plan is implemented, and after that no changes will be made to the infrastructure. In this case, the simulation was conducted in two steps.

First, we run the blueprint model from year 2000 to year 2007, when the planned bridge is finished. Then, the bridge is added to the road network and the travel times in the region are recomputed. The bridge will also affect proximities to infrastructure, city centers, employment centers, etc. At the same time, the economic model is run to assess the regional impact of the boost to the regional economy from this construction project. The simulation is run out to the year 2050 starting from the land use pattern at the end of 2007, with new development probabilities as a result of changed travel times, and new development targets from the economic model.

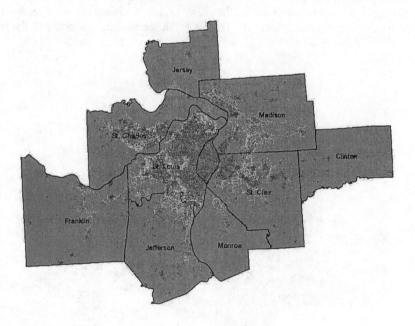

Figure 8.5   Summary map of the blueprint LEAM model (The lightest cells are residential developments, next are commercial developments. Darker gray areas are previously developed.)

The results are shown in the two regional maps (Figures 8.6 and 8.7). The first map summarizes change over time, and the second map compares change in this scenario with change in the blueprint model. The comparison map reveals how constructing the new Mississippi River Bridge is likely to pull more development to the Illinois side of the river, whereas the blueprint model had more development further away to the eastern and western fringes of development in the region. Urban growth can also be aggregated to counties and compared to the blueprint model. Figure 8.7 shows the extent to which development is likely to shift from Missouri to Illinois; within each sub-region, the relative share of different counties does not appear to change dramatically.

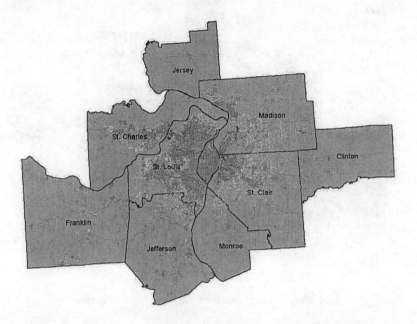

Figure 8.6   New bridge scenario summary map (The lightest areas are residential growth, next are commercial growth areas.)

Fiscal Impact Analysis

Land use change patterns have deeper implications. Fiscal impact is one of the further interpretations of urban growth. After considering various approaches already attempted by others, we tested a regression model based on per capita expenditure in the year 2000 using a sample of 73 jurisdictions in the Illinois portion of the St Louis metropolitan area. Our analysis suggests that there are not economies of scale: per capita expenditure increases as the number of households increase. At the same time, jurisdictions with greater population densities have lower per capita expenditures, and jurisdictions with greater economic activity (as measured by per capita sales tax collection) have higher per capita expenditures.

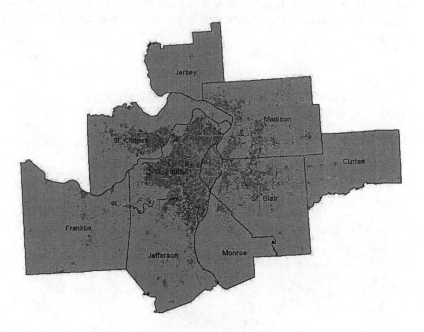

Figure 8.7   New bridge scenario and the blueprint model comparison

Table 8.1 illustrates the results of three scenarios for Belleville, IL, a fast-growing city. First, what if the population density were to increase by 50 per cent (along with a proportional decrease in land area to keep population at its present level)? Second, what if the number of households were to increase by 50 per cent (with a proportional increase in the land area to keep population density at its present level)? Third, what if per capita sales tax were to increase by 50 per cent (keeping number of households and population density constant)?

This model was also used to assess the fiscal impact of land use change around Belleville in a generic LEAM simulation of conditions in the year 2015. Table 8.2 compares two future scenarios with and without annexation to capture adjacent growth; the annexed area is indicated in Figure 8.8 and shows Belleville's existing municipal boundary laid over land use in the year 2015. The hatched area southwest of the city represents an area that might be annexed by the city to capture development, especially commercial growth. The St Louis LEAM project is an ongoing project. More detailed calibration will be conducted, more sub-models will be developed and dozens of scenarios will be implemented for local planners to consider. Exploring these scenarios will significantly enhance planners' insights into future land use and its impact. Although LEAM probably will not make decisions for planners, nor will it make planners smarter, it certainly will help them make smarter decisions.

Table 8.1   Fiscal impact scenarios for Belleville, IL

What If?	From	Change To	Per capita Expenditure Change	%	Amount	Total Expenditure
50% increase in population density	848	1272 People/ Sq Km	-$113	-17.3	$542	-$6,521,868
50% increase in number of households	17,603	26,405 Units	$27	4.1	$682	$1,122,625
50% increase in per capita sales tax collected	$154	$231 $/Person	$46	7.0	$701	$1,911,900

Table 8.2   The fiscal impacts of the Belleville growth and annexation, 2015 scenario

	Without Annexation	With Annexation	Difference
Population	59,861	64,963	5,102
Households	26,640	26,550	1,910
Per Capita Sales Tax	$142	$156	$14
Per Capita Expenditure	$562	$605	$43
Total Expenditure	$33,641,882	$39,392,615	$5,660,733

CONCLUSION

Planners need better tools to understand their cities and regions not just as economic systems or as static inventories of natural resources, but also as environmental systems that are part of regional and global networks (Campbell 1996). Remote Sensing and GIS are useful tools for planners, but inadequate to provide insights into possible urban futures. Urban systems, as complex systems, can best be understood by spatial dynamic modeling. To provide decision support tools for urban planners, LEAM was developed using an urban ecological approach. The LEAM environment enables users to capture stochastic influences and report the probable consequences of events in scenario format. What are the consequences of additional developments in

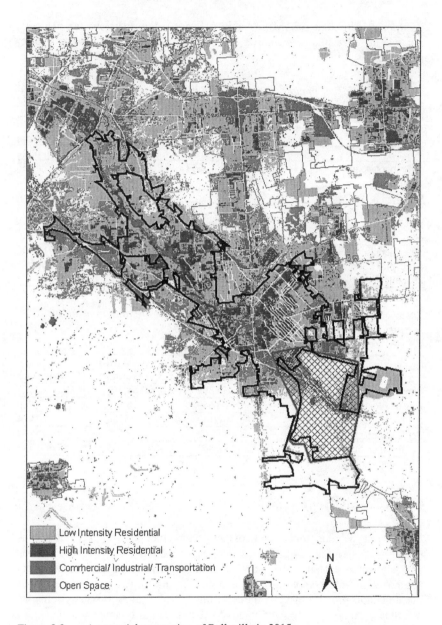

Figure 8.8   A potential annexation of Belleville in 2015

a particular part of a community or the impacts of a planned new road? How will growth policies impact the social wellbeing of existing residents? The completed work will enable planners and laypersons to assess the environmental impacts of urban land use policies and visualize the results.

LEAM was originally designed for analyzing relevant social, economic and environmental questions at community and regional scales. An open architecture however, enables the LEAM framework to be expanded, or incorporated within other macro simulation environments to address broader issues such as global change. The connections between climate change and urban land use dynamics have received increased attention. Urbanization is being related to climate change at both local (Chung, et al. 2004; Jauregui and Romales 1996) and continental scales (Bonan 1997); suggesting that urban land use change is affecting both micro and macroclimate patterns. Inverse relationships are also being expressed: that climate change, normally thought of in global terms, can have profound impacts on urban systems, such as transportation, utility infrastructure, air quality, water quality, energy and the general quality of life of urban residents (Patz, et al. 2001; Rosenzweig and Solecki 2001; Wilbanks 2003; Agrawala 2004; Duerden 2004). It seems imperative that climate change concerns should be woven into urban and regional planning efforts. It is critical for anticipating and responding to potential climate change impacts in order to minimize associated vulnerabilities. Leveraging existing planning, operations and investment to accommodate changes in climate and environmental concerns can have far-reaching implications for current policy and communal decision making. LEAM is a scenario-planning tool that enables planners to analyze and evaluate potential long-term policies or planning strategy under different climate change scenarios.

The importance of the collaborative approach and the democratization of the results in the LEAM process cannot be overstressed. This is the most important feature of the LEAM approach, which makes it unique when compared to other urban models. The LEAM dynamic urban modeling environment uses a multidisciplinary, distributed modeling and visual output approach to assess socially significant policy scenarios affecting land use change and its associated environmental impacts. Inefficiencies in some of the processes of developing competing computationally complex urban models may be hindering their progress toward application and utility. An open architectural approach to the LEAM environment exposes the fundamental modeling assumptions and variable interactions, increasing model transparency, transportability, validity and user trust in the reliability of the results.

LEAM has been successfully applied to Peoria, IL, and planners there are using LEAM in their daily decision making. Although the metropolitan St Louis project is still under development, some scenarios have been implemented and the results verified. The project demonstrates that LEAM can be a useful tool for planning decision support.

However, LEAM is not a finished product and probably will remain a dynamic work in progress. The causal mechanisms of urban system dynamics are still not well understood. Although LEAM may help to provide some insights, more sophisticated sub-models are needed to address the complexity of the social, economic and environmental issues inherent in urban system dynamics. The calibration of LEAM, as with other CA models, is still problematic, although recent research has shed light on possible solutions (Wu 2002; Maria de Almeida, et al. 2003). How to validate the model results is also being debated. Nevertheless, the spatial dynamic modeling process and the open framework of LEAM are not only useful to planners and decision makers, but also helpful to other academic researchers.

REFERENCES

Agrawala, S. (2004), 'Adaptation, development assistance and planning: Challenges and opportunities', *Ids Bulletin–Institute of Development Studies,* **35**(3): 50.
Almeida, C.B., M. Monteiro, M. Camara, et al. (2003), 'Stochastic cellular automata modeling of urban land use dynamics: empirical development and estimation', *Computers, Environment and Urban Systems,* **27**: 481–509.
Batty, M., H. Couclelis and M. Eichen (1997), 'Urban systems as cellular automata', *Environment and Planning B: Planning and Design,* **24**: 159–164.
Batty, M. and Y. Xie (1994), 'From Cells To Cities', *Environment and Planning B: Planning and Design,* **21**: S31–S38.
Batty, M., Y. Xie and Z. Sun (1999), 'Modeling urban dynamics through GIS-based cellular automata', *Computer, Environment and Urban Systems,* **23**: 205–233.
Birkin, M. (1994), 'Urban Landscape Dynamics–A Multilevel Innovation Process', in *Environment and Planning A,* Montanari, A., G. Curdes and L. Forsyth (eds), **26**: 1480–1480.
Bonan, G.B. (1997), 'Effects of land use on the climate of the United States', *Climatic Change,* **37**: 449–486
Brail, R.K. (2001), *Planning Support Systems: Integrating Geographic Information Systems, Models and Visualization Tools,* Redlands, CA: ESRI Press.
Campbell, S. (1996) 'Green Cities, Growing Cities, Just Cities? Urban Planning and the Contradictions of Sustainable Development', *Journal of the American Planning Association,* **62**: 296–312.

Chung, U., J. Choi and J.I. Yun (2004), 'Urbanization effect on the observed change in mean monthly temperatures between 1951–1980 and 1971–2000 in Korea', *Climatic Change,* **66**: 127–136.

Clarke, K.C. and L.J. Gaydos (1998), 'Loose-coupling a cellular automaton model and GIS: long-term urban growth prediction for San Francisco and Washington/Baltimore', *International Journal of Geographical Information Science,* **12**: 699–714.

Costanza, R. and V. Alexey (2004), *Landscape Simulation Modeling: A Spatially Explicit, Dynamic Approach Series,* New York, NY: Springer-Verlag.

Couclelis, H. (1985), 'Cellular Worlds–A Framework for Modeling Micro–Macro Dynamics', *Environment and Planning A,* **17**: 585–596.

Couclelis, H. (1987), 'Cellular-Dynamics–How Individual Decisions Lead to Global Urban Change', *European Journal Of Operational Research,* **30**: 344–346.

Couclelis, H. (1997), 'From cellular automata to urban models: New principles for model development and implementation', *Environment and Planning B: Planning and Design,* **24**: 165–174.

Deal, B. (2001), 'Ecological urban dynamics: the convergence of spatial modelling and sustainability', *Building Research and Information,* **29**: 381–393.

Duerden, F. (2004), 'Translating climate change impacts at the community level', *Arctic,* **57**(2): 204–212.

Engelen, G., R. White, I. Uljee, et al. (1995), 'Using Cellular-Automata for Integrated Modeling Of Socio-Environmental Systems', *Environmental Monitoring and Assessment,* **34**: 203–214.

Forrester, J.W. (1961), *Industrial Dynamics,* Cambridge, MA: MIT Press.

Forrester, J.W. (1970), *Urban Dynamics,* Cambridge, MA: MIT Press.

Hagerstrand, T. (1967), *Innovation diffusion as a spatial process,* Chicago, IL: University of Chicago Press.

Hannon, B. (1994), 'Sense of Place–Geographic Discounting by People, Animals and Plants', *Ecological Economics,* **10**: 157–174.

Hopkins, L.D. (1999), 'Structure of a planning support system for urban development', *Environment and Planning B: Planning and Design,* **26**: 333–343.

Jauregui, E. and E. Romales (1996), 'Urban effects on convective precipitation in Mexico City', *Atmospheric Environment,* **30**: 3383–3389.

Kammeier, H.D. (1999), 'New tools for spatial analysis and planning as components of an incremental planning-support system', *Environment and Planning B: Planning and Design,* **26**: 365–380.

Klosterman, R.E. (1999), 'The What If? Collaborative Planning Support System', *Environment and Planning B: Planning and Design,* **26**: 393–408.

Landis, J. and M. Zhang (1998), 'The second generation of the California urban futures model. Part 1: Model logic and theory', *Environment and Planning B: Planning and Design,* **25**: 657–666.

Landis, J. and M. Zhang (1998), 'The second generation of the California urban futures model. Part 2: Specification and calibration results of the land use change submodel', *Environment and Planning B: Planning and Design,* **25**: 795–824.

Landis, J.D. (1994) 'The California Urban Futures Model–A New-Generation Of Metropolitan Simulation-Models', *Environment and Planning B: Planning and Design,* **21**: 399–420.

Li, X. and A.G. Yeh (2002), 'Neural-network-based cellular automata for simulating multiple land use changes using GIS', *International Journal of Geographical Information Science,* **16**: 323–343.

Maria de Almeida, C., M. Batty, A.M. Vieira Monteiro, et al. (2003), 'Stochastic cellular automata modeling of urban land use dynamics: empirical development and estimation', *Computers, Environment and Urban Systems,* **27**: 481–509.

Maxwell, T. and R. Costanza (1997), 'An open geographic modeling environment', *Simulation,* **68**: 175–185.

Patz, J.A., M.A. McGeehin, et al. (2001), 'The potential health impacts of climate variability and change for the United States–Executive summary of the report of the health sector of the US National Assessment.' *Journal of Environmental Health,* **64** (2): 20–28.

Rosenzweig, C. and W.D. Solecki (2001), 'Climate change and a global city–Learning from New York', *Environment,* **43**(3): 8–18.

Schmidt, C.W. (1998), 'The Specter of Sprawl', *Environmental Health Perspectives,* **106**: 274–279.

Sipes, J.L. (2003), 'Visualizing community form–New digital tools help communities shape their own futures (CommunityViz, a program for landscape architects involved with community planning, land use planning, and natural resource management)', *Landscape Architecture,* **93**: 56.

Takeyama, M. and H. Couclelis (1997), 'Map dynamics: Integrating cellular automata and GIS through Geo-Algebra', *International Journal of Geographical Information Science,* **11**: 73–91.

Tobler, W. (1979), 'Cellular geography', in *Philosophy in geography,* G. Gale and S. Olsson (eds), pp. 379–386.

Torrens, P.M. and D. O'Sullivan (2001), 'Cellular automata and urban simulation: where do we go from here?', *Environment and Planning B: Planning and Design,* **28**: 163–168.

Von Neumann, J. (1966), *Theory of Self-Reproducing Automata,* Urbana, IL: University of Illinois Press.

Waddell, P (2002) 'UrbanSim–Modeling urban development for land use, transportation, and environmental planning', *Journal of The American Planning Association,* **68**: 297–314.

White, R. and G. Engelen (1997), 'Cellular automata as the basis of integrated dynamic regional modelling', *Environment and Planning B: Planning and Design,* **24**: 235–246.

Wilbanks, T.J. (2003), 'Integrating climate change and sustainable development in a place-based context', *Climate Policy,* **3**: S147–S154.

Wolfram, S. (2002), *A New Kind of Science*, Champaign, IL: Wolfram Media.

Wu, F. and C.J. Webster (1998), 'Simulation of land development through the integration of cellular automata and multicriteria evaluation', *Environment and Planning B: Planning and Design*, **25**: 103–126.

Wu, F.L. (2002), 'Calibration of stochastic cellular automata: the application to rural-urban land conversions', *International Journal of Geographical Information Science,* **16**: 795–818.

Wu, F.L. and D. Martin (2002), 'Urban expansion simulation of Southeast England using population surface modeling and cellular automata', *Environment and Planning A*, **34**: 1855–1876.

Wu, F.L. and C.J. Webster (2000), 'Simulating artificial cities in a GIS environment: urban growth under alternative regulation regimes', *International Journal of Geographical Information Science*, **14**: 625–648.

PART IV

Methods and Cases

9 Urbanization Effect on Rainfall: Implications for Drainage Infrastructure Performance and Design

Steven J. Burian

INTRODUCTION

Consider the hydrologic cycle divided into three compartments: the surface, subsurface and atmosphere, each containing stores of water and associated materials as well as providing pathways for fluxes within the compartment and between compartments. Urbanization augments residence times and fluxes of water (and pollutants) in the three compartments and between compartments. At the watershed surface the introduction of impervious surfaces and corresponding efficient drainage systems (Scheuler 1994), the removal of vegetative cover (Boyer and Burian 2002), and the compaction of the soil matrix during construction (Pitt, et al. 2003) have been documented to increase runoff volumes, pollutant loads and discharge rates. Increased pollution and runoff have in turn been linked to degraded water quality (EPA 2000) and altered stream geomorphology (EPA 1997), respectively. In the watershed subsurface compartment the effects of urbanization are similar to the effects of karstification (Sharp, et al. 2003). Pathways for enhanced fluxes of water within the subsurface and between the surface and subsurface are present. For example, urbanization enhances subsurface zones of permeability and water mains and sewer systems may develop leaks after construction and provide for enhanced recharge and transmission of pollutants to the hydrogeologic system (Foster 1996). The water content in the atmosphere and the fluxes between the watershed surface and the atmosphere can also be influenced by urbanization. Direct effects include the modified surface to atmosphere fluxes of water, energy and momentum caused by vegetation changes and the introduction of built materials and structures. Altered surface cover properties (such as albedo) and resultant fluxes are manifested in changes to local and regional temperature distributions (Bornstein 1968), wind patterns (Hjemfelt 1982) and air quality (Quattrochi, et al. 1998).

Urbanization's impacts on the hydrologic cycle produce myriad environmental consequences due to the numerous feed-forward extensions and non-linear feedbacks of perturbation. One compelling possibility is modification of rainfall, the subject of this chapter. Previous research has suggested that urban areas may be modifying rainfall due to one or a combination of the following four causes:

1. Atmospheric destabilization through enhanced thermal mixing due to low-level heating (such as from Urban Heat Islands [UHI]);
2. Increased turbulence and mechanical mixing due to increased aerodynamic roughness created by tall buildings;
3. Modification of low-level atmospheric moisture content, potentially caused by additions from urban-industrial sources as well as altered evapotranspiration; and
4. Modified microphysical and dynamic processes caused by the addition of cloud condensation nuclei (CCN) from automobiles and industry.

The effect on rainfall from the combination of these factors acting synergistically with local forcings (for example, terrain and coastline curvature) and global forcings (such as global climate change and El Niño) is difficult to isolate for a particular urban area. Decades of data collection and analysis and numerical simulations have provided limited insight into the interaction of factors and the potential consequences. Field experiments are difficult and expensive to conduct and to date have been impossible to control completely, while numerical models have been hindered by computational limitations. The results of urban-induced rainfall modification research therefore have often been difficult to validate, providing an open forum for debate. The following paragraphs review many of the important highlights of urban-induced rainfall modification research forming the foundation of the debate. The reader is invited to weigh the evidence before considering, later in the chapter, the assessment of drainage system performance and design impacts caused by modified rainfall patterns.

Some of the earliest observations of urban-induced rainfall modification were made by Horton (1921), who noted thunderstorm formation over two US cities (Albany, New York and Providence, Rhode Island) and dissipation of those storms within a short distance outside the limits when there were no other adjacent thunderstorms. In addition to urban areas, Horton identified shallow lakes with sandy shores and canyons and arroyos in the semi-arid western US as 'thunderstorm-breeding spots.' Horton surmised that if cities were affecting rainfall then this might have an important bearing on various engineering problems, including storm-sewer design.

At an international symposium on 'Man's Role in Changing the Face of the Earth,' Landsberg (1956) discussed the extent of climatic change caused by urban development. Among the various causes and effects described, a review of precipitation modification studies was included. Studies of rainfall in Munich (Schmauss 1927), Nürnberg (Kratzer 1937), and the Ruhr region (Weigel 1938) of Germany; Budapest, Hungary (Berkes 1947); Moscow, Russia (Bogolepow 1928); and Rochdale, England (Ashworth 1929) produced a range of evidence of urban-rural differences in rainfall totals, number of days with small amounts of rainfall and the number of heavy rainstorms. Landsberg (1956) built upon the evidence presented in these studies by analyzing rainfall data for Tulsa, Oklahoma in the Midwestern US. He found an increase of 5 to 10 per cent in mean annual precipitation in Tulsa compared to a background mean estimate based on rainfall data from surrounding rural regions. A seasonal analysis found the urban-rural difference to be greater for the cold months (October–March) compared to the warm months (April–September).

The detailed study of urban-induced rainfall modification in the US was advanced by the Illinois State Water Survey in the late 1950s and early 1960s with studies of cloud initiation and precipitation patterns over urban-industrial areas (for example see Pearson 1958; Changnon 1962; Stout 1962). The detailed climatological-statistical re-analysis of rainfall over La Porte, Indiana in the Midwestern US by Changnon (1968) identified significant warm season increases in total precipitation and in the frequency of rain days, thunderstorm days and hail days. The presentation of the La Porte rainfall anomaly incited significant scientific debate and spawned additional research of inadvertent rainfall modification in the US and elsewhere (see review by Lowry [1998] for more details on the surge of citations related to urban climatology that indicated the response of the scientific community to the work of the researchers at the Illinois State Water Survey). In one study responding to the identification of the La Porte anomaly, Ogden (1969) reviewed rainfall records from stations located downwind of a major steelworks in New South Wales and made a quantitative assessment of the processes potentially responsible for rainfall modification (through a quantifiable microphysical approach). Contrary to the conclusions made by Changnon (1968) regarding the effect of industry on rainfall, the records showed no influence of the steelworks on rainfall greater than 5 per cent of total rain, summer rain or light rain. Ogden concluded that the data suggested that the industrial effect was an unlikely explanation for the observed rainfall anomaly at La Porte.

Atkinson (1968; 1969; 1971) conducted a study of the effect of London, England on rainfall. The first part of the study used a climatological-statistical approach whereby a statistically significant maximum of thunderstorm rainfall was noted in London for the years 1951–1960 (Atkinson 1968; 1969). Ten summer storm events were identified as the cause of the maximum. Atkinson

(1970; 1971) then conducted a detailed study of two of the thunderstorms using radar echoes and a dense observation network of temperature, precipitation and other meteorological variables. The integration of the case study approach with the climatological evidence and a quantitative assessment of the microphysical processes provided a more comprehensive understanding of the cause-effect relationship than could be ascertained using one of the approaches independently. Changnon and Schickedanz (1971) voiced the value of this integrated approach for inadvertent weather modification studies and stressed the need to verify results from the climatological-statistical analyses with field experiments and to carefully devise cause-effect hypotheses during the early stages of the study. The conclusion from Atkinson's comprehensive study was that the urban effect was real, but it occurred only when conditions were 'just right.'

By the early 1970s studies of inadvertent rainfall modification by urban areas were following three basic approaches: climatological assessment of long-term rainfall records to identify spatial and temporal anomalies; microphysical approaches to quantify input of cloud condensation nuclei, heat and water vapor that could affect cloud microphysics; and intensive case studies of individual storm events (numerical modeling and large field experiment approaches had yet to evolve). Some cases made use of an integrated approach (see, for example, Atkinson's London, England study). Although the approaches to study the issue were being standardized, the results of the studies conflicted. The reality of the La Porte and other urban-induced rainfall anomalies and the causes were highly debated following their introduction.

As the debate was heightening in the early 1970s, an intensive field experiment and accompanying numerical modeling activities and laboratory investigations were organized into a major study of inadvertent rainfall modification caused by the urban area of St Louis, Missouri in the Midwestern US. The comprehensive goals of the Metropolitan Meteorological Experiment (METROMEX) were to:

1. Study the effects of urban environments upon the frequency, amount, intensity and duration of precipitation and related severe weather;
2. Identify physical processes of the atmosphere that are responsible for producing the observed urban weather effects;
3. Isolate the factors of the city complex which are the causative agents of the observed effects; and
4. Assess the impact of urban-induced inadvertent weather changes upon the wider issues of society (Changnon, et al. 1971).

The prodigious amount of data and analysis results derived from METROMEX are too extensive to review in their entirety here. Analyses were made of historical total rainfall, frequency and intensity of daily rainfall, frequency of thunderstorms, hail and severe rainstorms, weekday-weekend occurrence, diurnal rainfall distributions and urban effects caused by synoptic weather types (Huff and Changnon 1972). In addition, a dense network of observation stations collected new rainfall, hail and thunderstorm data and innovative numerical modeling studies were conducted. The compiled evidence suggested several urban effects on rainfall and meteorology (see Changnon, et al. 1977 for a detailed overview).

Although the amount of urban weather modification research declined in the 1980s, studies did continue to validate and extend the METROMEX investigations. For example, data analyses by Balling and Brazel (1987) found more frequent late afternoon and early evening storms in Phoenix, Arizona possibly linked to population growth and the unusual nocturnal wind flows. During the 1990s, climatological-statistical studies continued and more numerical modeling studies appeared. Several researchers reflected on previous studies and commented on the broader application of the results (for example, Changnon [1992] addressed global climate change). Others, such as Lowry (1998) questioned the research methods applied and the uncertainty associated with the explanations of results. These observations highlighted new scales of effect and summoned a renewed effort to verify the findings and reduce the uncertainty of results.

Recently the focus of urban-induced rainfall modification studies has been on re-visiting previous case studies using longer rainfall records and more sophisticated spatial and temporal statistical analyses, using newer satellite data sources and applying more complex and computationally intensive numerical models. For example, Shepherd, et al. (2002) performed a unique data analysis of rainfall rates measured by the Precipitation Radar (PR) aboard the Tropical Rainfall Measuring Mission (TRMM) satellite for the US cities of Atlanta, Georgia; Montgomery, Alabama; and Dallas, Waco and San Antonio, Texas. They found that the average percentage increase in mean rainfall rate in the identified urban impact zone over an upwind control area was 28 per cent. Several recent numerical modeling studies have provided insight into the cause-effect relationship between urban areas and the initiation and enhancement of convective thunderstorm activity (for example, see Bornstein and Lin 2000; Thielen, et al. 2000; Rozoff, et al. 2003). The urbanization of meso-scale meteorological models (Borstein and Craig 2002) and the work to incorporate urban representations in global climate models (Best and Betts 2002; Dickinson 2003; Jin and Shepherd 2005) signals the future development of new numerical studies of urban-induced rainfall modification at a range of space-time scales.

The sampling of studies of urban-induced rainfall modification reviewed above indicates the importance of the topic for those involved with weather prediction and modification, flood forecasting, hydrologic design and water management. Currently, the topic is receiving renewed attention because previous research focused on a limited cross section of cities and did not definitively identify the cause-effect relationship. A recently convened US Weather Research Panel recommended additional observational and modeling studies of the urban influence on rainfall (Dabberdt, et al. 2000). More research is needed because the world's population continues to urbanize at an unprecedented rate and the implications of urbanization-induced weather modification at the regional and global scales is not well understood. Moreover, the impact of local inadvertent weather modification on the design and operation of engineered urban infrastructure systems is not well-known and must be identified and quantified to develop appropriate mitigation protocols, if necessary.

Building upon the knowledge that urban areas may be affecting rainfall patterns, this chapter explores one possible feed back of rainfall modification. Urban-induced rainfall modification in general has the potential to feedback to the land surface and in numerous ways impact urban dwellers, infrastructure and ecosystems at a range of space-time scales. Clearly, alterations to rainfall patterns could have direct impacts on stormwater management, wastewater collection, water supply, agricultural production, reservoir management, stream geomorphology, biogeochemical cycling and ecosystem response. In addition, the aggregate effect of many urban areas may also impact the global climate through development of clouds and precipitation in and around cities (Changnon 1992). This chapter focuses specifically on the potential feedback impacts of urban-induced rainfall modification on stormwater drainage systems. The goal of the remainder of this chapter is to present an assessment of the potential effect of urban-induced rainfall modification on drainage infrastructure performance and design. The next section reviews previous studies of the effect of modified rainfall patterns on drainage infrastructure. The review will include both urban-induced rainfall modification and global climate change studies. The third section of this chapter presents an assessment of drainage infrastructure performance and design in response to possible levels of rainfall modification. The assessment is based on a case study analysis of drainage designs, design techniques and rainfall information specific to Houston, Texas, located in the southwest US. The final section summarizes the assessment, presents conclusions and outlines needs for future research.

BACKGROUND

Urban stormwater drainage systems are designed to limit, convey, store and treat rainfall runoff from urbanized areas. Drainage systems are composed of an intricate network of gutters, ditches, storm drains, culverts, channels and other hydraulic conveyance structures; detention, retention, infiltration, treatment and pumping facilities; and diversions, weirs, orifices, controls and other hydraulic complexities. The hydrologic and hydraulic design of the drainage system components and the analysis of the overall system performance are usually based on historical rainfall data most often in the form of frequency-duration relationships derived through statistical analysis of rainfall data. Consequently, if rainfall patterns were to change, the basis of design may be invalid and the design may prove to be inadequate or over-designed. Over-design needlessly wastes resources while flooding associated with system inadequacy could disrupt transportation, cause property damage and even loss of life in extreme cases (Changnon 1996). Of most interest from an urban drainage design perspective are the heavy rainstorms (more total rainfall and higher intensity) and the potential of urban areas to enhance the frequency and intensity of such events and consequently exacerbate flooding when not included in planning and design of storm drainage systems and flood control structures. Heavy rainstorms will be the focus of the assessment presented herein.

Several previous studies have investigated urban influences on higher intensity and larger total-accumulated-depth rainstorms, the type of storm events used to size drainage infrastructure components for flood control. One such study was a component of METROMEX that involved analyses of rainfall data collected by the dense rain gauge network established within and around St Louis to determine the impact of urban areas on heavy rainstorms (Huff and Vogel 1978). This work entailed analysis of the distribution of heavy rainstorms (defined as ≥ 25 mm of rainfall recorded at one of the rain gauges in the dense network) in 17 selected areas in and around the St Louis metropolitan area for a period of five summers. Higher ratios of normalized volumes of rainfall in the urban area to that of the upwind control area indicated that urban or topographic effects were present and important. This result, coupled with other work by the authors, suggested that the enhanced rainfall volume from heavy rainstorms in the urban-affect areas was due to stimulation of ongoing storms by modification of the dynamics and/or microphysics of cloud processes in the urban area.

Analysis of data from a dense rain gauge network in northeastern Illinois in and around Chicago for the summers of 1976 and 1977 suggested that the urban area experienced 176 per cent more heavy rainstorms (≥ 25 mm of rainfall) than the rural control area adjacent to the city (Changnon and Semonin 1977). Jauregui and Romales (1996) found that the daytime heat island in Mexico City seemed to correlate with intensification of rain showers during the wet season (May–October) and that frequency of intense rain showers had increased in recent decades in connection with the growth of the city. Changnon and Westcott (2002) analyzed 12 years of rainfall data from a dense rain gauge network in operation in Chicago since 1989 and compared the characteristics of heavy rainstorms to rainstorms that occurred from 1948 to 1980. Heavy rainstorms were defined as those lasting between one and 24 hours with intensities equal to or greater than the published two-year recurrence-interval event. Results indicated that 40 per cent more heavy storms occurred on average per year from 1989 to 2001 compared to 1948 to 1980. Furthermore, the spatial distribution of the total rainfall from the heavy storms for the more recent time period was found to be maximized over the city, confirming previous observations of enhanced rainfall in Chicago.

Some studies have expanded on the identification of a rainfall anomaly by translating the modified rainfall patterns to impacts on transportation systems and hydrologic response. Changnon (1980) defined urban flood events in Chicago to correspond to the one- to five-year recurrence-interval rainstorms. This information, coupled with previous work by Changnon and Semonin (1977) that found from 14 to 176 per cent more heavy rain events in the one- to four-year return periods occurred due to urban influences in Chicago, suggested that Chicago flooding events were increasing from 10 to 100 per cent due to urban effects. Changnon (1996) investigated the impacts of urban heat island enhanced rainfall events in Chicago on transportation systems. Analysis of transportation accident data indicated that on rainy days traffic accidents in the metropolitan area doubled, accident severity increased, and 57 per cent of the 30-minute or longer flight delays at Chicago O'Hare Airport occurred. The rainy-day influence on transportation accidents and flight delays leads one to the rational correlation between urban-enhanced rainfall activity and increased traffic accidents and flight delays, although research to quantify this relationship has not been performed.

The results of studies of climate change effects on urban drainage infrastructure are in most cases directly applicable to urban-induced rainfall modification studies. In general, climate change could potentially lead to more frequent extreme precipitation events, more frequent periods of rainfall and longer periods of drought. The increased frequency and magnitude of extreme rainfall is consistent with the potential effects of urban-induced rainfall modification. Several recent studies of climate change effects on drainage infrastructure are reviewed below for insight into methods to assess rainfall modification impacts on drainage system performance and design.

Denault, et al. (2002) developed an approach using rainfall trend analysis and numerical modeling to assess possible climatic change impacts on urban infrastructure and ecosystems of small watersheds. The linear trends of annual maximum rainfall amounts at numerous durations (five-minute, two-hour and so on) were determined and the linear model was used to project future rainfall intensities for the corresponding duration. This method assumes that the historical trend of short-duration rainfall intensities represents the future trend to be produced by climate change effects. The projected future intensities were then used in the United States Environmental Protection

Agency's (EPA) Storm Water Management Model (SWMM) (Huber and Dickinson 1988) to predict the effects of increased rainfall intensities on drainage infrastructure capacity. The case study of a small watershed in Vancouver, British Columbia, Canada found that the projected future rainfall intensities did not severely impact existing drainage infrastructure. Most of the system components in place had adequate capacity to handle the runoff generated by projected higher intensities. However, the authors stressed the site-specific nature of the study and suggested that the linear regression-SWMM approach could be used as a framework for assessing vulnerability of drainage systems in other cities.

Ruth and Kirshen (2002) presented a dynamic systems modeling framework to study climate impacts on the multitude of urban infrastructure systems and their interrelationships and interaction with other urban systems. The methodology was applied to study climate change impacts on five infrastructure systems of the Metro Boston area (transportation and communication, public health, coastal and riverine flood management, water supply and wastewater treatment and energy). A key component of the systems modeling process was to involve stakeholders and technical experts in the model component definition phase. One product of the work was the identification of six challenges for research and decision making about climate impacts on urban infrastructure.

Luijtelaar and Dirkzwawger (2002) studied the potential climate change effects on the functioning of common and alternative urban drainage systems. Climate change scenarios were incorporated into a time-series of rainfall from 1955 to 1979, and the precipitation series was used to check the design and performance of three types of drainage systems. The precipitation changes included increasing the highest precipitation intensities by 20 per cent, increasing the summer precipitation volume by 2 per cent, and increasing the winter precipitation volume by 12 per cent. For the reference drainage system, simulations using the modified rainfall time-series (6 per cent average rainfall increase) produced dramatic effects on the combined sewage overflow volume (40 to 70 per cent increase), overflow frequency (30 to 80 per cent increase), and overflow duration (25 to 85 per cent increase). For the second case study drainage system, the modified rainfall time-series increased the average duration of flooding by 50 to 80 per cent. And for the third drainage system the effect was an increased frequency of pond level exceeding the critical level.

These previous studies have noted rainfall modification (both urban-induced and global climate change related) impacts on urban infrastructure in general and drainage infrastructure in particular. The remainder of this chapter will present an assessment of the performance of hypothetical drainage system components in Houston, Texas and the implications for the design of future systems in response to potential urban-induced rainfall modification.

HOUSTON CASE STUDY

The goal of the case study assessment is to explore the implications of increased rainfall intensities on drainage system performance and design. The specific objectives of the case study are to:

1. Demonstrate a method to assess through simulation climate change impacts on the performance of drainage system components;
2. Explore potential design modifications of drainage system components necessary to respond to climate change; and
3. Determine if the City of Houston should be concerned with possible rainfall modification impacts on drainage systems.

The Houston metropolitan area was selected for this case study because it has three characteristics that make it an attractive location for possible urban-induced rainfall modification and because previous research has found evidence linking the urban area to spatial and temporal rainfall anomalies. The first characteristic that makes Houston an attractive location is its large sprawling metropolitan area. A size/population threshold for urban effects on rainfall has not been established, but urban effects have been noted for cities with populations as small as 200 000 (such as Tulsa, Oklahoma). Houston currently has a population of 1.9 million, making it the fourth largest city in the US. The entire Houston Urbanized Area, as defined by the US Census Bureau in 2000, has a population of 3.8 million, while the Houston-Galveston-Brazoria Consolidated Metropolitan Statistical Area (CMSA) has a population of 4.8 million. This relatively high population may not guarantee urban effects for Houston, but a population of this magnitude covering an area of 3350 km^2 in flat terrain (a variation of about 30 m from high point to low point) is equal to or exceeds the size of other cities with documented urban effects on rainfall. The second characteristic that makes Houston attractive for rainfall modification analysis is its subtropical humid climate with hot and humid summers and mild winters. In the summer the average maximum daytime temperature is 34°C. Humidity is greatest in the late summer and early fall, reaching a peak in July and August when the average dew point temperature is 22°C. The combination of a large city in a hot, polluted environment suggests potential for urban heat island effects, which are a suspected causative factor of rainfall modification. The third characteristic that makes Houston an attractive case study location is the frequent occurrence of convective rainfall during the warm season. A common conclusion from urban-induced rainfall modification studies is the presence of a warm season enhancement of convective activity, precipitation amounts and intensities. Average annual rainfall recorded at the Bush International Airport for the past two decades is 1200 mm, 310 mm during the warm season (June–August). Analysis of thunderstorm day and rainfall amount data stratified by month, as shown in Figure 9.1, suggests that rainfall during the warm season is dominated by subtropical convection, while spring and fall months (March, April, May, September and October) contain a mixture of convective and frontal storms, and the winter months (November, December, January and February) are dominated by frontal storms.

One disadvantage of Houston as the case study location is the complications introduced by the geography of the region. Although the metropolitan area is flat, thus eliminating the concern for orthographic effects on precipitation, the metropolitan area is located adjacent to Galveston Bay and near the Gulf of Mexico. The coastal influences on rainfall make the direct identification of the urban area as the causative factor of observed rainfall anomalies more difficult (Shepherd and Burian 2003).

Overall, the three characteristics of Houston reviewed above and the availability of rainfall data from long-term rain gauges and a dense rain gauge network outweigh reservations presented by the complexity introduced by coastal influences. The next subsection reviews previous research investigating rainfall modification caused by the Houston urban area.

PREVIOUS STUDIES OF HOUSTON: URBAN-INDUCED RAINFALL MODIFICATION

A thorough literature review uncovered several studies of urban-induced rainfall modification in Houston. Kelly (1972) analyzed 58 years of annual rainfall data from 22 rain gauges distributed throughout southeast Texas to determine if the data recorded by the Houston Weather Station were statistically different from the data collected by nearby rural gauges. Fourier analysis of that data indicated no significant difference between the rainfall trend at the Houston station and the trends of data at other stations outside the urban area. Additional analyses were performed on data from a 12-gauge Houston area network to determine monthly and annual spatial patterns for 1955 to 1970. The spatial patterns did not reveal a discernible maximum over the urban area. The rainfall patterns were also analyzed in conjunction with data from the Houston air pollution monitoring network to determine if increased air pollution was altering rainfall patterns. The analyses found no significant alteration of rainfall patterns due to air pollution.

Huff and Changnon (1973) studied weather records from eight US cities including Houston for indications of urban effects on rainfall. Their analyses of historical Houston weather data showed little evidence of an urban effect on monthly or seasonal rainfall patterns. However, a 17 per cent increase in rainfall from non-frontal storms within the city during the warm season (June–August) from 1964 to 1968 was found relative to areas outside the city. Analyses of thunder days and hail days related to growth of the Houston industrial sector suggested a possible urban-industrial effect on thunderstorms in the area of industrial growth.

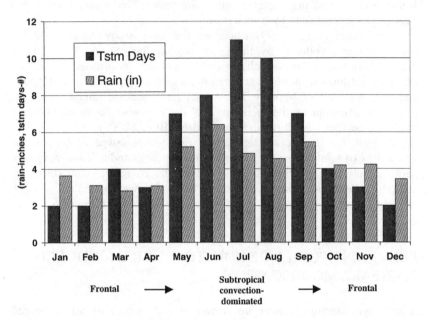

Figure 9.1   Mean thunderstorm days and monthly rainfall amounts for Houston (data from Texas Climate Center)

Data from 26 Houston area rain gauges for the time period 1901 to 1973 were analyzed by Crooker and Goldman (1974). Annual precipitation isohyets revealed significant precipitation modification along the axis of the mean annual near surface wind direction. The modification was attributed to urban development. Bouvette, et al. (1982) developed revised intensity-duration-frequency relationships for four Houston area rain gauges based on data up to 1981 and compared the revised intensities with those developed in 1961 by the US Weather Bureau (Hershfield 1961). The 24-hour, 100-year storm intensity had decreased by 13 per cent from 1961 to 1981 for the downtown gauge, but had increased by an average of 15 per cent for the three gauges in developing areas of the city.

A recent analysis of 12 years (1989–2000) of ground-based lightning data for the Houston area indicated that the highest flash densities recorded were over and downwind of the Houston metropolitan area (Orville, et al. 2001).

Meso-scale model simulations suggested that the elevated lightning densities were caused by either urban heat island-induced convergence or enhanced lightning efficiency by increased urban aerosols, or some combination of these effects. Since lightning is associated with convection in the atmosphere, the urban modification of lightning patterns suggests that the urban area may also be impacting rainfall.

Shepherd and Burian (2003) presented the results from the TRMM PR (Tropical Rainfall Measuring Mission Precipitation Radar) component of a downscaling analysis of Houston rainfall. Analysis of the mean monthly 'conditional' rainfall rates recorded by the TRMM PR at a height of 2 km supported the hypothesis that the central Houston urban area and the seasonally-variant downwind regions (generally northeast for Houston, but northwest-northeast during the warm season) exhibit enhanced rainfall relative to regions upwind of the city. The mean monthly rainfall rate was computed to be 2.97 mm/hr in the urban-impacted region (UIR), 2.66 mm/hr in the urban area (UA), and 2.06 mm/hr in the upwind control region (UCR). This represents an increased mean rain rate of 44 per cent in the UIR and 29 per cent in the UA compared to the UCR. The results are more compelling for the warm season. The mean monthly rain rate during the warm season increased 28 per cent in the UIR and 57 per cent in the UA. Results corroborated the findings from the Orville, et al. (2001) Houston lightning study, and they confirmed analyses conducted by Huff and Changnon (1973) and Bouvette, et al. (1982). The study also presented evidence that rainfall anomalies are linked to the urbanized region and not exclusively sea or bay breeze circulations.

Burian, et al. (2004) performed a downscaling analysis of rainfall data for southeast Texas to identify and quantify rainfall anomalies in Houston that may be caused by the urban area. Results from the conjunctive analyses of TRMM PR conditional mean monthly rain rates and rain gauge records provide strong evidence that Houston is modifying rainfall patterns in and downwind of the city. Rain gauge data analysis found the rain gauges in the urban-affected regions to have statistically significant higher average annual and warm season rainfall amounts from 1984 to 1997. The urban area had 22 per cent greater rainfall during the average warm season than the upwind control region and the downwind urban-impacted region. The isolated enhanced rainfall was consistent with the TRMM PR data analysis. To further refine the cause-effect relationship between urbanization and modification of rainstorms, the data from nine rain gauges were divided into independent storm events and analyzed for a relatively pre-urban time period and a post-urban time period. The average maximum one-hour rainfall intensity during the warm season increased from pre- to post-urban periods in the urban-affected region by 16 per cent, compared to a 4 per cent increase in the upwind control region. Moreover, the average number of 'heavy' (≥ 25 mm accumulated depth) rainstorms occurring during the warm season increased by 35 per cent in the urban-affected region from pre- to post-urban time periods, while a 3 per cent decrease was noted in the upwind control region. Thus, the cumulative evidence provided by the TRMM PR, rain gauge annual and seasonal totals and storm event characteristics indicates that the rainfall patterns are different in the urban-affected regions of Houston compared to the upwind control regions and the cause is likely related to urbanization.

Table 9.1   Changes in design rainfall amounts from 1961 to 1998

Duration	2-yr	5-yr	10-yr	25-yr	50-yr	100-yr
15-minute	-4.17	2.78	4.99	5.70	6.16	7.08
30-minute	-10.87	-10.40	-11.65	-14.52	-16.48	-17.94
1-hour	-15.22	-9.83	-7.52	-5.69	-3.96	-1.52
2-hour	-10.71	-5.79	-9.21	-7.01	-3.39	0.87
3-hour	-20.00	-13.04	-14.03	-10.53	-10.20	-8.99
6-hour	-17.33	-14.04	-10.10	-5.43	0.23	2.95
12-hour	-10.59	-12.70	-10.24	-5.49	-4.20	0.77
24-hour	-15.00	-14.18	-14.29	-3.84	-2.47	0.30

One additional step was taken to build upon the previous research efforts, explore the hypothesis of rainfall modification by Houston, and tie it to drainage performance and design. Design rainfall data is most often obtained from Technical Paper 40 (TP-40) published by the National Weather Service or the National Oceanic and Atmospheric Administration (NOAA) Hydro-35. A recent update of the Texas precipitation depth-duration-frequency data by the US Geological Survey (USGS) (Asquith 1998) provided for a simple comparison of how the design rainfall has changed from the circa 1961 TP-40 based on 10 to 15 years of rainfall data for most locations to the 1998 publication based on more than 50 years of rainfall data for most locations (see Table 9.1). Differences in data sources and frequency analysis methods may be responsible for some of the intensity differences, but general insight might be gained by observing how the short-duration rainfall amounts have changed with time and increased urbanization. One interesting observation is the decreased rainfall amounts for all durations for the two-year design event (the designated design event in Houston), indicating a potential historical over-design of storm drainage structures for present-day design rainfall. One other interesting observation that is consistent with other observations of urban-induced rainfall modification is the increase in 15-minute rainfall amounts. Although the changes are relatively small, their magnitude compared to the negative differences noted is substantial and identifies a potential short-duration rainfall intensity anomaly in the Houston dataset. Further analyses need to be performed to investigate how the design rainfall intensities have changed in rural areas.

The previous investigations have culminated in conflicting conclusions. However, the early studies were conducted using datasets with limited lengths of record or corresponded to periods when Houston was a large city, but not nearly as large (and influential over the weather) as the metropolitan area of today. More recent studies seem to be in agreement that convective rainfall activity (lightning, rainfall amounts and intensities) is different in the urban area compared to adjacent non-urban areas.

ASSESSMENT APPROACH

The assessment presented herein evaluated the impact of increasing rainfall intensities on the performance of existing drainage systems and the design of future systems using Houston as the case study location. The research addresses three questions:

1. What is the relationship between increased design rainfall intensity and system performance?
2. What magnitude of rainfall increase is necessary to affect performance significantly enough to mandate design modifications?
3. What alterations to design methods would produce a cost effective improvement to the system and provide the designated level of service for possible rainfall intensities of the future?

The ideal approach to assessing urban drainage infrastructure performance and design in response to potential climate change rainfall scenarios would involve predicting the modified rainfall characteristics and then simulating the response of the drainage systems. In addition, the approach would consider socioeconomic, political, cultural and other non-engineering influences on drainage systems as well as focusing on fundamental response processes that would produce results transferable across geographic, climatic, development and socioeconomic ranges. Given the potential myriad combinations of climate change and rainfall modification scenarios, infrastructure components, system layouts, design procedures, development patterns and receiving water bodies, a generalized analysis that incorporates detailed study of system components likely is not feasible. The approach taken in this study involves simulating the performance of drainage system components (and simple systems of components) and determining the required design modifications for the system components for incrementally increasing rainfall intensities and amounts. This is admittedly less than ideal by the above definition; therefore, the approach and the reasoning behind the process must be explained.

The assessment approach taken in this study focused on a subset of drainage system components and simple combinations of components designed according to widely accepted techniques in the US. There are many possible drainage system components that could have been included in the study. Table 9.2 lists several components and the primary performance issues and possible design modifications required in response to increasing rainfall amounts and intensities. The most common performance issues will be inadequate conveyance and storage capacity. Therefore, for this study, the storm drain and flood control detention basin components were selected to represent the conveyance capacity and storage capacity issues, respectively. Storm drains and detention basins are among the most common components of urban drainage systems.

Given the serious deficiencies in characterizing the global hydrologic cycle and thus the uncertainty in describing the global climate system, predictions of future climate scenarios are not reliable. And trying to dis-aggregate the global climate simulation predictions to regional or local levels is questionable. Thus, using global climate predictions as the basis for altering rainfall intensities and amounts was not chosen for this assessment. Instead, the basis for the assessment is to define a reasonable range of rainfall intensity (or amount) increases. Another approach eliminating the need for global climate predictions is to fit a model to historical rainfall data and use that model to project future rainfall intensities and amounts for a range of design durations. This is the approach that Denault, et al. (2002) used in their assessment of drainage system performance and design in response to climate change. They used a linear model fitted to the time-series of annual maximum intensities. This method provides limited information because it sets a single possible rainfall intensity or amount and because the use of a linear model to make the prediction incorporates significant uncertainty. Using a range of potential rainfall intensities and amounts allows for exploration of the gradient of change of performance and design aspects of the drainage system components in response to the gradient of change of rainfall characteristics. Further, a range of intensities accounts for the uncertainty of future rainfall characteristics.

The range of rainfall intensities and amounts selected for this analysis was based on the magnitude of the urban effect noted in previous studies of urban-induced rainfall modification. Burian, et al. (2004) noted approximately a 20 per cent increase of the one-hour maximum rainfall intensity for Houston rainstorms from a pre-urban to urban time period. This value was consistent with the magnitude of increase noted for studies in other cities such as St Louis, Missouri. To define the range of change, this 20 per cent magnitude increased to 50 per cent. A 10 per cent increment of change from 0 to 50 per cent was chosen for the incremental analysis.

In summary, the performance and design assessment conducted involved sizing underground storm drains and open-cut detention facilities using standard engineering techniques and current design rainfall data for Houston. Then, to assess the performance and design of the components for 'modified' design rainfall intensities, the design rainfall intensities (amounts) were systematically increased by 10 per cent increments up to 50 per cent for

Table 9.2   *Performance issues and possible design modifications for urban drainage infrastructure components in response to increased rainfall intensities*

Component	Performance Issue (possible rainfall modification effect)	Likely Design Modification
Storm Drain	Conveyance capacity insufficient leading to increased frequency of surcharge	Increase size
Inlets, Junctions and Manholes	Conveyance capacity insufficient to accept increased flow leading to increased surface flooding (possible safety risk on roadways)	Increase size or improve hydraulic efficiency of flow
Diversions	Probably used to divert higher flows and would not be affected by higher flows	Design modification not needed
Channel	Conveyance capacity insufficient leading to increased frequency of flooding; Flow rates increase leading to increased erosive forces	Increase conveyance capacity; Supplement erosion control
Culvert	Conveyance capacity unable to pass discharge leading to increased upstream flooding and increased erosion potential at entrance and exit	Increase conveyance capacity and modify erosion control at inlet and outlet
Flood Control Detention Basins	Inadequate storage capacity causing increased overflow/bypass	Modify outlet or increase storage capacity
Pumping Facility	Inadequate pumping capacity	Increase pumping capacity or alter operation strategy
Real-time control; SCADA	Control strategies may be inappropriate for higher discharges	Additional modeling might be necessary to identify correct operation strategies
Combined-Sewer Overflows	Inadequate storage or treatment capacity	Increase storage and/or treatment rate

(continued on next page)

*Table 9.2   Performance issues and possible design modifications for urban
drainage infrastructure components in response to increased rainfall
intensities (continued)*

Component	Performance Issue (possible rainfall modification effect)	Likely Design Modification
Infiltration Basins and Trenches	On-line devices will be overwhelmed more frequently and higher throughput will lead to earlier clogging of device	Increase storage capacity or convert to off-line device with appropriate pre-treatment
Water quality devices (sand filters, wet detention basins, biofilters, bioretention and so on)	These devices are sized to capture the water quality event (defined to approximate ~80% runoff volume capture or provide maximized cost effective control of annual runoff and pollutant load). In most cases these devices are designed off-line or to bypass excess flows, which does not alter their performance for water quality control.	Design modification may be necessary to provide additional erosion control if rainfall intensities of extreme events are exacerbated by urban effects

specified design durations. The performance of the components was assessed
using a numerical model (described in greater detail below). The design
assessment entailed re-designing the components using the modified rainfall
values and computing the change in component characteristics (drain diameter
and detention basin storage volume) necessary to provide the cost effective
design for the new rainfall intensity. Thus, the performance assessment results
will indicate the adequacy of existing components and the design evaluation
results will indicate the needs for design of future components. Additional
details of the assessment process specific to the performance or design
evaluations and the storm drain or detention basin components are included in
the following section.

ASSESSMENT PROCEDURES AND RESULTS

Performance

The assessment of rainfall modification impacts on the performance of storm
drains and detention basins designed with current rainfall information and
standard design techniques for the City of Houston is presented in this

subsection. The storm drain assessment is presented first, followed by the detention basin assessment.

Storm drains

A storm drainage system was designed for a 6.5-acre commercial catchment located in Houston. A schematic of the drainage system showing sub-catchments to each inlet and each conduit is displayed in Figure 9.2. A two-year return period was used to size reinforced concrete pipes to convey the design storm peak discharge. The 10-year design event was used to calculate the elevation of the hydraulic grade to be sure it was below the top of each drain segment and would not surcharge for the 10-year design event. The minimum pipe diameter permitted was set at 12 inches for this analysis and not the 24 inches mandated by the City of Houston to eliminate the over-design of the system with a 24-inch minimum. The 24-inch minimum will, however, be used below for the design assessment. Following the Rational Method of drainage design, the pipe sizes were calculated using the rainfall intensities that were determined from the City of Houston intensity-duration-frequency data for the calculated pipe times of concentration.

To assess the performance of the system, the EPA SWMM (Huber and Dickinson 1988) was used to simulate the runoff from each sub-catchment and the flow in the storm drain network in response to two-year, 10-year, 25-year, 50-year and 100-year Soil Conservation Service (SCS) Type III design storms. SWMM is a comprehensive deterministic stormwater runoff simulation program capable of simulating the transport of precipitation and pollutants washed off the ground surface, through pipe/channel networks and storage/treatment facilities and finally into receiving waters (Nix 1994). Given a suite of watershed surface cover parameters (for example imperviousness, slope and roughness) and a temporal and spatial distribution of rainfall, SWMM calculates the infiltration and surface storage of water and routes the rest as sheet flow. The sheet flow is routed to storm drain inlets and then to the discharge point using either a kinematic wave approximation or the full Saint-Venant equations (coupled continuity and momentum, see Chow, et al. 1988). Primary model inputs are:

1. The temporal and spatial distribution of rainfall;
2. Drainage catchment characteristics including area, per cent impervious-ness, slope, depression storage and drainage path roughness; and
3. Storm drain information including drain geometry, slope and roughness.[1]

The results of the storm drainage system assessment are contained in Table 9.3. The total number of pipes surcharged for different durations are listed for the 10-year design storm and larger (two-year not shown because there is no surcharging). Keep in mind that the surcharged pipes can be relieved with an incremental increase of rainfall because if an upstream pipe becomes surcharged it may alleviate surcharging in a downstream pipe. This unintended benefit of upstream surcharge can in some cases be used to optimize the operation of the drainage system (in-system storage). The results illustrate that an incremental increase in 24-hour rainfall depth could significantly increase the number of pipes operating under surcharge conditions and possibly increase flooding near the upstream junction. For example, the results for the 10-year design event suggest that a rainfall modification of 10 to 20 per cent is insignificant as it only floods one pipe (P-7 in Figure 9.2) for a significant time, but the 30 per cent rainfall modification produced surcharged conditions in nearly 30 per cent of the pipes, and a 40 per cent increase surcharged 65 per cent of the pipes. Other recurrence intervals display a similar outcome. An incremental increase in rainfall modification can trigger new flooding in 50 per cent or more of the network.

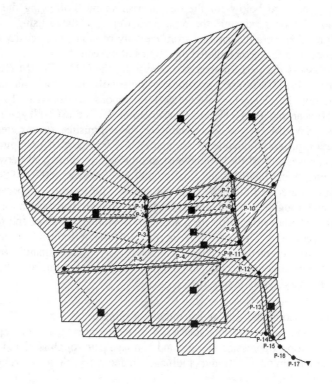

Figure 9.2   SWMM schematic of drainage system used for performance evaluation. Cross-hatched areas are sub-catchments, circles are junctions, and solid lines are pipes (The outfall of the system is the triangle located at the lower right corner.)

Table 9.3   Number of pipes surcharged for a range of design storm, duration and rainfall intensity increase combinations (total of 17 pipes)

Rainfall Intensity Increase	Number of pipes surcharged	Number of pipes surcharged at least 20 minutes	Number of pipes surcharged at least 40 minutes	Number of pipes surcharged at least 60 minutes
10-yr, 100% P	0	0	0	0
10-yr, 110% P	1	0	0	0
10-yr, 120% P	2	1	0	0
10-yr, 130% P	6	5	0	0
10-yr, 140% P	12	11	1	0
10-yr, 150% P	14	12	6	0
25-yr, 100% P	6	5	0	0
25-yr, 110% P	12	11	1	0
25-yr, 120% P	14	14	9	0
25-yr, 130% P	15	14	12	0
25-yr, 140% P	17	17	14	0
25-yr, 150% P	17	17	17	10
50-yr, 100% P	14	14	9	0
50-yr, 110% P	17	15	13	0
50-yr, 120% P	17	17	14	2
50-yr, 130% P	17	17	17	12
50-yr, 140% P	17	17	17	14
50-yr, 150% P	17	17	17	14
100-yr, 100% P	17	17	14	2
100-yr, 110% P	17	17	17	11
100-yr, 120% P	17	17	17	14
100-yr, 130% P	17	17	17	14
100-yr, 140% P	17	17	17	16
100-yr, 150% P	17	17	17	16

Part of the motivation for the initial demonstration of this assessment approach is to derive general observations applicable to other drainage components and locations and to identify areas of improvement for future assessments. One general observation is the potential benefit of the over-design requirements including minimum pipe diameters and the requirement that downstream pipe must have an equal or larger size than the upstream pipe. The first requirement was not instituted for this design, but considering the results one could conclude that the amount of surcharging would have been reduced in the pipes with diameters less than 24 inches (more than 50 per cent of the pipes). For the second requirement, the pipes that were sized by this requirement recorded lower durations of surcharge. Thus, the two over-design requirements instituted by most cities would produce system robustness to climate change rainfall intensity increases.

Based on the storm drain assessment, one improvement to the analysis would be to incorporate another measure of performance in addition to the total minutes surcharged. If a pipe is surcharged it indicates failure at the pipe, but looking at the extent of street flooding at the junction/inlet, the level of service impacted or the damage caused would translate the results into tangible system performance terms.

Detention basin

For the detention basin performance assessment, a basin was designed to control the post-development peak discharges from a hypothetical 100-acre watershed to pre-development levels. SWMM was used to simulate the pre-development and post-development runoff from the watershed. For both pre- and post-development conditions, the watershed was assigned reasonable sub-catchment parameters including depression storage, surface roughness and infiltration parameters that fell within the range of values used in other calibrated SWMM models of larger watersheds in the Houston area. For post-development conditions the drainage from the hypothetical watershed enters a detention basin with vertical walls 8-feet deep. The volume and outlet orifice size of the detention pond were determined by performing trial-and-error reservoir routing (McCuen 1998). Separate basin designs were completed for the two-year, five-year, 10-year, 25-year, 50-year and 100-year, 24-hour SCS Type III design storms. The performance of each detention basin was assessed only for the incremental range of design storms corresponding to its recurrence interval. For example, the performance of the two-year design was assessed for the two-year design storm with the total rainfall depth of that event increased by 10 per cent incrementally up to a 50 per cent increase. Two measures of detention basin performance were included in the analysis: total minutes facility was under emergency bypass operation and the total volume bypassed. Both measures indicate level of design failure.

Figure 9.3 shows the number of minutes the facility is operating in bypass mode for the six detention basin designs and six design storm recurrence intervals. Two noteworthy observations are apparent. First, note the relatively high number of bypass minutes for the first 10 per cent increment of 24-hour rainfall depth increase. For all design storms, the average minutes bypassed was 120 for the first 10 per cent increase of the design 24-hour rainfall amount. The gradient of increase for the bypass minutes reduces with increasing incremental rainfall amount. Second, note that the number of minutes of overflow generally decreases as the recurrence interval increases. This suggests that the larger design storage volumes and outlet orifices will have overflow durations for shorter periods for the same level of rainfall amount increase. In other words, detention basins designed for larger recurrence intervals provide more reliable control for variability of rainfall amount above the design level for that event. Table 9.4 presents the bypass volume for each scenario normalized to the design pond volume. The normalized bypass volumes suggest that the overflow volume relative to the design pond volume is nearly independent of the recurrence interval, except for the rainfall increases of 40 and 50 per cent.

Based on the detention basin performance assessment (and similar to the storm drain performance assessment conclusion) additional measures of performance should be included in future assessments. The objective of most detention basins is to reduce downstream peak discharges and thus reduce downstream flood impacts. Incorporating a general measure of downstream flood impact caused by rainfall intensity variability is needed.

Design

The assessment of the effect of increasing design rainfall intensities (amounts) on the design of storm drains and detention basins is presented in this subsection. The storm drain assessment is presented first, followed by the detention basin assessment.

Storm drain

An assessment of the design modifications required for a drainage system servicing a six-acre parking lot was performed. Two drainage design approaches were assessed: a traditional curb and gutter layout with raised island, and an alternative site design approach with depressed islands and on-site management (low-impact development [LID] approach).

Figure 9.5 shows the plan view drawings of the two design alternatives. The traditional development type includes raised islands, curb and gutter and a network of underground pipes. The LID layout replaces the raised islands with depressed bioretention areas, the overflow section of the parking lot with modular porous pavement blocks, and one of the underground conduits with a grassed swale containing a biofilter. Drainage systems for parking lots and other developments have been constructed in Houston following both the traditional and LID design concepts. Traditional designs are more common, but the LID concept, which is consistent with smart growth principles, is being used more frequently as designers and plan reviewers gain more experience working with the concept. A parking lot was chosen for this assessment (instead of a residential neighborhood or commercial strip mall) because it is a common, straightforward design allowing for exploration of rainfall intensity variability effects on design and how this effect differs between traditional and LID designs. In addition, variations of the elements included in the design (such as inlet location, pipe placement and so on) could have been changed, but again the goal was to provide a simple design that limited unique features in order to make the results more widely applicable.

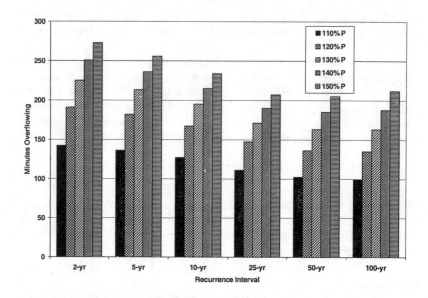

Figure 9.3   Total minutes detention pond is bypassing overflow for the range of recurrence interval storm event-design combinations and 24-hour rainfall depth incremental increases

To be consistent with drainage design practice for Houston, both parking lot designs followed the hydrologic and hydraulic design procedures set forth in 'Chapter 9: Storm Water Design Requirements' of the *City of Houston Design Manual*. For design of areas up to 600 acres the manual recommends using the Rational Method to determine the design discharge and Manning's equation to size the conduits. The traditional design was based on runoff coefficients of 0.85 for recurrence intervals less than 25 years and 0.95 for recurrence intervals of 25 years or greater (McCuen 1998). Representing LID practices in Rational Method calculations can be accomplished in two ways. First, the times of concentration for sub-catchments can be increased to represent increased flow paths, disconnected impervious areas, and roughened surfaces associated with LID practices. Second, the runoff coefficient can be reduced to represent impervious areas being disconnected and stormwater being retained or infiltrated on-site. The inability to account for detention storage in the conventional Rational Method is a major drawback for application to LID design, yet the simplicity of the method makes it attractive to designers. More appropriate techniques accounting for the distributed storage element of LID would use computerized rainfall-runoff models that can represent more detail in the sub-catchment. But to be consistent with standard design practice, complex numerical models (such as SWMM) were not used in the storm drain design assessment.

Table 9.4   Bypassed volume expressed as a per cent of the total design pond volume for the range of design storms and incremental rainfall depths tested

24-hr Rainfall Depth Incremental Change	2-yr	5-yr	10-yr	25-yr	50-yr	100-yr
110% P	13	14	13	14	14	15
120% P	28	28	29	31	30	32
130% P	44	44	44	45	49	48
140% P	57	59	60	64	65	71
150% P	73	77	79	80	89	91

For the LID design the addition of bioretention areas and porous pavement reduced the runoff coefficients to 0.75 and 0.85 for the less than 25-year and 25-year or greater recurrence intervals, respectively. The times of concentration for each conduit in the traditional design will be computed using the calculation methods presented in the *City of Houston Design Manual*. To represent the effect of the bioretention areas, porous pavement and the biofilter, the times of concentration were increased five minutes for each device (a reasonable design hydraulic residence time). Although the larger storm events will likely bypass or completely overwhelm the bioretention device, the hydraulic residence time was still applied for computing the time of concentrations for each downstream component. These assumptions were deemed reasonable and consistent with the design requirements for the City of Houston.

For the traditional design, the four underground storm drains were sized, while for the LID design the three underground storm drains and the entrance-way culvert were sized. The LID practices (bioretention areas, biofilters and so on) could also be included in this assessment, but their design is likely to be less influenced by the larger design events. The sizing of the on-site LID practices is based on smaller water quality capture volumes that would not be affected by the modification of the less frequent drainage design events. In most cases, LID practices are designed to bypass or divert the higher flow rates associated with the traditional drainage design events. Additional diversion/bypass capacity and erosion control or stability fortification would be possible design modifications. For storm drain design in Houston a minimum of a two-year recurrence interval and a minimum pipe diameter of

24 inches are required. For this assessment, a range of design storm recurrence intervals (two-year, five-year, 10-year, 25-year and 100-year) were included to increase the applicability to other cities and locations that may have other design requirements. The design process was as follows. The time of concentration for each pipe was determined following the *City of Houston Design Manual*. This time of concentration was then used to determine the design rainfall intensities for the two-year, five-year, 10-year, 25-year and 100-year recurrence intervals using the intensity-duration-frequency curve in the *City of Houston Design Manual*. The conduits for both parking lot layouts were then sized using Manning's equation and reinforced concrete pipe standard sizes, using slopes of 2 per cent for pipes 1 and 2 and 1 per cent for pipes 3 and 4. The rainfall intensities were then incrementally increased by 10 per cent up to 50 per cent and the design was repeated.

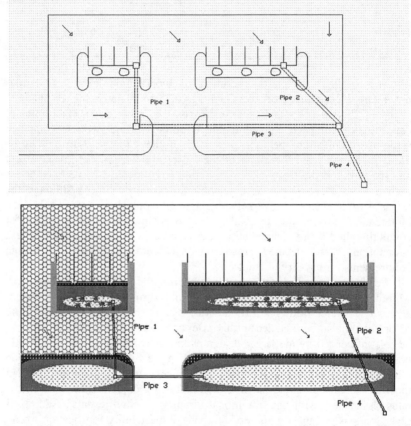

Figure 9.4   Plan views of two parking lot designs: (top) traditional curb and gutter design and (bottom) low-impact development design

The results of the storm drain design assessment indicated that the size of pipes 1 and 2 did not change with increasing intensity if a minimum pipe diameter of 24 inches was required. This observation holds for both design alternatives. The implication of this is that the 24-inch minimum pipe size mandated by the City of Houston (and other cities) is relatively conservative and permits a 50 per cent increase in intensity without increasing the required pipe size. This over-design benefit will only be present at upstream ends of the drainage system, areas where local flooding has less opportunity to create severe impacts because the flow rates are much smaller. If the minimum pipe size were set at 12 or 18 inches (as it is in some municipalities) then more changes of design pipe size would be noted for all pipes, especially numbers 3 and 4.

Tables 9.5 and 9.6 display the design pipe sizes for pipes 3 and 4, respectively. The pipe sizes shown in Table 9.5 indicate that the design size of pipe 3 would only change for the 25-year and 100-year recurrence intervals. For the 100-year recurrence interval event, a 20 per cent increase in rainfall intensity would require an increase in pipe diameter from 24 to 27 inches (following standard reinforced concrete pipe size increments). The pipe sizes in Table 9.6 indicate that the design size of pipe 4 would change for the two-year, 10-year, 25-year and 100-year intervals. For the two-year return period, the design pipe size does not change for the range of rainfall intensity increases. For a 100-year return period, a 10 per cent increase in intensity will change the design pipe diameter from 30 to 33 inches. The results in Tables 9.5 and 9.6 suggest that the design pipe diameter could be inadequate if rainfall intensities were altered by urban-induced rainfall modification. The required changes for an upstream area of the watershed, however, are limited due to the conservative minimum pipe diameter requirement (24 inches) and the standard incremental pipe sizes for reinforced concrete pipe. The LID layout results are contained in Tables 9.7 and 9.8. As expected, the results indicate that in general smaller pipe diameters would be needed for the LID approach. LID is meant to reduce the amount of runoff by promoting on-site infiltration and storage. Thus the necessary size of downstream drainage infrastructure is reduced. With the reduced runoff production, the number of pipe size increases caused by the increasing design rainfall intensity is less, as shown in Tables 9.7 and 9.8, compared with the traditional design.

One general observation from the storm drain design assessment is the increasing effect of rainfall intensity changes on required design size with downstream progression in the drainage system. The frequency and magnitude of pipe size changes is greatest in pipe 4 (the downstream most pipe), while pipes 1 and 2 did not require changes. This suggests that a more comprehensive impact assessment would be multi-scale, comparing lot, catchment, watershed and basin scale effects.

Table 9.5   Design pipe diameters (in) for increasing levels of intensity (pipe 3)

Return Period	Original i	110%i	120%i	130%i	140%i	150%i
2-yr	24	24	24	24	24	24
5-yr	24	24	24	24	24	24
10-yr	24	24	24	24	24	24
25-yr	24	24	24	24	27	27
100-yr	24	24	27	27	27	27

Table 9.6   Design pipe diameters (in) for increasing levels of intensity (pipe 4)

Pipe	Original i	110%i	120%i	130%i	140%i	150%i
2-yr	24	24	24	24	24	24
5-yr	24	24	27	27	27	27
10-yr	27	27	27	27	30	30
25-yr	30	30	30	30	33	33
100-yr	30	33	33	33	36	36

Table 9.7   Design pipe diameters (in) for increasing levels of intensity (pipe 3) in the LID layout

Pipe	Original i	110%i	120%i	130%i	140%i	150%i
2-yr	24	24	24	24	24	24
5-yr	24	24	24	24	24	24
10-yr	24	24	24	24	24	24
25-yr	24	24	24	24	24	24
100-yr	24	24	24	24	24	27

Table 9.8   Design pipe diameters (in) for increasing levels of intensity (pipe 4) in the LID layout

Pipe	Original i	110%i	120%i	130%i	140%i	150%i
2-yr	24	24	24	24	24	24
5-yr	24	24	24	24	24	24
10-yr	24	24	24	27	27	27
25-yr	27	27	27	30	30	30
100-yr	27	30	30	30	33	33

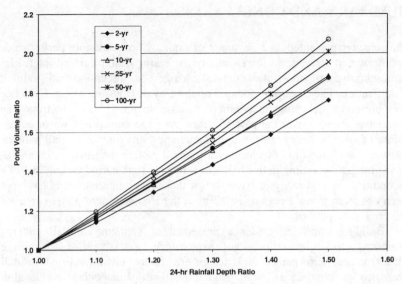

Figure 9.5   Variation of pond volume ratio to the 24-hour rainfall depth ratio for a range of design storms

Detention basin

The detention basin design assessment involved evaluating the necessary design volume modification for the previously analyzed detention pond scenario for six design storms (two-year, five-year, 10-year, 25-year, 50-year and 100-year). Again, SWMM was used to perform the modeling and the SCS Type III design storm was used to represent the rainfall temporal distribution. The design orifice size for each recurrence interval-rainfall intensity increase combination was determined and used in the assessment of the necessary volume modification. For each new orifice size the design storage volume was determined through trial-and-error. Figure 9.5 shows the variation of the ratio of new design storage volume (the size required to control the modified rainfall-runoff event) to old design storage volume (the size required to control the original rainfall-runoff event) for the range of incremental increases in design rainfall amount and recurrence intervals. The results indicate a greater than one-to-one incremental change in required storage volume per incremental change in design rainfall depth. In fact, there is a nearly uniform design modification of twice as much incremental storage volume required to handle the incremental rainfall increase. For example, for the 100-year design, an incremental rainfall change of 10 per cent requires a 20 per cent increase in pond storage volume. This is important because it indicates that relatively small changes in design rainfall depth could have significant impacts on required design pond storage volume.

SUMMARY AND CONCLUSIONS

This chapter presented an assessment of drainage infrastructure performance and design in response to incrementally increasing design rainfall intensities representative of possible climate change or urban-induced rainfall modification. The case study focused on the City of Houston, Texas. Evidence was presented indicating that rainfall patterns in the Houston metropolitan area have changed over the past 50 years. Average annual and warm season rainfall amounts, heavy rainstorm characteristics, and diurnal rainfall patterns have all been found to have increased (diurnal pattern modified) from an 18-year time period ending in the 1950s to a 16-year time period ending in 1999. In addition, spatial analyses have shown that these same increases have not been observed in rural regions adjacent to the Houston metropolitan area for the same time periods.

Building upon the evidence presented of changing rainfall patterns attributed to urbanization, an exploratory assessment of drainage infrastructure performance and design for future urban-modified rainfall scenarios was conducted. The drainage infrastructure components evaluated in the assessment were storm drains and detention basins, two of the more common elements of urban storm drainage systems. The assessment suggested that the performance of existing drainage system components would be impacted by increased design rainfall intensities if urbanization or global change increases rainfall amounts and intensities for a range of storm durations. The design modifications necessary are still uncertain because current drainage infrastructure is typically over-designed. Deriving widely applicable general conclusions based on one assessment of two infrastructure components in one city is not possible. Further assessments are necessary. However, several general and specific observations based on the performance and design assessment of hypothetical Houston storm drains and detention basins can be made:

- Incremental increases of the design rainfall intensity by 10 per cent can produce extensive surcharged conditions in a small drainage network. Higher intensity changes produce longer duration flooding throughout the network.
- Changes to 24-hour design rainfall amounts would increase pond overflow duration and volume, and the magnitude of the overflow changes increases as rainfall modification increases.
- Changes in design rainfall intensity as small as 10 per cent could potentially modify the design pipe size for the most basic of drainage systems for rarer design events (25-year and 100-year return periods) for both traditional and low-impact development parking lot designs.

- Potential implications of rainfall modification effects on sizing storm drains is limited at the site design level (upstream end of watershed) due to conservative minimum pipe size standards, rules requiring the size of downstream pipes to be at least as large as the upstream pipe, and incremental pipe sizes available for selection.
- The design pipe size would be reduced if sufficient LID practices are implemented. However, since LID practices are likely designed for smaller sized rainfall-runoff events, the urban-induced enhancement of larger events might impact the overall drainage system similarly whether LID is implemented or traditional drainage design approaches are used.
- The design storage volume of detention ponds using reservoir routing and SCS design storms would be increased by twice as much as the corresponding rainfall modification.

The effects of climate change and urban-induced rainfall modification are not singular to urban drainage systems. Rainfall modification affects the overall complex urban system, of which urban drainage is one piece. Detailed studies of potential climate change impacts on individual infrastructure systems must continue to be conducted, as should more general studies of infrastructure impacts and interdependencies. More studies should be performed that move towards integrating the detailed and general studies into comprehensive analyses to produce more comprehensive decision making and policy forming information. Other considerations to include in future studies are:

- What are the long-term life-cycle costs associated with drainage systems designed to accommodate potential climate change rainfall scenarios?
- What is the effect of the scale of design?
- Are there feedback mechanisms from development that may be influencing rainfall modification processes? For example, if LID is implemented vigorously might there be reduced alteration of the hydrologic cycle (for example, surface fluxes) and a potentially cooler urban environment (reduced urban heat island), which may mitigate the urban-induced rainfall modification?
- What are the implications of the modification of hydrologic drivers for ecosystem response under different rainfall modification scenarios?
- How might the level of expected service be modified instead of the design under different climate change scenarios? Might more frequent minor nuisance flooding of streets and low-lying property away from structures be more acceptable instead of the additional costs for more conveyance and storage capacity in the drainage system?

ACKNOWLEDGEMENTS

Much of the work reported in this chapter was supported by a grant from NASA's Earth Science Enterprise-Precipitation Measurement Missions Program, grant number NNG04GC94G. Several individuals made contributions to this chapter including J. Marshall Shepherd from NASA, Parastou Hooshialsadat from the University of Arkansas, and Shannon Reynolds and Cameron Hales from the University of Utah. Their efforts are gratefully acknowledged.

NOTE

1. For this assessment SWMM, version 5, available for download from the EPA website (http://www.epa.gov/ednnrmrl/swmm/) was used.

REFERENCES

Ashworth, J.R. (1929), 'The influence of smoke and hot gases from factory chimney's on rainfall', *Quarterly Journal of the Royal Meteorological Society*, **55**: 334–350.

Asquith, W.H. (1998), 'Depth-duration frequency of precipitation for Texas', *Water–Resources Investigations Report*, 98-4044, Austin, TX: US Geological Survey.

Atkinson, B.W. (1968), 'A preliminary investigation of the possible effect of London's urban area on the distribution of thunder rainfall, 1951–1960', *Transactions of the Institute of British Geographers*, **44**: 97–118.

Atkinson, B.W. (1969), 'A further examination of the urban maximum of thunder rainfall in London, 1951–60', *Transactions of the Institute of British Geographers*, **48**: 97–120.

Atkinson, B.W. (1970), *The reality of the urban effect on precipitation–A case study approach*, WMO Technical Note No. 108, pp. 342–360.

Atkinson, B.W. (1971), 'The effect of an urban area on the precipitation from a moving thunderstorm', *Journal of Applied Meteorology*, **10**: 47–55.

Balling, R.C. and S.W. Brazel (1987), 'Recent changes in Phoenix, Arizona Summertime Diurnal Precipitation Patterns', *Theoretical and Applied Climatology*, **38**: 50–54.

Berkes, Z. (1947), 'A Csapadek eloszlasa Budapest teruleten', *Idöjaras*, **51**: 105–111.

Best, M.J. and R.A. Betts (2002), 'Urban areas in climate simulations', *Preprints of the Fourth Symposium on the Urban Environment*, 20–24, Norfolk, VA, May 2002.

Bogolepow, M.A. (1928), 'Über des Klima von Moskau', *Meteorologische Zeitschrift*, **45**: 152–154.

Bornstein, R.D. (1968), 'Observations of the urban heat island effect in New York City', *Journal of Applied Meteorology*, **7**: 575–582.

Bornstein, R.D. and K.J. Craig (2002), 'Survey of the history of the urbanization of numercal mesoscale models', *Preprints of the Fourth Symposium on the Urban Environment*, 20–24, Norfolk, VA, May 2002.

Bornstein, R. and Q. Lin (2000), 'Urban heat islands and summertime convective thunderstorms in Atlanta: three cases studies', *Atmospheric Environment*, **34**: 507–516.

Bouvette, T.C., J.L. Lambert and P.B. Bedient (1982), 'Revised rainfall frequency analysis for Houston', *Journal of the Hydraulics Division*, ASCE, **108**: 515–528.

Boyer, M. and S.J. Burian (2002), 'The effects of construction activities and the preservation of indigenous vegetation on stormwater runoff rates in urbanizing landscapes', *Proceedings, Indigenous Vegetation within Urban Development*, 14–16, Uppsala, Sweden, August, 2002.

Burian, S.J., J.M. Shepherd and P. Hooshialsadat (2004), 'Chapter 1: Urbanization impacts on Houston rainstorms', in *Innovative modeling of urban water systems*, W. James (ed.), pp. 1–22.

Changnon, S.A. (1962), 'A climatological evaluation of precipitation patterns over an urban area', *Air over cities*, USPHS SEC Tech, Report A62–5, 37–67.

Changnon, S.A. (1968), 'The La Porte weather anomaly–fact or fiction?' *Bulletin of the American Meteorological Society*, **49**: 4–11.

Changnon, S.A. (1980), 'Summer flooding at Chicago and possible relationships to urban-induced heavy rainfall', *Water Resources Bulletin*, **16**: 323–325.

Changnon, S.A. (1992), 'Inadvertent weather modification in urban areas: Lessons for global climate change', *Bulletin of the American Meteorological Society*, **73**: 619–627.

Changnon, S.A. (1996), 'Effects of summer precipitation on urban transportation', *Climatic Change*, **32**: 480–494.

Changnon, S.A., F.A. Huff, P.T. Schickedanz, et al. (1977), *St Louis precipitation anomalies and their impact*, Vol. 1, METROMEX Final Summary, Illinois State Water Survey, p. 196.

Changnon, S.A., F.A. Huff and R.G. Semonin (1971), 'METROMEX: An investigation of inadvertent weather modification', *Bulletin of the American Meteorological Society*, **52**(10): 958–967.

Changnon, S.A. and P.T. Schickedanz (1971), 'Statistical studies of inadvertent modification of precipitation', *Preprints, International Symposium of Probability and Statistics in the Atmospheric Sciences*, 137–142.

Changnon, S.A. and R.G. Semonin (1977), 'Chicago area program: A major new atmospheric effort', *Bulletin of the American Meteorological Society*, **59**: 153–160.

Changnon, S.A. and N.E. Westcott (2002), 'Heavy rainstorms in Chicago: Increasing frequency, altered impacts, and future implications', *Journal of the American Water Resources Association*, **38**(5): 1467–1475.

Chow, V.T., D.R. Maidment and L.W. Mays (1988), *Applied hydrology*, New York, NY: McGraw-Hill, Inc.

Crooker, C.B. and J.L. Goldman (1974), *The changing climate, an analysis of rainfall and temperature for Houston–Galveston and a 13 county area, 1901–1973*, Houston, TX: Institute for Storm Research (now the Weather Research Center).

Dabberdt, W.F., J. Hales, S. Zubrick, et al. (2000), 'Forecast issues in the urban zone: Report of the tenth prospectus development team of the US Weather Research Program', *Bulletin of the American Meteorological Society*, **81**: 2047–2064.

Denault, C., R.G. Millar and B.J. Lence (2002), 'Climate change and drainage infrastructure capacity in an urban catchment', Proceedings, Annual Conference of the Canadian Society for Civil Engineering, Montréal, Québec, Canada, 5–8 June 2002.

Dickinson, R.E. (2003), 'Framework for inclusion of urbanized landscapes in a climate model', 2003 AGU Fall Meeting, San Francisco, California, 8–12 December 2003.

EPA (2000), *National water quality inventory: 2000 report*, EPA-841-R-02-001, Washington, DC: US Environmental Protection Agency Office of Water.

EPA (1997), *Urbanization and stream: Studies of hydrological impacts.* EPA-841-R-97-009, Washington, DC: US Environmental Protection Agency Office of Water.

Foster, S. (1996), 'Groundwater quality concerns in rapidly developing countries', in *Hydrology and hydrogeology of urbanizing areas*, J.H. Guswa, et al. (eds), St Paul, MN: American Institute of Hydrology.

Hershfield, D.M. (1961), *Rainfall frequency atlas of the United States for durations from 30 minutes to 24 hours and return periods from 1 to 100 years*, Technical Paper No. 40, Washington, DC: National Weather Service, Deptartment of Commerce.

Hjemfelt, M.R. (1982), 'Numerical simulation of the effects of St Louis on mesoscale boundary layer airflow and vertical motion: Simulations of urban vs non-urban effects', *Journal of Applied Meteorology*, **21**: 1239–1257.

Horton, R.E. (1921), 'Thunderstorm breeding spots', *Monthly Weather Review*, **49**: 193.

Huber, W.C. and R.E. Dickinson (1988), *Storm Water Management Model, Version 4, Part A: User's Manual, EPA-600-3-88-001a*, Athens, GA: US Environmental Protection Agency.

Huff, F.A. and S.A. Changnon (1972), 'Climatological assessment of urban effects on precipitation at St Louis', *Journal of Applied Meteorology*, **11**: 823–842.

Huff, F.A. and S.A. Changnon (1973), 'Precipitation modification by major urban areas', *Bulletin of the American Meteorological Society*, **54**: 1220–1232.

Huff, F.A. and J.L. Vogel (1978), 'Urban, topographic and diurnal effects on rainfall in the St Louis Region', *Journal of Applied Meteorology*, **17**(5): 565–577.

Jauregui, E. and E. Romales (1996), 'Urban effects on convective precipitation in Mexico City', *Atmospheric Environment*, **30**: 3383–3389.

Jin, M. and J.M. Shepherd (2005), 'Inclusion of urban landscape in a climate model', *Bulletin of the American Meteorological Society*, **86**(5): 681–689.

Kelly, T.J. (1972), 'An investigation of the possible urban effects on precipitation in the Houston, Texas area', *MS thesis*, Norman, OK: University of Oklahoma, p. 58.

Kratzer, A. (1937), 'Das Stadtklima', *Die Wissenschaft*, Vol. 90, Braunschweig: Friedrich Vieweg and Sohn.

Landsberg, H.E. (1956), 'The climate of towns', *Man's Role in Changing the Face of the Earth*, Chicago: University of Chicago Press.

Lowry, W.P. (1998), 'Urban effects on precipitation amount', *Progress in Physical Geography*, **22**(4): 477–520.

Luijtelaar, H.V. and A.H. Dirkzwager (2002), 'Quickscan climatic change and urban drainage', *Global Solutions for Urban Drainage*, Proceedings of the Ninth International Conference on Urban Drainage, 8–13 September 2002, Portland, OR.

McCuen, R.H. (1998), *Hydrologic analysis and design,* 2nd edn, Upper Saddle River, NJ: Prentice Hall.

Nix, S.J. (1994), *Urban stormwater modeling and simulation*, Boca Raton, FL: Lewis Publishers.

Ogden, T.L. (1969), 'The effect of rainfall on a large steelworks', *Journal of Applied Meteorology*, **8**: 585–591.

Orville, R.E., G. Huffines, J. Nielsen-Gammon, et al. (2001), 'Enhancement of cloud-to-ground lightning over Houston, Texas', *Geophysical Research Letters*, **28**: 2597–2600.

Pearson, J.E. (1958), 'The influence of lakes and urban areas on radar observed precipitation echoes', *Bulletin of the American Meteorological Society*, **39**: 79–82.

Pitt, R., S.E. Chen, S. Clark, et al. (2003), 'Chapter 12: Infiltration through compacted urban soils and effects on biofiltration design', in *Practical Modeling of Urban Water Systems*, W. James (ed.), Guelph, CA: CHI.

Quattrochi, D., J. Luvall, M. Estes, et al. (1998), 'Project Atlanta (Atlanta Land use Analysis: Temperature and Air Quality): a study of how urban landscape affects meteorology and air quality through time', *Preprint Volume Second AMS Urban Environment Conference*, pp. 104–107, Albuquerque, NM.

Rozoff, C. M., W.R. Cotton and J.O. Adegoke (2003), 'Simulation of St Louis, MO landuse Impacts on thunderstorms', *Journal of Applied Meteorology*, **42**(6): 716–739.

Ruth, M. and P. Kirshen (2002), 'Dynamic investigations into climate change impacts on urban infrastructure: Background, examples, and lessons', *Western Regional Science Association* Annual Meeting, 18–20 February 2002, Monterey, CA.

Scheuler, T.S. (1994), 'The importance of imperviousness', *Watershed Protection Techniques*, **1**(4): 100–111.

Schmauss, A. (1927), 'Grosstädte und Niederschlag', *Meteorologische Zeitschrift*, **44**: 339–341.

Sharp, J.M. Jr., J.N. Krothe, J.D. Mather, et al. (2003), 'Effects of urbanization on groundwater systems', in *Earth science in the city: A reader*, G. Heiken, R. Fakundiny and J. Sutter (eds), Washington, DC: American Geophysical Union.

Shepherd, J.M. and S.J. Burian (2003), 'Detection of urban-induced rainfall anomalies in a major coastal city', *Earth Interactions*, **7**(4): 1–17.

Shepherd, J.M., H.F. Pierce and A.J. Negri (2002), 'Rainfall modification by major urban areas: Observations from spaceborne rain radar on the TRMM satellite', *Journal of Applied Meteorology*, **41**: 689–701.

Stout, G.E. (1962), 'Some observations of cloud initiation in industrial areas', *Air over cities,* USPHS SEC Tech. Report A62-5, pp. 147–153.

Thielen, J., W. Wobrock, A. Gadian, et al. (2000), 'The possible influence of urban surfaces on rainfall development: a sensitivity study in 2D in the meso-gamma scale', *Atmospheric Research*, **54**: 15–39.

Wiegel, H. (1938), *Niederschlagsverhältnisse und Luftverunreinigung des Rheinisch–Westfälischen Industriegebiets und seiner Umgebung*, Veröffentlichungen des Meteorologischen Instituts, Universität Berlin, Vol. III, No. 3, Berlin, Verlag von Dietrich Reimer.

10 Flood Risk Institutions and Climate Change in the Netherlands

Nicolien M. van der Grijp, Alexander A. Olsthoorn, Richard S.J. Tol and Peter E. van der Werff

INTRODUCTION

Running averages of 30-year climate records are changing all over the world. Concurrently, in many places flood risks seem to be on the rise, not only due to altering hydrological cycles but also because of changes in land use and economic developments. This chapter discusses the scope for flood risk institutions to adapt to climate change, in the context of various other arrangements that channel socioeconomic developments (Olsthoorn, et al. 2001). The area of study is the Netherlands, a small (41 000 km^2) but densely populated (about 16 million inhabitants) country that is economically highly developed. About half of the country would be inundated without flood risk management, so water management is a necessary condition for the very existence of the Netherlands. For those who face an increase in flood risks it might be of considerable interest to gain some insight into the Dutch institutions that deal with water management, and how they respond to climate change *vis-à-vis* several other societal interests, such as demand for land for development schemes. The key challenge to address is how to claim land for water management given the many other interests, institutions and variety of stakeholders related to land use. In the Netherlands, the idea that hydrology should become a guiding principle in land use planning is increasingly put forward in the public debate on these matters. Therefore, in this way climate change may have a direct impact on the institutions that govern land use, and eventually on the Dutch landscape.

The issue is complex, with a range of possibilities to form its description. We choose the following structure, while acknowledging that these topics are to some extent mutually dependent, so there is some risk of repetition. We present the physical–both natural and human-made–characteristics of the 'action arena,' the delta formed by the rivers Rhine and Meuse, as well as describe two specific cases of water management studied in detail. Moving on, we provide a taste of the study methodology and briefly describe four broad trends in society: naturalization, democratization, integration and internationalization. These represent the changing societal context against which flood risk management responds to climate change. We use these concepts in the analysis of institutions that govern water management and the descriptions to analyze stakeholders and interests.

GEOGRAPHY OF FLOOD RISK AND CASE STUDIES

This section presents some geographical information about the study area. First, we present some essential data about the Netherlands and its system of flood defenses. Then we present details of two areas-at-risk that are or might be affected by major infrastructure works to secure flood safety in the future.

The Netherlands

In the following map of the Netherlands.the hatched area represents the part of the country that is not at risk to either riverine floods or floods due to sea surges. The non-gray area is divided into dike ring areas. Each dike ring area constitutes an area protected from inundation by flood defense structures along its boundaries, which are either human-made (dikes) or natural (dunes). Flood risks vary with dike ring area (dike ring areas 13 and 14 are best protected against sea surges with a probability of flooding once in 10 000 years. Along the rivers (dike ring areas 40, 41 and 43), flood risk is highest (probability of once in 1250 years).

Riverine floods arise mainly from two rivers, the Rhine and the Meuse. The rivers Rhine (mean discharge 2200 m^3 per second, measured maximum discharge 26 000 m^3 per second) and Meuse (mean discharge 230 m^3 per second, measured maximum 1500 m^3 per second) are most important with respect to flood risks. The catchments areas of both rivers extend across various countries. For instance, the 160 000-km^2 watershed of the river Rhine covers parts of Switzerland, Germany and France.

Flood safety used to be a local concern. It became a national concern with economic, administrative and political developments in the nineteenth century (Langen and Tol 1998). These developments and corresponding engineering works have resulted in the 'human-made' nature of the country; much of the geography of the Netherlands is now a technological artifact. Polders, dikes, levies and systems for pumping water are the most well-known elements of the Dutch landscape. River discharges are controlled in real-time by moveable

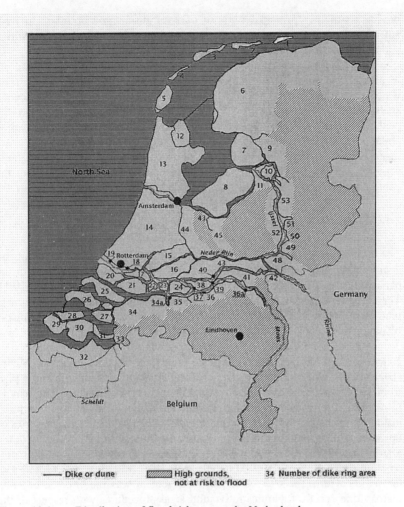

Figure 10.1   Distribution of flood risks across the Netherlands

dams in the rivers Lower Rhine (*Neder Rijn*), *Lek* and Meuse. In case of low discharges, these dams are closed in order to maintain sufficient flow in the main river artery–the river *Waal* (between dike ring areas 41 and 43)–to prevent silting by seawater from the mouth of this river and to control navigability for inland shipping. Navigability is important since the river Rhine links Rotterdam Seaport, the world's largest harbor, with major centers of industry and population in northwestern Europe. With the industrial revolution in the nineteenth century, the Rhine became a major transportation artery, in particular for bulk commodities such as coal, ores and petroleum products. Another principal purpose of river discharge control is to have sufficient fresh water flow in the sub-sea level areas in order to prevent silting and drought induced subsidence of organic soils (bogs).

Next to climate change, causing changes in precipitation patterns and sea level rise, two other geophysical processes call for a re-evaluation of current water management strategies. First, due to the movements of the continental shelf, the Netherlands is slowly sinking. Second, peat-type soils in the Netherlands are subsiding because of oxidation processes when desiccating. On top of this, there are socioeconomic motives for reconsidering water management: changes in land use, increasing population and economic activity, and the development of new transport infrastructure all affect the context water management must accommodate.

The Maaswerken

The *Maaswerken* refers to a series of civil engineering works along an approximately 80 km section of the Meuse (in Dutch *Maas*) located in the panhandle area in the southeastern part of the Netherlands (see Figure 10.1). The *Maaswerken* involves reconstruction of embankments, creation of gravel pits, construction of bypass canals, retention basins and weirs, improvements of navigability, creation of nature areas (from abandoned gravel pits), and deepening of the riverbed. It originated in a plan from 1990 to issue a new concession for gravel mining in the upstream section of river Meuse (*Grensmaas*), while simultaneously creating a natural area, and also in a plan from 1992 to improve navigability of the river. River discharge events heavily influenced the ongoing public discussion about this plan, prompting institutional change. Officials reconsidered flood risk policies after a series of upstream floods, along the river Meuse in 1993 and 1995. Then, in the aftermath of the 1995 near-flood of the Rhine (an event which led to the pre-emptive evacuation of 250 000 people from dike ring areas 48, 43 and 41), legislation with respect to flood risk management was modified in order to increase the speed of administrative and legal procedures with respect to the reinforcement of weak spots in the river embankments.

Meanwhile, the main administrative stakeholders (provincial authorities, national ministries, funding agencies and so on) saw a need for an integrative approach, incorporating public and private financing, for all the works going on along the Meuse. In 1997, these administrative bodies created the project group *Maaswerken*, which was responsible for implementing the strategic level plans. In the same period, the plans were extended to cover the downstream part of the Meuse, the *Zandmaas*. For this part, the plan also aimed to improve navigability. A major idea behind the project was that the revenues from gravel mining would be used to finance other elements of the project, in particular the creation of natural areas. In 2000, the project became part of a larger program involving works in the whole of the floodplain of the Meuse in the province of Limburg and beyond.

Green River

The second case that illuminates a series of aspects of flood risk management in the Netherlands is the plan of the 'green river.' In the public debate on how to cope with increased flood risk from climate change, a group of Dutch water management institutions led by Delft Hydraulics (1998) launched a plan that included a proposal to construct a bypass at the beginning of the Rhine delta, where the river enters the Netherlands. This plan was in fact a scenario for flood safety management based on the principle of 'give room to the river.' Instead of building ever-higher dikes, low-level areas are designated to store excess water temporarily or to constitute additional temporary rivers to channel excess water. The core of the plan is to redirect the flow of the Rhine over its different branches. Figure 10.2 (lower panel) shows the current situation. The numbers indicate the discharge capacity of the river branches and the proposed future situation (left panel). A bypass to the river IJssel diverts excess water through sparsely populated dike ring areas 49, 50, 51, 52, 53, 10 and 14 (see Figure 10.1). The planners engineered the bypass as part of a green river, a natural area that occasionally would be flooded. The envisaged bypass, however, would lead through the 200-inhabitant village of Helhoek (Hell's Angle), which would have to be abandoned.

TRENDS

We analyze developments in terms of a series of broad societal trends that frame both the developments and the methods of analysis–naturalization, democratization, integration and internationalization.

Naturalization

A most influential trend is naturalization (or ecologicalization), which we understand here as the ever-increasing importance of the concept of nature in many domains of modern society. A striking example of naturalization is the emergence of the concept of 'ecological main structure' becoming a guiding principle in the Netherlands' system of strategic land use planning. This concept says that natural areas within the Netherlands must be connected by corridors that enable the interchange of species. For instance, rivers are no longer just transport channels and fresh water resources, but important recreational areas and parts of the ecological main structure.

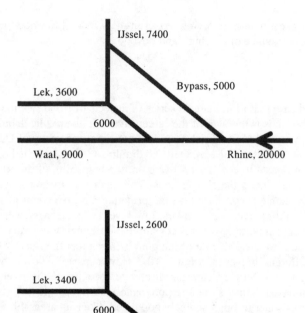

Figure 10.2   Current (lower panel) and proposed future (upper panel) distribution of the Rhine's peak flows (15 000 m³/s) over its branches. The 5000 m³ per second branch is to be constructed and would only be used in times of excess discharges. It involves digging a new canal but largely relies on an earlier branch of the river (Delft Hydraulics 1998).

The development in the thinking about flood safety management is a second example of naturalization. Water and flood safety management used to be decided using a narrow economic and engineering calculus, and biased by typical civil engineering thinking. The upsurge of the environmental movement in the 1970s, reinforcing older movements aiming to protect landscapes and cultural heritage, changed this bias. Notably, during that time, plans to impolder the IJssel Lake (bordered by dike rings 6, 7, 8, 12 and 13 in Figure 10.1) and the Waddensea (the wetlands south of dike rings 1, 2, 3, 4 and 5) were abandoned, and plans to close the Eastern Scheldt Estuary were changed, all in favor of nature preservation (Hisschemöller 1985). Without 'naturalization,' Figure 10.1 would have looked quite different. Similarly, in the 1970s, after years of struggle between environmental interest groups and riverine flood management authorities, dike engineering adopted the concept of 'smart' dike design. Smart design (see also Chapter 5 in this volume) implies consideration of local conditions–including local landscape and local cultural heritage–in the engineering of structures to reinforce flood defense along the rivers. Government funding was made available for this approach.

The ever-higher value placed on nature and cultural heritage inspires engineering philosophy to make use of natural dynamics, rather than concrete and steel, in designing flood risk management structures (Van Hall 1997). The other argument is that, given the expectations of increasing probabilities of extreme river discharges, merely heightening dikes would be a dead-end management strategy.

Today, the national government has explicitly rejected the management of flood safety through heightening embankments along the rivers. The overall strategy is now based on the idea of 'giving room' to water. This strategy implies that, along the branches of the Rhine, certain areas must be designated as spillover basins to be used for once-in-a-thousand-year flood events. Obviously, an area selected for excess water storage will be constrained in its possibilities for socioeconomic development. However, the potential for development of nature areas are enhanced. The green river scheme described in the previous section is an example of an ultimate consequence of such a shift in values for flood risk management.

Democratization

The second trend is democratization, the change in the mode of governance towards more direct stakeholder involvement in policy making or, in other words, towards more public participation (see also Chapter 5 in this volume). Democratization can be seen as a process of improving the coordination of political decision making.

Flood safety and other services of water management, such as drainage, are indivisible public goods of which the provision requires collective action. In the Netherlands, this action is organized by water boards (*Waterschappen*), which date back to medieval times. These political-administrative bodies, concerned solely with water management, are governed by elected members. Voting rights (and political power) used to be based on ownership of land in the area at risk of flooding since, presumably, the types of activities at risk, usually agricultural were related to the size of land owned. Shifts in economic structure and population led to different patterns of interests. This led to the gradual extension of voting rights in water boards, the political bodies that govern water management of watershed regions. A mark in this shift in political stakeholder involvement, from large landowners to all inhabitants, was the adoption of the new Water Board Act in 1991 (Gilhuis and Menninga 1996; Katsburg 1996). One may note, however, that the water board maintains a low political profile. Voter turnout at elections is about 20 per cent.

These bodies are concerned with water management and tend to be one-issue agencies. Environmental interests are watched over by the legal requirement of environmental impact assessment (EIA) for large works such as dike heightening. Simultaneously, *inspraak* procedures (procedures for public participation) allow for public participation in the process of granting permits for carrying out such large projects. Although this increases the democratic nature of decision making and presumably the quality of planning and implementation, it may also increase costs and slow down the process considerably. In the period 1980 to 1995 little dike reinforcement occurred, one of the reasons being public resistance, which led to time-consuming legal controversies. Actually, in reaction to the near floods of 1995, new legislation was put in place (the *Deltaplan Grote Rivieren*–delta plan for major rivers). An accompanying law, the State Government Project Procedure (*Rijksprojectenprocedure*), introduces legal shortcuts in decision making procedures. This law applies also to procedures for decision making on infrastructure developments other than those related to flood safety, such as transport infrastructure (Kroon 1997).

Democratization implies that stakeholders are ready to defend their interests. This was the case in Helhoek. People from Helhoek and the nearby village of Groessen were not unprepared for a public discussion since they had participated in a local interest group, initiated in 1990, when the Dutch government launched the plan to build a new railway from Rotterdam seaport to Germany that would cross the area. Members of this group explicitly and wisely acknowledged that if, eventually, they had to negotiate individually about damage and compensation, then they were free to do so, without blame from other members.

Integration

In the 1970s and the 1980s, the concept of integration received a high profile in policy science and policy making. This is the type of trend that refers to a frame for analyzing institutional change. The term integration stands for the organization of decision making, specifically, the attempt to systematically involve all stakeholders in decision making procedures. Democratization and integration led, in the 1980s and 1990s, to the development of the concept of 'open planning.' Open planning, particularly of large development or infrastructure schemes, means public empowerment by government bodies and policy makers soliciting opinions on proposals from all stakeholders (individuals, NGOs and other government entities). The development of the *Maaswerken* is one of the first examples of such an attempt.

Internationalization

Finally we mention internationalization, the trend of extending the geographical policy area from the local scale to the watershed, a region that transcends current political borders. In the Netherlands, water management policy, traditionally a matter of local and regional authorities, was first nationalized by Louis Napoleon, viceroy for his brother Boneparte (see Langen and Tol 1998 and Tol and Langen 2000, for a more extensive review of the history of flood management in the Netherlands). The responsibility of the central government for water issues was confirmed in the Constitution of 1848, and strengthened again in the Constitution of 1983. Operational and financial responsibility for flood safety rested with the water boards. The flood of 1953 led to a reorganization of the water boards; the number shrinking from over 2500 in 1950 to less than 50 now (Van den Berg and Van Hall 1997). Professionalism of the water boards rose simultaneously. Geographical scaling-up of institutions continues at an international level. First, the riparian states of the Rhine set up the International Rhine Committee (IRC). The 1986 Sandoz incident in which a large amount of poisonous chemicals were flushed into the river after a fire in the Sandoz chemical plant in Switzerland helped to give teeth to the IRC, though initially only to chew on water quality and pollution issues. In the 1990s, the geographic scope widened further when water management became an area of EU (European Union) competence. In 1995, the EU Council of Environment Ministers signed the Declaration of Arles, stating that action plans on flood protection should be prepared for the Rhine and the Meuse. The Helsinki Convention provided a framework for treaties on the Meuse (De Villeneuve 1996). The new EU Water Directive is likely to reinforce the trend of internationalization of river water management.

Since the floods of 1995, mostly in Germany, the mandate of the IRC has included flood control (Van der Grijp and Olsthoorn 2001). The IRC adopted a Rhine Flood Action Plan that aims to:

1. Stabilize the damage potential by 2005, and decrease it by 10 per cent by 2020;
2. Lower high water levels by 30 cm in 2005 and by 70 cm by 2020;
3. Improve early flood warning; and
4. Increase public awareness of flood risks.

Cooperation is more than just planning. Dutch and German water management agencies also increasingly cooperate during implementation. In Germany, locations for retention basins (spillover areas) have been identified and the Netherlands will bear part of the costs of making these retention basins, such as the *Bislicher Insel* near Wezel, operational.

One may wonder what the drivers are behind internationalization, democratization and integration. What are their origins? This is a big question. A small part of the answer can be found under a set of simple economics assumptions applying simple game theory insights (Tol 2001). It says that for economic actors at risk from flooding it pays to cooperate on flood risk management and to accept a central authority if there is transparency in everybody's contribution to risk reduction.

Demographic and economic development will change the Netherlands as well as its geographical characteristics. These developments, together with climate change, do not, however, constitute the sole origin of ongoing changes in flood risk policies. Perhaps even more profound are cultural changes, a series of trends that culture theorists summarize as a shift from modernity to post-modernity (see del Moral, et al. 2003). Presently occurring climate change has confirmed that the future climate is inherently uncertain. This idea fits neatly into the new style of post-modern policy making which views the future as uncontrolled, full of uncertainty and even chaotic. Consequently, policy making should be flexible in order to adapt to changing circumstances. Unfortunately, flexibility is hard to achieve in a complex and still partly modern world. There are many inhibitors of change, notably all kinds of vested interests. History has shown that disastrous events may bring about the momentum required to change institutions, but only if other societal conditions, such as economic circumstances, do not act as barriers (Kingdon 1988).

THE INSTITUTIONAL LANDSCAPE

Being at risk of floods is an ongoing condition of life in the Netherlands. Effective policies and institutions that address a public good such as flood safety require collective action and consensus. The institutions that govern water management have a centuries-old history, and the high value that is placed on consensus in decision making in the Netherlands can be traced back to the need for collective action in flood risk policies.

Flood risk, however, is just one of the issues that relates water management to quality of life. Table 10.1 lists different resources and hazards associated with water around which institutions have evolved. Many formal and informal national institutions that deal with these aspects have evolved over the years. We limit our scope to the policy fields of protection against flooding, quality and quantity management in relation to ground and surface water, and navigation. Beyond water management, there are other policy areas and stakeholder networks (land use planning, environmental management, nature protection, recreation, fisheries and agriculture) with special relevance to water management.

Table 10.1   Functions and hydrological risks as distinguished in the Netherlands water management

Resources and services	Associated risk
Transport of water and ice from indigenous precipitation, but primarily from Germany, Belgium and beyond to the sea	Floods
Source of water for domestic purposes, agriculture and industry	Drought
Source of minerals (clay for bricks, gravel, sand)	Depletion of mineral resources such as gravel and sand
Transport infrastructure (inland navigation)	Navigation interrupts
Resource for flushing stagnant water bodies	Silting, and other water pollution
Resource for control of water levels in stagnant water bodies, and of groundwater levels	Subsidence (through oxidation of dry peat soil), depletion of ground water resources
Providing cooling water to power plants	Production interrupts, higher production costs
Fisheries	Depletion of stocks of fish
Tourism and leisure activities	Shortage of leisure facilities
Biodiversity, nature, cultural heritage	Loss of biodiversity and nature

Public water management was first introduced in the Netherlands in the twelfth century (Van den Berg and Van Hall 1997). Compared with today it had a local character, resulting in a large regional variety of public bodies dealing with water issues. The Constitutions of 1814 and 1815 laid out codified the basic principles of water management–with reference to the powers of water management bodies relative to the authorities of other administrative entities such as municipalities. Since then, local and regional water management has rested with the water boards (*waterschap*) under the supervision of the provinces and the supreme supervision of the central government. The Constitution of 1848 established a strict separation of water management and other administrative concerns.

The 1953 sea surge, during which 1835 people drowned, was a landmark in flood safety policy making. This disaster resulted in new legislation, and most importantly in the national government, providing funds for flood defense works. Hitherto, local water boards were to finance works from local funds. With respect to the completion of the Delta plan it must certainly be recognized that the works were carried out in a period of high economic growth. Today the national expenditures on flood safety are about 1.2 billion euro annually, which is about 0.25 per cent of the Gross National Product (GNP).

Table 10.2 presents an overview of the prevailing Dutch water management legislation and Dutch disaster management legislation relevant to flood disasters.

A main provision of the Disaster Act is that administrative authorities such as municipalities and provinces should have in place contingency plans for disasters that could occur under their jurisdiction. The recent act on financial compensation for disaster losses regulates hitherto ad-hoc relief and financial support from the government.

Integrated Water Management

The multitude of functions of water and associated risks (conceptualized as the water system) and the long history of water management are reflected in legislation that has become increasingly complex over the years. Much of policy making in recent decades was aimed at resolving the administrative inconsistencies in legislation and providing ways to better facilitate the coordination of legal procedures. This focus of policy developments became known as 'integrated water management' (Van Rooy and de Jong 1995). The Act on Pollution of Surface Waters is one of the first examples of this view. It fully materialized with the entry into force of the Water Management Act (*Wet op de waterhuishouding*) in 1989, which provided the instruments to align the policies of different water management authorities. In addition, regional responsibilities were rearranged with the aim of creating a situation of ownership, management and maintenance by only one administrative unit, preferably an all-in water board. Integrative water management relies on planning and careful policy analysis, since cooperation of different authorities requires overarching common principles and aims. Actually, the 1989 Water Management Act codified the already existing practice of strategic planning in water management. The first integrated plans were laid out in the Third Strategic Water Policy Plan (NW3) from 1989, together with the preceding white paper 'Dealing with Water' from 1985.

The Fourth Strategic Water Policy Plan (NW4), covering the 1998–2006 period, dates from December 1998. This plan is the product of close cooperation between the ministry of Transport, Public Works and Water Management (V&W), the ministry of Agriculture, Nature Management and Fisheries (LNV), the ministry of Housing, Spatial Planning and the Environment (VROM), and the Union of Water Boards (UvW). Its implementation process involves the consultation of the different government bodies and other stakeholders in order to develop widely agreed on operational targets. Consultation is emphasized as an important part of the process to create integration of policies. The NW4 outlines management at the national level and includes policies for the (Perdok 1996):

- Allocation of functions to the national surface water bodies;
- Allocation of functions to regional surface waters as far as national interests are involved;
- Formulation of objectives concerning water systems including time tables;
- Formulation of measures to achieve the objectives set; and
- Indication of financial, economic and physical consequences.

Table 10.2   Overview of water management legislation in the Netherlands

Classic water management legislation	
Water Administration Act 1900	*Waterstaatswet 1900 (stb. 1900, 176)*
Rivers Act of 1908	*Rivierenwet van 1908 (stb. 1908, 339)*
Delta Act	*Deltawet (stb. 1958, 2460)*
Delta Damage Compensation Act	
Modern water management legislation	
Act on Pollution of Surface Waters	*Wet verontreiniging oppervlaktewateren (stb. 1971, 444)*
Groundwater Act	*Grondwaterwet (stb. 1981, 392)*
Water Management Act	*Wet op de waterhuishouding (stb. 1989, 285)*
Delta Act Major Rivers	*Deltawet grote rivieren (stb. 1995, 210)*
Water Embankment Act	
Act of State Water Authority	*Wet op de waterkering (stb. 1996, 8)*
Operations	*Wet beheer rijkswaterstaatswerken (stb. 1996, 654)*
Disaster management legislation	
Disaster Act	*Rampenwet (stb. 1985, 88)*
Act on Compensation of Financial Losses due to Disasters and Serious Accidents	*Wet tegemoetkoming schade bij rampen en zware ongevallen (stb. 1998, 325)*
Institutional legislation	
Water Board Act	*Waterschapswet (stb. 1991, 444)*

These plans are issued under the auspices of the ministries mentioned above. There is, however, consultation with many other stakeholders: consumer organizations, environmental organizations, press, farmers, industry, drinking water suppliers, professionals (especially technicians), scientists, politicians and public officials. In the Netherlands, there are no NGOs around the topic of flood risk, which may point at the lack of controversy about the need for flood risk policies.

Some analysts such say that water management policy in the Netherlands is not the result of an open debate in formal arenas such as parliament, but is formulated in an 'iron ring' around the formal arenas. This ring consists of civil servants and various affected parties. Because of the rather low political profile of water management and the technical expertise required, most water management policy is in practice formulated by civil servants in consultation with economic stakeholders and environmental NGOs (Mostert 1997).

Open Planning

The key assumption behind integrated management is that it is possible to foresee the major obstacles (for example, physical, legal, financial and psychological) that might result in policies or plans being unworkable. Such an assumption may come true under careful planning. If not, integrated management may become stuck in the details. A possible way out would be through open planning. Open planning, or interactive policy making, refers to extensive stakeholder involvement in finding appropriate and agreed-upon operational level approaches to reach strategic objectives (see also Chapter 5 in this volume). There is, however, no guarantee of success. The *Maaswerken* (Van der Grijp and Warner 2001) constitutes an example of open planning and integrated water management that failed. Van der Grijp and Warner also came across a great number of institutions that caused this project to get stuck in planning and negotiations between stakeholders without reaching conclusions. These institutions vary from the issuing of concessions for gravel mining and associated policies regarding resources of construction material, policies to create natural areas, views on 'what is a natural area,' spatial planning procedures, rules for public procurement, procedures for technical/hydrological engineering, historic tensions between local and central administrative and political bodies and international complications. A principal issue is the finance structure of the *Grensmaas* part of the program: the revenues of the gravel mining should fully cover the costs of turning the gravel pits into nature conservation areas. This idea of public-private financial governance was, in 1991, put forward as the 'green for gravel' approach.

Acceptable Risk and Flood Safety Standards

Flood risk, in the sense of a numerical probability of a flood event, is not something to avoid at all costs. Somewhere, the costs will not outweigh the avoided risk. Acceptable risk is the probability of flooding that warrants no more risk reduction measures. This probability is associated with the probability of high water levels, or high river discharge levels. For instance, in the 1970s, a 13 000 m^3 per second discharge in the Rhine was expected to occur once in 1000 years. Today one is less sure about probability distributions.

Acceptable risk is associated with possible highest river discharges. Operational water and flood risk management takes this value as the guiding principle in design of water defense operations. In Dutch, this number is called *Maatgevend HoogWater* (MHW). The MHW is the highest river flow that flood defenses should be able to withstand.

Traditionally flood risk strategies, as expressed in MHWs, were based on historical high water levels, taking into account a safety margin. In the 1950s, however, risk strategies became based on advanced hydrological and statistical analyses. Nowadays, however, under uncertainty in the rate of climate change, the importance of the MHW as the single indicator for risk has dwindled. The MHW still exists as an engineering guideline, but, by law, it is now subject to periodical revisions (when expected discharge frequency distributions and/or required safety levels are revised). Today's white papers and publications of advisory bodies (see for example TAW 2000; RLG 1998) point at the inherent uncertainty of water discharge probability distributions under climate change and other developments, while stressing the likelihood of high water being on the rise. Risk management is no longer restricted to efforts to contain water between dikes. Now it includes discussion of measures such as controlled flooding through retention basins and green rivers that extend beyond dikes into sparsely populated areas. One might say 'structural flood protection' integrates with contingency planning, if controlled flooding is seen as such.

Institutions in Helhoek

Risk and approaches to risk differ with the nature of the stakeholder that experiences the risk. At the individual level, much of the cost of risk manifests as anxiety. An individual's benefit from reducing risk is psychological in nature: the reduction of fear. One may presume that fear has different origins, it may embody evolutionary cumulated hazard experience, it may be based on the actual personal experience of a hazard, and it may be based on social constructions that imprint on one's mind. An impression of the social significance of flood risk is presented in Table 10.3, which illustrates perceived flood risk in the Netherlands. Although a large majority of the population is actually at risk of floods, most people (80 per cent) seem to feel safe. Since all know the flood situation, Table 10.3 can best be interpreted as a vote of confidence in the flood protection system in the Netherlands.

Table 10.3   Perception of flood risk in the Netherlands

	Do you think you are at risk to floods?	
Do you live near dikes or embankments?	Yes	No
Yes	9%	51%
No	1%	39%

Source: Lijklema and Koelen (1999). The survey was conducted two years after the 1995 flood events. (N=1810)

People that live in the areas that might be designated as spillover areas or as green rivers (people living near dikes or embankments) clearly appreciate flood risk differently than those who live on high ground. How would these people in flood plains react to initiatives that would restrict their potential socioeconomic development? Or in anthropological terms, what institutions, patterns of thought or worldviews would channel their reactions? The people of Helhoek (discussed above) might offer a partial answer. In Helhoek, in a series of interviews local people were confronted with the plan *Rijn op Termijn*, which implies that their village would fall victim to infrastructure works (a green river) that would decrease flood risks elsewhere in the river Rhine Delta (Van der Werff 2004).

Helhoek is a relatively isolated village with strong social ties, possibly due to its isolation. Heloekers interact via a large network of associations including sports clubs, music bands, farmer's organizations and a carnival association,. They constitute a remarkably strong pre-modern, close-knit community based on personalized relationships. Forced relocation could result in the loss of these pre-modern acquisitions and therefore could be seen as the most important disadvantage of the new room-for-water oriented approaches to address riverine flood risk.

Helhoekers also have instrumental, single-stranded relationships that deal with only one aspect of life, mostly in contacts with actors outside their own village community. In this way, they benefit from and contribute to modern state arrangements, technological innovations and economic growth. They are informed about and contribute to trends such as increased openness and flexibility in decision making. They understand the wisdom of combining the priority of safety with ecological management of the river basin. They increasingly participate in planning processes. They consider the necessity of international cooperation for managing the Rhine and think about the long-term sustainability of projects. In this sense, Helhoekers also take part in post-modern developments.

KEY STAKEHOLDERS AND INTERESTS

Table 10.1 above lists the essential interests linked to the field of water management. Most of the policies that target one of the resources and risks mentioned in Table 10.1 have implications for other functions and risks. The topic that is most affected by the expected climate change is floods. A small effort to identify stakeholders associated with each of the items will quickly result in a very long list since there are stakeholder networks associated with each function and with each risk. We restrict ourselves to the network of stakeholders who are closest to flood risk management. Table 10.4 summarizes the domain of actors and their activities related to flood risk management.

At the heart of the stakeholder network is *Rijkswaterstaat* (the state Water Management Authority). This body, a subsidiary of the Ministry of Transport and Water Management, is involved in both the development and implementation of water management strategies, the latter at strategic positions in the Dutch water system (such as sea defense works and major rivers). Most of the funding (approximately 90 per cent) for flood risk management comes from the national budget; therefore the *Rijkswaterstaat*'s position in the stakeholder network is clearly most important.

These stakeholders may exert influence individually, or as indicated in Table 10.4, in some kind of organizational arrangement. An influential body is the *Technische Adviescommissie Water* (Technical advisory committee for water, or TAW). This body, bundling scientific and civil engineering expertise in the Netherlands, also advises the government on major flood policy issues. The civil engineering department of Delft Technical University functions as an informal focal point providing education and research on flood risk strategies.

Table 10.1 shows that policies that target flood risks potentially touch on a great number of water-related policy topics. The origins of taking a systems view on water management date back to the 1970s. Earlier, flood risk was considered a structured problem (Hisschemöller, et al. 1999) and there was little dispute about the facts (such as the probability distributions for high water and dike engineering methods), as well as little dispute about values (the value of nature that was to be sacrificed for the sake of flood safety). Narrow cost-benefit analysis that only considered items that could be monetarily valued was sufficient to identify adequate policy options.

Table 10.4   Stakeholder network in flood risk management

Administrative and political body	Competencies and activities	Other stakeholders, NGOs
European Commission	Integrated directive Declaration of Arles	-
International Rhine Committee	Rhine Action Plan on Flood Defence	NGOs
National ministries of water management, land use planning, environment, nature *Rijkswaterstaat*	Strategic national water policy, strategic land use planning, water management legislation, management of national surface waters, supervision over provinces, water boards and municipalities. *Rijkswaterstaat* is also operational in management of main water bodies.	NGOs for conservation of nature and culture Water management/ engineering complex (TAW)
Provinces (12) The Association of Provinces (IPO)	Strategic ground and surface water policy, operational land use planning, operational groundwater policy, supervision over water boards and municipalities	NGOs (for example, *Provinciale Milieufederatie*)
Water boards (65) The Union of Water Boards (UvW)	Operational surface water management, flood risk management	Local residents and farmers' associations
Municipalities (572) The Association of Dutch Municipalities (VNG)	Sewerage management, operational land use management	Local residents

In the 1970s and 1980s this type of approach to flood risk management met more and more opposition because of the emergence of stakeholders that defended nature, landscapes and cultural heritage. Nowadays the importance of these values is undisputed within policy making bodies, and policy strategies took these values on board and developed appropriate procedures (integrative policy making). In the 1990s, the probability distribution of the chance of high discharges became uncertain under climate change; in other words, the flood risk problem lost structure. Newer approaches require both government involvement (distributive justice) and participation of stakeholders with conflicting views in order to find common ground for solutions. This type of approach is termed 'interactive policy making,' which is another name for open planning, referred to in the preceding section.

The *Maaswerken* project, introduced earlier, is one of the first efforts to follow this approach. The complexity of the *Maaswerken* evolves from the many stakeholders and the differences in the nature of their interests: flood risk, gravel mining, nature development and navigability. The principal strategic level stakeholders are: the provincial authorities, the ministry of Transport and Water Management, the Panheel group (a consortium of gravel mining companies), several environmental NGOs (notably *Natuurmonumenten*, which is the Netherlands's largest organization for nature conservation) and the *Maaswerken* project group (the administrative body set up to execute the program and set up by the ministries of V&W and LNV, the province of Limburg, and led by the regional department of *Rijkswaterstaat*). Gravel mining companies, civil engineering and construction firms and *Natuurmonumenten* have formed the *Consortium Grensmaas BV*, a firm that will carry out the actual mining operations and construction of natural areas. Table 10.5 summarizes the various interests of the main stakeholders involved in the development of the *Maaswerken* project.

With respect to the *Grensmaas* part of the works, the issue to be decided was as follows: what was the maximum amount of gravel that could be extracted given the need for revenues to appropriate for both the reduction of flood risk and the creation of nature areas from the eventually depleted gravel mining sites? The negotiations started in the beginning of the 1990s. At that time flood risk safety was not an important topic–it only became so after the floods of 1993 and 1995. The four principal strategic interests, as agreed on by governmental authorities and the consortium *Grensmaas BV* in the beginning of 2001, are:

1. The extraction of at least 60 million tons of gravel between 1995 and 2015 along the *Grensmaas*. The riverbed of the Meuse constitutes the principal Dutch source of gravel and therefore of strategic interest to Dutch construction activities. Private companies carry out the actual mining under a concession system.
2. The creation of about 1500 ha of natural areas.
3. The reduction of flood risk along the river to a once-in-250-years event.
4. Improvement of navigability (refers to the *Zandmaas* part).

There are various reasons the negotiations haven't taken a long time; for instance, the differences in time-horizons of private and public policy making and the intricacies of reconciling the different interests. A circumstance particular to the negotiations is that the mining companies have united to form the *Panheel* group; therefore, anti-trust rules may apply. In 1991, the *Panheel* group asked the Dutch anti-trust authority (NMA)[1] for dispensation from anti-trust rules, arguing that the complexity of the project warranted this specific consortium rather than open tendering. 'Higher interest' would be the legal argument that would override anti-trust rules.

Table 10.5　Stakeholders and their interest in the Maaswerken project

Stakeholder	Relevant interests
Ministry of V&W	Responsibility for water management, including flood risk management and navigability. Responsibility for transport infrastructure and resources for construction materials (50–60 million tons gravel). Funds for flood protection.
Ministry of LNV	Responsible for nature conservation.
Ministry of VROM	Interest in environment, notably handling of contaminated dredging material and mine waste.
Province of Limburg (provincial government)	General interest. Finances. Design of nature area.
Municipalities	Plans and implementation at the local level. Issue local permits. Nuisance caused by carrying out mining and construction works.
Project group *Maaswerken*	Administrative body formed to execute the program. Set up by the ministries of V&W and LNV and the province of Limburg. Communication with the municipalities along the Meuse, regional water boards, nature protection groups, tourist organisations, farmers' organisations, industry associations, water companies, the regional Chambers of Commerce, and local interest groups (Van Leusen, et al. 2000).
Dutch anti-trust regulator	Anti-trust rules. Gravel mining companies, united in the Panheel group, pleaded for exemption.
Private companies	Gravel mining companies and construction companies are involved in gravel mining and in the construction of nature areas.
Natuurmonumenten	The national NGO for conservation of nature and cultural heritage. Design of new nature areas.
Grensmaas BV	The Grensmaas BV consortium was founded by the gravel mining companies, construction companies and *Natuurmonumenten*.
Milieufederatie	The provincial association of local environmental NGOs. Brought forward the notion that gravel mining destroys nature.
Farmers' association	Gravel mining in floodplains is at the expense of agricultural activity.
Local citizens	Nuisance (e.g. noise, road safety) due to the construction of the pits and operation of the gravel extraction.

Another reason for the slow progress is historic sensitivities at several levels–between core and peripheral areas, between provinces, and between riparian states. In March 2000, the tension between the provincial and the national administrations diminished after the national government agreed to provide a large share of the budget (about 35 billion euro) for the *Zandmaas* part of the *Maaswerken* project.

Public support for the *Maaswerken* project, however, is feeble. The long negotiation period, the changes in the project's objectives and fragmentary public communication have made people weary. When confronted with the impacts on the local environment (such as the nuisance due to ongoing works), additional resistance evolved.

Currently this project is led by the *Maaswerken* project group, installed in 1997, which is a public partnership of two national governmental agencies and a regional body: the V&W, LNV and the province of Limburg (Van Leussen, et al. 2000). Strikingly, the ministry of Housing, Spatial Planning and Environment (VROM) is only loosely and informally involved in monitoring land use planning and environmental aspects of contaminated dredging material.

In its communications with the public the project is explicitly framed as having three targets: improving flood safety, increasing nature areas and improving navigability.[2] For the *Grensmaas* part of the project, the link between gravel mining and nature development (mostly wetlands) is obvious. For the *Zandmaas* part, this framing seems more cosmetic than real. For that part of the *Maaswerken,* measured in terms of numbers of separate projects, flood safety appears to be the most important (32 projects), followed by projects that improve navigability (16 projects) and then nature developments (10 projects).

Helhoek

Although the village of Helhoek is geographically isolated, the interviewed inhabitants (about 25) were informed and aware of both actual and planned flood risk interventions. Also, most interviewed people were aware of the conflicts between personal and public interests. Major elements focus of the *Rijn op Termijn* plan (and other strategies to address future flood risk that are being discussed today) are the plans to create natural areas in the extended floodplains. The people of Helhoek proved positively sensitive to this idea.

There were mixed reactions from the inhabitants of Helhoek to the idea of losing their homes for the good of flood safety elsewhere (and the creation of a new natural area). Not unexpectedly, there were not-in-my-backyard (NIMBY) reactions. Also, questions were raised about both the idea that climate change enhances flood risk and, among those who felt flood risks are indeed on the rise, and what proposed works would offer the most desirable solution (locals were not consulted in the development of the plans). Some mistrust of authorities was behind these rejections of the plan. There was, however, also evidence of trust in the authorities, in that the inhabitants expected to receive ample financial compensation for possible losses.

CONCLUSIONS

What happened?

The long history of floods in the Netherlands explains much of the contemporary thinking about flood safety in the country. The 1953 coastal flood catastrophe is still a vivid reference for flood risk management. During most of the post-war period, high river discharges failed to occur. However, in the 1990s, floods along the Meuse and near-flood disasters along the Rhine confirmed the reality of flood risk.

Both events prompted institutional change. The 1953 catastrophe resulted in the national government taking formal responsibility for flood risks and establishing guidelines for management. A principal guideline requires minimum heights for dikes along the rivers. This guideline, however, reflects fixed expectations of very high water discharges, and implementation failed initially. One reason is that traditional engineering approaches manage flood risks at the expense of nature, landscapes and cultural heritage, resources whose values are on the rise (through naturalization). In flood risk management, the resulting conflicts proved very hard to resolve and concrete risk management to implement the safety standards has been limited.

A new spur occurred after the 1993 and 1995 (near) flood events. The direct effects were mending weak spots in dikes, making improvements to flood warning systems and improving municipal contingency plans. These floods also helped conclude a discussion on new legislation (Water Embankment Act).

In the Netherlands, flood risk management is part of the larger water policy domain. Since the 1960s, policy makers put forward integrated water management as a principal element of policy. Strategic planning that considers all interests related to water is an important and necessary element of this approach.

In a debate on long-term strategies, climate change naturally comes into view. Current thinking about climate change refers to two things. First, the probability of very high river discharge is on the rise in the Netherlands. Second, the rate of change is not well-known.

This analysis asks for approaches to flood risk management that are more robust with respect to assumptions than the traditional dike-heightening approach. These approaches will extend beyond the current water policy domain. For instance, Dutch policy makers turn to their upstream colleagues and influence policies beyond Dutch borders. However, a more profound approach is needed. The key is to find and reserve land for temporary storage or for discharge capacity of occasional excess water.

Concrete proposals for designating areas to process excess water have already been put forward. For such areas, it would mean that the possibilities for development would be constrained and that occasionally people living in those areas would be confronted with inundations. This is in contrast with the notion of a zero-risk society, as is shown by the emotions in some reactions of locals to concrete ideas put forward by the ministry of Transport and Water Management.

Adaptive capacity

The focus of this study is on the ability of institutions to adapt to climate change. In the first section we argued that institutions might be the crucial element of adaptive capacity in the Netherlands. We also argued that adaptation to changes in flood risks in the Netherlands would take the shape of major interventions in the riverbeds and catchments. Further, we questioned whether current flood management institutions would be capable of successfully planning and implementing large projects. From the previous section, one may conclude that strategic level institutions adapted (if climate change is revealed by events). However, adaptation should occur at other levels too. Two questions emerge:

- How do people feel when confronted with plans that concern their village? (public acceptability of adaptation)
- Is the current institutional structure–the intricate system of laws, procedures and customs–fit to accommodate changes in a timely manner? (administrative feasibility of adaptation)

The people of Helhoek, a village in the middle of a planned overflow area, gave answers to the first question. These answers reveal post-modern, modern and pre-modern social dynamics. Acceptance stems from a post-modern appreciation of a necessity to address increasing flood risk and a democratic attitude to policy making. A third reason relates to the way these new approaches are framed. Reserving land for water discharge implies the creation of natural areas. So, bypasses are framed as 'green rivers.' Under a naturalization trend people are sensitive to these arguments (or vice versa). Rejection results from a defense of pre-modern societal attributes of close communities, which would be torn apart by forced, permanent evacuation. From a modern stance, people will negotiate financial compensation from the state. We note that Helhoek may not be an exemplary village because, for instance, an important contextual factor is the existence of other plans for infrastructure works (railway, motorways). Nevertheless, the indications are that, in the Netherlands, people are potentially ready to accept adaptation projects, provided that they see the need and that project planning and implementation follows acceptable procedures and delivers acceptable outcomes.

People may be ready under certain conditions, but how about institutions that govern the required negotiations? The area in which changes are likely to be necessary is the shared domain of flood risk policy and land use planning. In other words, flood risk management should become a major topic in spatial planning. Our analysis of the planning and execution of a river basin project in the valley of the river Meuse (the *Maaswerken*) provides examples of the various conflicts that should be dealt with. In the case of the *Maaswerken*, these include the distribution of costs between (governmental) stakeholders, the handling and storage of heavily contaminated dredging material, the accuracy of technical calculations, the restriction in land use options, and frustrations of the local population about their peripheral position in decision making. One of the options for breaking deadlocks is to declare the future State Government Project Procedure (*Rijksprojectenprocedure*) applicable. In the meantime, the responsible authorities have to work with the large number of procedures that are prescribed in the various laws that the many issues touch upon.

The legal and administrative instruments to facilitate planning, negotiations, decision making and execution of major infrastructure works in the catchment area of the Rhine/Meuse seem inadequate. This inadequacy has to do with the complexity of the problems and the range of interests and stakeholders that are involved. Under such conditions, interactive policy making, learning processes and open planning are likely the ways to identify and decide on operational level policies that have public support.

In sum, decision makers in the Netherlands are well aware of the risks of increased flooding due to climate change. The technologies and economic means to cope with potentially increased risks are available. Current planning and implementation procedures, however, are not adequate. This is acknowledged, and there are plans to overcome these shortcomings. Since unpredictable contextual factors (such as the occurrence of floods) may eventually be decisive, time will tell whether these plans are sufficient.

ACKNOWLEDGEMENTS

This paper is one of the outcomes of the project 'Societal and Institutional Responses to Climate Change and Climatic Hazards' (SIRCH), which was conducted with the financial support of the Environment and Climate Program of CEC-DG12 (ENV4 CT97 0447).

NOTES

1. For more information on the NMA visit http://www.nma-org.nl.
2. For more information on public communication and the Maaswerken project group visit http://www.demaaswerken.nl.

REFERENCES

Delft Hydraulics (1998), *De Rijn op Termijn*, Delft, the Netherlands: Delft Hydraulics.
del Moral, L., P.E. Van der Werff, K. Bakker, et al. (2003), 'Global Trends and Water Policy in Spain', *Water International*, **28**(3): 358–366.
De Villeneuve, C.H.V. (1996), 'Consistentie, Transparantie en Subsidiariteit: Naar Samenhang in het Internationaal Waterbeheer?', *M en R*, **12**.
Gilhuis, P.C. and H. Menninga (1996), 'Natuur en milieu in de Waterschapswet', *M en R*, **12**: 227–233.
Hisschemöller, M. (1985), 'Afzien Van Afsluiten: De Dienst Rijkswaterstaat in de Jaren Zeventig', in *Succes–en Faalfactoren bij Bestuurlijke Reorganisaties*, H.A. Van de Heijden, J. Kastelein and J. Kooiman (eds), Groningen: Wolters-Noordhoff.
Hisschemöller, M and A.A. Olsthoorn (1999), 'Identifying barriers and opportunities for policy responses to changing climatic risks', in *Climate, Change and Risk*, T. Downing, A.A. Olsthoorn and R.S.J. Tol (eds), London: Routledge, pp. 365–390.
Katsburg, P.R.A. (1996), 'De verkiezing verkozen', *Het Waterschap*, **81**(4): 122–128.
Kingdon, J.W. (1984), *Agendas, Alternatives and Public Policies*, Boston/Toronto: Addison-Wesley.
Kroon, J. (1997), 'Voeten Blijven Droog', NRC, 7 May 1997.
Kwadijk, J. and H. Middelkoop (1994), 'Estimation of Impact of Climate Change on the Peak Discharge Probability of the River Rhine', *Climatic Change*, **27**: 199–224.
Langen, A. and R.S.J. Tol (1998), 'A concise history of riverine floods and flood management in the Dutch Rhine Delta', in *Climate, Change and Risk*, T. Downing, A.A. Olsthoorn and R.S.J. Tol (eds), London: Routledge, pp. 162–173.
Lijklema, S. and M.A. Koelen (1999), *Draagvlak voor waterbeheer*, Stichting Toegepast Onderzoek Waterbeheer, Utrecht.
Mostert, E. (1997), *Water Policy Formulation in the Netherlands*, RBA Series on River Basin Administration 6, Delft University of Technology.
Mostert, E. (1998), 'River Basin Management in the European Union', *European Water Management*, June/July.

Olsthoorn A.A. (2001), 'The evolution of acceptable risk', in *Floods, flood management and climate change in the Netherlands*, A.A. Olsthoorn and R.S.J. Tol (eds), Amsterdam, pp. 43–58, IVM-VU Report R-01/04, IVM.

Olsthoorn A.A. and R.S.J. Tol (eds) (2001), *Floods, flood management and climate change in the Netherlands,* Amsterdam, IVM-VU Report R-01/04, IVM.

Perdok, P.J. (1996), *Institutional Framework for Water Management in the Netherlands*, RBA Series on River Basin Administration 3, Delft University of Technology.

RLG (1998), *Overvloed en schaarste: water als geld. Advies over de gevolgen van klimaatverandering, zeespiegelrijzing en bodemdaling voor het landelijk gebied*, Raad voor het Landelijk Gebied, RLG98/5, Ministerie LNV, Den Haag, www.rlg.nl.

TAW (2000), *From overtopping risk to flood risk*, Technische Adviescommissie voor de Waterkeringen, Delft.

Tol, R.S.J. and A. Langen (2000), 'A Concise History of Dutch River Floods', *Climatic Change*, **46**: 357–369.

Tol, R.S.J. (2001), 'Games of flood control', in *Floods, flood management and climate change in the Netherlands*, A.A. Olsthoorn and R.S.J. Tol (eds), Amsterdam, IVM-VU Report R-01/04, IVM-VU, pp. 59–65.

Van den Berg, J.T. and A. Van Hall (1997), *Waterstaats- en Waterschapsrecht*, W.E.J. Tjeenk Willink, Deventer.

Van der Grijp, N.M. and A.A. Olsthoorn (2001), 'Institutional Framework for the Management of the Rivers Rhine and Meuse in the Netherlands–An Overview', in *Floods, flood management and climate change in the Netherlands*, A.A. Olsthoorn and R.S.J. Tol (eds), Amsterdam, IVM-VU Report R-01/04, IVM-VU, pp. 5–40.

Van der Grijp, N.M. and J. Warner (2000), 'Planning and decision making related to the Maaswerken project', in *Floods, flood management and climate change in the Netherlands*, A.A. Olsthoorn and R.S.J. Tol (eds), Amsterdam, IVM-VU Report R-01/04, IVM-VU, pp. 67–88.

Van der Werff, P.E. (2004), 'Stakeholder Responses to Future Flood Management Ideas in the Rhine River Basin: Nature or Neighbor in Hell's Angle', *Regional Environmental Change*, 4: 145–158.

Van Hall, A. (ed.) (1997), *Waterbeheerswetgeving*, Koninklijke Vermande: Lelystad.

Van Leusen, W., G. Kater, and P. Van Meel (2000), *Multi-level approach to master the floods in the Netherlands' part of the Meuse,* Government of the Netherlands to the Seminar on Flood Prevention in Berlin, Germany, 7–8 October 1999.

Van Rooy, P.T.C.J. and J. de Jong (1995), 'Towards Comprehensive Water Management in the Netherlands (1): Developments', *European Water Pollution Control*, **5**(4): 59–65.

11 From the Ground Up: Local Land Use Policies, Transportation Choices and the Potential for Improved Air Quality

Kelly J. Clifton and Carolina V. Burnier

INTRODUCTION

The desire to achieve more sustainable development patterns has many communities reconsidering the relationship between land use, transportation systems and overall climate change. Emissions from the transport sector are the fastest growing source of greenhouse gas emissions and of these transport-related emissions, cars and light trucks account for nearly one-third. Thus, public policy has attempted to mitigate their contribution to climate change through a number of strategies. These efforts to reduce emissions from personal vehicles tend to be grouped into three approaches: vehicle efficiency; fuel composition; and travel demand. Improvements in vehicle technology and fuel composition have been successful in producing a significant decline in the amount of pollutants emitted per vehicle mile; however, these improvements in air quality have been offset by the increasing amount of vehicular travel. Hence, policies to reduce demand for automobile travel have received more attention of late. Local and state governments are giving more consideration to fostering strong linkages between the land development processes and transportation planning with the hope that more efficient use of urban land will lead to a decline in automobile dependence. The end goal is to decrease automobile usage by reducing the length and frequency of automobile trips and shifting demand to mass transit or non-motorized transport modes.

The federal government has prompted local consideration of these issues directly through legislative action and indirectly by setting spending priorities. For example, the EPA air quality non-attainment designation mandates that urban areas must reconcile their air pollution problems with their future transportation decisions. Metropolitan areas that suffer from high levels of air pollution are required by the federal government to develop air quality plans to limit emissions, to which ensuing short- and long-range transportation plans are required to conform. In cases where future mobile source emissions are expected to exceed the limits set forth in the plan, efforts must be directed toward transportation projects that will reduce vehicular emissions and improve regional air quality. Indirectly, federal transportation spending priorities, the Intermodal Surface Transportation Efficiency Act (ISTEA) and the Transportation Efficiency Act for the twenty-first Century (TEA-21), call for a balanced multi-modal system that integrates land development and transportation planning decisions and allocates funding to plan, build and maintain such systems.

In response to these federal initiatives, many metropolitan areas have implemented smart growth strategies to curb urban sprawl, provide mobility alternatives and create environments conducive to walking, cycling and transit use. The intent of these land use strategies is to reduce automobile travel by shortening distances between trip origins and destinations, and/or increasing the share of alternate modes by increasing their availability and relative attractiveness. Improvements in air quality would be, in principle, derived from the corresponding reduction in automobile emissions resulting from less vehicular travel, especially during congested peak periods. The ability of these locally-based policies to achieve success remains to be tested. Nonetheless, these policies represent powerful possibilities to transform the urban landscape and have the potential to affect regional climate change as they seek to change human activity patterns, behavior and their environmental consequences 'from the ground up.' They are deserving of a closer look.

Toward this end, the following chapter presents some of the theoretical links, empirical evidence and analytical methods used to understand the relationship between smart growth policies, transportation and travel, air quality and overall climate change. The chapter begins by outlining one conceptual framework for how human behavior interacts with the built environment and the resulting environmental effects. In the next section, several land development strategies or smart growth policies that have been implemented with the intent to reduce automobile use are presented. Various attempts to evaluate the success of smart growth to curb automobile dependence have been made over the years and the empirical evidence to date has been mixed. The chapter continues by summarizing some of the major findings of this thread of research. The relationships between travel behavior and emissions and air quality are also discussed. This chapter, reviewing the work that has been done to understand each of the separate processes in the path from smart growth, transportation and climate change, concludes by pointing to the lack of a coherent framework for understanding and examining this system of relationships and suggests a reconciliation of the various perspectives, approaches and disciplines involved in aspects of this research area.

LAND USE, TRANSPORTATION AND AIR QUALITY: TRENDS AND CONCEPTS

American land use patterns have undergone radical transformations over the years (see USEPA 2001 for a review). The most dramatic changes have occurred in response to technological innovation, including transportation and communications technologies. Over the last 100 years, the automobile has been at the forefront of those factors driving changes in urban spatial structure. The mobility changes brought on by transportation investments allow for a greater range of spatial access and have fostered the dispersion and decentralization of human activities. The ability to reach more distant destinations quickly has broadened the spatial extent of daily interaction and the quantity of choices available. But, the benefits of this spatial restructuring come with environmental and social costs. The re-orientation of the urban landscape to accommodate the automobile has raised concerns about urban sprawl and its consequences for the natural environment, economic efficiency and quality of life.

Parallel to the trends in land development, vehicular travel has increased substantially. In recent years the annual growth in vehicle miles traveled (VMT) has outpaced population growth. The amount of VMT on US roads has been increasing at a rate of 3.1 per cent per year since 1980, while the population has increased at an annual rate of 1.1 per cent for the same time period (BTS 1996). This growth is due in part to demographic and market changes, such as increasing numbers of women in the workplace, vehicle ownership rates and driver licensure. But these social trends explain only part of the story. The increasing numbers of trips and longer distance traveled are also contributing factors (Handy, et al. 2002b).

As a result of this increased automobile travel, urban areas are experiencing growing traffic congestion. According to the 2003 Annual Urban Mobility Report conducted by the Texas Transportation Institute, traffic congestion has spread to more cities, affects more of the road system, and extends over more time during the day and to more days of the week. According to the study, the amount of traffic experiencing congested conditions in the peak travel periods has doubled in 20 years, from 33 per cent in 1982 to 67 per cent in 2001. The percentage of the major roadway system that is congested has risen from 34 per cent in 1982 to 59 per cent in 2001 (Shrank and Lomax 2003). In addition to loss in productivity, driver frustration and safety issues, these conditions raise concerns about the impacts on the environment and air quality.

Vehicle emissions have been drastically reduced due to innovations and technological improvements in engine efficiencies, exhaust controls and fuel composition, and the air quality in US cities has improved as a result. However, the growth in VMT and increasing levels of congestion threaten to offset these improvements. As a result, policies to address congestion and to reduce VMT have been the focus of local, regional and state efforts (Frank 2000). Among the strategies to curb automobile use are attempts to alter the built environment in ways that influence activity and travel decisions of the population.

A conceptual diagram of the relationships between the built environment, human activity, travel behavior and air quality is shown in Figure 11.1. The built environment consists of land use and urban form elements interacting with transportation and communications infrastructure to influence local and regional accessibility. This, in turn, impacts the residential and employment location decisions of individuals, households and firms. The decision to purchase an automobile is strongly tied to where one lives as well as the other transportation and accessibility options available. Local and regional accessibility and the transportation options available influence decisions about daily activities and the travel needed to reach destinations. These travel patterns, combined with the fleet of vehicles on the roadway, determine the amount and type of vehicular emissions. Other sources of pollutants in the area and the atmospheric conditions in the region are subject to the land use patterns of the area, including the locations of manufacturing and utilities, the amount of vegetation and ground cover and overall levels of urbanization. Ultimately, these factors all interact to affect the overall air quality of a region. From this conceptual diagram, it is evident that the ways that the built environment influences air quality are many and the relationships are complex. This chapter focuses on those land use strategies that aim to influence travel demand by increasing accessibility and transportation options.

LAND USE STRATEGIES FOR CURBING AUTO-DEPENDENCE

Since the mid-1990s, the smart growth movement has attempted to make more direct linkages to the environment, transportation and quality of life. Smart growth principles include the mixing of land uses, encouraging compact development, producing a range of housing choices, creating walkable environments, fostering distinct, attractive communities, preserving open space, directing development toward existing urbanized areas, providing transportation alternatives, streamlining decision making and encouraging public participation (Tregoning, et al. 2002). Specific policies have been put in place at various levels of government with the intent of creating urban development that is consistent with these principles. Motivated by smart growth policies, research has focused on characterizing urban sprawl and development patterns with the intent of informing the policy discussion about how best to craft responsive policies.

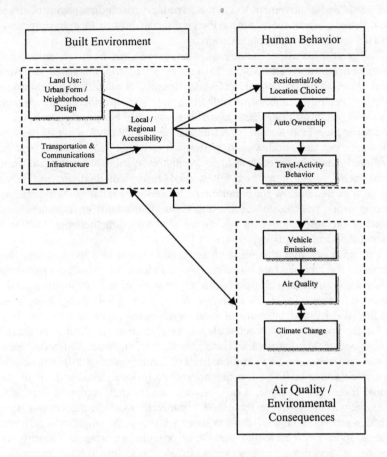

Figure 11.1   Built environment effects on travel behavior and air quality

Traditionally, the location and density of residential populations have been used to characterize the intensity of land development. Fulton, et al. (2002) compare population growth to changes in urbanized land area using aggregate population densities across a number of cities. The share of population growth of the suburbs relative to that of the central city is frequently used to describe the extent of urban decentralization and dispersion. Recently, Wassmer (2000) used this measure, as well as other demographic statistics, to describe the degree of centralization. The need for additional measures has been punctuated by research examining the land use and transportation interaction, where measures that capture the local or micro-scale built environment are required (Handy, et al. 2002a). In response to these needs and a movement to characterize the various dimensions of urban sprawl better, the measures to describe land use and urban form have recently increased in number and sophistication.

The multi-dimensional nature of urban growth has been recognized and operationalized in recent work. Galster, et al. (2001) identified different spatial dimensions of sprawl including density, continuity, concentration, clustering, centrality, nuclearity and proximity. Song (forthcoming) expands upon these and contributes measures of urban form. The specific attributes of urban form examined include street design and circulation systems, density, land use mix, accessibility and pedestrian access. Song created several operational measures for each attribute, which were validated using data from several metropolitan areas over 50 years. Measures of land use and urban form such as these allow for better characterization of urban growth patterns, directing urban policies to specific attributes of the built environment, and enhancing the resolution with which we study the link between land use, transportation and air quality.

The strategies that attempt to direct urban growth into more sustainable patterns can be grouped into broad categories in terms of how they operate on the landscape, including those various dimensions of urban growth patterns mentioned above. Table 11.1 shows one grouping of these categories, including density and intensity of land development, type and mix of land uses, street connectivity, street scale of development, aesthetic and design elements and regional structure (Handy, et al. 2002a). Policies affecting each of these categories can be operationalized or implemented at different spatial scales from site-specific to the neighborhood, to local area, and up to the regional level. For example, a mix of uses can be employed in a particular development project, where retail and commercial exist on the ground floor and office and residential inhabit the space above. At the neighborhood level, the term applies to residential areas that provide opportunities nearby for shopping, entertainment and services, usually in commercial corridors or neighborhood cores. Jobs-housing balance describes how this might be operationalized at the regional level to ensure an even distribution of residential and employment opportunities across a larger geographic area.

Promoting a mix of land uses and housing types also acts to desegregate the current land use patterns, which locate residential areas away from retail, service and employment opportunities. A variety of mixes places opportunities for human activity such as work, recreation, shopping and leisure near the home, again enhancing the attractiveness of alternative modes of travel. Another benefit is the provision of more options in residential location and housing type, giving consumers more choices in housing type, neighborhood and lifestyle. Like more intensely developed land, mixed-use development has the potential to alter travel patterns and the residential, employment and firm location decisions and automobile ownership rates.

Street connectivity and network design refers to the availability of alternative routes in the transportation network. A dense grid-like network provides more direct routes, which act to shorten the paths between origins and destinations. Networks that are more curvilinear have fewer alternate paths, more dead-end streets, and have more circuitous routes. The shorter trip lengths and increased connectivity of the grid network are conducive to the use of non-motorized transport but the increased number of intersections does have the disadvantage of increased pedestrian delay and exposure to vehicular traffic. The network design does not affect the use or intensity of the developed land directly, although the density of the road network does affect block size and can partition land areas. Curvilinear streets, while more indirect, may offer safer alternatives for pedestrians and bicyclists since routes tend to have fewer intersections and may have more local traffic.

The scale of the street and how it relates to the adjacent buildings is also an important consideration. This dimension of development describes the 'human scale' or orientation toward non-motorized transportation. Similar in concept are the aesthetic qualities of a place. These are measures of attractiveness that can be highly subjective and less tangible concepts to control through policy. Nonetheless, the concept has potential to exert influence over residential location choices and the decision to walk, bike or take transit in an area.

Finally, the overall urban structure is a critical factor. The spatial distribution of land use, urban form transportation infrastructure and services across a region influences the availability of competing opportunities and the ease with which those destinations can be accessed by various modes. This last dimension describes the aggregate characteristics of a region, such as the degree of centrality, poly-nuclearity and continuity of land development, to name a few. This dimension is perhaps the most difficult to control via policy since, in some ways, it represents a composite of many policies across a number of jurisdictions.

Although strategies that affect each of these dimensions of the built environment can be employed individually, smart growth approaches tend to adopt a set of these policies that work in concert to shape aspects of the built environment and to create more sustainable urban patterns. Overall, the intended effect is to create environments that provide choices that enable different travel decisions. Many of these strategies are implemented on a state, regional or metropolitan scale, while others target new or infill development at the local scale. In addition to their direct transportation impacts, these policies are relevant when trying to understand regional climate change and mediate its impacts. For example, building redundancies into the transportation system such as more choices in travel routes and modes can decrease the adverse effects of severe weather and natural hazards on local populations. On the other hand, these strategies may create additional concerns about evacuation and emergency response if higher levels of congestion result from higher development densities.

Table 11.1   *Dimensions of the built environment that influence travel choices*

Dimension	Definition	Example of measures
Density and intensity	Amount of activity in a given area	Persons per acre or jobs per square mile Ratio of commercial floor space to land area
Land use mix	Proximity of different land uses	Distance from house to nearest store Share of total land area for different uses Dissimilarity index
Street connectivity	Directness and availability of alternative routes through the network	Intersections per square mile of area Ratio of straight-line distance of network distance Average block length
Street scale	Three-dimensional space along a street as bounded by buildings	Ratio of building heights to street width Average distance from street to buildings
Aesthetic qualities	Attractiveness and appeal of a place	Per cent of ground in shade at noon Number of locations with graffiti per square mile
Regional structure	Distribution of activities and transportation facilities across the region	Rate of decline in density with distance from downtown Classification based upon concentrations of activity and transportation network

Source: Handy, et al. (2002a)

The State of Maryland provides one example of a state-level approach to managing growth and development. In 1997, the State of Maryland passed a set of policies under the collective umbrella of smart growth. Maryland's Office of Smart Growth now directs development by targeting programs and funding mechanisms that support established communities, direct efforts toward designated growth areas and act to protect rural and agricultural areas. The following initiatives comprise the core of Maryland's smart growth strategy: Priority Funding Areas, Brownfields Development, Live Near Your Work, Job Creation Tax Credits and Rural Legacy. The Priority Funding Areas Act is the centerpiece of Maryland's approach and exerts influence by directing state investment in infrastructure, including transportation, to those geographic areas designated for growth by state, county and local governments. The remaining four components complement this legislation through preservation of agricultural and rural lands that exist outside of these Priority Funding Areas and by encouraging growth within them through a mix of regulations and incentives.

Much attention has been given to attempts to employ land use change at the neighborhood level to affect travel. New Urbanism and Transit Oriented Development are two taxonomies of strategies that have received the lion's share of interest and debate among planners, developers, policy makers and academics. Both of these development approaches offer a mix of land uses–esidential with retail and services nearby, at varying densities and with a focus on promoting alternative transportation options including walking, transit and cycling. Many new and infill developments have been built in the US in accordance with these development philosophies. Early efforts include the developments of Seaside, Celebration, Kentlands and Laguna West, which have achieved near iconic status (see Bernick and Cervero 1997 and Katz 1994 for a review of early examples). More recently, the movement has produced a more diverse selection that caters to a variety of incomes, lifestyles and urban environments, while holding steadfast to the fundamental tenets of earlier development (see Dittmar and Ohland 2004 and Steuteville and Langdon 2003 for more recent reviews of best practices). New Urbanist developments have typically been successful in attracting homebuyers desiring these attributes and willing to pay a premium for them (Song and Knaap 2003). However, the overall impact of these types of developments on travel behavior is the subject of continuing debate among supporters and cynics.

Policies that attempt to alter the spatial distribution and character of activities, in terms of those dimensions above, are expected to affect the travel decisions made by individuals and households. The relationships between land use and urban form and travel behavior have been the topic of focused academic study for the last twenty-five years. The next section explores the evidence from this research and what the results tell us about the relationships between land use and travel.

LAND USE AND AUTOMOBILE TRAVEL

One goal of smart growth is to strengthen the policy relationships between urban land development and the transportation system; however, much remains uncertain about how these two systems interact with each other and with the activity and travel decisions of system users. The interaction between land use and travel behavior has been recognized within the transportation planning community for some time; however, the specific relationships between the two remain the subject of inquiry and debate among researchers. Several reviews of the literature in this area exist (Handy 1996; Badoe and Miller 2000; Crane 2000; Ewing and Cervero 2001) and document the various attempts to quantify these relationships.

Many studies aim to test the effect of smart growth principles, including New Urbanism and Transit-Oriented Development, by comparing the travel patterns of individuals living and working in different development types. These empirical studies attempt to tease out relationships between different elements of land use, urban form and travel choices by examining the effect of various qualities of the built environment and characteristics of the individual trip-maker and her household on travel behavior. The operationalized urban form and land use measures employed vary but the basic dimensions included are those discussed in the previous section. Travel itself has been expressed a variety of ways, including trip frequency, trip length, mode choice and VMT (Handy 2002).

From their extensive review of the research in this area, Ewing and Cervero (2001) summarize some important findings that characterize the relationship between the different expressions of travel and urban form and socioeconomic variables. For one, socioeconomic characteristics of individuals and their households tend to have greater influence on the frequency of trips than those of the built environment. Two, trip lengths are primarily a function of the urban form with socioeconomic characteristics having lesser influence. Three, the built environment and traveler characteristics both influence the mode of travel. Finally, land use and urban form characteristics contribute significantly toward explaining VMT, a product of the three other measures of travel. From their review of previous studies, Ewing and Cervero summarized the typical elasticities of travel variables (number of trips and VMT) with respect to a number of different land use variables, shown in Table 11.2. Although these results do not point to a large magnitude of influence for each of these variables, the cumulative effects are not insignificant in reducing automobile travel.

Other studies have generated empirical evidence supporting the ability of smart growth interventions to affect travel, particularly among receptive populations. Handy and Clifton (2001) found that residents who want transportation alternatives make residential location decisions that facilitate these desired behaviors. In a study of households making a change in residential location (Krizek 2003), households that moved to neighborhoods with pedestrian-friendly characteristics tend to walk more than others. While these studies point to the potential of smart growth policies to provide transportation choices that residents will take advantage of, one limitation is that they only uncover correlations between smart growth land use patterns and declines in automobile use and do not go farther in defining causal relationships. This question of self-selection–do residents who desire less dependence on the automobile seek out neighborhoods where less auto travel is possible–has been a caveat in nearly all studies on this topic. Moreover, land use intervenes into the travel decision process in a number of ways, including residential location, automobile ownership and daily travel, as shown in Figure 11.1. Understanding the complexities of these linkages in an integrated fashion will be a challenge for future work in this area (Miller, et al. 2004).

Table 11.2   Typical elasticities of travel with respect to the built environment

	Vehicle Trips	Vehicle Miles Traveled
Local Density	-0.05	-0.05
Local Diversity (Mix)	-0.03	-0.05
Local Design	-0.05	-0.03
Regional Accessibility	-	-0.20

Source: Ewing and Cervero (2001)

Study of the land use-travel behavior relationship has evolved as the methods, data and modes of inquiry have become more advanced. But this line of research has produced many more questions than answers, particularly in its ability to give definitive answers that can guide policy. The question of whether relationships exist between the spatial arrangements of activities and transportation is not in doubt. Rather, the debate centers on the degree to which land use affects the amount of travel, the modes chosen and the locations frequented. These findings point to ways that various policy relevant variables might impact automobile use but they fall short of quantifying a causal relationship. As a whole, the body of research does not offer strong suggestions about which specific dimensions of land use and urban form influence travel behavior. Also, we know little about how these characteristics of the physical environment interact with the decision making of the traveler. The ability to find definitive answers has been hampered in the past by lack of data–relatively poor information on land use and urban form and travel data that is based upon a limited number of days. While data issues are still a concern, the problem now centers on how best to examine the complexities of these interactions. The relationships between transportation, air quality and climate change are even more elusive and the next frontier of research will wrestle with linking land use and travel behavior to air quality, which is discussed in the next section.

IMPACTS ON AIR QUALITY

Transportation is a major contributor to air pollution and is responsible for a large percentage of emissions controlled by the Federal Clean Act Air (Bae 1993). The US Environmental Protection Agency (USEPA) has set national air quality standards for the criteria pollutants controlled by the federal Clean Air Act of 1977. These pollutants are the six principal air pollutants: nitrogen dioxide (NO_2), ozone (O_3), sulfur dioxide (SO_2), particulate matter (PM), carbon monoxide (CO) and lead (Pb) (USEPA 2003). Since the Clean Air Act of 1977, metropolitan planning organizations (MPOs) and state transportation programs have had to conform to the National Ambient Air Quality Standards (NAAQs) in their State Implementation Plans (SIPs) (USDOT 2000). These plans have to demonstrate how states and metropolitan areas will achieve and maintain air quality goals through regulation and measures that reduce emissions, including travel demand management, transportation systems management and vehicle fuel and emissions control technology. The intended effects of each of these approaches on emissions are shown in Figure 11.2.

Since the late 1970s, automobile emissions control has been an important area of research and air quality has improved dramatically due to technological advances in cleaner fuels and exhaust emission control equipment. By the 1990s, with the great increase in the number of vehicles, it was becoming apparent that these new technological improvements in emissions were soon going to be surpassed by the large number of vehicle miles traveled. In fact, there has been a 32 per cent decrease in emissions per vehicle but a 29 per cent increase in population and a 121 per cent increase in VMT since the 1970s (USEPA 1998).

With the Clean Air Act Amendments of 1990, travel demand strategies were given greater emphasis as a means to deal with future emissions. These strategies included increasing public transportation facilities and implementing land use and growth management techniques. As mentioned in the previous section, evaluations of land use strategies and their ability to reduce VMT have resulted in mixed findings. If the relationships between land use and travel behavior are intricate, those between travel and emissions are no less complicated. The study of land use and travel behavior focuses on the amount of travel as measured by travel frequency, trip length, vehicle and person miles traveled and travel mode. The literature has less to say about how land use affects travel speeds, a key factor in determining the amount and type of emissions.

Vehicle Miles Traveled, Travel Speeds and Emissions

Air quality impacts of transportation strategies are typically evaluated in terms of the reductions in mobile source emissions brought about by these strategies

(Cambridge Systematics 2001). Although there is considerable variation in the methodologies used, the typical framework for evaluating the emissions outcomes of transportation strategies in current practice has two main stages:

1. Estimating the emission-producing activities resulting from transportation sources; and
2. Quantifying emissions caused by these activities. VMT is one important component of emissions evaluation; vehicle speeds are another.

The quantification of emission-producing activities, like number of trips, VMT and speeds, is performed in practice using transportation demand models such as the Urban Transportation Planning System (UTPS) generation of models. The inputs to these models include characteristics of the population, land use and activity system, and the transportation network and services. The output from these planning models is considered sufficient to estimate emissions on a regional basis, though there is considerable debate about the extent to which these models are sensitive to many of the strategies that regions might introduce to induce change in travel patterns and reduce emissions. Neither are these models sensitive to changes in the spatial distribution of activity opportunities that are expected to come about through contemplated smart growth policies.

USEPA (1999) supports a series of emission factor models called MOBILE. At present, these are the only EPA approved models and they are required for preparing SIPs and conformity analysis. These emission factor models employ highly aggregated fleet estimates and average emission rates that are not specific to the fleet in operation, mode of vehicle operation or grade of the highway facility (Bachman 1997). For estimating total vehicle emissions in a given time period, estimates of VMT are combined with pollution rates per mile traveled (USEPA 2003b). The EPA's 1996 National Air Quality and Emission Trends Report states that 'emissions estimates are derived from many factors, including the level of industrial activity, technology changes, fuel consumption, VMT and other activities that affect air pollution.' Motivated by a growing need among transportation planners, several studies have proposed modal emission models, which are highly dis-aggregated and can explicitly model emissions resulting from a wide range of vehicle operating modes (see for example, TU-Graz 1998 re: European experience; Guensler, et al. 1998 re: MEASURE model at Georgia Tech; Yu 1997).

With these evaluation methods, studies have examined the extent to which the number of vehicle miles traveled affects overall regional air quality. The empirical findings from studies examining travel behavior reviewed above show limitations on the impact of travel demand strategies alone, including land use approaches, to improve air quality. A study conducted by

Bae (1993) is more hopeful. The study reports that based on the South Coast Air Quality Management District's projections in the 1991 Draft Air Quality Management Plan, growth management accounted for around two-fifths of VMT-related emissions reductions. But, the use of VMT as a primary determinant of future air quality has been questioned. For example, Ho and Fauver (1997) challenged the current method of using VMT as the basis for future air quality estimates. Their results find a correlation between the number of ozone exceedances and daily VMT; however, the relationship is not a strong one and points to the importance of other factors in determining air quality.

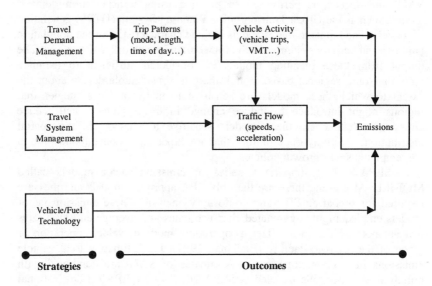

Figure 11.2   Analytical process for evaluating congestion management air quality (CMAQ) projects (Cambridge Systematics 2000)

While there has been a focus on automobile emissions control due to the number of vehicle miles traveled, more attention should be directed to the speed of travel. Several studies suggest that travel speeds may be a better determinant of emissions outcomes than VMT because vehicles emit criteria pollutants at different quantities at different speeds. For example, Tang, et al. (2003) modeled the effect of speed on volatile organic compounds (VOC), nitrous oxides (NO_x) and carbon monoxide (CO) emission rates using MOBILE 6. The results show that the emission rates for all three pollutants are remarkably sensitive to varying speeds. The Metropolitan Washington Council of Governments (MWCOG) developed air quality speed charts to show how automobile emissions vary according to speed. These charts show that NO_x emissions are higher at low speeds (< 15 mph) and at high speeds (> 45 mph). It also shows that VOC emissions are highest at low speeds (< 15 mph) and are lowest at high speeds (> 45 mph). These graphs show that both VOC and NO_x emissions are low in the speed range of 35–40 mph. The US EPA (1996) demonstrated how speed affects emission rates using their MOBILE 5 model. Their results, in Figure 11.3, show that VOC and CO emission rates typically decrease as speed increases, but increase at high speeds. NO_x emission rates turn up at very low speeds (USEPA 1996). Finally, a study by Roberston, et al. (1998) concludes that a reduction in speed leads to a significant reduction in NO_x emissions. However, the effects of speed are not as evident in the rate of CO and hydrocarbon emissions. The study also notes that driving behaviors that produce an increase in acceleration and deceleration events increase emissions and fuel consumption. The importance of these relationships in emissions are subject to change with the introduction of new technologies, such as hybrid vehicles, and the importance of driver behavior and speed will have different implications as new fuels and power mechanisms are established in the marketplace.

These findings point to the complexities in estimating emissions, particularly when relating emissions outcomes directly to land use and smart growth strategies. Transportation planning research efforts have centered on linking land use arrangements to travel behavior outcomes, particularly overall VMT. Air quality analysis has aimed to link VMT and/or travel speeds to emissions rates. However, a comprehensive, integrated framework that considers all the manifestations of land use on vehicle emissions has not been widely employed in practice, although some have been proposed (Marquez and Smith 1999; Miller, et al. 2004; Waddell 2002). As it stands, the present state of research recognizes that land use and urban form play a role in decisions about residential location, auto ownership, daily activity and travel, but the specific relationships and interactions are not well defined nor understood. Moreover, little is known about how land development patterns affect vehicle speeds and the consequences for air quality, a key relationship given·the findings of the studies above.

This chapter has focused on climate change linkages between development, transportation investments, personal lifestyle choices and consequences for air quality. Of specific interest here is the contribution of personal motor vehicle travel to regional climate change via the emission of greenhouse gases and other pollutants. It is important to recognize that the changes in regional climatic conditions may in turn have profound impacts on transportation and land use, although very little is known about the ways in which climate change may ultimately impact transportation demand (Mills and Andrey 2002). Regional climate change and the resulting consequences

Methods and cases

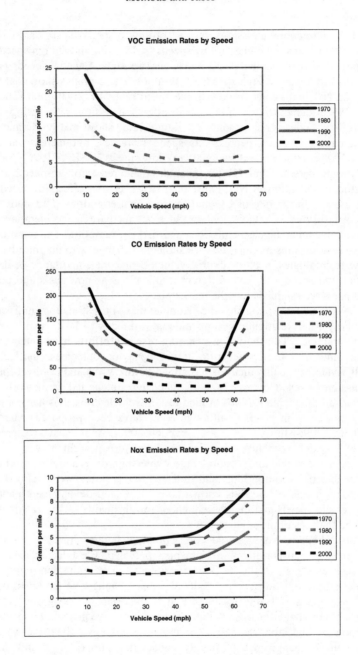

Figure 11.3   Relationship between speed and emissions for VOC, CO and NO_x

$$NO_x$$

(Source: USEPA 1996)

such as changes in weather patterns, precipitation, sea levels, coastlines and natural hazards may impact future transportation and land use decisions. For example, elevated sea levels may redirect coastal development and the location of roadways and other infrastructure. Increasing occurrence of natural hazards such as hurricanes, blizzards, floods and tornados will create greater need for emergency response and evacuation planning. The distribution of environmentally sensitive areas will require attention in planning processes for land development and transportation. Relative to the discussion in this chapter, climate change may also impact the ability for urban areas to meet air quality goals. Studies have linked weather patterns to ozone production and mobile source emissions rates (Grambsch 2002). Temperatures influence atmospheric chemical reactions, including ozone generation and acid deposition from NO_x and SO_2. These dynamic relationships and interactions between transportation, land use, air quality and climate change present real challenges for planners and policy makers to understand and mitigate the environmental impacts of policy interventions and future urban development scenarios.

CONCLUSIONS

From the results of empirical investigations discussed above, the ability of land use strategies to curb automobile travel is mixed at best. But, before policies are dismissed as ineffective, several key aspects should be considered. Most of the structure and form of urban development patterns is fractured. There are few, if any, cases in the United States that offer the coherent and continuous urban landscape to which most smart growth approaches aspire. This being the case, empirical studies are forced to examine small, incongruous areas that possess land use and urban form with the normative qualities of mixed-use, compact development that accommodates alternative modes of travel, and contrast them with equally discontinuous areas with characteristics of the opposite extreme. For smart growth strategies to reach their full potential, they must be applied in a comprehensive, regional context and allowed to promote change across the entire continuum of a metropolitan area.

Evaluation and ultimately implementation of specific smart growth policies in a given area requires addressing several challenges. This would entail a richer and deeper understanding of the interactions between land use, travel and activity behavior, and vehicular emissions over time and space than is currently available or is reflected in existing tools used in transportation and regional/urban planning practice. Analysis to support decision making has been largely predicated on the output from regional model systems that relate traffic congestion and air quality to help determine the effects of various alternative transportation investment schemes. However, the models can be insensitive to many policy effects, especially those that seek to influence travel behavior by affecting the underlying spatial distribution of activity opportunities, as is the intent of certain smart growth policies. Characteristics of land use and urban form have not been adequately modeled. Likewise the land use changes that result from transportation investments, and the interactions between the two, are rarely considered. These drawbacks limit the range of policies that can be realistically evaluated, and hence limit the usefulness of known models to inform the decision making process in the realm of smart growth planning coupled with transportation system planning.

The limitations in the ability of current state-of-practice methodology are deeply rooted in the historical origins of transportation and land use models. These were conceived at and for a time when the role of planning was limited to building support for roadway projects intended to open up development opportunities in the suburbs. The notion of integrating land use and transportation planning to achieve efficient patterns of land and transportation capacity utilization was not a guiding concern of transportation planners or decision makers. Mitigating the externalities of growth and hyper-congestion, including air quality, climate change and other impacts to the social and physical environment, did not become a major policy driver until much later. As the policies evolved, and society's expectations and preferences started shifting, the tools available for analysis and decision making remained largely static.

Meeting these challenges requires advances in both methodology and underlying theory, supported by carefully gathered empirical analysis. In addition, it is critical to consider the dynamics of the associated processes, as well as the spatial dimension of the changes under consideration. For instance, it is essential to examine the processes by which smart growth policies affect and determine development patterns of metropolitan areas, the time frames over which changes in development patterns might be expected to occur, and to document the spatial scales of such change. However, existing methods have been most deficient in the linkages between land development patterns and travel demand and, specifically, in relating land use characteristics to levels of automobile use, and more generally to the associated travel and activity patterns. These are particularly important because they establish a critical bridge between land use, which characterizes the spatial distribution of activity opportunities, and transportation patterns resulting from the activity-travel choices of users. Forging the link between urban structure, automobile use and air quality remains an area of critical importance and one where our fundamental knowledge is insufficient. Smart growth policies, then, should not be dismissed as ineffective until both the policies and the evaluation methodologies mature, and more is understood about the influence of these policies and other exogenous drivers.

REFERENCES

Bachman, W.H. (1997), *Towards a GIS Based Modal Model of Automobile Exhaust Emissions*, Doctoral Dissertation, Department of Civil Engineering, Georgia Institute of Technology.

Badoe, D. and E. Miller (2000), 'Transportation–land use interaction: empirical findings in North America, and their implications for modeling', *Transportation Research Part D*, 5(4): 235–263.

Bae, C-H C. (1993), 'Air quality and travel behavior–Untying the knot. Journal of the American Planning Association', *ABI/INFORM Global*, 59(1): 65–74

Bernick, M. and R. Cervero (1997), *Transit villages in the 21st century*, New York: McGraw Hill.

BTS (1996), *National Transportation Statistics 1996*, US Department of Transportation, Bureau of Transportation Statistics, November.

Cambridge Systematics, Inc. (2000), *A Sampling of Emissions Analysis Techniques for Transportation Control Measures*, Washington, DC: Federal Highway Administration, US Department of Transportation.

Cambridge Systematics, Inc. (2001), *Quantifying Air–Quality and Other Benefits and Costs of Transportation Control Measures*, National Cooperative Highway Research Program (NCHRP) Report 462, Transportation Research Board, Washington, DC: National Academies.

Crane, R. (2000), 'The influence of urban form on travel: an interpretive review', *Journal of Planning Literature*, 15(1): 3–24.

Dittmar, H. and G. Ohland (2004), *The new transit town: Best practices in transit-oriented development*, Washington, DC: Island Press.

Ewing, R. and R. Cervero (2001), 'Travel and built environment', *Transportation Research Record*, 1780: 87–114.

Frank, L. (2000), 'Improving air quality through growth management and travel reduction strategies', *Journal of Urban Planning and Development*, 124(1): 11–32.

Fulton, W., R. Pendall, M. Nguyen and A. Harrison (2002), *Who sprawls most? How growth patterns differ across the US*, Washington, DC: Brookings Institution.

Galster, G., R. Hanson, M.R. Ratcliffe, H. Wolman, S. Coleman and J. Freihage (2001), 'Wrestling sprawl to the ground: Defining and measuring an elusive concept', *Housing Policy Debate*, 12(4): 681–717.

Grambsch, A. (2002), *Climate Change and Air Quality*, The Potential Impacts of Climate Change on Transportation Federal Research Partnership Workshop, Washington, DC: US Department of Transportation, Center for Climate Change and Environmental Forecasting, 1–2 October 2002, http://climate.volpe.dot.gov/workshop1002/workshop.pdf.

Guensler, R., S. Washington and W. Bachman (1998), *Overview of the MEASURE Modeling Framework*, Transportation Planning and Air Quality III: Emerging Strategies and Working Solutions, Transportation Research Board 77th Annual Meeting, January, pp. 51–70.

Handy, S. (1996), 'Methodologies for exploring the link between urban form and travel behavior', *Transportation Research D*, **1**(2): 151–165.

Handy, S. (2002), 'Smart growth and the transportation–land use connection: what does the research tell us?', in *New Urbanism and Smart Growth: A Research Symposium*, National Center for Smart Growth Research and Education, University of Maryland, 3 May 2002.

Handy, S. and K. Clifton (2001), 'Local Shopping as a Strategy for Reducing Automobile Travel', *Transportation*, **28**: 317–346.

Handy, S., M. Boarnet, R. Ewing and R. Killingsworth (2002a), 'How the built environment affects physical activity: views from urban planning', *American Journal of Preventative Medicine*, **23**(2S): 64–73

Handy, S., A. De Garmo and K. Clifton (2002b), *Understanding the Growth in Non-work VMT*, Report No. SWUTC/02/167802-1, Southwest Region University Transportation Center, The University of Texas at Austin, February.

Ho, C. and K. Fauver (1997), 'VMT vs ozone exceedances: An analysis of correlation', in *Conference Proceeding: Transport Land use Air Quality ASCE*, Reston, VA, pp. 286–295.

Katz, P. (1994), *The new urbanism: Toward an architecture of community*, New York, NY: McGraw Hill.

Krizek, K. (2003), 'Residential Relocation and Changes in Urban Travel: Does Neighborhood-Scale Urban Form Matter?', *Journal of the American Planning Association*, **69**(3).

Marquez, L and N. Smith (1999), 'A framework for linking land use and air quality', *Environmental Modeling and Software*, **14**: 541–548.

Miller, E.J., J.D. Hunt, J.E. Abraham and P. Salvini (2004), 'Microsimulating Urban Systems', *Computers, Environment and Urban Systems*, **28**: 9–44.

Mills, B. and J. Andrey (2002), *Climate Change and Transportation: Potential Interactions and Impacts*, The Potential Impacts of Climate Change on Transportation Federal Research Partnership Workshop, Washington, DC: US Department of Transportation, Center for Climate Change and Environmental Forecasting, 1–2 October 2002, http://climate.volpe.dot.gov/workshop1002/workshop.pdf.

Robertson, S.A., H.A.Ward, G.Marsden, U. Sandberg and U. Hammerström (1998), *The effect of speed on noise, vibration and emissions from vehicles*, Master Working Paper. R 1.2.1, Report for the EC (DGVII).

Shrank, G. and T. Lomax (2003), *The 2003 Annual Urban Mobility Report*, Texas Transportation Institute, Texas A & M University.

Song, Y. (forthcoming), 'Comparing Urban Growth in US Metropolitan Areas: A Spatial Analysis of Urban Form', *International Regional Science Review*.

Song, Y. and G. Knaap (2003), 'New urbanism and housing values: a disaggregate assessment', *Journal of Urban Economics*, **54**(2): 218–238.

Steuteville, R. and P. Langdon (2003), *The new urbanism: Comprehensive report and best practices guide*, Ithaca, NY: New Urban Publications, Inc.

Tang, T., M. Roberts, and C. Ho (2003), *Sensitivity Analysis of MOBILE6 Motor Vehicle Emission Factor Model*, FHWA Resource Center, Report Number FHWA-RC-Atlanta-03-0007.

Tregoning, H, J. Agyeman, and C. Shenot (2002), 'Sprawl, Smart Growth, and sustainability', *Local Environment*, **7**(4): 341–347.

TU-Graz (1998), 'Instantaneous Emission Data and their use in Estimating Passenger Car Emissions', Institute of Internal Combustion Engines and Thermodynamics, Technical University Graz, VKM-THD, **94**, August.

USDOT (2000), *Transportation Conformity: A Basic Guide for State and Local Officials*, Washington, DC: United States Department of Transportation, Federal Highway Administration.

USEPA (1996), *Mobile5B, fleet average, low altitude, including NLEV and Heavy Duty Vehicle Standards*, Washington, DC: United States Environmental Protection Agency, Office of Air Quality Planning and Standards.

USEPA (1998), *1996 National Air Quality and Emission Trends Report* (EPA 454/R-97-013), Washington, DC: United States Environmental Protection Agency, Office of Air Quality Planning and Standards.

USEPA (1999), *Description of the MOBILE Highway Vehicle Emission Factor Model*, Washington, DC: United States Environmental Protection Agency, Office of Mobile Sources, April.

USEPA (2001), *Our built and natural environment: A technical review of the interactions between land use, transportation, and environmental quality* (EPA 231-R-01-002), Washington, DC: United States Environmental Protection Agency, Development, Community and Environment Division, January.

USEPA (2003), *2003 National Air Quality and Emission Trends Report–Special Studies Report*, EPA Document Number EPA 454/R-03-005, Washington, DC: United States Environmental Protection Agency, Office of Air Quality Planning and Standards.

Waddell, P. (2002), 'UrbanSim, modeling urban development for land use, transportation, and environmental planning', *Journal of the American Planning Association*, **68**: 297–314.

Wassmer, R. (2000), *Urban sprawl in a US metropolitan area: ways to measure and a comparison of the Sacramento area to similar*

metropolitan areas in California and the US, Lincoln Institute of Land
    Policy Working Paper.
Yu, L. (1997), *Collection and evaluation of modal traffic data for
    determination of vehicle emission rates under certain driving conditions*,
    Technical Report No. TxDOT 1485-1, Texas Southern University,
    Houston, TX.

12 Regional Energy Demand and Adaptations to Climate Change: Methodology and Application to the State of Maryland, USA

Matthias Ruth and Ai-Chen Lin[1]

MERGING RESEARCH AGENDAS

To date, the bulk of climate change research has concentrated on biogeochemical processes, and where this research interfaced with human systems, it was much concerned with the identification of strategies to mitigate climate change through the reduction of greenhouse gas emissions and the quantification of impacts on agriculture, forestry and fisheries (IPCC 2001). Only very recently did researchers start to investigate potential impacts and adaptation strategies in urban areas–the places of much economic and social activity (Rosenzweig and Solecki 2001; Ruth and Kirshen 2001). Since these are also the areas in which most energy is consumed, significant synergies may exist between mitigation to reduce greenhouse gas emissions and adaptation to reduce climate impacts.

This chapter concentrates on the potential impacts of climate change on energy demand in the residential and commercial sectors of one state in the US–Maryland–and explores demand changes in the broader context of economic and population changes. Impacts on manufacturing energy use are not analyzed here because previous studies as well as our own preliminary analyses strongly suggest that manufacturing energy use is not temperature sensitive.

Due to adequate empirical data, possible impacts of severe weather events on the reliability of regional energy transmission and distribution are not dealt with here. However, anecdotal evidence suggests that severe weather impacts–in the form of ice storms, heat waves, high winds and so on–can seriously impact local energy supply.

In the following section we briefly review climate-related drivers behind energy demand in the US and in Maryland. We then describe the data used in this study and address the methodology used to simulate–on the basis of sub-regional climate and population data, as well as energy prices–possible future scenarios under a range of socioeconomic assumptions. We close the chapter with conclusions about adaptation strategies for the region.

ENERGY DEMAND SENSITIVITY TO CLIMATE AND CLIMATE CHANGE

Much of society's use of energy is to satisfy heating and cooling preferences. In the United States, residential households devote 58 per cent (EIA 1999), commercial buildings 40 per cent (EIA 1995), and industrial facilities 6 per cent (EIA 2001) of energy consumption to space-conditioning requirements, not including water heating. As these sectors account for 20, 16 and 38 per cent of total US end use energy demand, respectively, roughly 22 per cent of all end use energy is directly utilized for space-conditioning purposes. Such a large share of energy devoted to heating and cooling suggests climatic change may have real and measurable effects on energy consumption and, subsequently, emissions from the combustion of fossil fuels. Clearly, while emphasis has been placed on the influence of energy consumption in a changing climate, 'it is equally important to realize that climate variability and climatic change can itself impact both energy supply and demand' (Sailor 1997, p. 313).

The link between climatic variables and energy use has been widely documented and used to explain energy consumption and to assist energy suppliers with short-term planning (Quayle and Diaz 1979; Le Comte and Warren 1981; Warren and LeDuc 1981; Downton, Stewart, et al. 1988; Badri 1992; Lehman 1994; Lam 1998; Yan 1998; Morris 1999; Pardo, Meneu, et al. 2002). However, to date few analyses address the longer-term implications of climate change for energy use patterns and investment decisions. The results of the few studies that have examined the effects of climate change on the energy sector suggest, in general, noticeable impacts on energy demand, capital requirements or expenditures (Linder 1990; Belzer, et al. 1996; Rosenthal, et al. 1995; Morrison and Mendelsohn 1998).

The majority of studies examining the consequences of climate change for the energy sector typically quantify impacts at relatively coarse spatial resolutions, usually at the national level. As a consequence, they capture only an average response for a large geographic area. However, average responses have little value in guiding place-specific adaptation response (Wilbanks and Kates 1999) and may result in the prescription of inappropriate policy recommendations. Therefore, if the objective of a study is not only to quantify impacts but also to identify policy solutions, it must be conducted at a scale where, as the IPCC notes, 'the impacts of climate change are felt and responses are implemented' (IPCC 2001, p. 25).

The research within this chapter is based on the premise that for policy analyses, energy demand sensitivities to climate and climate change should be performed at the regional scale for a number of reasons. First, global climate change is anticipated to have geographically distinct impacts. For example, global climate models predict that the Mid-Atlantic region of the US (within which Maryland is situated) will experience warming trends that differ from the US average (Barron 2002). As a consequence, analyses that apply a uniform temperature increase over the entire nation may miss important geographic impacts on energy use.

A second justification for carrying out a regional assessment lies in the regional differences of energy infrastructures. Regional energy systems differ in terms of energy sources, efficiencies and characteristics of supply and conversion infrastructure, age of transmission and distribution systems, end use technologies, and characteristics of end users. In part, structural differences between regional energy systems have arisen as the built end use infrastructure and housing stock have evolved to service a unique mix of heating and cooling requirements under relatively stationary historic regional climate regimes (Pressman 1995).

A third justification for energy demand sensitivity analysis at regional scales is that residential, commercial and industrial sectors exhibit distinct demand sensitivities to climate. Since sectoral compositions vary across regions, the structure of a region's economy significantly influences the sensitivity of regional energy demand to climate (Lakshmanan and Anderson 1980; Sailor and Munoz 1997).

Several empirical studies support these arguments for regional assessments of climate impacts on the energy sector. For example, in a state-level analysis of residential and commercial electricity, Sailor (2001) observes significant variation in sectoral demand sensitivities between states. He finds a temperature increase of 2°C is associated with an 11.6 per cent increase in residential per capita electricity use in Florida, but a 7.2 per cent decrease in Washington. Even in neighboring states, such as Florida and Louisiana, residential and commercial demand sensitivities are noticeably different. Similarly, Sailor and colleagues estimate the sensitivity of state-level electricity and natural gas consumption to temperature variables and find considerable variation (Sailor and Munoz 1997; Sailor, et al. 1998). Warren and LeDuc (1981) statistically relate natural gas consumption to prices and heating degree-days in a nine-region model of the US and find noticeable regional differences. Scott, et al. (1994) use a building energy simulation model to assess the impacts of climate change on commercial building energy demand in four US cities (Seattle, Minneapolis, Phoenix and Shreveport). Each city was found to have a unique demand response to climates changes with, for instance, a 7°F increase in daily temperature increasing cooling energy use 36.6 per cent in Phoenix and 93.3 per cent in Seattle.

The observed spatial and temporal variations in energy demand across the US and across seasons suggest that it is important to treat climate impacts on heating-related energy needs separate from those for cooling. Analyses focusing on total energy use may find only negligible changes in aggregate, annual physical quantities or in monetary expenditures because changes in cooling and heating may offset one another. Yet, differences in intra-annual energy use profiles will have different implications for cooling and heating energy system expansion and contraction. For example, higher electricity demand in summer months may–in physical terms–be offset by lower heating oil demand in winter, requiring larger investment in peak load electricity generation without comparable changes in heating oil delivery capacities.

DATA SOURCES

Our analysis uses monthly energy consumption and degree-day data. Time-series data on a monthly interval may produce more robust estimates of the energy-climate relationship than annual time-series data since there are more observations and variability between observations. Additionally, the use of monthly data allows for the assessment of non-uniform seasonal climatic changes, such as a more pronounced warming during the winter season than in other seasons of the year for higher latitude regions, as predicted by global climate models (Greco, et al. 1994). In contrast, analyses that apply a uniform temperature increase over the entire year may miss important seasonal impacts on energy use. The following sections describe the data used in our regional energy demand sensitivity analysis.

Energy Data

The Maryland energy consumption data used in this study comes from the US Energy Information Administration (EIA). Monthly electricity sales and price to residential and commercial end users are available from the Electric Power Monthly (EIA various years). The electricity sales data span from January 1977 to December 2001, while monthly electricity price data is limited to the January 1990 to December 2001 period (Figure 12.1). The overall upward trends for both the residential and commercial sector's electricity use are driven, in large part, by changes in the size of the local population, combined with changes in household sizes, building stock and increased proliferation of electric heating and air conditioning, as well as increases in overall economic activity in the region.

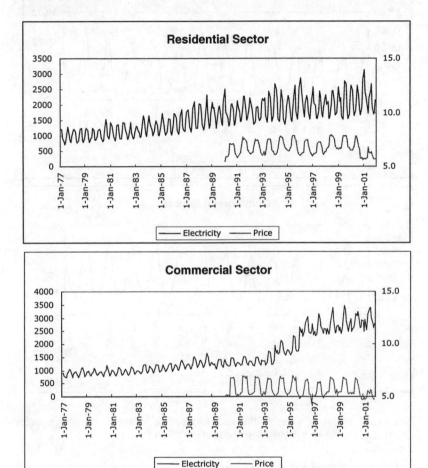

Figure 12.1   Maryland's residential and commercial monthly electricity consumption (million kWh) and price (constant 1990 cents per kWh), 1977–2001

Prices of electricity demonstrate intra-annual oscillation but, in general, no inter-annual trend. To adjust for inflation, the electricity price data is deflated with the Bureau of Labor Statistics' consumer price index for electricity in the Mid-Atlantic region (BLS 2003).

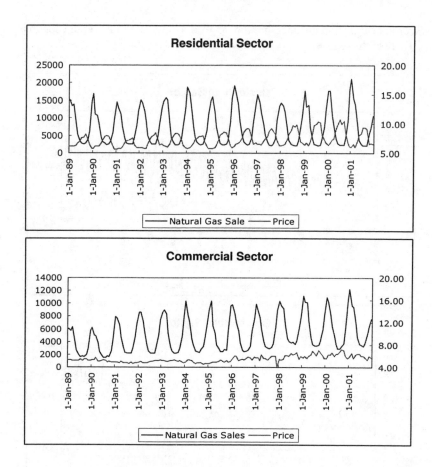

Figure 12.2   Maryland's residential and commercial monthly natural gas sales (MMcf) and price (constant 1990 $ per 1000 cf), 1989–2001

Monthly natural gas sales to residential and commercial end users are from the Natural Gas Monthly (EIA various years). Natural gas sales and price data for the residential and commercial sectors span from January 1989 to December 2001 and are shown in Figure 12.2. Monthly sales of heating oil (distillate fuel oil No. 2) to all end users are published in the Petroleum Marketing Monthly (EIA various years). Because sales to individual end use sectors are not available and the majority of heating oil is consumed by the residential sector, we assume that all heating fuel sales are to residential end users. Heating oil sales and price data cover the January 1983 to December 2002 period (see Figure 12.3). The prices of both natural gas and heating oil are adjusted for inflation using the Bureau of Labor Statistics' consumer price index for fuels in the Mid-Atlantic region (BLS 2003).

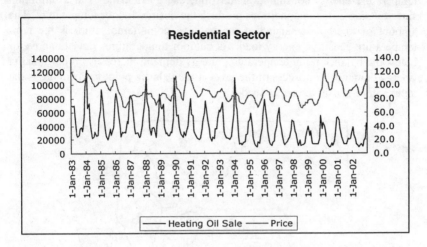

Figure 12.3   Maryland's monthly heating oil sales (MMgal/d) and price (constant 1990 cents per gallon), 1983–2002

Socioeconomic Data

Annual population estimates for Maryland come from the US Census Bureau (2004) and employment data from the US Bureau of Economic Analysis (2002). Commercial employment data were dis-aggregated from overall Maryland employment data based on commercial enterprises that compose commercial energy use as defined in the State Energy Report 1999 (EIA 2001). To coincide with the time-step of the monthly energy data the annual population and commercial employment data are held constant throughout each month of the year.

Climate Data

The historic climate data consist of monthly average temperature series generated by the National Weather Service of the National Oceanic and Atmospheric Administration (NOAA) for eight different climate divisions in Maryland and Washington, DC (NCDC 2004). From that data we derive monthly heating degree-days (HDD) and cooling degree-days (CDD) for each of the eight divisions (see Figure 12.4) to coincide with the time-step of the energy data. Degree-days are a common energy accounting practice for forecasting energy demand. The degree-day methodology presumes a V-shaped temperature-energy consumption relationship as shown in Figure 12.5 (Jager 1983). At the balance point temperature (the bottom of the V-shaped temperature-energy consumption function) energy demand is at a minimum since outside climatic conditions produce the desired indoor temperature. The amount of energy demanded at the balance point temperature is the non-temperature-sensitive energy load. As outdoor temperatures deviate above or below the balance point temperature, energy demand increases proportionally. Energy demanded in excess of the level at the balance point temperature is the temperature-sensitive energy load.

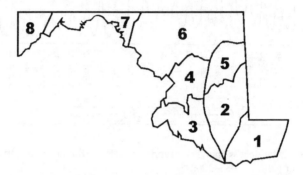

Figure 12.4   Climate divisions in Maryland[2] (Source: National Climate Data Center)

Each degree deviation from a predefined balance point temperature is counted as a degree-day. For example, if a balance point temperature of 65°F is chosen for a region and the average temperature in that region is 70°F, this would result in five cooling degree-days in that region. Aggregate, state-wide degree-day data for the residential sector can be generated by weighting region-specific temperatures by population in the respective climate division. Those population-weighted temperatures are then used to calculate heating and cooling degree days for given base temperatures. Similarly, aggregate degree-day data for the commercial sector can be generated by weighting region-specific temperature by commercial employment in the respective climate division.

In addition to the climatological variables, we calculated daylight hours in each month of the year. Information on daylight hours helps us reduce bias in the econometric estimates of demand sensitivity because daylight hours are correlated with temperature and affect energy use. Daylight hours influence energy use for lighting needs as well as other energy use that may change as individuals are more likely to be indoors. We use the hours of daylight on the 15th day of each month, calculated as the time elapsing between sunset and sunrise, as a proxy for the number of daylight hours per month in Maryland (NOAA 2003).

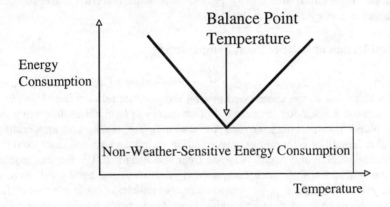

Figure 12.5   Theoretical relationship between temperature and energy consumption

METHODOLOGY

In order to estimate climate impacts on regional energy demand, we follow a three-step modeling and estimation procedure similar to the one used by Amato, et al. (2005). First, we empirically identify region-specific heating and cooling degree-days as outlined above. Second, we use the monthly time-series data of heating and cooling degree-days, together with energy prices, daylight hours and trend variables, in a fixed-effects regression model to quantify the historic sensitivity of end use energy demand by the residential and commercial sectors.

For each sector the demand for electricity, natural gas and heating oil is separately estimated. We assume the separation of energy forms used predominantly for heating (namely natural gas and fuel oil) and those for cooling (typically electricity) is important because climate change is anticipated to have unique impacts on the use of each form of energy and, subsequently, on the different energy delivery systems. Furthermore, to better isolate the influence of climate on energy use from socioeconomic factors we modify the raw electricity and heating fuels data by accounting for consumption on a per capita level in the residential sector and a per employee level in the commercial sector.

In the third part of the analysis we estimate future energy consumption in Maryland under various climate change and socioeconomic scenarios, using the energy sensitivity relationships developed in the first step of the analysis. A comparison of model results against a base case, which assumes average historic temperature and energy prices, then helps discern climate-induced changes in energy demand in the region.

Identification of Balance Point Temperatures

Energy analyses commonly use a base temperature of 65°F as the balance point threshold in the space-conditioning temperature relationship. However, the actual balance point temperature of an energy system varies depending on the place-specific characteristics of the building stock, non-temperature weather conditions (humidity, precipitation, wind and so on), and cultural preferences (Nall and Arens 1979; de Dear and Brager 2001). For example, a region with a housing stock comprised of well-insulated homes will have a relatively low balance point temperature. Nonetheless, while place-specific variations in base temperatures exist, most assessments continue to use the 65°F base because of the ease of data collection since degree-days are commonly calculated with 65°F as the base. However, using 65°F as a universal base temperature implicitly assumes that the temperature where energy is demanded for heating and cooling service is the same everywhere.

The method used in this paper is to tailor the balance point temperature to the characteristics of Maryland, using a quantitative approach, rather than *a priori* postulating it. In this way, the functional relationship between energy demand and temperature will be better specified. Similar to the methodology used by Belzer and colleagues (Belzer, et al. 1996), a set of statistical models are iteratively run for the state over a range of balance point temperatures. Each iteration is performed using degree-days formulated with a different base temperature at 1°F intervals. Then energy use is regressed against degree-days, energy prices, daylight hours, and trend variables. The base temperature that explains the largest share of changes in energy use (the one that produces the highest R-square) is then designated as the balance point temperature. The approach is used for each energy type in each end use sector.

We assume that balance point temperatures for heating- and cooling-related electricity use are identical. Consequently, the electricity use-temperature function is V-shaped and any temperature difference from the balance point results in some temperature-sensitive electricity demand. However, we do not make the simplifying assumption that for all fuels all heating degree-days are derived from the same balance point temperature. Instead, we empirically find a balance point temperature for electricity of 60°F in the residential sector and 53°F for the commercial sector (Figure 12.6). The balance point temperature for natural gas used for heating is 71°F in both the residential sector and commercial sector (Figure 12.7) while the balance point temperature for heating oil used in the residential sector is 64°F (Figure 12.8). Because natural gas and heating oil are predominantly used for heating purposes, the relationship with temperature is a downward sloping function.

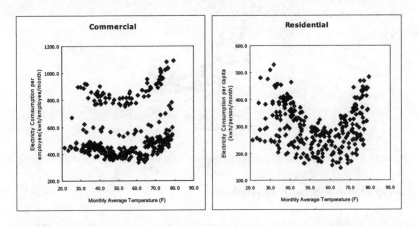

Figure 12.6   Monthly average temperature and sectoral electricity consumption, 1977–2001

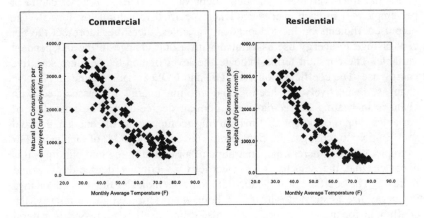

Figure 12.7   Monthly average temperature and sectoral natural gas sales, 1989–2001

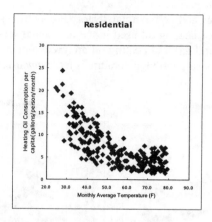

Figure 12.8   Monthly average temperature and heating oil sales, 1989–2001

Energy Demand Sensitivity Analysis

We use a fixed effects regression model to estimate end use energy demand in the residential and commercial sectors for each of the different energy types as a function of heating and cooling degree-days, energy prices, daylight hours and trend variables. The dependent variable (energy use per capita or per employee) in each energy model is specified in natural log format. The output coefficients on the independent variables, therefore, represent the per cent change in energy use associated with a unit change in the independent variable. The constant terms indicate the level of non-temperature-sensitive energy use. The coefficient on the HDD and CDD variables indicate per cent changes, respectively, in heating and cooling energy use associated with changes in heating degree-days and cooling degree-days. The annual trend variables capture potential time-varying components of energy demand sensitivities to changes in degree-days over the period of analysis. For example, with the increasing penetration of air conditioning into buildings it is expected that the sensitivity of electricity to cooling degree-days would increase. The coefficient of the daylight variable indicates the per cent change in energy use associated with a one hour change in daylight. Similarly, the coefficient for the energy price variable, which itself is expressed in natural log form, represents the per cent change in energy use associated with a per cent change in the price of energy.

Residential sector

The regression results for monthly residential per capita electricity consumption in Maryland are shown in Table 12.1. The analysis is restricted to the 1990 to 2003 period due to limited data for monthly sectoral electricity prices. Heating and cooling degree-days used in the residential electricity model are derived from a 60°F base temperature.

Table 12.1   Regression results for residential sector

	Log Electricity per capita (kWh/person/month)
Constant	5.35969***
Annual Trend	0.0127386***
Monthly HDD (base 60°F)	0.0006528***
Monthly CDD (base 60°F)	0.0010355***
Hours of Daylight	0.0005867
Log Electricity Price	-0.0499648
R-square (adjusted)	0.8441
Durbin-Watson statistic (transformed)	1.942146
N	143

*Significant at the 10% level **Significant at the 5% level ***Significant at the 1% level

The constant term in the regression model is representative of non-temperature-sensitive electricity demand or the amount of energy demanded at the balance point temperature. The annual trend variable suggests per capita consumption increases slightly more than 1.2 per cent per year. The coefficient on the degree-day variables indicates a 100 unit increase in monthly heating degree-days is associated with a 6.5 per cent increase in monthly per capita electricity consumption, while a 100 unit increase in monthly cooling degree-days is associated with a 10.3 per cent increase in monthly per capita electricity consumption. However, the regression result shows there is no obvious relationship between residential electricity consumption and daylight hours. Electricity use is somewhat inversely related to electricity price but the coefficient is not statistically significant. The regression model explains 84 per cent of the historic variation in per capita electricity consumption.

Table 12.2 contains the natural gas and heating oil regression models for the residential sector, which use degree-days derived from 71°F and 64°F temperatures respectively. The annual trend variable suggests natural gas consumption increases 3.3 per cent per year. The coefficient on the heating degree-day variables indicates a 100 unit increase in monthly heating degree-days is associated with a 9.7 per cent increase in monthly per capita natural gas consumption. The regression result shows there is no obvious relationship between residential natural gas consumption and daylight hours. However, natural gas use is statistically inversely related to gas price. The regression model explains over 90 per cent of the historic variation in per capita natural gas consumption.

As for heating oil, the annual trend variable shows that heating oil sales have been decreasing with time by 5.9 per cent per year, which in part could be explained by the increasing use of natural gas or electric heaters in the region. Monthly heating degree-days are positively and significantly correlated with an increase in heating oil sales. A 100 unit increase in heating degree-days is associated with a 10.9 per cent increase in heating oil sales. Also, residential heating oil sales are inversely and statistically significantly associated with the number of daylight hours. In contrast, the regression result shows no significant relationship between residential heating oil sales and the price of heating oil. The regression model explains 83 per cent of the historic variation in per capita electricity use.

Table 12.2   Regression results for residential sector

	Log Natural Gas per capita (cubic ft / person / month)	Log Heating Oil per capita (gallons / person / month)
Constant	9.665865***	2.585665***
Annual Trend	0.0335183***	-0.0590547***
Monthly HDD (base 71°F)	0.0009751***	
Monthly HDD (base 64°F)		0.0010945***
Hours of Daylight	0.0051253	-0.0384377**
Log Natural Gas Price	-1.984442***	
Log Heating Oil Price		0.0463627
R-square (adjusted)	0.9069	0.8324
Durbin-Watson statistic (transformed)	2.004448	2.132796
N	155	239

*Significant at the 10% level **Significant at the 5% level ***Significant at the 1% level

Commercial sector

Table 12.3 shows the regression analyses for electricity and natural gas use per employee. The annual trend variable for electricity suggests electricity consumption increases each year by 7.7 per cent. The heating degree-day variable (derived from a temperature base of 53°F) implies that a 100 unit increase is associated with a 2 per cent increase in per employee monthly electricity use whereas a 100 unit increase in monthly cooling degree-days is associated with a 4 per cent increase in per employee electricity use. Electricity for cooling is used more intensively than that for heating as suggested by the larger coefficient of the cooling degree-day variable.

Commercial electricity use is inversely related to hours of daylight but the coefficient of the daylight variable is not statistically significant. No obvious relations between electricity use and price are detected. The regression model explains about 62 per cent of the historical variation in per employee electricity use.

As for commercial natural gas use, the annual trend variable for electricity suggests electricity use increases each year by 5.5 per cent. Natural gas use is highly related to the number of heating degree-days: a 100 unit increase in heating degree-days (derived from temperature base 71°F) is associated with an 11 per cent increase in per employee natural gas use. Commercial natural gas use is inversely related to the price of natural gas. The regression model explains 81 per cent of the historical variation in per employee natural gas use.

Table 12.3   Regression results for commercial sectors

	Log Electricity per employee (kWh / person / month)	Log Natural Gas per employee (cubic ft / person /month)
Constant	4.929313***	5.876947***
Annual Trend	0.0772271***	0.0554748***
Monthly HDD (Base 53°F)	0.0002052***	
Monthly CDD (Base 53°F)	0.0004013***	
Monthly HDD (Base 71°F)		0.0011024***
Hours of Daylight	-0.0062064	0.0259723
Log Electricity price	0.0010849	
Log Natural Gas price		-0.2968363*
Adjusted R-Square	0.6243	0.8119
Durbin-Watson statistic (transformed)	2.418751	1.925123
N	143	155

*Significant at the 10% level **Significant at the 5% level ***Significant at the 1% level

SCENARIOS OF FUTURE ENERGY USE

In the third part of our analysis we use the regression results for electricity, natural gas and heating oil use in conjunction with climate change and energy price scenarios to explore possible future energy use in the residential and commercial sectors. Since our historical time-series used to estimate past relationships between energy use and temperature is rather short, and since any trend variables used to explain past behavior are less valid the further we project into the future, we limit our future scenarios to explore potential energy use only until 2025.

To explore potential impacts of future climate conditions on energy use, we calculate average monthly temperatures for each of the eight climate regions in Maryland and Washington DC, using historical data from 1977 to 2001. We then calculate new monthly population-weighted heating and cooling degree-days from population forecasts for each of the regions (Maryland Department of Planning 2004; US Census Bureau 2004) and assume that regional employment remains at the historic average ratio of employment to population. The result is a future scenario for regional climate that is consistent with average past climate. This scenario establishes a benchmark against which we compare alternative futures.

To reflect climate change, we gradually adjust the temperatures in the eight climate regions in accordance with trends from the United Kingdom Hadley Centre climate model (HadCM2) for the mid-Atlantic region. According to HadCM2, which accounts for the effects of changes in both atmospheric greenhouse gas concentrations and aerosols, temperatures in Maryland could increase by 3°F (with a range of 1 to 7°F) in spring and 4°F (with a range of 2 to 9°F) in summer, fall and winter by the year 2100. Results for the low and high assumptions of future temperature changes are not qualitatively different from the mid-range projections and therefore not discussed in detail here. On the basis of these future temperature scenarios, and forecasts of population and employment in the eight climate regions, we calculate new population-weighted future heating and cooling degree-days for each fuel.

The assumptions about temperature changes can be combined, for example, with a range of assumptions about future energy prices. One scenario posits that future energy prices remain at current (2003) levels. Alternatively, future energy prices could be at the average observed over the historic record. The latter assumption implies higher energy cost and thus, *ceteribus paribus*, lower energy demand, because historic prices on average are above current prices. In contrast, assuming current prices will persist is tantamount to assuming that the lowest historical prices can be maintained over the next 25 years.

The following graphs show results for the mid-range of temperature changes (+3°F in spring and +4°F in summer, fall and winter), as well as energy prices at their average historic levels. To filter out the potential effects of climate change on energy demand, we compare the results to a scenario of average energy prices and average temperatures.

The projections for residential monthly electricity use are shown in Figure 12.9. The results suggest that demand for residential electricity by 2025 would closely resemble average demand over the 1977–2000 time period, and that if future prices were like the historical average, then residential electricity use in the near future would be noticeably below average use. However, all future use of electricity in this scenario is within two standard deviations of historical per capita electricity use, implying that the amount of electricity used in the future may not significantly differ from past use.

The bar chart of Figure 12.9 shows the percent change in monthly per capita energy use attributable to climate change–the difference between the amount projected for a year with and without climate change. The graph suggests that total change attributable to climate change is small, though seasonally not uniform.

If we assume, in contrast, that electricity prices will stay at their current, historically low levels, future electricity use per capita would increase with warmer climate scenarios (see Figure 12.10). As with the previous scenario, electricity use per capita lies within two standard deviations of historical electricity demand, and thus should be considered consistent with past electricity use patterns. However, since energy prices are assumed to remain low, climate impacts on electricity use are felt more in the region, resulting consistently throughout each year of the forecast period in increased per capita use by more than 20 per cent (see bar chart of Figure 12.10).

Figure 12.11 shows that residential per capita gas consumption in the future, with climate change, would decrease during the early and late parts of the year, yet increase during summer months, in part because of increased non-energy-sensitive demand. While much of the change in natural gas use is outside the historically observed range, the percentage change in per capita natural gas use that is attributable to climate change is rather small (see bar chart of Figure 12.11).

Figure 12.12 shows future heating oil consumption per capita. Because of persistent trends to replace heating oil as a residential energy source, per capita demand drops significantly, and climate change slightly speeds up that trend.

Results for the commercial sector differ from those for the residential sector, with future electricity use per employee clearly exceeding the range of the historically observed pattern (Figure 12.13). In contrast, natural gas use per employee largely falls within two standard deviations around the historical mean (Figure 12.14).

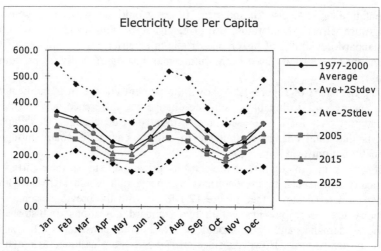

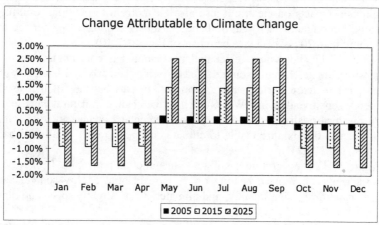

Figure 12.9   Residential electricity use per capita and percentage change attributable to climate change (Future electricity price is assumed to be equal to the average historical price)

SUMMARY AND DISCUSSION

This study investigates the potential impacts of climate change on the use of electricity, natural gas and heating oil in the residential and commercial

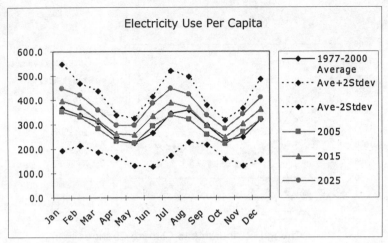

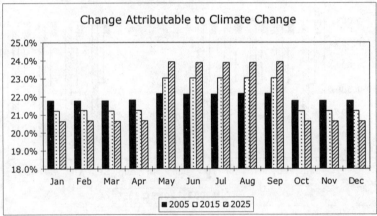

Figure 12.10   Residential electricity use per capita and percentage change attributable to climate change (Future electricity price is held constant at current levels)

sectors at the sub-national level, using a three-step process. First, region-specific, population-weighted climate data were used to identify balance point temperatures above and below which energy use is temperature sensitive. Second, energy use by energy type and sector was regressed against heating and cooling degree-days, length of daylight hours, energy prices and trend variables to establish statistical relationships on the basis of past behaviors. Those relationships were then used in the third step of the analysis to explore

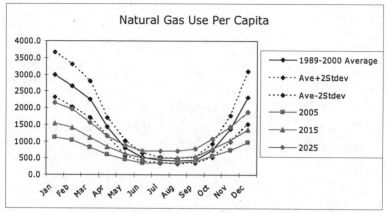

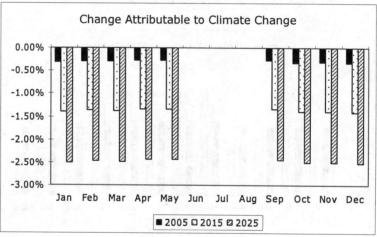

Figure 12.11 Residential natural gas use per capita and percentage change attributable to climate change (Future natural gas price is assumed to be equal to the average historical price)

how energy use may differ for different assumptions about future climate, population and energy prices.

The results of this analysis suggest that assumptions about future energy prices and regional population changes may have much larger impacts on future energy use in Maryland's residential and commercial sector than assumptions about future climate. Although there are noticeable seasonal and annual impacts of climate change–all of which differ for electricity, natural

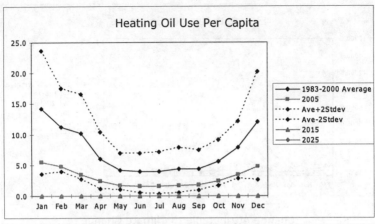

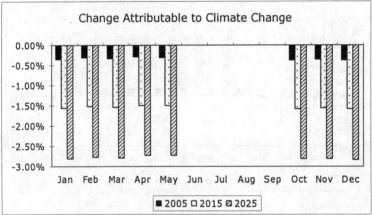

Figure 12.12   Residential heating oil use per capita and percentage change attributable to climate change (Future natural gas price is assumed to be equal to the average historical price)

gas and heating oil use–few of the impacts fall well outside the historically observed ranges. Several conclusions emerge from this analysis. First, even moderate changes in energy prices can trigger demand responses that help revert climate-induced increases in demand. Second, there is no immediate need for large-scale investment in electricity generation and energy delivery systems. However, because there are typically long lead times between changes in demand and expansion in the infrastructure to meet that demand, an opportunity exists to prepare carefully for climate-induced changes in

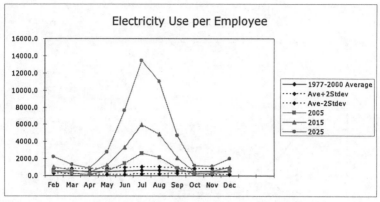

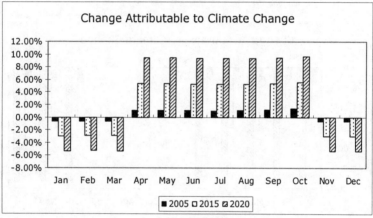

Figure 12.13 Commercial electricity use per employee and percentage change attributable to climate change (Future electricity price is assumed to be equal to the average historical price)

energy use in the region. Third, climate-induced increases in electricity use in the commercial sector are larger than in the residential sector. These impacts are most pronounced during the summer months–a period in which the region already on occasion battles peak load capacity constraints. Furthermore, these impacts noticeably increase non-linearly in later years. Since the commercial sector provides an important base for economic activity in the region and is particularly sensitive to power supply disruptions, prudent capacity planning becomes even more important now than it has been in the past.

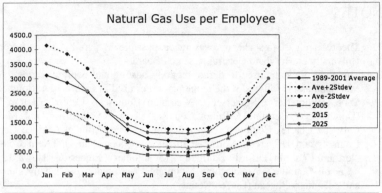

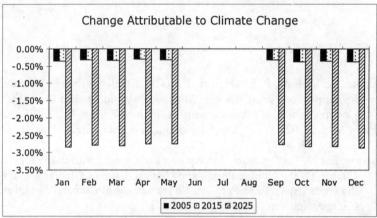

Figure 12.14 Commercial natural gas use per capita and percentage change attributable to climate change (Future natural gas price is assumed to be equal to the average historical price)

Taken together, all three conclusions give hope for the region to adjust its energy use profiles gradually, assuming energy prices provide adequate signals to consumers in the residential and commercial sectors to reduce energy use, and to modify the existing supply structures and capacities to meet future demand. As these adjustments are undertaken, opportunities are opened up to reduce greenhouse gas emissions through reductions in energy use and through changes in the relative shares of the energy types used in the region.

NOTES

1. The research of this chapter was made possible in part by a grant from the University of Maryland General Research Board.
2. The eight divisions used to derive monthly heating and cooling degree-days for Maryland are as follows in the numerical order used in Figure 12.4: Southeastern Shore (Worcester / Somerset / Wicomico Counties); Central Eastern Shore (Dorchester / Caroline / Talbot Counties); Lower Southern (Saint Mary's / Calvert / Charles Counties); Upper Southern (Anne Arundel / Prince George's Counties and DC area); Northeastern Shore (Queen Anne's / Kent Counties); Northern Central (Harford / Baltimore / Montgomery/ Frederick / Howard / Cecil / Carroll Counties); Appalachian Mountain (Washington / Allegany Counties); and Allegheny Plateau (Garrett County).

REFERENCES

Amato, A., M. Ruth, P. Kirshen, et al. (2005), 'Regional Energy Demand Responses to Climate Change: Methodology and Application to the Commonwealth of Massachusetts', *Climatic Change*, **71**(1): 175–201.

Badri, M.A. (1992), 'Analysis of demand for electricity in the United States', *Energy*, **17**(7): 725–733.

Barron, E. (2002), 'Potential Consequences of Climate Variability and Change for the Northeastern United States', Climate Change Impacts on the United States: The Potential Consequences of Climate Variability and Change, National Assessment Synthesis Team.

Belzer, D.B., M.J. Scott, et al. (1996), 'Climate change impacts on US commercial building energy consumption: An analysis using sample survey data', *Energy Sources*, **18**(2): 177–201.

BLS (2003), *'Consumer Price Index for Fuels'*, Washington, DC: Bureau of Labor Statistics, http://www.bls.gov.

de Dear, R. and G.S. Brager (2001), 'The adaptive model of thermal comfort and energy conservation in the built environment', *International Journal of Biometeorology*, **45**: 100–108.

Downton, M.W., T.R. Stewart, et al. (1988) 'Estimating historical heating and cooling needs: Per capita degree days', *Journal of Applied Meteorology*, **27**(1): 84–90.

EIA (1999), *A Look at Residential Energy Consumption in 1997*, Washington, DC: Energy Information Administration.

EIA (2001), *Annual Energy Review 2000*, Energy Information Administration, Washington, DC: US Department of Energy.

EIA (2001), *State Energy Data Report 1999*, Energy Information Administration, Washington, DC: US Department of Energy.

EIA (various years), *Electric Power Monthly*, Energy Information Administration, Washington DC: US Government Printing Office.

EIA (various years), *Natural Gas Monthly*, Energy Information Administration, Washington, DC: US Government Printing Office.

EIA (various years), *Petroleum Marketing Monthly*, Energy Information Administration, Washington, DC: US Government Printing Office.

EPA (1998), *Climate Change and Maryland* (Report 236-F-98-0071), Washington, DC: US Environmental Protection Agency, Office of Policy, September 1998.

Greco, S., R.H. Moss, et al. (1994), *Climate Scenarios and Socioeconomic Projections for IPCC WG II Assessment*, Washington, DC: IPCC-WMO and UNEP: 67.

IPCC (2001), *Climate Change 2001: Impacts, Adaptation and Vulnerability*, Geneva, Switzerland: Intergovernmental Panel on Climate Change.

Jager, J. (1983), *Climate and Energy Systems: A Review of their interactions*, New York, NY: John Wiley and Sons.

Lakshmanan, T.R. and W. Anderson (1980), 'Residential energy demand in the United States: A regional econometric analysis', *Regional Science and Urban Economics,* **10**: 371–386.

Lam, J.C. (1998), 'Climatic and economic influences on residential electricity consumption', *Energy Conversion and Management,* **39**(7): 623–629.

Le Comte, D.M. and H.E. Warren (1981), 'Modeling the impact of summer temperatures on national electricity consumption', *Journal of Applied Meteorology,* **20**: 1415–1419.

Lehman, R.L. (1994), 'Projecting monthly natural gas sales for space heating using a monthly updated model and degree-days from monthly outlooks', *Journal of Applied Meteorology,* **33**(1): 96–106.

Linder, K.P. (1990), 'National Impacts of Climate Change on Electric Utilities', in *The Potential Effects of Global Warming on the United States*, J.B. Smith and D.A. Tirpak (eds), Washington, DC: US Environmental Protection Agency.

Maryland Department of Planning (2004), *Historical and Projected Total Population for Maryland's Jurisdiction Average Annual Growth Rates, Planning Data Service,* http://www.mdp.state.md.us/msdc/dw_popproj.htm, 12 November.

Morris, M. (1999), *The Impact of Temperature Trends on Short-Term Energy Demand*, Energy Information Administration, Washington, DC: US Government Printing Office.

Morrison, W. and R. Mendelsohn (1998), *The Impacts of Climate Change on Energy: An Aggregate Expenditure Model for the US*, Washington, DC: US Department of Energy.

Nall, D. and E. Arens (1979), 'The Influence of degree-day base temperature on residential building energy prediction', *ASHRAE Transactions,* **85**: 1.

NCDC (2004), *Climate Division in Maryland*, National Climate Data Center, http://www.ncdc.noaa.gov/oa/ncdc.html.

NCDC (2004), *1971–2000 United States Climate Normals:Monthly*, Daily and Divisional Products, Environmental Information Series C-23, National Climate Data Center.

NOAA (2003), Sunrise/Sunset Calculator, National Climate Data Center, National Oceanic and Atmospheric Administration, http://www.srrb.noaa.gov/highlights/sunrise/sunrise.html.

Pardo, A., V. Meneu, et al. (2002), 'Temperature and seasonality influences on the Spanish electricity load', *Energy Economics,* **24**(1): 55–70.

Pressman, N. (1995), *Northern Cityscape:Linking Design to Climate*, Yellowknife, Canada: Winter Cities Association.

Quayle, R.G. and H.F. Diaz (1979), 'Heating Degree Day Data Applied to Residential Heating Energy Consumption', *Journal of Applied Meteorology,* **19**: 241–246.

Rosenthal, D.H., H.K. Gruenspecht, et al. (1995), 'Effects of global warming on energy use for space heating and cooling in the United States', *The Energy Journal,* **16**(2).

Rosenzweig, C. and W.D. Solecki (eds) (2001), *Climate Change in a Global City: The Impacts of Potential Climate Variability and Change in the New York Metropolitan Region*, New York: Columbia Earth Institute, p. 241.

Ruth, M. and P. Kirshen (2001), 'Integrated impacts of climate change upon infrastructure systems and services in the Boston metropolitan area', *World Resources Review*, **13**(1): 106–122.

Sailor, D.J. (1997), 'Climatic change feedback to the energy sector: developing integrated assessments', *World Resource Review,* **9**(3): 301–316.

Sailor, D.J. (2001), 'Relating residential and commercial sector electricity loads to climate–Evaluating state level sensitivities and vulnerabilities', *Energy,* **26**: 645–657.

Sailor, D.J. and J.R. Munoz (1997), 'Sensitivity of electricity and natural gas consumption to climate in the USA–Methodology and results for eight states', *Energy,* **22**(10): 987–998.

Sailor, D.J., J.N. Rosen, et al. (1998), 'Natural gas consumption and climate: A comprehensive set of predictive state-level models for the United States', *Energy,* **23**(2): 91–103.

Scott, M.J., L.E. Wrench, et al. (1994), 'Effects of climate change on commercial building energy demand', *Energy Sources,* **16**: 317–332.

US Bureau of Economic Analysis (2002), *Total full-time and part-time employment by industry*, http://www.bea.doc.gov.

US Census Bureau (2004), *State Population Estimates*, Washington, DC: US Government Printing Office.

Warren, H.E. and S.K. LeDuc (1981), 'Impact of climate on energy sector in economic analysis', *Journal of Applied Meteorology,* **20**: 1431–1439.

Wilbanks, T.J. and R.W. Kates (1999), 'Global change in local places: How scale matters', *Climatic Change,* **43**: 601–628.

Yan, Y.Y. (1998), 'Climate and residential electricity consumption in Hong Kong', *Energy,* **23**(1): 17–20.

13   Physical Planning and Urban Heat Island Formation: How Cities Change Regional Climates

Brian Stone, Jr

INTRODUCTION

As explored in the preceding chapters, there is a significant and mounting body of evidence to suggest that the earth is experiencing a shift in global climate that may be unprecedented in both its magnitude and rate of change. While the effects of this shift on the functioning of cities over time remain uncertain, a regional warming phenomenon known as the 'urban heat island effect' provides an important present-day window for investigating the impacts of future climate change on cities. Driven by changes in the surface character of urban land and the emissions of waste heat energy, the urban heat island effect is responsible for a rise in ambient temperatures of between about 5 to 9°F in many cities (McPherson 1994)–a localized shift in climate that approximates changes in global climate projected to occur over the next 100 years (IPCC 2001). Through exploring how cities affect and, in turn, are affected by regional scale changes in climate, we may begin to formulate strategies for mitigating and adapting to rising urban temperatures attributable to both regional and global warming phenomena.

This chapter explores the linkages between the physical design of cities and urban warming. It begins with an overview of the basic science of urban heat island formation. Why do large cities exhibit higher temperatures than their rural hinterlands? How is the urban heat island effect measured, and how does the phenomenon vary by geographic region and city size? In examining these questions, a particular emphasis is placed upon the role of urban infrastructure in the formation of heat islands and on the differing mechanisms through which the physical design of cities influences the regional and global processes of climate change. This overview will conclude with an examination of the many climatological feedbacks between the urban heat island effect and global warming.

The second component of the chapter will consider the implications of the urban heat island effect for public health in cities. As the global urban population is projected to double between 2000 and 2038, there is a critical need for the planning and public health communities to address the threat of rising temperatures to rapidly growing urban populations (United Nations 2002). In recent years, the large number of heat-related fatalities resulting from extreme weather events in North American and European cities attests to the direct effects of urban temperatures on human health. Yet, even more significant are the detrimental effects of heat through its role in regional air pollution formation. To this end, we explore the physiological effects of heat on the human respiratory system, as well as the role of heat in ground level ozone (smog) formation.

The concluding components of the chapter focus on a set of physical planning strategies that have proven effective in reducing surface and air temperatures in cities. Three general classes of strategies will be considered: first, strategies designed to increase the reflectivity of the urban surface, thereby offsetting the quantity of heat absorbed by buildings, roadways, and other infrastructure; second, strategies designed to conserve undeveloped land at the urban periphery and to increase tree canopy cover within the developed core; and, finally, strategies designed to reduce the quantity of waste heat emitted from buildings and vehicles. The chapter concludes with the presentation of an integrated approach for combating both regional and global scale climate change phenomena.

THE MAKING OF A HEAT ISLAND

The relationship between the built environment and urban climate has been observed for centuries. Dating back to ancient Rome, it was widely noted that 'parts of the [city] became hotter during the summer ... after the streets had been widened during the reign of Emperor Nero.' To address this problem it was recommended that streets be 'made narrow, with houses high for shade' (Bosselmann, et al. 1995, p. 226). In addition to street design, the significance of building materials for thermal comfort was also widely recognized by ancient architects. Characterized by a higher surface reflectivity, white-hued materials and coatings have been used for centuries to moderate heat gain in the hot and arid climates of the Middle East. In the more temperate urban climates of North America and Europe, planners also have long recognized the benefits of green space for urban cooling. In his writings on urban design, for example, Thomas Jefferson called for the uniform spacing of built and green spaces in cities to promote the flow of air between hotter and cooler surfaces (Bosselmann, et al. 1995).

In each instance, traditional planners have sought to counteract the warming tendencies of cities through modification of the form or surface properties of the built environment. Today, these warming tendencies are more formally classified as the urban heat island effect. Characterized by an elevation in the air temperature of urban centers relative to adjacent rural zones, the urban heat island effect is driven by three principal mechanisms:

1. An increase in the heat absorbing and storage potential of surface features;
2. A reduction in the natural cooling mechanism of evapotranspiration; and
3. The emission of waste heat energy.[1]

Through examining each of these mechanisms in turn, we can better understand how the physical design of cities influences regional climate.

Urban Infrastructure and Ambient Temperatures

The development of urban infrastructure entails substantial modifications to the natural landscape. In displacing the natural land covers of forests, fields and waterways with the mineral-based construction materials of cement, asphalt and roofing shingle, the physical properties of the natural landscape are altered in profound ways. One important change pertains to the heat absorption and storage capacity of urban surfaces. Both the structure and material composition of the built environment enhance the ability of the surface to absorb and retain solar radiation. For example, the dense geometry of downtown districts greatly increases the surface area of urban zones, enhancing the ability of these surfaces to absorb incoming solar energy and trap outgoing longwave radiation. A second important property, the surface reflectivity or 'albedo,' measures the ability of surface features to reflect away incoming solar radiation. In general, materials characterized by dark hues and rough surfaces, such as asphalt or brick, are efficient absorbers and poor reflectors of solar energy.

Urban land covers also tend to absorb and retain large quantities of heat energy due to the high heat capacity of mineral-based materials. A measure of the quantity of heat energy absorbed (or released) per unit volume of a material in response to a rise (or fall) in temperature of one degree, heat capacity governs the ability of surface materials to store thermal energy (Oke 1987). Because cement and asphalt tend to have higher heat capacities than vegetation, urban environments absorb and store large quantities of heat energy during daylight hours. The gradual release of this heat energy in the late afternoon and into the evening serves to increase the intensity and duration of warming in cities relative to adjacent rural areas, a classic indicator of the urban heat island effect. Figure 13.1 illustrates the generalized distribution of temperature throughout an urban heat island.

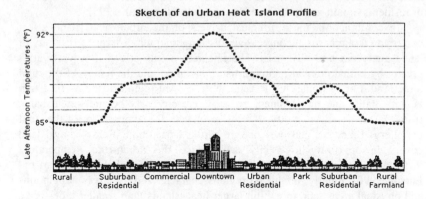

Figure 13.1   Temperature profile for the urban heat island effect (USEPA 1992)

In addition to enhancing the thermal properties of the urban surface, the displacement of natural land covers by urban infrastructure greatly diminishes regional rates of evapotranspiration. The combined processes of evaporation and transpiration, evapotranspiration is the physical mechanism through which heat energy is used by soils and plants to convert water to water vapor. Because heat energy received from the sun and atmosphere is used in this conversion process, it is no longer available to raise the temperature of surface features. Rather, the energy is effectively locked up within the water vapor molecules and is transported away from the earth's surface as the vapor dissipates into the atmosphere. As a result, the evapotranspiration process provides a natural cooling mechanism for urban areas that is lost through deforestation and other forms of natural land conversion (McPherson 1994).

A final significant driver of the urban heat island effect is the emission of waste heat energy from industries, autos and buildings. A byproduct of any fuel combustion process, waste heat is emitted in large quantities from industrial smokestacks and automotive tailpipes. The mechanical removal of heat from buildings by air conditioning systems provides another significant source of waste heat in cities. While the climatological effect of waste heat emissions from any single source is unlikely to be significant, the combined effects of numerous sources distributed throughout a dense urban region can measurably impact ambient temperatures. As concluded in a study conducted in Tokyo, Japan, the intensity of waste heat emissions in that city's downtown district is sufficient to elevate nighttime air temperatures by approximately 5°F (Saitoh, et al. 1995). Combined with the thermal energy emitted from the urban surface, such excessive emissions of waste heat could result in future summer temperatures of over 109°F in Tokyo's downtown district, rendering the district largely uninhabitable for sensitive populations, such as the elderly, or residents of non-air conditioned buildings (Saitoh, et al. 1995).

In combination, these principal drivers of the urban heat island effect contribute to a measurable increase in urban temperatures across a diversity of landscape types and city sizes. The intensity of the effect, however, varies greatly by climatological region, urban population and the nature of the rural hinterland. For example, in the densely developed region of the northeastern United States, the development zone of one city may be indistinguishable from that of an adjacent city, serving to elevate the temperature of the rural periphery. Likewise, the presence of barren agricultural fields or arid land covers in proximity to a city can reduce the urban-rural temperature differential by increasing the temperature of the rural periphery (Carnahan and Larson 1990). Finally, urbanized regions characterized by larger populations and physical areas tend to exhibit larger heat islands than smaller cities (Oke 1987).

Regional versus Global Mechanisms of Climate Change

In seeking to develop strategies to combat the problem of rising temperatures, it is important to distinguish between regional and global mechanisms of climate change. A primary distinction pertains to the spatial and temporal dimensions across which each phenomenon is measured. In contrast to the phenomenon of global warming, which is measured as an increase in mean global temperatures between two points in time, the urban heat island effect is measured as an increase in localized temperature between two points in space, the center and periphery of a metropolitan region. Thus, while global scale changes can be measured only over the temporal dimensions of years and decades, the intensity of the heat island effect can be measured across space on an instantaneous basis.

A second important distinction pertains to the physical mechanisms through which the regional and global warming phenomena influence urban temperatures. Driven by a rise in atmospheric concentrations of greenhouse gases, the global greenhouse effect is a process through which outgoing terrestrial radiation is absorbed in the lower layer of the atmosphere (the troposphere). Once absorbed this thermal energy elevates the temperature of the atmosphere, which in turn increases surface temperatures (Tarbuck and Lutgens 1997). Characterized by an enhanced flux of energy from the atmosphere to the earth's surface, the greenhouse effect can be understood to produce a principally downwelling warming effect. In contrast, the urban heat island effect is driven by the physical alteration of the earth's surface and the direct release of waste heat from surface activities. As this production of surface heat warms the atmosphere from below, the urban heat island effect can be understood to produce an upwelling warming effect.

The opposing direction of these effects gives rise to a number of important climatological feedbacks between the regional and global warming mechanisms. For example, the urban heat island effect creates a greater demand for air conditioning in the warm season, elevating regional energy demand. This increase in energy demand increases emissions of greenhouse gases, contributing to the global greenhouse effect, which in turn further elevates near surface air temperatures and requires additional energy demand for cooling (Rosenfeld, et al. 1995). Deforestation associated with urban development also fuels regional and global warming by diminishing both evapotranspiration, which cools the city, and carbon sequestration, which provides a sink for atmospheric carbon dioxide. Finally, an increase in ambient temperatures in cities enhances ground level ozone formation, which, in addition to its direct impacts on human and environmental health, is a significant greenhouse gas.

These distinctions in the causal mechanisms of regional and global climate change, in concert with the many feedbacks between the two warming phenomena, suggest a number of important directions for urban climate change management. Before examining the ways in which physical planning may be employed as a tool to combat regional and global scale warming, it is important to understand the significant threat ambient heat poses to public health and environmental quality in metropolitan regions. To this end, the following section provides an overview of the effects of ambient heat on human heat stress and ground level ozone formation.

AMBIENT HEAT AND PUBLIC HEALTH

During the summer of 2003, Europe experienced the most intense heat wave in over 100 years of record keeping. For eleven consecutive days in Paris, France, maximum daily temperatures were an average of 25.6°F higher than the normal temperature, while daily lows were 15.7°F above normal. London, England, posted a daily maximum of 100°F for the first time in recorded history, while Rome, Italy, experienced temperatures over 95°F for 21 days between June and August. According to Dr Laurence Kalkstein (2003) of the Center for Climatic Research at the University of Delaware, were a comparable heat wave to occur in Washington, DC, daily maximum temperatures would average 110°F, constituting the worst heat wave ever experienced in the United States. Through an analysis of regional press accounts, it has been estimated that approximately 35 000 heat-related fatalities occurred in Europe during the month of August alone (Earth Policy Institute 2003).

The outcome of this warming episode signals an important warning to urban populations of the developed world. Despite the availability of highly advanced public health response systems and medical technologies, a sustained rise in maximum daily temperatures can create a significant public health emergency. Such high levels of ambient heat threaten human health through two mechanisms. First, high levels of heat can elevate core body temperatures and, after prolonged duration, overwhelm the body's ability to cool itself, resulting in heat stress or, in the most extreme cases, heat stroke. Second, high ambient temperatures are associated with ground level ozone formation and thus may indirectly threaten human health through the enhancement of regional air pollution. The following sections examine the many linkages between urban warming and public health in cities.

Ambient Heat and Human Welfare

High levels of ambient heat most directly impact public health through the occurrence of heat stress and heat stroke. As reported by the National Oceanic and Atmospheric Administration (NOAA), ambient heat is now responsible for more annual fatalities in the US than any other form of extreme weather (NOAA 2000). Heat poses a particular threat to human health in urbanized regions for two reasons. First, cities are often home to large lower income populations, which may lack access to air conditioning or adequate health care facilities (Kilbourne 1997). Second, the urban heat island effect serves to magnify the effects of summer heat waves, with cities often experiencing a rise in temperatures several degrees higher than in rural areas. Figure 13.2 illustrates the urban-rural temperature differential in Chicago, Illinois, and St Louis, Missouri, during a 1999 heat wave. In each instance, urban areas clearly experienced a more significant increase in temperatures than did rural areas during the period of the heat wave. Not surprisingly, the majority of heat-related fatalities in Illinois and Missouri occurred in these large urban centers (Palecki and Chagnon 1999).

Ambient heat directly impacts human health by diminishing the body's ability to regulate internal temperature. The human body cools itself through the release of heat to the surrounding atmosphere via the heat transfer mechanisms of convection, radiation and evaporation. When the temperature of the air is higher than that of the body, heat energy is transmitted from the atmosphere to the skin, serving to elevate body temperatures. Likewise, under conditions of high humidity, the ability of human skin to cool itself through the evaporation of sweat is diminished, also serving to elevate body temperatures. Under extreme conditions, the human body may be unable to regulate internal temperatures efficiently, potentially resulting in increased coagulability of the blood and heat stroke. More common is the occurrence of heat stress, a condition resulting in fatigue and, in some cases, an exacerbation of pre-existing heath problems, such as heart and respiratory diseases. Studies have shown that heat strokes account for 5 to 20 per cent of all heat-related fatalities, with an exacerbation of pre-existing cardiac and respiratory conditions accounting for the remainder (Kilbourne 1997).

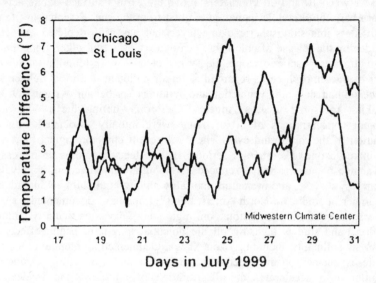

Figure 13.2   Urban-rural temperature difference in Chicago and St Louis during the July 1999 heat wave (Palecki and Changnon 1999)

High levels of ambient heat can also threaten public health and welfare by disrupting the normal operation of urban infrastructure and services. The elevated demand for air conditioning during heat waves, for example, can place tremendous pressures on urban electrical grids, resulting in blackouts. The vast majority of heat wave victims are those who lack air conditioning or experience a disruption in electrical service. During the 1999 heat wave in Chicago, for example, power outages left 92 000 residents without electricity for between four hours and three days. Other, generally non-life-threatening disruptions to urban infrastructure include the failure of electrified rail systems due to power outages and the buckling of roadway paving from exposure to extreme temperatures (Palecki and Changnon 1999).

Ambient Heat and Urban Air Quality

In addition to its effects on human health, ambient heat plays a significant role in regional ozone formation. Ozone is a colorless gas that is formed in the presence of sunlight through the chemical interaction of nitrogen oxides (NO_x)

and volatile organic compounds (VOC), two classes of pollutants produced from the combustion of fossil fuels. Ozone consists of three atoms of oxygen (O_3) and, like its close cousin diatomic oxygen (O_2), is present in several layers of the atmosphere. When found in the stratosphere–the layer extending from between 10 and 50 kilometers above the earth's surface–ozone acts to absorb harmful ultraviolet radiation emitted from the sun. Essential to life on Earth, it is this stratospheric ozone layer that has been depleted in recent decades by the release of chlorofluorocarbons (CFCs) and other compounds. By contrast, tropospheric ozone, the same molecule when found in the lowest layer of the atmosphere, is regarded as an air pollutant due to its deleterious effects on human health, vegetation and buildings (Nebel and Wright 1998).

First measured in Los Angeles, California, during the 1940s, high ambient concentrations of urban ozone were initially associated with an irritation of the throat and eyes. The more recent epidemiological literature has linked ozone to a range of serious health effects, including an increased prevalence of acute asthma, reduced cardiopulmonary function, aggravated respiratory disease, and premature mortality among both children and adults. A number of studies in North America and Europe have documented a sharp increase in hospital admissions on high smog days, particularly among children, and studies focusing on the potential long-term health effects of urban air pollutants, including ozone, have documented a potential reduction in life expectancy on the order of years (Touloumi, et al. 1997). Ozone air pollution also accelerates the deterioration of buildings and is deemed responsible for annual crop losses in this country valued in the hundreds of millions of dollars (USEPA 2000a).

Ambient heat influences ground level ozone formation through its effects on the rate of emission of ozone precursors from both human and natural sources. As noted above, the ozone precursors of VOC and NO_x are emitted from vehicle tailpipes and industrial smokestacks as a byproduct of fuel combustion. In addition to these exhaust emissions, VOC is also emitted in an evaporative form directly from vehicle engines and gas tanks, and during vehicle refueling. Highly sensitive to ambient heat, these evaporative VOC emissions increase in response to rising temperatures, whether a vehicle engine is running or not. For example, evaporative VOC emissions in the Atlanta, Georgia region have been found to increase by 5 per cent with each degree Celsius rise in temperature (Cardelino and Chameides 1990).

In addition to VOCs emitted by automobiles and industrial sources various species of trees produce natural forms of VOC, such as isoprene (Sillman 1995). The effects of temperature change on such 'biogenic' precursor emissions can be substantial. For example, in modeling the effects of temperature change on ozone formation in the Atlanta, Georgia region, a 3.5°F (2°C) rise in temperature was found to be associated with an approximately 45 per cent increase in biogenic isoprene emissions (Cardelino and Chameides 1990). Similarly, the thermal decomposition of an atmospheric compound known as peroxyacetyl nitrate (PAN) can also promote ozone formation. With rising ambient temperatures, the PAN compound decomposes into peroxyalkyl radicals and nitrogen dioxide. Through the liberation of sequestered nitrogen dioxide, the chemical decomposition of PAN increases the atmospheric reservoir of NO_x (Cardelino and Chamedies 1990).

The sensitivity of ozone formation to ambient temperature is creating a significant obstacle to improving regional air quality in large cities. Data obtained from the country's largest metropolitan regions indicates that, despite the hundreds of billions of dollars invested in pollution control, ozone formation has persisted and, in many cases, increased in recent years. Figure 13.3 depicts the average number of national ozone standard violations in the 50 most populous US cities during the 1990s. In each panel of the figure, these standard violations, also referred to as ozone exceedances, are plotted against average annual emissions of VOCs and NO_x, and, in the bottom panel, mean annual temperatures. As suggested by the top two panels, despite a significant decrease in VOC emissions and a general stabilization of NO_x, ozone formation continued to fluctuate during the 1990s, with a higher number of ozone exceedances experienced in 1999 than in 1990. The non-significant correlation coefficients derived for each of these graphs indicates that trends in the emission of ozone precursors from anthropogenic sources were not closely associated with ozone formation during this period, raising important questions about the efficacy of our national ozone management program.

In contrast, mean annual temperatures were closely associated with ozone exceedances in large metropolitan regions. As illustrated in the bottom panel of Figure 13.3, the warmer years of 1991, 1995 and 1998 corresponded with high ozone years, while the cooler years of 1992 and 1996 corresponded closely with a relatively low number of ozone exceedances, on average. As indicated by the significant correlation coefficient of 0.86, mean annual temperatures were strongly associated with ozone exceedances during this decade, a level of correlation that was far more significant than that observed between ozone formation and precursor emissions from mobile and stationary sources.

The results of this analysis confirm the existence of a well-established relationship between ambient temperature and ozone formation. In light of this sensitivity of urban air quality to ambient heat, urban climate modification may provide a viable approach to ozone abatement. Even so, can regional climates be altered through physical planning? The answer to this question depends upon the scale of the phenomenon to be addressed. At the global level, most climatologists believe the process of global warming ultimately can be reversed only through a substantial reduction in the

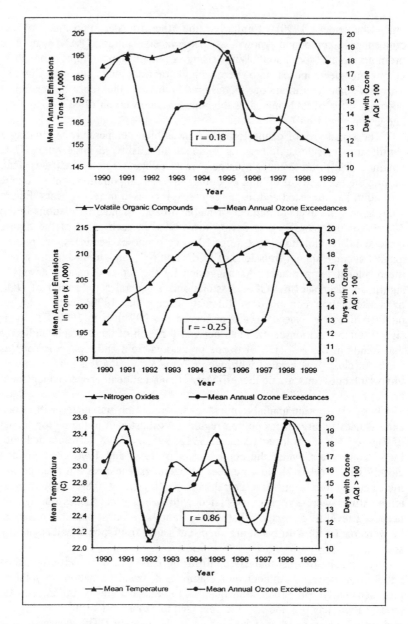

Figure 13.3   Precursor emissions, temperature and ozone exceedances in the fifty largest US cities[2]

emissions of greenhouse gases. Yet, due to the prolonged residence times of many greenhouse gases—over a century for some species—the planet will likely continue to warm for many decades despite corrective measures (IPCC 2001). At the regional level, reductions in the urban heat island effect of just a few degrees could yield measurable improvements in urban air quality and human health. The remainder of the chapter explores a set of physical planning strategies demonstrated to offset surface heat production within cities.

MITIGATING THE URBAN HEAT ISLAND EFFECT

Driven by physical changes to the urban landscape and the emission of waste heat, the urban heat island effect may be mitigated through physical planning strategies designed to offset the thermal enhancing properties of urban land uses and to promote energy conservation. While still formative, the literature on urban heat islands identifies three general strategies that may be employed to cool cities over the near to medium term. These strategies include: the enhancement of surface albedo through the use of highly reflective paving and building materials; the enhancement or protection of natural vegetative cover within cities and at the urban periphery; and the reduction of waste heat emissions through energy efficient building design and transit and pedestrian oriented development. The following paragraphs examine these two approaches in detail and highlight the advantages and limitations of each for growing metropolitan regions.

Painting the City White: Cooling Cities through Albedo Enhancement

As discussed above, the built environment can elevate surface and near surface air temperatures by reducing the natural reflectivity of the landscape. The displacement of natural land covers by the darkly hued and high heat capacity materials of asphalt, brick and roofing shingle greatly enhances the quantity of solar energy absorbed at the surface by reducing the surface albedo. Unable to reflect away radiation received from the sun and atmosphere, low albedo surface materials often absorb a large proportion of this energy, which serves to elevate surface temperatures and increase the quantity of thermal energy returned to the atmosphere in the form of sensible heat. Albedo enhancement strategies seek to increase the reflectivity of the surface through the use of highly reflective materials and surface treatments. For example, the use of light gray or white roofing materials can significantly reduce the heat absorption and temperature of building roofs. Likewise, white-pigmented paving aggregates have been developed and used in hot climates to reduce the thermal absorption of roads and parking lots.

The potential for albedo enhancement techniques to reduce surface temperatures is well established. Figure 13.4 presents solar reflectance values for a number of common urban construction materials. A measure of the proportion of incident radiation reflected back to the atmosphere, the solar reflectance index provides an important metric for gauging the cooling effects of alternative albedo enhancement strategies. As indicated by the graph, the use of bright white surface treatments can achieve a solar reflectance of over 80 per cent, significantly reducing heat gain and surface temperatures. While such a high level of reflectivity would be undesirable for street surfaces, in that the resulting glare could impede visibility, such materials could be used safely in roofing shingle, particularly for multi-story structures with flat roofs. The use of paving materials with a solar reflectivity around 20 per cent would further reduce the quantity of solar energy absorbed in cities.

In the interest of gauging the benefits of an aggressive albedo enhancement strategy, scientists at the Lawrence Berkeley National Laboratory developed a computer simulation of urban surface structure and heat island formation for Los Angeles, California. The results of this modeling process indicated that the use of highly reflective roofing and paving materials throughout the LA metropolitan region would reduce mean summer temperatures by as much as 2.7°F (1.5°C) (Rosenfeld, et al. 1998), a cooling effect sufficient to offset several decades of projected global warming. If achievable, such a reduction in ambient temperatures would hold the potential to improve regional air quality significantly. As suggested by Figure 13.3, changes in average temperatures of just a few degrees could yield significant changes in annual ozone exceedances.

The great appeal of an albedo enhancement strategy is that it could be achieved incrementally over time at relatively low cost. As the periodic resurfacing of streets and building roofs is required every 10 to 20 years, urban albedo could be increased gradually through the process of routine maintenance. Estimated to cost an additional \$25 per 100 m^2 (1076 ft^2) of roof area, most residential structures could be re-shingled with high albedo materials for an additional cost of about \$50, a periodic expense that would be more than offset through energy savings resulting from a reduced demand for air conditioning. For example, the Rosenfeld, et al. study suggests that the adoption of an albedo enhancement and tree planting program would reduce annual residential air conditioning costs in Los Angeles by approximately \$78 for older homes (those built prior to 1978) and \$60 for newer homes. While Rosenfeld, et al. did not assess the costs of tree planting and maintenance, many other studies have found tree planting to be cost effective. In a recent study of tree benefits in Davis, California, Maco and McPherson found the annual benefits of trees to exceed planting and maintenance costs by a ratio of 3.8:1, with about 40 per cent of these benefits attributable to energy savings and reduced air pollution (Maco and McPherson 2003). If this ratio holds true for the Los Angeles region, a large-scale tree planting and albedo enhancement program would be expected to generate environmental and property value benefits far in excess of costs over a 10 to 20 year period.

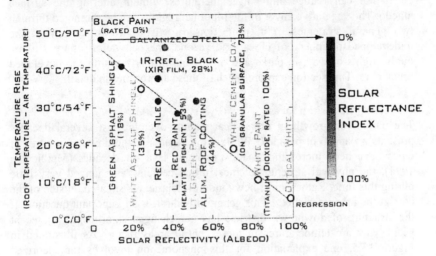

Figure 13.4   Solar reflectance index (Heat Island Group, Lawrence Berkeley National Laboratory)

While albedo enhancement strategies hold great promise for reducing urban temperatures over time, there are two principal limitations to this approach. The first obstacle is cultural. While the use of light hued building materials throughout the hot and arid climates of the Middle East is common, North American and European architecture has been characterized historically by darker hues, a cultural preference that may be difficult to overcome. A second and perhaps more significant limitation to this approach is that it fails to address the root cause of urban heat island formation: the conversion of natural land covers to the mineral-based surfaces of urban construction. While high albedo surfaces can reduce heat gain, for many regions an albedo enhancement strategy is unlikely to restore the thermal properties of the natural landscape. Such an outcome may only be achieved through strategies designed to restore and preserve a region's natural land covers.

Growing the City Green: Cooling Cities through Evapotranspiration

If albedo enhancement strategies are designed to paint the city white, the enhancement of natural land covers within and around cities may be conceptualized as a green strategy. Rather than increase the solar reflectivity of the urban surface, tree planting and protection strategies promote cooling through evapotranspiration and surface shading. By enhancing the ability of the urban surface to use intercepted radiation for the combined processes of evaporation and transpiration in green plants, the planting of trees and other vegetation can reduce ambient temperatures without altering the surface albedo. The vegetative cover of metropolitan regions can be promoted through two general strategies: first, protection of existing forest canopy at the undeveloped periphery of cities; and second, the cultivation of trees along public rights-of-way, in parks and on private property within the developed urban core. This section explores each of these approaches in detail.

Protecting the urban forest
The pattern of growth in urban heat islands over the last several decades presents an apparent paradox. While temperatures in the downtown cores of cities have been increasing steadily over the last few decades (McPherson 1994), the physical structure of most urban centers has changed very little during this time. Rather, most new land development is situated outside of the core at the urban periphery. This general trend raises an important question. If the structure of downtown districts has not changed significantly in recent years, why are temperatures in these central areas rising? As illustrated in Figure 13.5, one explanation for this phenomenon involves the theorized movement of heat and air within an urban heat island. Under calm conditions, the highly impervious urban core acts as a regional thermal engine, causing heated air at the city center to rise and drawing in cooler air from the urban periphery. As natural land covers at the urban periphery are converted to urban land uses, both surface and air temperatures in these areas increase, which ultimately increases the temperature of the air drawn toward the city center. If this theory of a circulating, convective wind regime is accurate, development in both the core and at the urban periphery can be expected to elevate air temperatures throughout a metropolitan region.

The role of both centralized and peripheral land uses in regional heat island formation suggests a second important question for urban planning. What pattern of new development, high or low density, is most conducive to additional urban warming? While higher density patterns of growth tend to concentrate impervious materials and reduce the area of greenspace in each parcel, lower density patterns of growth are associated with higher rates of deforestation at the urban periphery. To address this question, Stone and Rodgers (2001) used high resolution thermal imagery to measure the quantity of surface heat emitted by high and low density residential parcels throughout the Atlanta, Georgia metropolitan region. The results of this analysis suggest that the area of the residential parcel has a strong positive relationship with surface heat production. As illustrated in Figure 13.6, each quarter-acre increment in lot size was found to increase excess parcel heat emissions by more than a third.

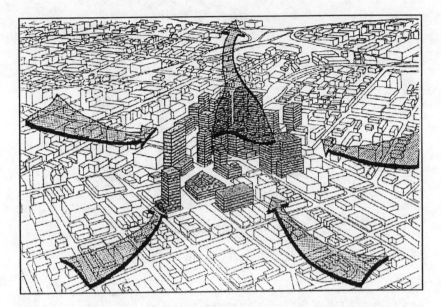

Figure 13.5 Hypothesized movement of heat and air in a heat island (Golany 1996)

Lower density development patterns were found to produce more heat energy than higher density patterns for two simple reasons:

1. Larger lot sizes are characterized by larger building footprints and driveways than smaller lot sizes; and
2. Larger lot sizes are associated with larger lawn areas, which, for cities situated in naturally forested areas, results in more deforestation per parcel than do higher density patterns.

As forested areas were found to be significantly cooler than unshaded lawn areas, the displacement of tree canopy by lawn areas was identified as a significant driver of surface warming in low density residential zones of the Atlanta region (Stone and Rodgers 2001).

In light of these findings, municipal governments interested in promoting higher density development as a means of mitigating a range of environmental impacts, such as auto emissions and stormwater runoff, may also enjoy thermal benefits associated with regional forest conservation. Consistent with the principles of smart growth planning, development policies designed to encourage smaller lot sizes, shorter building setbacks and narrow street widths, among many other design attributes, can potentially slow the rate of heat island expansion by conserving rural land covers. In combination with albedo

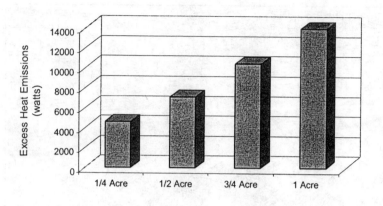

Figure 13.6   Heat emissions by parcel size in Atlanta, Georgia

Note: The measure of excess heat emissions is derived by subtracting the estimated pre-development radiant flux of thermal energy from the post development radiant flux (for a more detailed explanation see Stone and Rodgers 2001).

enhancement within the urban core, the protection and cultivation of rural tree canopy provides a highly effective and natural mechanism for cooling cities.

Tree planting in cities

While the preservation of peripheral land covers slows the regional expansion of urban heat islands, the planting of trees within cities offsets the thermal impacts of the existing built environment. The cultivation of trees along roadways and in proximity to buildings promotes cooling by increasing local rates of evapotranspiration and by reducing the quantity of solar radiation received by the impervious surfaces of streets, sidewalks and buildings. In shading houses and other buildings, strategic tree planting can also help reduce waste heat emissions generated by air conditioning units. The benefits of tree planting for energy consumption are well documented. In a study of vegetative cover and energy consumption for residential parcels, for example, Meier (1991) found the placement of mature shade trees to the south and west of single-family homes to offset cooling costs by 25 to 80 per cent during the summer months. Likewise, McPherson (1991) estimates that the strategic positioning of trees in Tucson, Arizona can yield over $20 per tree in annual energy savings.

    In perhaps the most comprehensive analysis of urban design and heat island mitigation to date, the Lawrence Berkeley National Laboratory study referenced above modeled the effects of an aggressive tree planting program on summer ambient temperatures throughout the Los Angeles, California region. The results of computer simulations indicated that the planting of 11 million trees in proximity to houses and streets and within public parks would effect a reduction in summer temperatures of 2.7°F (1.5°C), a cooling effect equivalent to that found to result from an aggressive albedo enhancement program (Rosenfeld, et al. 1998). Through the development of an ozone formation and transport model, the cooling benefits of a combined tree planting and albedo enhancement program—a reduction in temperatures of 5.4°F (3°C)—were found to be associated with a 12 per cent reduction in annual ozone exceedances (Rosenfeld, et al. 1998). Significantly, the air quality benefits of this modeled program were found to surpass those achieved by California's ongoing programs to phase in cleaner fuels and low to zero emission vehicles.

Similar to albedo enhancement strategies, the strong appeal of tree planting programs is that they can be implemented gradually over time and may be achieved through both public and private sector actions. An additional advantage of this approach to heat island mitigation is that most metropolitan regions have already enacted some form of tree conservation ordinance (Duerksen and Richman 1993). While the strength and enforcement of these ordinances varies considerably throughout the country, the existence of an established legal mechanism for promoting urban tree planting provides a valuable foundation for this heat island mitigation strategy.

Cooling Cities Through Waste Heat Reduction

A final important driver of urban warming is the emission of waste heat from industrial processes, mobile sources and buildings. As noted above, great quantities of waste heat are produced from fuel combustion and released into the atmosphere from smokestacks and tailpipes. In addition, heat that is mechanically removed by air conditioning systems from houses and buildings can be a significant source of warming in cities. While the magnitude of waste heat emissions varies widely among and within cities, in some instances the flux of artificial energy can be quite substantial. For example, in comparison to an average solar input of 106 watts per square meter (W/m^2) within central London, McGoldrick (1980) found the flux of waste heat energy to range between 100 and 234 W/m^2. Similarly, Landsberg (1981) found the flux of anthropogenic heat within parts of Manhattan, New York to register over 600 W/m^2.

Physical planning approaches to waste heat reduction include climate responsive building design and transit and pedestrian supportive development. Climate responsive building design involves the use of highly insulating building materials, energy efficient heating, ventilation and lighting systems, and, as outlined above, highly reflective surface treatments and the strategic orientation of windows and landscaping to maximize seasonal warming and cooling. The development of rooftop gardens presents another increasingly effective approach for reducing building energy consumption. Through the retention of rainwater and the promotion of evapotranspiration, vegetative rooftops can significantly cool buildings and near-surface air temperatures. A study of green roof installation in Philadelphia, Pennsylvania, for example, found vegetative roof covers to reduce surface temperature fluctuations in the spring and summer by approximately 80 per cent relative to conventional tar-based roofing materials (USEPA 2000b).

The physical design of cities has also been demonstrated to influence the quantity of vehicle travel and tailpipe emissions. As concluded by a number of studies, moderate to high levels of population and employment density, land use mix and the provision of transit facilities–the principal elements of transit and pedestrian oriented development–can significantly reduce auto travel and emissions. For example, in a study of land use and vehicle travel in the Sacramento, California region, Johnston, et al. (2000) found the combined impacts of transit improvements and land use strategies to reduce vehicle miles traveled (VMT) between 4 and 7 per cent over 20 years. In one of the most widely cited studies of this nature, the Land Use, Transportation and Air Quality (LUTRAQ) analysis conducted in Portland, Oregon, a development scenario emphasizing transit oriented development, pedestrian infrastructure improvements and transportation demand management policies, was found to reduce daily VMT by 8 per cent relative to the business-as-usual scenario of highway expansion. Significantly, this study also found the emissions of nitrogen oxides and carbon monoxide to be reduced by 6 and 3 per cent, respectively (Cambridge Systematics, et al. 1996). While not a direct surrogate for heat emissions, reductions in vehicle miles of travel and pollutant emissions resulting from physical planning strategies are likely to yield associated reductions in waste heat emissions as well.

CONCLUSION: AN INTEGRATED APPROACH TO CLIMATE CHANGE MANAGEMENT

The existence of a physical linkage between the structure of the built environment and urban air temperatures suggests an emerging role for physical planning in the process of climate change management. Generally viewed as a long-term strategy for environmental remediation, environmentally responsive design may prove to be the most viable approach in the near term for abating urban warming trends and associated air quality problems. Due to the long atmospheric residence times of greenhouse gases, a reduction in current emissions through technological controls would be unlikely to yield measurable results for many decades.[3] In contrast, changes to the physical characteristics of cities can produce cooling benefits at the time of implementation. If aggressively pursued, the installation of highly reflective roofing and paving materials, the preservation and replanting of urban trees, and the minimization of waste heat emissions through energy conservation can produce substantial cooling benefits over the period of a decade or two–far sooner than benefits would accrue under the climate change management strategies outlined in the Kyoto Protocol.

This significant distinction in the temporal dimensions of the regional and global mechanisms of climate change highlights a potential integrated approach for climate change management in cities. Rather than seeking to combat climate change through greenhouse gas emission reductions alone, urbanized regions also may focus on heat island mitigation to slow the rate of growth in regional air temperatures over the near to medium term. Due to the many positive feedback mechanisms linking regional and global scale warming phenomena, any strategy that serves to reduce air temperatures in cities is likely to reduce greenhouse gas emissions associated with energy consumption and ozone formation. Achievable with the aid of conventional technologies and planning strategies, heat island mitigation programs may be implemented in the present time period and at a relatively modest cost to municipal governments and city residents. In short, the mitigation of urban heat islands may prove to be the most effective adaptation strategy for climate change in cities.

A partial re-orientation in focus from the global to the regional process of climate change would require a number of important institutional shifts in the national framework for air quality management. Most significantly, a shift in focus from technological emissions controls to physical planning strategies is needed to reduce ambient heat in cities most effectively. Currently structured to reduce air pollutant emissions from industrial processes and mobile sources through emissions control technologies, our national air quality management framework provides no legal basis for improving air quality through the regulation of land use. As material use, tree planting and urban form are key drivers of urban heat island formation, climate change management strategies must focus on the physical dimensions of cities in addition to the emission of greenhouse gases from smokestacks and tailpipes.

A second important institutional shift needed to promote climate change management in cities is an expanded role for local and regional governments in the realm of air quality management. Traditionally the mandate of federal and state government agencies, the national framework for air quality management has failed to emphasize physical planning as a control strategy due to the statutory limitations on land use regulation (Stone 2003). The purview of local and, in a few cases, regional governments, land use controls embodied in municipal ordinances, such as zoning and subdivision regulations, set the standards for urban development patterns and, as such, provide an essential set of tools for enhancing the climate responsiveness of cities. In light of this jurisdictional divide between environmental management and land use controls, the effective control of climate and air quality in cities will require greater institutional coordination between federal, state and local planning agencies. Such coordination must entail a more integrated approach to land use, transportation and air quality management strategies, as well as the provision of federal and state funding mechanisms for climate change management at the local level.

In closing, it is important to emphasize that physical planning does not constitute a comprehensive solution for managing climate change and climate-induced air pollution. Driven by global patterns of energy consumption and land use, the phenomenon of global warming may only be stabilized over the long-term through a widely coordinated reduction in the emission, or an increase in the sequestration, of greenhouse gases. Yet changes to the physical structure and surface character of cities provides a near to medium term strategy for adapting to global changes in climate through actions implemented at the regional level. Oriented toward both the spatial and technological bases of climate change, climate responsive design embodies a viable and pragmatic strategy that may be enacted in concert with larger scale reductions in greenhouse gas emissions. It is a strategy that is cost effective, politically tenable, and highly compatible with other elements of sustainable urban growth. In short, it is a no regrets option for cities concerned about the growing impacts of ambient heat on urban air quality and public health.

NOTES

1. As described by Oke (1987), a reduction in wind speeds also can diminish surface cooling within urban zones. However, as the physical structure of cities can both promote and abate wind speeds, the significance of this meteorological variable to heat island formation remains uncertain.
2. An ozone exceedance is defined as a day in which the EPA's Air Quality Index (AQI) for ozone exceeds a value of 100. The correlation coefficients derived for VOC and NO_x emissions and ozone exceedances were not found to be significant at the $p < .05$ level. The correlation coefficient derived for mean temperature and ozone exceedances was found to be significant at the $p < .001$ level (Stone 2005).
3. While the cooling benefits of greenhouse gas mitigation strategies may only be realized over the long-term, it is important to note that efforts to reduce energy consumption in the near term can yield significant economic savings to households and businesses, and for this reason alone should be pursued.

REFERENCES

Bosselmann, P., E. Arens, K. Dunker, et al. (1995), 'Urban form and climate: case study, Toronto', *Journal of the American Planning Association,* **61**(2): 226–239.

Cambridge Systematics, Inc. and Parsons Brinkerhoff Quade, Douglas, Inc. (1996), *Making the land use, transportation, air quality connection: Analysis of alternatives,* Portland, OR: 1000 Friends of Oregon.

Cardelino, C. and W. Chameides (1990), 'Natural hydrocarbons, urbanization, and urban ozone', *Journal of Geophysical Research,* **95**(D9): 13971–13979.

Carnahan, W. and R. Larson (1990), 'An analysis of an urban heat sink', *Remote Sensing of Environment, 33:* 65–71.

Duerksen, C. and S. Richmann (1993), *Tree Conservation Ordinances,* Planning Advisory Service Report 446, Chicago, IL: American Planning Association.

Earth Policy Institute (2003), *Record heat wave in Europe takes 35,000 lives,* Retrieved 2 March 2004, http://www.earth-policy.org/updates/ update29.htm.

Golany, G. (1996), 'Urban design morphology and thermal performance', *Atmospheric Environment,* **30**(3): 455–465.

IPCC (2001), *Climate change 2001: Impacts adaptation, and vulnerability,* Cambridge, UK: Intergovernmental Panel on Climate Change.

Johnston, R., C. Rodier, M. Choy, et al. (2000), 'Air quality impacts of regional land use policies', Washington, DC: US Environmental Protection Agency, Urban and Economic Development Division.

Kalkstein, L. (2003), 'The great European heat wave of 2003', *EPA Heat Island Reduction Initiative Conference,* University of Delaware, December.

Kilbourne, E. (1997), 'Heat waves and hot environments', in *The public health consequences of disasters,* Eric K. Noji (ed.), New York, NY: Oxford University Press, pp. 245–269.

Landsberg, H. (1981) *The urban climate,* New York, NY: Academic Press.

Maco, S. and E.G. McPherson (2003), 'A practical approach to assessing structure, function, and value of street tree populations in small communities', *Journal of Arboriculture,* **29**(2): 84–97.

McGoldrick, B. (1980), 'Artificial heat release from greater London, 1971', *Physics Division Energy Workshop Report,* Sunderland, UK: Sunderland Polytechnic, Department of Physical Science.

McPherson, E.G. (1991), 'Economic modeling for large-scale urban tree plantings', in *Energy Efficiency and the Environment: Forging the Link,* Washington, DC: American Council for an Energy Efficient Economy.

McPherson, E.G. (1994), 'Cooling urban heat islands with sustainable landscapes', in *The Ecological City: Preserving and Restoring Urban Biodiversity*, R. Platt, R. Rowntree and P. Muick (eds), Amherst, MA: University of Massachusetts Press.

Mier, A. (1991), 'Measured cooling savings from vegetative landscaping', in *Energy efficiency and the environment: Forging the link*, E. Vine (ed.), Washington, DC: American Forest Association, pp. 4133-4144.

Nebel, B. and R. Wright (1998), *Environmental Science*, Upper Saddle River, NJ: Prentice Hall.

Oke, T.R. (1987), *Boundary Layer Climates*, New York, NY: Methuen and Co.

Palecki, M. and S. Changnon (1999), *The nature and impacts of the July 1999 heat wave in the Midwest*, Midwestern Climate Center, Retrieved 2 March 2004, http://mcc.sws.uiuc.edu/hw99/hw99.html.

Rosenfeld, A., H. Akbari, S. Bretz, et al. (1995), 'Mitigation of urban heat islands: Materials, utility programs, updates', *Energy and Buildings*, **22**: 255-265.

Rosenfeld, A., H. Akbari, J. Romm, et al. (1998), 'Cool communities: Strategies for heat island mitigation and smog reduction', *Energy and Buildings*, **28**: 51-62.

Saitoh, T.S., T. Shimada and H. Hoshi (1995), 'Modeling and simulation of the Tokyo urban heat island', *Atmospheric Environment*, **30**(20): 3431-3442.

Sillman, S. and P. Samson (1995), 'Impact of temperature on oxidant photochemistry in urban, polluted rural and remote environments', *Journal of Geophysical Research*, **100**(D6): 11497-11508.

Stone, B. Jr (2003), 'Air quality by design: Harnessing the Clean Air Act to manage metropolitan growth', *Journal of Planning Education and Research*, **23**(2): 177-190.

Stone, B. Jr (2005), 'Urban heat and air pollution: An emerging role for planners in the climate change debate', *Journal of the American Planning Association*, **71**(1): 13-25.

Stone, B. Jr. and M. Rodgers (2001), 'Urban form and thermal efficiency: How the design of cities influences the urban heat island effect', *Journal of the American Planning Association*, **67**(2): 186-198.

Tarbuck, E. and F. Lutgens (1997), *Earth Science*, Upper Saddle River, NJ: Prentice Hall.

Touloumi, G., K. Katsouyanni, D. Zmirou, et al. (1997), 'Short-term effects of ambient ozone exposure on mortality: A combined analysis within the APHEA project', *American Journal of Epidemiology*, **146**(2): 177-185.

United Nations (2002), *World urbanization prospects: The 2001 revision*, United Nations Population Division, Department of Economic and Social Affairs, United Nations Secretariat: ESA/P/WP.173, March.

USEPA (2000a), *National air quality and emissions trends report, 1998* (EPA 454 / R-00-003), Washington, DC: United States Environmental Protection Agency.

USEPA (2000b), *Vegetated roof cover, Philadelphia, Pennsylvania* (EPA 84-B-00-005D), Washington, DC: United States Environmental Protection Agency.

14 Climate Change and Public Health: Focusing on Emerging Infectious Diseases

Paul R. Epstein

Epidemics are like signposts from which the statesman of stature can read that a disturbance has occurred in the development of his nation– that not even careless politics can overlook.

Dr Rudolf Virchow, 1848

BACKGROUND ON CLIMATE CHANGE

The climate system can remain stable over millennia due to interactions and feedbacks among its basic components: the atmosphere, oceans, ice cover, biosphere and energy from the sun (Albritton, et al. 2001). Harmonics among the six orbital (Milankovitch) cycles (such as tilt and eccentricity) of the earth about the sun have–as revealed by analyses of ice cores and other 'paleothermometers' such as tree rings and coral cores (Mann, et al. 1998)– governed the oscillations of Earth's climate between ice ages and warm periods–until the twentieth century. To explain the global warming over the twentieth century of close to 1°C, according to all studies reviewed by the Intergovernmental Panel on Climate Change (Houghton, et al. 2001), one must invoke the role of heat-trapping greenhouse gases (GHGs)–primarily carbon dioxide (CO_2), nitrogen oxides (NO_x), methane and chlorofluorocarbons (CFCs). These gases have been steadily accumulating in the lower atmosphere (or troposphere) out to about 10–16 km, and have altered the heat budget of the atmosphere, the world ocean, land surfaces and the cryosphere (ice cover) (Houghton, et al. 2001).

For the past 420 000 years, as measured by the Vostok ice core in Antarctica, CO_2 has stayed within an envelope of between 180 parts per million (ppm) and 280 ppm in the troposphere (Petit, et al. 1999). Today CO_2 is found in concentrations of 379 ppm, and the rate of change over the past century surpasses that observed in ice core records (World Health Organization 1996). Ocean and terrestrial sinks for CO_2 have presumably played feedback roles throughout the millennia. Today, the combustion of fossil fuels (oil, coal and natural gas) is generating CO_2 and other GHGs, and the decline in sinks, primarily forest cover, accounts for 15 to 20 per cent of the buildup (Houghton, et al. 2001).

Climate Stability

As important as the warming of the globe is to biological systems and human health, the effects of increasingly extreme and anomalous weather patterns that accompany the excess energy in the system may be even more profound (Epstein 1999). As the rate of warming accelerated after the mid-1970s, anomalies and wide swings away from norms increased (Epstein and McCarthy 2004), suggesting that feedback, corrective mechanisms in the climate system, are being overwhelmed. Some ecological change may be irreversible over long time periods (Maslin 2004). Indeed, increased variability may presage transitions. Ice core records from near the end of the last ice age (about 10 000 years ago) indicate that increased variability was associated with rapid change in state (NRC 2001).

Further evidence for instability comes from the world oceans. While the oceans have warmed overall in the past century, a region of the North Atlantic has cooled in the past several decades. Several aspects of global warming are apparently contributing.

Recent warming in the Northern Hemisphere has melted a lot of North Polar ice. Since the 1970s the floating North Polar ice cap has thinned by almost half (Rothrock, et al. 1999). A second source of cold fresh water comes from Greenland, where continental ice is now melting at higher elevations each year (Parkinson, et al. 1999). Some melt water is trickling down through crevasses–lubricating the base, accelerating ice 'rivers,' and increasing the potential for sudden slippage. A third source of cold fresh water is rain at high latitudes. Overall, ocean warming speeds up the water cycle, increasing evaporation (Albritton, et al. 2001). The warmed atmosphere can also hold and transport more water vapor from low to high latitudes. Water falling over land is enhancing discharge from five major Siberian rivers into the Arctic (Peterson, et al. 2002), and water falling directly over the ocean adds even more fresh water to the surface.

The cold, freshened waters of the North Atlantic accelerate transatlantic winds, and this may be one factor driving frigid fronts down the eastern US seaboard and across to Europe and Asia, as in the winter of 2003. The North Atlantic is also where deep-water formation drives thermohaline circulation, the 'ocean conveyor belt' considered key to climate stabilization (Broecker 1997).

The ice itself, as well as pollen and marine fossils, reveal that cold reversals have interrupted warming trends in the past. The North Atlantic Ocean can freshen to a point where the North Atlantic deep water pump–driven by sinking cold, salty water that is, in turn, replaced by warm Gulf Stream waters–can suddenly slow down. Some 13 000 years ago, when the globe was emerging from the last Glacial Maximum and continental ice sheets were thawing, the Gulf Stream abruptly changed course and shot straight across to France (NRC 2001). The Northern Hemisphere refroze–for the next 1300 years–before temperatures jumped again in just several years, warming the world to its present state. Calculations (of orbital cycles) indicate that our hospitable climate regime was not likely to end due to natural causes any time soon (Berger and Loutre 2002). But due to the burning of fossil fuels, atmospheric levels of carbon dioxide are now greater than at any time in the last half million years. The recent buildup of heat-trapping greenhouse gases is forcing the climate system in new ways and into uncharted seas.

The Hydrological Cycle

Warming is also accelerating the hydrological (water) cycle. As heat builds up in the deep ocean–down to 3 km (Levitus, et al. 2000)–more water evaporates and sea ice melts. Over the past century, droughts have lasted longer and heavy rainfall events (defined as > 5 cm/day) have become more frequent (Karl, et al. 1995a-b). Enhanced evapotranspiration dries out soils in some regions, while the warmer atmosphere holds more water vapor, fueling more intense, tropical-like downpours elsewhere (Trenberth 1999; Easterling, et al. 2000). Prolonged droughts and intense precipitation have been especially punishing for developing nations.

Global warming is not occurring uniformly. It is occurring twice as fast as overall warming during the winter and nighttime (Easterling, et al. 2000), and the winter warming is occurring faster at high latitudes than near the tropics (Houghton, et al. 2001). These changes may be due to greater evaporation and increased humidity in the troposphere, as water vapor is a natural greenhouse gas, and can account for up to two thirds of all the heat trapped in the troposphere. Together, warming nights and winters along with the intensification of extreme weather events have begun to alter marine life and weather patterns that impact the ecological systems essential for regulating the vectors, hosts and reservoirs of infectious diseases. Other climate-related health concerns include:

1. Temperature and mortality, especially the role of increased variability in heat and cold mortality (Braga, et al. 2001);

2. Synergies between climate change and air pollution (including CO_2 fertilization of ragweed and excess pollen production), asthma and allergies (Wayne, et al. 2002);
3. Travel hazards associated with unstable and erratic winter weather (EPA 2003); and
4. Genetic shifts in arthropods and rodents induced by warming. (Bradshaw and Holzapfel 2001).

CLIMATE AND INFECTIOUS DISEASE

Climate is a key determinant of health. Climate constrains the range of infectious diseases, while weather affects the timing and intensity of outbreaks (Dobson and Carper 1993). A long-term warming trend is encouraging the geographic expansion of several important infections (McCarthy, et al. 2001), while extreme weather events are spawning 'clusters' of disease outbreaks and sparking a series of surprises (Epstein 1999; 2000). Ecological changes and economic inequities strongly influence disease patterns. But a warming and unstable climate is playing an ever-increasing role in driving the global emergence, resurgence and redistribution of infectious diseases (Leaf 1989; McMichael, et al. 1996).

The World Health Organization (1996) reports that over thirty diseases have appeared since 1975 that are new to medicine. Included are HIV/AIDS, Ebola, Lyme disease, Legionnaires,' toxic *E. coli*, a new hantavirus and a rash of rapidly evolving antibiotic-resistant organisms. Of equal concern is the resurgence of old diseases, such as malaria and cholera. Declines in social conditions and public health programs underlie the rebound of diseases transmitted person-to-person (for example, tuberculosis and diphtheria). The resurgence and redistribution of infections involving two or more species– mosquitoes, ticks, deer, birds, rodents and humans–reflect changing ecological and climatic conditions as well as social changes (such as suburban sprawl).

Waves of infectious diseases come in cycles. Many upsurges crest when populations overwhelm infrastructures or exhaust environmental resources, and at times pandemics can cascade across continents. These transitional periods can, in turn, affect the course of history (Epstein 1992). The Justinian Plague emerged out of the ruins of the Roman Empire in the sixth century AD, and arrested urban life for centuries. When the plague–carried by rodents and fleas–reappeared in the repopulated and overflowing urban centers of the fourteenth century, it provoked protests and helped end feudal labor patterns. In *Hard Times*, Charles Dickens describes overcrowded nineteenth century England: 'full of tall chimneys, out of which interminable serpents of smoke trailed themselves forever and ever, and never got uncoiled ... where the piston of the steam-engine worked monotonously up and down like the head of an elephant in a state of melancholy madness–that bred smallpox, cholera and tuberculosis' (Matossian 1989). But society responded with sanitary and environmental reform, and the epidemics abated. Just how will our society respond to the current threat to our health and biological safety?

An Integrated Framework for Climate and Disease

All infections involve an agent (or pathogen), host(s) and the environment. Some pathogens are carried by vectors or require intermediate hosts to complete their life cycle. Climate can influence pathogens, vectors, host defenses and habitat.

Diseases carried by mosquito vectors are particularly sensitive to meteorological conditions. These relationships were described in the 1920s (Gill 1920a-b). Excessive heat kills mosquitoes, but within their survivable range warmer temperatures increase their reproduction, biting activity (Leeson 1939) and the rate at which pathogens mature within them. At 20°C, falciparum malarial protozoa take 26 days to incubate, but at 25°C, they develop in 13 days (MacArthur 1972). *Anopheline* mosquitoes–carriers of malaria–live only several weeks. Thus, warmer temperatures permit parasites to mature in time for the mosquito to transfer the infection.

Temperature thresholds limit the geographic range of mosquitoes. Transmission of *Anopheline*-borne falciparum malaria occurs where temperatures exceed 16°C (Martens, et al. 1997). The range of yellow fever (with a high rate of mortality) and dengue fever (characterized by severe headaches and bone pain, with mortality associated with dengue hemorrhagic fever and dengue shock syndrome) are both carried by *Aedes aegypti*, which is restricted by the 10°C winter isotherm. Freezing kills *Aedes* eggs, larvae and adults. Thus, given other conditions, such as small water containers, expanding tropical conditions can enlarge the ranges and extend the season with conditions allowing transmission.

Warm nights and warm winters favor insect survival. Fossils from the end of the last Ice Age demonstrate that rapid, poleward shifts of insects accompanied warming, especially of minimum temperatures (TMINs) (Elias 1994). Insects, notably Edith's Checkerspot butterflies today, are superb 'paleothermometers,' outpacing the march of grasses, shrubs, trees and mammals in response to advancing frost lines (Parmesan 1996; Parmesan, et al. 1999). In addition to the direct impacts of warming on insects, volatile weather and warming can disrupt co-evolved relationships among species that help to prevent the spread of nuisance species (Epstein, et al. 1997).

Pest Control: One of Nature's Services

Systems at all scales have self-correcting, feedback mechanisms. In animal cells, errors in structural genes (mismatched base pairs) resulting from radiation or chemicals, are 'spell-checked' by proteins propagated by regulatory genes. Malignant cells that escape primary controls must confront an ensemble of instruments that compose the immune surveillance system. A suite of messengers and cells also awaits invading pathogens–some that stun them, and others, like phagocytes, which consume them.

Natural systems have also evolved a set of pheromones and functional groups (like predators, competitors and recyclers) that regulate the populations of opportunistic organisms. The diversity of processes provides resistance, resilience and insurance, while the mosaics of habitat–stands of trees about farms that harbor birds and nectar-bearing flowers that nourish parasitic wasps–provide generalized defenses against the spread of opportunists. Against the steady background beat of habitat fragmentation, excessive use of toxins and the loss of stratospheric ozone are driving climate change towards fast becoming a dominant theme, disrupting relationships among predators and prey that would otherwise prevent the proliferation of pests and pathogens.

Climate Change and Biological Responses

Northern latitude ecosystems are subjected to regularly occurring seasonal changes, but prolonged extremes and wide fluctuations in weather may overwhelm ecological resilience, just as they may undermine human defenses. Repeated winter thawing and refreezing depresses forest defenses, increasing vulnerability to pest infestations. And sequential extremes and shifting seasonal rhythms can alter synchronies among predators, competitors and prey, releasing opportunists from natural biological controls (Epstein, et al. 1997).

Several aspects of climate change are particularly important to the responses of biological systems. First, global warming is not uniform. Warming is occurring disproportionately at high latitudes, just above Earth's surface and during winter and nighttime (Easterling, et al. 2000). Parts of Antarctica, for example, have already warmed almost 1°C this century and the temperatures within the Arctic Circle have warmed 5.5°C in the past 30 years (Houghton, et al. 2001). Since 1950, Northern Hemispheric springs begin earlier and falls appear later.

While inadequately studied in the US, warm winters have been demonstrated to facilitate over-wintering, thus we have seen northward migration of the ticks that carry encephalitis and Lyme disease (Lindgren, et al. 2000). Agricultural zones are shifting northward–though not as swiftly as are key pests, pathogens and weeds that, in today's climate, consume 52 per cent of the growing and stored crops worldwide (Rosenzweig and Hillel 1998; Rosenzweig, et al. 2000).

An accelerated hydrological cycle–ocean warming, sea ice melting and rising atmospheric water vapor–is demanding significant adjustments from biological systems, along with ocean warming (Levitus, et al. 2000). Communities of marine species have shifted (Barry, et al. 1995). A warmer atmosphere also holds more water vapor (6 per cent for each 1°C warming), insulates escaping heat and enhances the greenhouse effect. More evaporation also fuels more intense, tropical-like downpours, while warming and parching of Earth's surface intensifies the pressure gradients that draw in winds (for example, causing winter tornados) and large weather systems (Karl, et al. 1995a-b, 1997; 2003). Elevated humidity and lack of nighttime relief during heat waves directly challenge human and livestock health. These conditions also favor mosquitoes.

Range Expansion of Mosquito-borne Diseases

Today, one half of the world's population is exposed to malaria on a daily basis. Deforestation, drug resistance and inadequate public health measures have all contributed to a recent resurgence. Warming and extreme weather add new stresses. Dynamic models project that global warming will increase the transmission capacity of mosquitoes 100-fold in temperate zones, and that the area capable of sustaining transmission will grow from that containing 45 per cent of the world's population to 60 per cent (Martens, et al. 1997), though recent statistical models project less of a change (Martin and Lefebvre 1995). Notably all these analyses rely on average temperatures, rather than the more rapid changes in minimum temperatures being observed, and thus may underestimate the biological responses.

In addition, historical approaches to understanding the role of temperature and infectious disease have argued that the relationships do not hold for periods such as the Medieval Warm Period and the Little Ice Age (Reiter 2000). It is important to note, however, that the change of CO_2 and temperature–and their rates of change–over the twentieth century are outside the bounds of those observed during the entire Holocene (the last 10 000 years).

Some of these projected changes may be under way. Since 1975 several vector-borne diseases have reappeared in temperate regions. *Anopheline* mosquitoes have long been present in North America and malaria circulated in the US earlier this century. But by the 1980s transmission in the US was limited to California, after mosquito control programs were put in place. Since 1990, however, small outbreaks of locally transmitted malaria have occurred during hot spells in Texas, Georgia, Florida, Michigan, New Jersey, New

York and Toronto (Zucker 1996). Malaria has returned to South Korea, parts of southern Europe and the former Soviet Union. Moving southward, malaria has re-colonized the Indian Ocean coastal province of South Africa, while dengue fever has spread into northern Australia and Argentina (Epstein, et al. 1998).

These changes are consistent with projections, though some authors stress the compounding issues, including land clearing, population movements and drug and pesticide resistance for malaria control. Sets of changes occurring in tropical highland regions are internally consistent and are indicative of long-term warming.

Climate Change in Montane Regions

In the nineteenth century European colonists sought refuge from lowland 'mal arias' by settling in the highlands of Africa. These regions are now getting warmer. Since 1970 the height at which freezing occurs (the freezing isotherm) has climbed approximately 160 meters within the tropical belts, equivalent to almost 1°C warming (Diaz and Graham 1996). Local changes, such as mountainside deforestation, cannot account for this global change, for the measurements are drawn from released weather balloons and satellites.

Plants are migrating to higher elevations in the European Alps, Alaska, the US Sierra Nevada and New Zealand (Pauli, et al. 1996). This is a sensitive gauge, for a plant shifting upward 500 m would have to move 300 km northward to adjust to the same degree of global warming (Peters 1991).

Insects and insect-borne diseases are now being reported at high elevations in East and Central Africa, Latin America and Asia. Malaria is circulating in highland urban centers, like Nairobi, and rural highland areas, like those of Papua New Guinea. *Aedes aegypti*, once limited by temperature to about 1000 m in elevation, has recently been found at 2000 m high in Mexico and 2200 m in the Colombia Andes (Epstein, et al. 1998).

These insect and botanical trends, indicative of gradual, systematic warming, have been accompanied by the hardest of data: the accelerating retreat of summit glaciers in Argentina, Peru, Alaska, Iceland, Norway, the Swiss Alps, Kenya, the Himalayas, Indonesia, Irian Jaya and New Zealand (Thompson, et al. 1993; Mosley-Thompson 1997; Irion 2001). Glaciers in the Peruvian Andes retreating 4 m annually in the 1960s and 1970s were melting 30 m a year by the mid-1990s and 155 m per year in 2000 (Irion 2001). Many small ice fields may soon disappear, jeopardizing regional water supplies critical for human consumption, agriculture and hydropower.[1] Highlands–where the biological, glacial and isotherm changes are especially apparent–are sensitive sentinel sites for monitoring the long-term impacts of climate change.

Extreme Weather Events and Epidemics

While warming encourages the spread of infectious diseases, extreme weather events are having the most profound impacts on public health and society. The study of variability also provides insights into the stability of the climate regime itself.

A shift in temperature norms alters the variance about the means, and high-resolution ice core records suggest that greater variance from climate norms indicates instability. Today, the enhanced hydrological cycle is changing the intensity, distribution and timing of extreme weather events (Trenberth 1999; Easterling, et al. 2000). Over the past century droughts have become longer and bursts of intense precipitation (> 5 cm over 24 hours) more frequent (Karl, et al. 1995a). Large-scale weather patterns have shifted. Warming of the Eurasian land surface, for example, has apparently intensified the monsoons (Kumar, et al. 1999) that are strongly associated with mosquito- and water-borne diseases in India and Bangladesh. Monsoons in the US southwest may also have shifted, with implications for disease patterns in that region.

Extremes can be hazardous for health (Bouma, et al. 1997a-b; Checkley, et al. 1997; Kovats, et al. 1999). Prolonged droughts fuel fires, releasing respiratory pollutants. Floods promote fungi, such as the house mold *Stachybotrys atra* associated with an emerging hemorrhagic lung disease among children (Dearborn, et al. 1999). Floods leave mosquito breeding sites and flush pathogens, nutrients and pollutants into waterways, precipitating water-borne diseases like Cryptosporidium (Mackenzie, et al. 1994). Runoff from flooding can also trigger harmful algal blooms along coastlines that can be toxic to birds, mammals, fish and humans; can generate hypoxic 'dead zones;' and can harbor pathogens like cholera (Epstein 1993).

The El Niño Southern Oscillation (ENSO) phenomenon is one of Earth's coupled ocean-atmospheric systems that help to stabilize the climate system by undulating between states every four to five years. ENSO events are accompanied by weather anomalies that are strongly associated with disease outbreaks over time and spatial clusters of mosquito-, water- and rodent-borne illnesses (Epstein 1999). The ENSO cycle also affects the production of plant pollens, which are themselves directly boosted by CO_2 fertilization (Wayne, et al. 2002; Ziska and Caulfield 2000), warranting further investigation as a possible contributor to the dramatic rise in asthma since the 1980s.

Other climate modes contribute to regional weather patterns. The North Atlantic Oscillation (NAO) is a seesaw in sea surface temperatures (SSTs) and sea level pressures that governs windstorm activity across Europe (Hurrell, et al. 2001). Warm SSTs in the Indian Ocean (that have bleached over 80 per cent of regional coral reefs) also contribute to increased precipitation in East Africa. A warm Indian Ocean added moisture to the rains drenching the Horn of Africa in 1997/98 that spawned costly epidemics of cholera, mosquito-borne Rift Valley fever and malaria (Linthicum, et al. 1999), and catalyzed the southern African deluge in February 2000.

Weather extremes–especially intense precipitation–have been especially punishing for developing nations, and the aftershocks ripple through economies. Hurricane Mitch, nourished by a warmed Caribbean, stalled over Central America in November 1998 for three days, dumping precipitation that killed over 11 000 people and caused over \$5 billion in damages. In the aftermath, Honduras reported 30 000 cases of cholera, 30 000 cases of malaria and 1000 cases of dengue fever (Epstein 2000). The following year Venezuela suffered a similar catastrophe, followed by malaria and dengue fever. Then in February 2000 torrential rains and a cyclone inundated large parts of southern Africa. Floods in Mozambique killed hundreds, displaced hundreds of thousands, and spread malaria, typhoid and cholera (Pascual, et al. 2000).

Developed nations have also begun to experience more severe and unpredictable weather patterns. Hurricane Floyd hit North Carolina in September 1999, bringing an abrupt and devastating end to an extended summer drought. Prolonged droughts are also afflicting parts of Europe, while growing temperature contrasts between cold poles and warm tropics generate windstorms (Hurrell, et al. 2001), like the twin winds that raced across the Atlantic over Christmas 1999, destroying France's forests. Extreme weather events are having long-lasting ecological and economic impacts on a growing number of nations, affecting infrastructure, trade, travel and tourism.

The 1990s was a decade of extremes, each year marked by El Niño (warm) or La Niña (cold) conditions (Trenberth 1999; Trenberth and Hoar 1996). Since 1976 the pace, intensity and duration of ENSO events have quickened, and extremes have become more pronounced. Accumulating heat in the oceans certainly intensifies weather anomalies, and may be modifying the natural ENSO mode itself. Understanding how the various climate modes are influenced by human activities, and how the modes interact, is a central scientific challenge, and the results will inform multiple sectors of society. Disasters, such as the \$10 billion European windstorms and Hurricane Floyd, suggest that the costs of climate change will be borne by all (IFRC and RCS 1999).

Case Study: West Nile Virus

West Nile virus (WNV) was first reported in Uganda in 1937. WNV is a zoonosis (is transmitted by mosquitoes to birds and other animals), with spill-over to humans, which also poses significant risks for wild, zoo and domestic animal populations. While it is not known how WNV entered the New World, in 1999 anomalous weather conditions may have helped amplify its spread among urban mosquitoes, birds and mammals (Epstein and Defilippo 2001;

Shaman and Stieglitz 2002). Analysis of weather patterns coincident with a series of US urban outbreaks of St Louis encephalitis (SLE), a disease with a similar life cycle, revealed that drought was a common feature. *Culex pipiens*, the primary mosquito vector (carrier) for WNV, thrives in city storm drains and catch basins, especially in the organically rich water that forms during drought and the accompany warm temperatures. As the potential risks from pesticides for disease control must be weighed against the health risks of the disease, an early warning system of conditions conducive to amplification of the enzootic cycle could help initiate timely preventive measures, and potentially limit chemical interventions.

WNV is primarily a disease of wildlife and there is evidence of infection in birds (120 species) and other animals, primarily horses. Raptors (such as owls and kestrels) have been particularly affected. West Nile virus likely caused thousands of birds of prey to die in Ohio and other states in July 2002. Zoo animals have also died (for example, eight Humboldt penguins and numerous macaques in the Milwaukee Zoo).

Equine cases totaled 14 045 in 38 states, reported to the US Department of Agriculture Animal and Plant Health Inspection Service (APHIS) by state health officials in 2002. WNV has now been associated with illness and death in several other mammal species, including squirrel, wolf and dog in Illinois (which leads the country in the number of human cases), and mountain goat and sheep in Nebraska (which leads the country in numbers of equine cases).

Moreover, because of the bird and mammal reservoirs for WNV, there is the potential for outbreaks in all eastern and gulf states of the US and into Canada in the coming years. However, the impacts of WNV on wildlife populations and biodiversity have not been adequately evaluated. The impacts of declines in birds of prey could ripple through ecological systems and food chains, and could in itself contribute to the emergence of disease.

Outbreaks of St Louis Encephalitis in the US

SLE first emerged in the city of St Louis in 1933, during the dust bowl era. Since 1933, there have been 24 urban outbreaks in the US. SLE is an appropriate surrogate for study because of its similarity to WNV, and because of the significant number of SLE outbreaks in the US and the availability of accurate weather data. For the US outbreaks we examined meteorological data using the Palmer Severity Drought Index (PSDI), a measure of dryness that is a function of precipitation and soil moisture, compared with 30 years of data in the same location. The PSDI ranges from -4 (dry) to +4 (wet).[2] The examination revealed that from 1933 to the mid-1970s 10 of the 12 urban SLE outbreaks–regionally clustered in Kentucky, Colorado, Texas, Indiana, Tennessee and Illinois–were associated with two months of drought (one of the other two with one month of drought). After the mid-1970s the relationship shifts and outbreaks are associated with anomalous conditions that include droughts and heavy rains. Outbreaks of SLE during the 1974–76 period and after show a variable pattern in relation to weather: occurring with drought or, alternatively, after anomalous rains. Once established in a region, summer rains may boost populations of *Aedes japonicus* and other *Aedes* species (spp.) that can function as 'bridge vectors,' efficiently carrying the virus from birds to humans. The roles of 'maintenance' (primarily bird-biting mosquitoes) and bridge vectors in WNV transmission are under study.

International Outbreaks of West Nile Virus

Romania 1996

A significant European outbreak of WNV occurred in 1996 in Romania, in the Danube Valley and in Bucharest. This episode, with hundreds experiencing neurological disease and 17 fatalities, occurred between July and October and coincided with a prolonged drought (May through October) and excessive heat (May through July). Human cases in Bucharest were concentrated in blockhouses situated over an aging sewage system where *C. pipiens* were breeding in abundance.

Russia 1999

A third large outbreak of WNV occurred in Russia in the summer of 1999, following a drought. Hospitals in the Volgograd Region admitted 826 patients; 84 with meningoencephalitis, of which 40 died.

US 1999

In the spring and summer of 1999, a severe drought (following a mild winter), affected the northeastern and mid-Atlantic states. The prolonged drought culminated in a three-week July heat wave that enveloped the northeast. Then the pendulum swung in the opposite direction, bringing torrential end-of-August rains (and later Hurricane Floyd to the Mid-Atlantic states). *Culex* spp. thrived in the drought months, and *Aedes* spp. bred in the late summer floodwaters. In the New York outbreak seven people died and of the 62 people who suffered neurological symptoms and survived, most report chronic disabilities, such as extreme muscle weakness and fatigue.

Israel 2000

WNV was first reported in Israel in 1951, and sporadic outbreaks followed. Israel, a major stopover for migrating birds, usually receives little precipitation from May to October. In 2000, the region was especially dry, as drought conditions prevailed across southern Europe and the Middle East, from Spain to Afghanistan. Between 1 August and 31 October 2000, 417 cases of serologically confirmed WNV were diagnosed in Israel, with 35 deaths. *C. pipiens* was identified as a vector.

US 2002

In the summer of 2002 much of the west and mid-west of the US experienced severe spring and summer drought. Lack of snowpack in the Rockies (warming winters leading to more winter precipitation falling as rain) contributed. Forest fires burned over 6.1 million acres, and haze and respiratory disease affected several Colorado cities. There was also an explosion of WNV cases, with humans or animal WNV being documented in 43 states and the District of Columbia. Drought conditions were present in June in Louisiana, the first epicenter of WNV in 2002. Widespread drought conditions and heat waves may have amplified WNV and contributed to its rapid spread throughout the continental US. Health officials have also become convinced that WNV can be transmitted via organ transplant and blood transfusion.

Public Health Implications

Multi-month drought, especially in spring and early summer, was found to be associated with urban SLE outbreaks from its initial appearance in 1933 through 1973 and with recent severe urban outbreaks of WNV in Europe and the US. Other factors, such as inadequate sanitation, sluggish urban waterways and abandoned tires, may increase vulnerability to urban arbovirus outbreaks. Each new outbreak requires introduction or reintroduction of the virus, primarily via birds or wildlife–so there have been seasons without SLE outbreaks despite multi-month drought. Spread of WNV and sporadic cases may occur, even in the absence of conditions amplifying the enzootic cycling. In Bayesian parlance, drought increases the 'prior probability' of a significant outbreak once the virus becomes established in a region; other factors, such as rains that increase populations of bridge vectors, may affect transmission dynamics.

Further investigation and modeling are needed to determine the role of meteorological factors, and to identify reservoirs, over-wintering patterns and the susceptibility of different species associated with WNV. The migration path of many eastern US birds extends from Canada across the Gulf of Mexico to South America.[3]

Factors other than weather and climate contribute to outbreaks of SLE and WNV. Antiquated urban drainage systems leave more fetid pools in which mosquitoes can breed, and stagnant rivers and streams do not adequately support healthy fish populations that consume mosquito larvae in isolated standing pools. Such environmental vulnerabilities present opportunities for environmentally-based public health interventions following early warnings of meteorological conditions conducive to outbreaks. State plans to prevent the spread of WNV have four components:

- Mosquito surveillance and monitoring of dead birds;
- Community communications and media outreach;
- Source (breeding site) reduction though larviciding, using *Bacillus sphaericus* and Altocid (methoprine), and neighborhood clean-ups; and
- Pesticide (synthetic pyrethrins) spraying, when deemed necessary.

The information on predisposing climatic conditions and their predictions may be most applicable for areas that have not yet experienced WNV, but lie in the flyway from Canada to the Gulf of Mexico. Projections of droughts (such as for northeast Brazil during an El Niño event) could help focus attention on those areas, enhancing surveillance efforts (including active bird surveillance), public communication and environmentally friendly public health interventions. They may also help to set the stage for earlier chemical interventions once circulating virus is detected.

Finally, in terms of the public perception and concern over the risks of chemical interventions, understanding the links of WNV to climatic factors and mobilizing public agency departments, such as water and sewage services, to address a public health threat may prove helpful in garnering public support for the combined set of activities needed.

West Nile Virus may have recently evolved new strength, as it took an unusual toll on birds in New York. Alternatively, the North American birds were sensitive, as they were immunologically naive. But the unexpected outbreak of a mosquito-borne disease in New York City and rapid spread across the nation in 2002 also serve as reminders of the potential for exponential spread of pests and pathogens, and that pathogens evolving anywhere on the globe–and the social and environmental conditions that contribute to those changes–can affect us all.

DISCONTINUITIES

Climate change may not prove to be a linear process. Polar ice is thinning (Rothrock, et al. 1999), Greenland ice is retreating (Parkinson, et al. 1999), and since 1976 several small step-wise adjustments appear to have reset the climate system (CLIVAR 1992). In 1976, Pacific Ocean temperatures warmed significantly, still further in 1990, and cooled in 2000. The intensity of ENSO has surpassed the intensity it had 130 000 years ago during the previous warm interglacial period (Tudhope, et al. 2000). Cold upwelling in the Pacific in

2000 could portend a multi-decadal correction that stores accumulating heat at intermediate ocean layers. Meanwhile, two decades of warming in the North Atlantic have melted Arctic ice, plausibly contributing to a cold tongue from Labrador across to Europe and enhancing the Labrador Current that hugs the US east coast. Such paradoxical cooling from warming and ice melting could alter projections for climate, weather and disease for northern Europe and the northeast of the US. It is the instability of weather patterns that is of most concern for public health and society.

Winter is a blessing for public health in temperate zones, and deep cold snaps could freeze *Culex pipiens* in NYC sewers, for example, reducing the risk of WNV during those years. Thus the greatest threat of climate change lies not with year-to-year fluctuations, but with the potential for a more significant abrupt change that would alter the life support systems underlying our overall health and wellbeing.

CONCLUSIONS

The resurgence of infectious diseases among humans, wildlife, livestock (Daszak, et al. 2000), crops (Rosenzweig, et al. 2001; Anderson, et al. 2004), forests and marine life (Harvell, et al. 1999) in the final quarter of the twentieth century may be viewed as a primary symptom integrating global environmental and social change. Moreover, contemporaneous changes in greenhouse gas concentrations, ozone levels, the cryosphere, ocean temperatures, land use and land cover challenge the stability of our epoch, the Holocene–a remarkable 10 000-year period that has followed the retreat of ice sheets from temperate zones. The impacts of deforestation and climatic volatility are a particularly potent combination creating conditions conducive to disease emergence and spread. Given the rate of changes in local and global conditions we may expect more synergies and new surprises.

Warming may herald some positive health outcomes. High temperatures in some regions may reduce snail populations, which act as intermediate hosts for schistosomiasis. Winter mortality in the Northern Hemisphere from respiratory disease may decline. But the consequences of wide swings in weather, such as more winter precipitation falling as rain, followed by freezing nighttime temperatures and extended cold snaps, may overshadow the potential health benefits.

The aggregate of air pollution from burning fossil fuels and felling forests provides a relentless destabilizing force on the earth's heat budget. Examining the full life cycle of fossil fuels also exposes layers of injury. Environmental damage from mining, refining and transport of fossil fuels must be added to direct health effects of air pollution and acid precipitation. Returning CO_2 to the atmosphere through their combustion reverses the very biological process by which plants draw down atmospheric carbon and generate oxygen and ozone, helping to cool and shield the planet sufficiently to support animal life.

NEXT STEPS

Measures to address climate change must be guided by the precautionary principle (Kriebel, et al. 2001). Solutions may be divided into three levels. First-order solutions to the resurgence of infectious disease include improved surveillance and response capability, drug and vaccine development and greater provision of clinical care and public health services.

Second is improved prediction. Integrating health surveillance into long-term terrestrial and marine monitoring programs–ecological epidemiology–can benefit from advances in satellite imaging and climate forecasts that complement fieldwork. Early warning systems based on the integrated mapping of conditions, consequences and costs can facilitate timely, environmentally-friendly public health interventions and inform policies. Anticipating the health risks posed by the extreme conditions facing the US east coast in the summer of 1999 could have enhanced mosquito surveillance, heightened sensitivity to bird mortalities (that began in early August) and allowed treatment of mosquito breeding sites, avoiding large-scale spraying of pesticides.

The third level then is prevention, and rests upon environmental and energy policies. Restoration of forests and wetlands–'nature's sponges and kidneys'–is necessary to reduce vulnerabilities to climate, changing or not. Population stabilization is also necessary, but World Bank figures demonstrate that that is a function of income distribution. The underlying question, then, is not whether to develop, but how.

Developing clean energy sources is the first step. Providing basic public health infrastructure–sanitation, housing, food, refrigeration and cooking–requires energy. Clean energy is needed to pump and purify water, and desalinate water for irrigation from the rising seas. Meeting energy needs with non-polluting sources can be the first step towards the rational use of Earth's finite resources and reduction in the generation of wastes.

Addressing all these levels will require resources. Just as funds for technology development were necessary to settle the Montreal Protocol on ozone-depleting chemicals, substantial financial incentives are now needed to propel clean energy technologies into the global market. International funds are also needed to support common resources, like fisheries, and for vaccines and medications for diseases lacking lucrative markets.

Human and ecological systems can heal after time-limited assaults, and the climate system can also re-stabilize, but only if the tempo of destabilizing factors is reduced. The Intergovernmental Panel on Climate Change (IPCC) calculates that stabilizing atmospheric concentrations of greenhouse gases requires a 60 per cent reduction in emissions (Houghton, et al. 2001).

Worldviews can shift abruptly. Just as we may be underestimating the true costs of business-as-usual, we may be vastly underestimating the economic opportunities afforded by the energy transition. A distributed system of non-polluting energy sources can help reverse the mounting environmental assaults on public health and can provide the scaffolding on which to build clean, equitable and healthy development in the century before us.

NOTES

1. More information is available at http://www.acia.uaf.edu.
2. More information on the Palmer Severity Drought Index is available through the National Climatic Data Center, part of the National Oceanographic and Atmospheric Administration, US Department of Commerce (http://www.ncdc. noaa.gov).
3. More information on migration patterns is available at http://www.npwrc. usgs.gov/resource/birds/migratio/migratio.htm.

REFERENCES

Albritton, D.L., M.R. Allen, A.P.M. Baede, et al. (2001), *IPCC Working Group I Summary for Policy Makers, Third Assessment Report: Climate Change 2001: The Scientific Basis*, New York, NY: Cambridge University Press.

Anderson, P.K., A.A. Cunningham, N.G. Patel, et al. (2004), 'Emerging infectious diseases of plants: Pathogen pollution, climate change and agriculture drivers', *Trends in Ecology and Evoution,* **19**: 536–544.

Barry, J.P., C.H. Baxter, R.D. Sagarin, et al. (1995), 'Climate-related, long-term faunal changes in a California rocky intertidal community', *Science,* **267**: 672–675.

Berger, A. and M.F. Loutre (2002), 'Climate: An exceptionally long interglacial ahead?', *Science,* **297**: 1287–1288.

Bouma, M.J., S. Kovats, J. Cox, et al. (1997a), 'A global assessment of El Niño's disaster burden', *Lancet,* **350**: 1435–1438.

Bouma, M.J., G. Poveda, W. Rojas, et al. (1997b), 'Predicting high-risk years for malaria in Colombia using parameters of El Niño Southern Oscillation', *Tropical Medicine and International Health,* **2**: 1122–1127.

Bradshaw, W.E. and C.M. Holzapfel (2001), 'Genetic shift in photoperiodic response correlated with global warming', *Proceedings of the National Academy of Sciences*, **98**: 14509–14511.

Braga, A.L.F., A. Zanobetti and J. Schwartz (2001), 'The time course of weather related deaths', *Epidemiology*, **12**: 662–667.

Broecker, W.S. (1997), 'Thermohaline circulation, the Achilles heel of our climate system: Will man-made CO_2 upset the current balance?', *Science*, **278**: 1582–1588.

Checkley, W., L.D. Epstein, R.H. Gilman, et al. (1997), 'Effects of El Niño and ambient temperature on hospital admissions for diarrhoeal diseases in Peruvian children', *Lancet*, **355**: 442–450.

CLIVAR (1992), *A study of climate variability and predictability*, World Climate Research Program, Geneva: World Meteorological Organization.

Daszak, P., A.A. Cunningham and A.D. Hyatt (2000), 'Emerging infectious diseases of wildlife–threats to biodiversity and human health', *Science*, **287**: 443–449.

Dearborn, D.G., I. Yike, W.G. Sorenson, et al. (1999), 'Overview of investigations into pulmonary hemorrhage among infants in Cleveland, OH, *Environmental Health Perspecives*, **3**: 495–499.

Diaz, H.F. and N.E. Graham (1996), 'Recent changes in tropical freezing heights and the role of sea surface temperature', *Nature*, **383**: 152–155.

Dobson, A. and R. Carper (1993), 'Biodiversity', *Lancet*, **342**:1096–1099.

Easterling, D.R., G.A. Meehl, C. Parmesan, et al. (2000), 'Climate extremes: observations, modeling, and impacts', *Science*, **289**: 2068–2074.

Elias, S.A. (1994), *Quaternary Insects and Their Environments*, Washington, DC: Smithsonian Institution Press, p. 284.

EPA (2003), Workshop on Climate Change and Climate Variability: Potential for Personal Injuries and Travel Hazards, Washington, DC: US Environmental Protection Agency.

Epstein, P.R. (1992), 'Pestilence and poverty–historical transitions and the great pandemics [Commentary]', *American Journal of Preventive Medicine*, **8**: 263–265.

Epstein, P.R. (1993), 'Algal blooms in the spread and persistence of cholera', *BioSystems*, **31**: 209–221.

Epstein, P.R. (1999), 'Climate and health', *Science*, **285**: 347–348.

Epstein, P.R. (2000), 'Is global warming harmful to health?', *Scientific American*, **8**: 50–57.

Epstein, P.R. and C. Defilippo (2001), 'West Nile virus and drought', *Global Change and Human Health*, **2**: 105–107.

Epstein, P.R., H.F. Diaz, S. Elias, et al. (1998), 'Biological and physical signs of climate change: focus on mosquito-borne disease', *Bulletin of the American Meteorological Society*, **78**: 409–417.

Epstein, P.R., A. Dobson and J. Vandemeer (1997), 'Biodiversity and emerging infectious diseases: integrating health and ecosystem monitoring', in *Biodiversity and Human Health*, F. Grifo and J. Rosenthal (eds), Washington, DC: Island Press.

Epstein, P.R. and J.J. McCarthy (2004), 'Assessing climate stability', *Bulletin of the American Meteorological Society*, **85**(12): 1863–1870.

Gill, C.A. (1920a), 'The relationship between malaria and rainfall', *Indian Journal of Medical Research*, **8**: 618–632.

Gill, C.A. (1920b), 'The role of meteorology and malaria', *Indian Journal of Medical Research*, **8**: 633–693.

Harvell, C.D., K. Kim, J.M. Burkholder, et al. (1999), 'Diseases in the ocean: emerging pathogens, climate links, and anthropogenic factors', *Science*, **285**: 1505–1510.

Houghton, J.T., Y. Ding, D.J. Griggs, et al. (2001), *IPCC Working Group I Third Assessment Report: Climate Change 2001: The Scientific Basis*, New York, NY: Cambridge University Press.

Hurrell, J., Y. Kushnir and M. Visbeck (2001), 'The North Atlantic Oscillation', *Science*, **291**: 603–604.

IFRC and RCS (1999), *World Disasters Report*, International Federation of Red Cross and Red Crescent Societies, New York, NY: Oxford University Press.

Irion, R. (2001), 'The melting snows of Kilimanjaro', *Science*, **291**: 1690–1691.

Karl, T.R., R.W. Knight, D.R. Easterling, et al. (1995a), 'Trends in US climate during the twentieth century', *Consequences*, **1**: 3–12.

Karl, T.R., R.W. Knight and N. Plummer (1995b), 'Trends in high-frequency climate variability in the twentieth century', *Nature*, **377**: 217–220.

Karl, T.R., N. Nicholls and J. Gregory (1997), 'The coming climate', *Scientific American*, **5**: 78–83.

Karl, T.R., K.E. Trenberth and K.E. Modern (2003), 'Global climate change', *Science*, **302**: 1719–1723.

Kovats, R.S., M.J. Bouma and A. Haines (1999), *El Niño and Health*, Geneva, Switzerland: World Health Organization.

Kriebel, D., J. Tickner, P. Epstein, et al. (2001), 'The precautionary principle in environmental science', *Environmental Health Perspectives*, **109**: 871–876.

Kumar, K.K., B. Rajagopalan and M.A. Cane (1999), 'On the weakening relationship between the Indian monsoon and ENSO', *Science*, **284**: 2156–2159.

Leaf, A. (1989), 'Potential health effects of global climate and environmental changes', *New England Journal of Medicine*, **321**: 1577–1583.

Leeson, H.S. (1939), 'Longevity of Anopheles maculipennis race atroparvus, Van Theil, at controlled temperature and humidity after one blood meal', *Bulletin of Entomological Research,* **30**: 103–301.

Levitus, S., J.I. Antonov, T.P. Boyer, et al. (2000), 'Warming of the world ocean', *Science,* **287**: 2225–2229.

Lindgren, E., T. Lars, and T. Polfeldt (2000), 'The impact of climactic change on the northern latitude limit and population density of the disease-transmitting European tick, Ioxodes ricinus', *Environmental Health Perspectives,* **108**: 119–123.

Linthicum, K.J., A. Anyamba, C.J. Tucker, et al. (1999), 'Climate and satellite indicators to forecast rift valley fever epidemics in Kenya', *Science,* **285**: 397–400.

MacArthur, R.H. (1972), *Geographical Ecology,* New York, NY: Harper and Row.

Mackenzie, W.R., N.J. Hoxie, M.E. Proctor, et al. (1994), 'A massive outbreak in Milwaukee of cryptosporidium infection transmitted through public water supply', *New England Journal of Medicine,* **331**: 161–167.

Mann, M.E., R.S. Bradley and M.K. Hughes (1998), 'Global-scale temperature patterns and climate forcing over the past six centuries', *Nature,* **392**: 779–787.

Martens, W.J.M., T.H. Jetten and D. Focks (1997), 'Sensitivity of malaria, schistosomiasis and dengue to global warming', *Climatic Change,* **35**: 145–156.

Martin, D.H. and M. Lefebvre (1995), 'Malaria and climate: sensitivity of malaria potential transmission to climate', *Ambio,* **24**: 200–209.

Maslin, M. (2004), 'Ecological versus climatic thresholds', *Science,* **306**: 2197–2198.

Matossian, M.K. (1989), *Poisons of the Past: Molds, Epidemics, and History,* New Haven, CT: Yale University Press.

McCarthy, J.J., O.F. Canziani, N.A. Leary, D.J. Dokken and K.S. White (eds) (2001), *Climate Change 2001: Impacts, Adaptation and Vulnerability Contribution of Working Group II to the Third Assessment Report of the Intergovernmental Panel on Climate Change,* UK: Cambridge University Press, p. 1000.

McMichael, A.J., A. Haines, R. Slooff and S. Kovats (eds) (1996), *Climate Change and Human Health,* Geneva, Switzerland: World Health Organization, World Meteorological Organization, United Nations Environmental Program.

Mosley-Thompson, E. (1997), *Glaciological evidence of recent environmental changes,* Paper presented at the annual meeting of the Association of American Geography, Fort Worth, TX, 3 April 1997.

NRC (2001), *Abrupt Climate Change: Inevitable Surprises*, National Research Council, National Academy of Sciences, Washington, DC: National Academy Press.

Parkinson, C.L., D.J. Cavalieri, P. Gloersen, H.J. Zwally and J.C. Comiso (1999), 'Spatial distribution of trends and seasonality in the hemispheric sea ice covers', *Journal of Geophysical Research*, **104**: 20827–20835.

Parmesan, C. (1996), 'Climate and species' range', *Nature*, **382**: 765.

Parmesan, C., N. Ryholm, et al. (1999), 'Poleward shifts in geographical ranges of butterfly species associated with regional warming', *Nature*, **399**: 579–583.

Pascual, M., X. Rodó, S.P. Ellner, R. Colwell and M.J. Bouma (2000), 'Cholera dynamics and El Niño-Southern Oscillation', *Science*, **289**: 1766–1769.

Pauli, H., M. Gottfried and G. Grabherr (1996), 'Effects of climate change on mountain ecosystems–upward shifting of alpine plants', *World Resource Review*, **8**: 382–390.

Peters, R.L. (1991), 'Consequences of global warming for biological diversity', in *Global Climate Change and Life on Earth*, R.L. Wyman (ed.), New York, NY: Routledge.

Peterson, B.J., R.M. Holmes, J.W. McClelland, C.J. Vörösmarty, R.B. Lammers, B.J. Shiklomanov, et al. (2002), 'Increasing river discharge to the Arctic Ocean', *Science*, **298**: 2171–2173.

Petit, J.R., J. Jouze, D. Raynaud, N.I. Barkov, J.M. Barnola, I. Basile, et al. (1999), 'Climate and atmospheric history of the past 420,000 years from the Vostok Ice Core, Antartica', *Nature*, **399**: 429–436.

Reiter, P. (2000), 'From Shakespeare to Defoe: Malaria in England in the Little Ice Age, *Emerging Infectious Diseases*, **6**: 1–11.

Rosenzweig, C. and D. Hillel (1998), *Climate change and the global harvest*, New York, NY: Oxford University Press, pp. 101–122.

Rosenzweig, C., A. Iglesias, X.B. Yang, P.R. Epstein and E. Chivian (2000), *Implications of Climate Change for US Agriculture: Extreme Weather Events, Plant Diseases and Pests*, Center for Health and the Global Environment, Harvard Medical School.

Rosenzweig, C., A. Iglesias, X.B. Yang, P.R. Epstein and E. Chivian (2001), 'Climate change and extreme weather events: Implications for food production, plant diseases, and pests', *Global Change and Human Health*, **2**: 90–104.

Rothrock, D.A., Y. Yu and G.A. Marykut (1999), 'Thinning of the Arctic Sea-ice cover', *Journal of Geophysical Research Letters*, **26**: 3469–3472.

Shaman, J., J. Day and M. Stieglitz (2002), 'Drought-induced amplification of St Louis encephalitis virus, Florida', *Emerging Infectious Diseases*, **8**(6): 575–580.

Thompson, L.G., E. Mosley-Thompson, M. Davis, P.N. Lin, T. Yao, M. Dyurgerov, et al. (1993), 'Recent warming: Ice core evidence from tropical ice cores with emphasis on Central Asia', *Global and Planetary Change*, **7**: 145.

Trenberth, K.E. (1999), 'The extreme weather events of 1997 and 1998', *Consequences*, **5**: 3–15.

Trenberth, K.E. and T.J. Hoar, (1996), 'The 1990–1995 El Niño-Southern Oscillation event: longest on record', *Journal of Geophysical Research Letters*, **23**: 57–60.

Tudhope, A.W., C.P. Chilcott, M.T. McCulloch, E.R. Cook, J. Chappell, R.M. Ellam, et al. (2000), 'Variability in the El Niño-Southern Oscillation through a glacial-interglacial cycle', *Science*, **291**: 1511–1517.

Wayne, P., S. Foster, J. Connolly, F. Bazzaz and P. Epstein (2002), 'Production of allergenic pollen by ragweed (*Ambrosia artemisiifolia L.*) is increased in CO_2-enriched atmospheres', *Annals of Allergy, Asthma and Immunology*, **8**: 249–253.

World Health Organization (1996), *The World Health Report 1996: Fighting Disease, Fostering Development.* World Health Organization, [available from Distribution and Sales, World Health Organization, CH-1211 Geneva 27, Switzerland].

Ziska, L.H. and F. Caulfield (2000), 'The potential influence of rising atmospheric carbon dioxide (CO_2) on public health: pollen production of common ragweed as a test case', *World Resource Review*, **12**: 449–457.

Zucker, J.R. (1996), 'Changing patterns of autochthonous malaria transmission in the United States: A review of recent outbreaks', *Emerging Infectious Diseases*, **2**: 37.

15 Impacts of Changing Temperatures on Heat-related Mortality in Urban Areas: The Issues and a Case Study from Metropolitan Boston

Matthias Ruth, Anthony Amato and Paul Kirshen

INTRODUCTION

Climate asserts a significant influence on human health, as is evidenced by the geographic distribution and seasonal fluctuations of many diseases and causes of mortality (Tromp 1980). The connection between climate and human health strongly suggests that climatic change may alter the incidence and distribution of a wide range of diseases (Stone 1995) and causes of mortality (Martens 1998). Public health researchers have, however, only recently begun to investigate the potential impacts of climate change and to identify adaptation strategies to reduce public health vulnerabilities to climate variability and change (Longstreth 1991; Kovats, et al. 1999; Patz, Engelberg et al. 2000; Patz, McGeehin et al. 2000; WHO 2000; Watson and McMicheal 2001).

This chapter assesses potential changes in temperature-related mortality in the United States. Specifically, we focus on the effect of high temperatures, which are among the most prominent causes of weather-related human mortality in the US, especially in its northern cities (Bridger, et al. 1976; Kalkstein and Greene 1997; Changnon, et al. 1996; Gaffen and Ross 1998; Davis, et al. 2002; 2003) and explore how temperature-related mortality has changed in the trends that may emerge as climate change manifests itself over the following decades. Our own exploration and a review of findings from related studies then suggest a set of implications for regional planning and other adaptations that will help reduce mortality rates in the future. The methodologies used to assess potential climate impacts on temperature-related mortality are illustrated with an application to the metropolitan Boston region of the US, consisting of the 101 communities shown in Figure 15.1. The study is part of a larger assessment of 'Climate's Long-term Impacts on Metro Boston' (CLIMB) which explores potential impacts on a variety of local infrastructure systems and services, including energy, transportation, communication and water quality and supply, as well as an integrated assessment of interactions among all these urban infrastructure components (Ruth and Kirshen 2001). The impact work is used to identify, in collaboration with stakeholders in the region, whether and when adaptation should be pursued, what alternative adaptation strategies might look like and how vigorously to pursue them (Kirshen, et al. 2004).

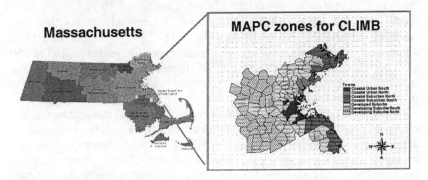

Figure 15.1   Study region and zones defined by the Metropolitan Area Planning Council (MAPC)

The scientific consensus is that globally averaged surface air temperature will warm between 1.4 and 5.8°C by 2100, relative to 1990, and globally averaged sea level will rise 0.09 to 0.88 meters by 2100 (IPCC 2001a). In the New England region, in which metropolitan Boston is located, climatic changes are projected by global change models to be relatively less drastic than in other parts of the United States. For example, the Hadley Model projects a 5.7°F (3.2°C) warming in annual minimum temperatures and a 30 percent increase in precipitation by 2100, whereas the Canadian Climate Model projects a 9.7°F (5.4°C) minimum temperature increase and a 10 per cent increase in precipitation over the course of the century (Rock and Moore 2001). If either of the average temperature increases suggested by the Hadley Model or the Canadian Climate Model is correct, then Boston's future temperature will be approximately the current 30-year average for Richmond, VA or Atlanta, GA, respectively. An increase in Boston's mean temperature would increase the probability of new record high temperatures, as depicted in Figure 15.2a, unless a compensating change occurs in the variance of the temperature regime. In contrast, if mean temperature is unchanged and variance increases then the probability of both hot and cold extremes increases (Figure 15.2b). Finally, increases in both the mean and variance likely result in changes in extreme hot and cold events (Figure 15.2c).

Several empirical studies support the assumption of increased frequency of extreme temperature events under climate change. For example, one study finds that an average temperature increase of 3°C (5.4°F) in Toronto, Canada is likely to result in an eight-fold increase in the probability of a five-day consecutive run over 30°C (86°F) (Colombo, et al. 1999). Similarly, researchers assessing the impacts of climate change in Victoria, Australia, using a high resolution climate model, find significant changes in the frequency of days with temperatures below freezing (32°F) and above 35°C (90°F) (Whetton, et al. 2002). They project, for example, that with a low warming scenario the number of days above 35°C (90°F) increases by 15 to 40 per cent in 2070, whereas the high warming scenario leads to a 150 to 350 per cent increase. As a general rule of thumb, in temperate climates the frequency of very hot days will approximately double for a 2 to 3°C increase in average summer temperature (CCIRG 1991).

Changes in the frequency of extreme weather events will accompany the changes in average temperatures. From a societal perspective, changes in extreme events may be an even larger concern than changes in climatic averages (Katz and Brown 1992; Changnon 2000). Past research predominantly suggests that for the range of usual projections of future temperatures, mortality in the United States will significantly increase in the early twenty-first century (Chestnut, et al. 1998; Gaffen and Ross 1998). However, the empirical record is far from conclusive, because the ultimate impact of temperature changes on mortality rates for a specific region depends on the age structure and other demographic characteristics of the region, the effectiveness of early health warning systems, access to heating and air conditioning, and other infrastructure-related adaptations such as heat-reflection or retention properties of the built environment, access to shade and more (Seretakis, et al. 1997; Chestnut, et al. 1998; Keatinge, et al. 2000; McGeehin and Mirabelli 2001; Donaldson, et al. 2003).

In assessing the potential climate impacts on mortality in metropolitan Boston, we follow a three-step approach. First, we determine, on the basis of historical data, the temperature thresholds for heat- and cold-related mortality in the region. In step two, we use these thresholds to investigate the functional relationship between mortality rates and climatological variables controlling for seasonal effects on mortality. In step three, we create a set of potential future local weather scenarios using moving block bootstrapping techniques in conjunction with climate forecasts from global circulation models (GCM), which we then combine with forecasts of future population and the functional relationship of temperature-related mortality developed in step two to simulate changes in mortality.

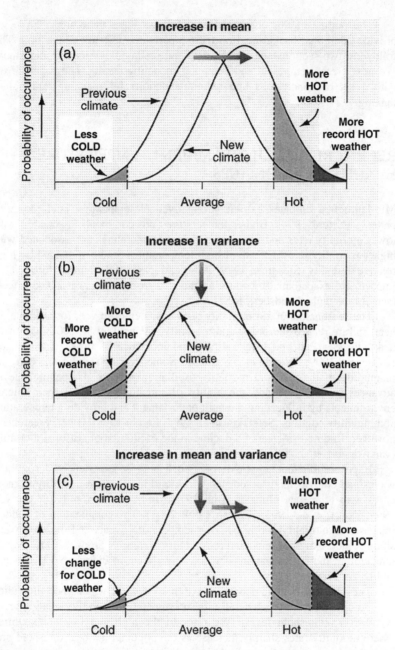

Figure 15.2   Influence of changes in mean and variance on temperature (IPCC 2001a)

The outline of this chapter closely follows these three steps. First, we provide additional background on the temperature-mortality connection. The following two sections address the data and methodology used in our study. We next present empirical and computer modeling results. The paper closes with a set of conclusions and recommendations for planning and policy making.

RECENT RESEARCH ON AMBIENT TEMPERATURE-HEALTH RELATIONSHIPS

Mid-latitudinal climates exhibit strong cyclical temperature and mortality patterns (Lerchl 1998). Higher temperatures are commonly associated with lower mortality rates and, conversely, lower temperatures are associated with higher mortality rates. Effects of high temperatures are compounded by high relative humidity (Steadman 1979; 1984) and many of the temperature-related impacts are exacerbated by warming induced from urban heat island effects (see, for example, Landsberg 1981).

The seasonal nature of mortality rates has been observed, for example, in heart failure-related morbidity and mortality (Steward, et al. 2002), coronary heart disease (Pell and Cobbe 1999) and incidence of stroke (Lanska and Hoffmann 1999; Oberg, et al. 2000). Some research indicates that the magnitude of the seasonal mortality oscillation may be dampening due to advances in medicine and the ability of humans to control their micro-environments by influencing the built environment and providing temperature and humidity controls (Seretakis, et al. 1997; Lerchl 1998). Other researchers, however, find no evidence of a decline in the oscillation of seasonal mortality (van Rossum, et al. 2001).

Exposure to temperature extremes, such as those experienced during heat waves and cold spells, is associated with rapid increases in mortality in most cities with temperate climates (Bull 1973; Bull and Morton 1978; Curwen 1991; Kunst, et al. 1993; Huynen, et al. 2001). The combination of sudden increases in mortality during extreme temperature events and the downward sloping non-extreme temperature-mortality relation produces an overall temperature-mortality relation schematically shown in Figure 15.3 (Kalkstein and Davis 1989).

The hot and cold temperature extremes beyond which mortality rates deviate upward from the generally linear temperature-mortality relation are a population's threshold levels. We refer to the high and low temperatures where mortality rates sharply increase as the population's heat threshold and cold threshold, respectively. Rapid escalation in mortality associated with temperatures exceeding heat and cold thresholds is a consequence of physiological stress due to increased requirements on the body's thermoregulatory system to maintain a comfortable physiological state. With exposure to non-extreme temperatures the body is able to maintain a comfortable state through perspiration and vasodilatation of cutaneous vessels. However, when the body is exposed to extreme temperatures an excessive number of deaths occur either directly as a result of mortality causes such as heat stroke or hypothermia, or indirectly by exacerbating pre-existing health conditions. Some research suggests that the majority of temperature-related deaths are a result of pre-existing cardiovascular and respiratory conditions (Keatinge, et al. 1986; Kilbourne 1997; Larsen 1990).

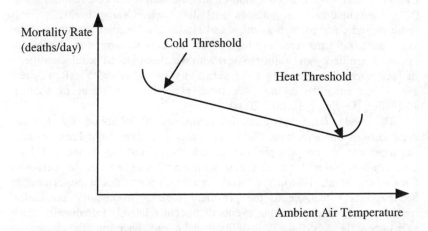

Figure 15.3   Theoretical temperature-mortality relationship for a population

Extreme heat events can cause rapid increases in mortality. For example, more than 700 deaths in Chicago were attributed to the July 1995 heat wave (Semenza, et al. 1996). Extreme heat events increase requirements on the cardiovascular system to produce physiological cooling, which in turn may lead to excess deaths (Kilbourne 1997). In particular, infants, the elderly, individuals with pre-existing illnesses, the poor, the overweight and individuals living in urban areas are vulnerable to heat-related morbidity and mortality (Blum, et al. 1998; Smoyer, et al. 2000; CDC 2002; National Weather Service 2002).

Extreme cold temperature events are also associated with increases in mortality rates, controlling for influenza (Kunst, et al. 1993; Eurowinter Group 1997). Sharp increases in mortality during cold events have been identified, mainly due to thrombolic and respiratory disease (Donaldson and Keatinge 1997). Other mechanisms through which cold affects mortality include increases in blood pressure, blood viscosity and heart rate. Coronary and stroke mortality have been shown to be associated with cold temperatures in the United States (Rogot and Padgett 1976). In Russia mortality is found to increase by 1.15 per cent for each 1°C drop in temperature (Donaldson, et al. 1998). A study of the impacts of temperature and snowfall on mortality in Pennsylvania found exposure to snow and temperatures below -7°C (19°F) to be dangerous to health (Gorjanc, et al. 1999).

The effects of extreme temperature events on mortality are not solely determined by physiological variables, but also by the degree of acclimation of the local population to the regional climate regime (Kalkstein and Davis 1989; Kalkstein and Greene 1997; Smoyer 1998; Keatinge, et al. 2000; Curriero, et al. 2002). Acclimation entails the adaptation of communities to their environmental surroundings including behavioral patterns, societal fashions and customs such as dress and siestas, the thermal attributes of the local built infrastructure, availability of air conditioning and the health system's familiarity and ability to deal with weather-induced health conditions. In fact research suggests that the sensitivity of mortality to extreme heat events has been decreasing over time, possibly as a result of societal adaptation (Davis, et al. 2002; 2004).

The wide range of climatic environments inhabited by humans demonstrates our enormous ability to buffer ourselves from harsh macro-environments. As an example, in Yakutsk–the coldest city in the world–no association is present between mortality rates and extremely cold temperatures (Donaldson et al. 1998). Yet, while acclimation enables a population to become less vulnerable to the prevalent weather events, the population remains susceptible to weather events that occur relatively infrequently (such as events at the tails of the probability distribution). Therefore, the changes in the frequency of extreme events accompanying climate change need to be examined in order to identify adaptation strategies such that the population can adapt to the characteristics of the new climate regime.

Studies investigating the impacts of climate on human health often employ a place-based approach in consideration of the importance of local acclimation in determining a population's morbidity and mortality (Martens 1998; Smoyer 1998). Place-specific mortality responses to changes in temperature have been found to be present even after controlling for differences in meteorological, demographic and economic variables (Smoyer, et al. 2000). In general, mortality rates of populations in cool climates are more sensitive to heat events, whereas populations in warmer climates have mortality rates more sensitive to cold events (Curriero, et al. 2002). To illustrate, Keatinge finds that for every 1°C decrease in temperature below 18°C (64.4°F) mortality rates in south Finland increases by only 0.27 per cent, while in Athens, Greece mortality rates increase by 2.15 per cent (Keatinge 1997). Likewise, Kalkstein and Davis evaluate temperature-related mortality rates in 48 US cities and find considerable variation in heat threshold levels.

For example, heat thresholds in Phoenix and Las Vegas equal or exceed 109°F (43°C), whereas in Boston and Pittsburgh the thresholds are below 86°F (30°C) (Kalkstein and Davis 1989). A city-level study examining minimum mortality temperatures in 11 large US cities finds temperature differences of up to 15°F between cities (Curriero, et al. 2002).

The following section provides a discussion of the data used in our study to estimate temperature-related mortality in metropolitan Boston–a region with typically cold winters and mild summers, and a local population experienced in dealing with frequent cold events. Acclimation to the traditionally cold climate is reflected, for example, by the fact that a significant portion of the region's urban housing stock is made from heat-retaining red bricks while few have central air conditioning.

DATA

Socioeconomic Data

The future socioeconomic outcomes in metropolitan Boston will result from complex interactions between global and national forces in a fast evolving global economy, on the one hand, and regional and local factors, which define the competitiveness and the quality of life in the region, on the other hand. The former forces include technological and socioeconomic drivers which define the national economic arena in an increasingly global economy. The latter regional and local factors pertain to: the physical and human capital resources of the metropolitan Boston region, which define the region's competitiveness; and the relevant public policies related to the environment, land use and transportation, which determine the quality of life in the various parts of the region. To capture and incorporate these multiple level influences, the CLIMB project relates the local and regional knowledge base on spatial land use and development patterns in metro Boston to the broader demographic and socioeconomic national level change drivers, which determine the national level demographic and economic outcomes. Regional information on spatial patterns of residences and industrial economic activity, as influenced by the environmental, land use and transportation policies and regulations in various towns, can be discerned from the Metropolitan Area Planning Council's (MAPC) Long Term Demographic and Employment Forecasts. The MAPC forecasts to 2025 at the town level represent the best regional judgments (based on MAPC's analysis of town level development policies) on the likely spatial evolution of people and economic activity in the region.

Climate Data

The climate data used in this study consists of meteorological records from a monitoring station located at Boston Logan Airport and has been collected and compiled by the National Weather Service (NOAA 2002). These records are used as proxies for the entire metropolitan Boston region. The historic record contains detailed information on daily maximum temperature, minimum temperature, average temperature (average of maximum and minimum temperature), snowfall and so on. Descriptive statistics are shown in Table 15.1.

Table 15.1   Descriptive statistics for CLIMB climate data (1970–1998)

Climate Variable	Mean	Standard Deviation	Minimum	Maximum
Max. Temperature (°F)	59.3	18.4	7	102
Min. Temperature (°F)	44.0	16.7	-7	83
Avg. Temperature (°F)	51.8	17.3	1.5	93
Snowfall (inches)	0.12	0.80	0	22.4

The historical weather data was used as the basis for regional forecasts of weather conditions until 2050. To generate future weather patterns that are consistent with past patterns, we applied a moving block bootstrapping (Vogel and Shallcross 1996; Harmel, et al. 2002). This is a non-parametric statistical method that maintains probability relationships of time-series values both within years and over years, and consists of sampling with replacement from the existing time-series of annual climate events until a time-series of desired length is obtained. The technique retains the region's non-normal temperature distribution (Figures 15.4 and 15.5).

To model time-series of climate change scenarios, trends of climate changes are applied to the set of time-series representing the present climate. These trends have been derived from regional outputs of two major climate models, the Canadian Center for Modeling and Analysis's Canadian Global Coupled Model (CCC model) and the Hadley Model. By bootstrapping local weather data and superimposing trends from more aggregate global climate models, we have created a set of time-series data for potential future weather conditions that are consistent with past patterns and global warming trends. This set of time-series data is used in the third step of our analysis to simulate potential impacts of climate change on temperature-related mortality in metropolitan Boston.

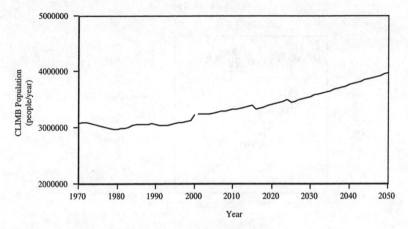

Figure 15.4   CLIMB population estimate and forecast

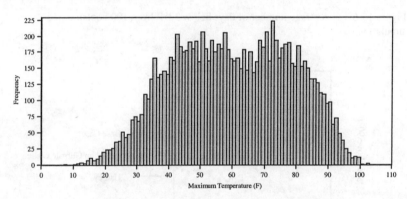

Figure 15.5   Maximum temperature frequencies in Boston, 1970–1998

For our analysis we generated time-series of potential future climate, noting the number of days below and above various temperature thresholds. For illustrative purposes, Figure 15.6 shows the average number of days below 32°F from 100 bootstrapped model runs with and without trends from the Canadian Climate Center and Hadley models. The average number of days below 32°F across the 100 bootstrapped runs and across 100 years is 22.3 days (standard deviation 0.8 days) in the base case, which drops to 15.7 days (standard deviation 3.6) in the case of the Hadley Model trends and 13.8 days (standard deviation 4.4) in the case of climate trends from the Canadian Climate Center model. But even within shorter time frames climate signals are present, albeit much less pronounced. For example, the average number of

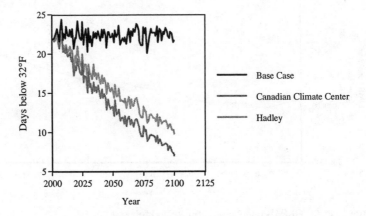

Figure 15.6   Average number of days below 32°F from 100 bootstrapped
simulation runs

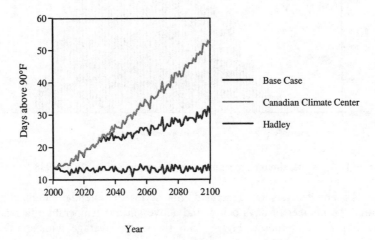

Figure 15.7   Average number of days above 90°F from 100 bootstrapped
simulation runs

days below 32°F across the 100 bootstrapped runs for the first 25 years without climate change is 22.5 (standard deviation 0.9) while for the Canadian Climate Center and Hadley models that number is, respectively, 20.0 (standard deviation 1.6) and 20.6 (standard deviation 1.3).

Figure 15.7 shows the average number of days above 90°F with and without climate trends. Averaged over 100 bootstrapped runs and 100 years of model simulation, the number of days above 90°F rises from 13.0 (standard deviation 0.7) in the base case to 30.6 (standard deviation 11.6) with assumptions from the Canadian Climate Center model and 23.4 (standard deviation 4.9) with trends from the Hadley model. For the first 25 years of the simulation these averages are 12.7 (standard deviation 0.6), 16.3 (standard deviation 2.3), and 16.3 (standard deviation 2.2), respectively.

Regional Mortality Data

The Massachusetts Department of Public Health[1] provided the mortality records used in this study. The records were presorted on the basis of the deceased residing in one of the 101 towns in the CLIMB region. We retain mortality observations on the basis of residence because we are interested in examining changes in mortality attributable to metropolitan Boston's weather. Accordingly, mortality records were excluded for individuals who died in the region but did not reside within the region.

A wide range of causes of death are impacted by weather, and therefore discerning exactly what constitutes 'weather-related' is problematic (Kalkstein and Davis 1989). For example, in the US there exists no uniform definition of heat-related mortality (CDC 1995). Therefore, we investigate all causes of mortality so as not to underestimate changes in mortality associated with heat and cold extremes.

Consistent data records, extending for the years 1970 to 1998, contained mortality information for 754 778 deaths, or on average 25 000 deaths per year, in the CLIMB region. The mortality data is aggregated to daily totals for each day between 1 January 1970 and 31 December 1998 generating 10 592 observations in the data set. The daily mortality rate–expressed as deaths per million people–is the daily mortality divided by the population in the CLIMB region in the respective year (see Figure 15.8). The mean daily mortality rate during the 1970 to 1998 period is 23.5 deaths per million people with a standard deviation of 3.7. The large spike in the mortality rate on 3 August 1975 to 66 deaths per million people occurred a day after Boston experienced an August all-time maximum temperature of 102°F. On the day of the extreme heat event the mortality rate increased by 100 per cent followed by a 200 per cent increase on the following day, relative to the 1970 to 1998 average August daily mortality rate.

METHODOLOGY

Our methodology for estimating climate-induced changes in mortality for the CLIMB region entails a three-step approach. As detailed in this section, we first determine heat and cold threshold temperatures indigenous to the region. We then statistically analyze changes in mortality associated with daily temperatures in excess of the thresholds derived in the first step. Finally, in the last step we use the threshold-mortality relationships along with population and climate forecasts to simulate potential future mortality impacts in the CLIMB region.

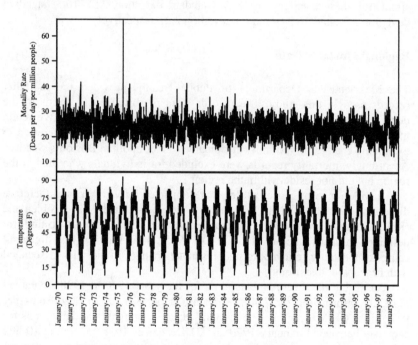

Figure 15.8   Daily mortality rates and average temperatures for the CLIMB study region, 1970–1998

Figure 15.9 illustrates average daily mortality rates for each month of the year based on the 1970–1998 daily data. Mortality rates in the CLIMB study region, as with most mid-latitudinal areas, exhibit significant seasonal fluctuations. The average daily mortality rate peaks in January at approximately 26.4 deaths per million people and reaches a minimum in August at approximately 21.5 deaths per million people, resulting in a 22.8 per cent peak-to-trough difference. Similar patterns of mortality rates being higher in winter than summer can be seen elsewhere in the United States and other countries (Donaldson and Keatinge 1997; Eurowinter Group 1997; Lerchl 1998; Laschewski and Jendritzky 2002). Despite the generally inverse relation between average monthly mortality rates and monthly temperatures, the extent of changes in mortality directly attributable to low temperatures is difficult to determine. One body of literature argues that mortality rates are more influenced by 'seasonal' factors such as influenza epidemics and that little of the variation in winter mortality can be explained by changes in temperature (Kalkstein and Greene 1997). Other researchers suggest, after controlling for influenza, that there is a consistent association between winter mortality and temperature (Langford and Bentham 1995; Donaldson and Keatinge 2002) and find that by 2050 climate change potentially could reduce winter mortality by nearly 9000 deaths per year in England and Wales (Langford and Bentham 1995).

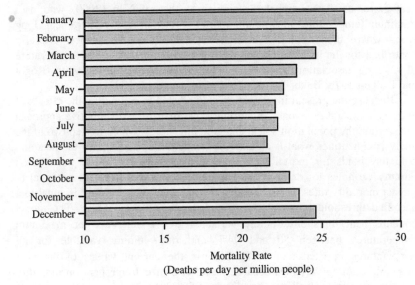

Figure 15.9   Monthly average daily mortality rates, 1970–1998

In this study we control for seasonal fluctuations in mortality rates by capturing monthly mortality variation using a fixed-effects regression model. This approach enables us to compare the actual daily mortality rate to the expected mortality rate within a given month and consequently observe if mortality anomalies at extreme temperatures are present. The model contains dummy variables for each month of the year allowing the intercept term, which in this case is a month's expected daily mortality rate, to vary throughout the year. The coefficient of each dummy variable (February-

December) indicates the change in the intercept relative to the predetermined monthly base mortality rate, which we designated as January. For example, the coefficient on the February dummy variable indicates the difference between February's average daily mortality rate and January's average daily mortality rate in the same year. The January average daily mortality rate is in turn adjusted each year by the annual trend variable, which accounts for longer-term trends in mortality rates such as demographic changes, changes in the housing stock, availability of air conditioning, advances in the health care system, behavioral adaptations, or other variables that relate to changes in the population's vulnerability to temperature.

Maximum daily temperature and incidence of snowfall are the independent weather variables in the statistical model. The maximum temperature is used rather than an average or minimum temperature due to the fact that the region has a colder climate than the US average and hence the population has acclimatized to cooler weather but remains unaccustomed to heat extremes. The rationale is similar to that of Yan (2000) who uses minimum temperatures in assessing mortality rates in relatively tropical Hong Kong where the population is unaccustomed to cold extremes. We also controlled for the incidence of snowfall given some evidence in the literature of a strong association between snowfall and increases in mortality (Rogot and Padgett 1976; Baker-Blocker 1982; Gorjanc, et al. 1999).

Because the present investigation is interested in estimating the effects of extreme temperature events on mortality, we first use a quantitative approach to ascertain the population's heat and cold thresholds, which in step two of the analysis constitutes what is an extreme temperature. To identify the heat and cold thresholds for mortality rates in metropolitan Boston we constructed dummy variables for daily maximum temperatures that have the potential to impact mortality rates. Days in which the maximum temperature is equal to a specified threshold temperature are coded one, otherwise zero. The model contains heat threshold dummy variables at 1°F intervals for maximum temperatures between 80 and 94°F and one dummy variable for all temperatures in excess of 95°F. We use the current values of the heat threshold dummy variables because the effects of extreme heat on mortality occur immediately (Kalkstein and Davis 1989; Curriero, et al. 2002).

Likewise, cold threshold dummy variables for maximum temperatures between 20 and 35°F and one dummy variable for all maximum temperatures below 20°F are included in the model. On account of previous research findings (Rogot and Padget 1976; Bull and Morton 1978; Gorjanc, et al. 1999; Donaldson and Keatinge 2002) and our initial results of a time-delay between extreme cold temperature events and effects on mortality rates, we include in the model time-lagged values for cold thresholds of two and three days. Finally, incidence of snowfall on the current and two succeeding days are modeled with dummy variables.

The coefficients on the temperature thresholds represent the difference in the mortality rate on days with temperatures at the specified temperature relative to the expected mortality rate on days within the reference temperature range conditional on the month. In essence, the fixed-effects model is a difference of means test between the mortality rates on days with temperatures at a respective threshold compared to mortality rates on days with maximum temperatures in the reference range, after controlling for seasonal fluctuations, annual trends and snowfall. Consequently, based on statistical significance we are able to determine the extreme hot and cold temperatures at which mortality rates sharply increase over what would be expected in a given month.

RESULTS

Temperature Thresholds

The results of our quantitative investigation into the temperature thresholds for the CLIMB region are presented in Table 15.2. The variables for all months (February-December) are strongly associated with changes in the mortality rate and show a statistical difference from the 27.2 deaths per million people in January. August has the largest decrease in mortality rate, at 4.4, compared with the January rate. The annual trend variable indicates that the region's mortality rate has been decreasing at an average annual rate of 0.1 deaths per day per million people over the period under investigation. With the annual trend variable we assume uniformity across all monthly mortality rates. This assumption is supported by a variety of preliminary analyses and hypotheses tests.

Days in which the maximum temperature reaches between 80°F and 89°F have no significant association with changes in the mortality rates on the current day as indicated by their respective heat threshold dummy variables. However, each of the dummy variables for maximum temperatures of 90°F or higher suggest a significant increase compared to the expected mortality rate. The results unambiguously suggest a heat threshold of 90°F for the CLIMB region, which coincides with the temperature at which heatstroke, heat cramps and heat exhaustion begin to occur (National Weather Service 2002) and is consistent with previous findings for Boston (Kalkstein and Davis 1989).

The results of the model indicate no clear association between extreme cold and mortality rates after controlling for season. Therefore, we elect to use 28°F as the cold threshold level for the CLIMB region, which is the coinciding maximum temperature threshold below which temperatures occur at the same frequency as temperatures 90°F or above. Our underlying assumption is that the population adapts to a particular temperature probability distribution and is susceptible to temperatures occurring at the tails of the distribution.

Table 15.2   Regression results of mortality rates in the CLIMB study region

	Mortality per day per million people		Mortality per day per million people
Constant (January)	27.24***	High Temp. = 34°F (t-3)	0.79**
February	-0.47**	High Temp. = 33°F (t-2)	-0.01
March	-1.37***	High Temp. = 33°F (t-3)	0.08
April	-2.33***	High Temp. = 32°F (t-2)	0.40
May	-3.17***	High Temp. = 32°F (t-3)	0.29
June	-3.81***	High Temp. = 31°F (t-2)	0.99***
July	-3.86***	High Temp. = 31°F (t-3)	0.74
August	-4.40***	High Temp. = 30°F (t-2)	-0.12
September	-4.08***	High Temp. = 30°F (t-3)	0.68
October	-2.73***	High Temp. = 29°F (t-2)	0.59
November	-2.23***	High Temp. = 29°F (t-3)	0.68
December	-1.44***	High Temp. = 28°F (t-2)	0.51
Annual Trend	-0.10***	High Temp. = 28°F (t-3)	0.29
High Temp. = 80°F (t)	-0.07	High Temp. = 27°F (t-2)	0.02
High Temp. = 81°F (t)	-0.30	High Temp. = 27°F (t-3)	0.54
High Temp. = 82°F (t)	0.00	High Temp. = 26°F (t-2)	0.73
High Temp. = 83°F (t)	0.44	High Temp. = 26°F (t-3)	1.07**
High Temp. = 84°F (t)	-0.13	High Temp. = 25°F (t-2)	1.21**
High Temp. = 85°F (t)	0.47*	High Temp. = 25°F (t-3)	0.98*
High Temp. = 86°F (t)	0.13	High Temp. = 24°F (t-2)	1.05*
High Temp. = 87°F (t)	-0.08	High Temp. = 24°F (t-3)	0.96
High Temp. = 88°F (t)	0.35	High Temp. = 23°F (t-2)	1.08
High Temp. = 89°F (t)	0.51*	High Temp. = 23°F (t-3)	0.21
High Temp. = 90°F (t)	0.93***	High Temp. = 22°F (t-2)	0.27
High Temp. = 91°F (t)	1.93***	High Temp. = 22°F (t-3)	-0.9
High Temp. = 92°F (t)	1.26***	High Temp. = 21°F (t-2)	1.23*
High Temp. = 93°F (t)	1.59***	High Temp. = 21°F (t-3)	-0.29
High Temp. = 94°F (t)	1.79***	High Temp. ≤ 0°F (t-2)	0.95**
High Temp. ≥ 95°F (t)	3.48***	High Temp. ≤ 20°F (t-3)	0.37
High Temp. = 35°F (t-2)	0.05	Snow (t)	0.74***

(continued on next page)

Table 15.2   Regression results of mortality rates in the CLIMB study region (continued)

	Mortality per day per million people		Mortality per day per million people
High Temp. = 35°F (t-3)	-0.33	Snow (t-1)	0.56***
High Temp. = 34°F (t-2)	0.65*	Snow (t-2)	-0.05
High Temp. = 34°F (t-2)	0.65*	R^2	0.1872
Durbin-Watson (DW) Statistic	2.04		

*Significant at the 10% level   **Significant at the 5% level   ***Significant at the 1% level

Temperature-Mortality Relationships

On the basis of the analysis presented above, we designate 90°F as the heat threshold and 28°F as the cold threshold temperatures. We include in the model a trend variable of the heat-related mortality to capture changes in the sensitivity of mortality to extreme heat over the period of analysis because some recent research suggests a de-sensitizing of populations to extreme heat events (Davis, et al. 2002). Additionally, we extend the lag lengths on the cold threshold to five days in light of the prolonged effect on mortality rates. The results of the statistical model are presented in Table 15.3.

The coefficients on the February-December dummy variables show the differences between expected daily mortality rates in each month relative to the expected daily mortality rate for January of that year. Daily mortality rates in February to December are lower than in January, with the largest difference appearing in August. The annual trend variable indicates that over the 1970 to 1998 period the daily mortality rate had an annual decrease of 0.10 deaths per day per million people.

Extreme heat has an immediate and prolonged effect on mortality rates. For example, our results suggest that on an August day in 1970 with a temperature of at least 90°F the mortality rate increases by 2.21 deaths per day per million people, or by 9.8 per cent, compared to a day with temperature in the reference range. The sensitivity of mortality rates to extreme heat events has, however, decreased over the period of analysis by, on average, 0.05 per year. Consequently, the results suggest that heat-related mortality decreased by roughly 50 per cent over the 1970 to 1992 period. The results also indicate that the effect of extreme heat on mortality is prolonged as the day after an extreme heat event has a mortality rate 2.37 higher and the following day 0.76 higher relative to a non-extreme temperature day. Similar to the immediate effects of extreme heat on mortality the delayed effects have also been decreasing by roughly the same amount over the period of analysis.

The effect of extreme cold on mortality is inconclusive. For example, mortality rates are 0.62 lower on the current day if the maximum temperature is below 28°F and then, three and four days later, increase by 0.59 and 0.42, respectively. The delayed effect of extreme cold on mortality has also been found in other studies (Donaldson and Keatinge 2002). Snow on the current and previous day is positively and significantly associated with mortality rates. The incidence of snowfall is associated with increases of 0.69 on the current day and 0.63 the succeeding day. The results suggest that mortality rates are more sensitive to snowfall than to days with maximum temperatures 28°F or below. Such findings may, in part, explain the 22 per cent increase in deaths from ischemic heart disease in Boston in the week following a blizzard (Glass and Zack 1979). Similar high mortality sensitivity to snow has been observed in Minneapolis-St Paul, Minnesota (Baker-Blocker 1982).

Since our choice of a 28°F cold threshold was not strongly supported by statistical criteria and the temperature-mortality relationship was similarly ambiguous for the effects of temperature on cold-related mortality, we choose not to investigate further in our scenario analysis potential impacts of future climates on cold-related mortality. The inconclusive results of the historical analysis, though, are by themselves noteworthy and correspond to similar findings in the literature (Kalkstein and Greene 1997).

Table 15.3   Regression results of mortality rates in the CLIMB region given extreme temperatures

	Mortality per million people per day	% Change in Mortality with Extreme Heat (1970)	% Change in Mortality with Extreme Heat (1990)
Constant (January)	27.33***		
February	-0.46**		
March	-1.48***		
April	-2.50***		
May	-3.36***		
June	-4.14***		
July	-4.41***		
August	-4.75***		
September	-4.31***		
October	-2.90***		
November	-2.38***		
December	-1.51***		
Annual Trend	-0.10***		

(continued on next page)

Table 15.3   Regression results of mortality rates in the CLIMB region given extreme temperatures (continued)

	Mortality per million people per day	% Change in Mortality with Extreme Heat (1970)	% Change in Mortality with Extreme Heat (1990)
High Temp. >= 90°F (t)	2.21***	+9.8% †	+5.9% †
Trend High Temp. >= 90°F (t)	-0.05**		
High Temp. >= 90°F (t-1)	2.37***	+10.5% †	+5.7% †
Trend High Temp. >= 90°F (t-1)	-0.06**		
High Temp. >= 90°F (t-2)	0.76***	+3.4% †	+2.7% †
Trend High Temp. >= 90°F (t-2)	-0.01		
High Temp. >= 90°F (t-3)	0.42		
Trend High Temp. >= 90°F (t-3)	-0.03		
High Temp. <= 28°F (t)	-0.62***		
High Temp. <= 28°F (t-1)	0.26		
High Temp. <= 28°F (t-2)	0.38*		
High Temp. <= 28°F (t-3)	0.59***		
High Temp. <= 28°F (t-4)	0.42**		
High Temp. <= 28°F (t-5)	0.11		
Snow (t)	0.69***		
Snow (t-1)	0.63***		
Snow (t-2)	0.05		
R^2	0.20		
Durbin-Watson (DW) Statistic	2.04		

*Significant at the 10% level   **Significant at the 5% level   ***Significant at the 1% level
† Relative to August's mortality rate

CLIMATE CHANGE SCENARIOS

In this section we examine, based on the findings presented above, the effects of climate change on heat-related mortality in the CLIMB region. We use scenarios of future weather specifically developed for the region to assess changes in annual heat-related mortality, which is the annual sum of the daily mortality predicted by the statistical model.

Simulation results indicate for the base case, Hadley Centre and Canadian Climate Centre scenarios a decline in regional mortality. That decline is more pronounced under the two climate model scenarios in which the frequency of extreme heat events increases. These findings are predominantly caused by the assumed continuation of past trends in mortality declines and are discussed in more detail in the following section. The simulation results further show on average slightly higher mortality until about 2010 under climate change, compared to the base case. From 2010 onward mortality declines more rapidly under climate change than without it, and from approximately 2012 onward the number of deaths actually declines as the number of heat events increases. One explanation behind this observed reversal lies in the effects that repeated events may have on a population's adaptive behavior–the more frequent the number of events, the more may the population be prepared to deal with them.

CONCLUSIONS

There is overwhelming empirical evidence that ambient temperatures (low and high) still to this day influence mortality rates in urban areas and that the extent to which those influences manifest themselves varies with, among other things, geographic location. Our analysis for metropolitan Boston indicates that there is no clear, discernible cold threshold for the population in the region, nor is there a strong statistical association between historically observed low temperatures and cold-related mortality. In contrast, we do find a heat threshold of 90°F and a strong influence on heat-related mortality by the number of days above that threshold. Using the derived statistical relationship between mortality rates and the number of days above 90°F in conjunction with simulations of alternative future climate, we find that more frequent occurrence of heat episodes will not result in higher mortality in metropolitan Boston, presumably because of more aggressive adaptation to those events.

These findings are subject to several interrelated assumptions about socioeconomic characteristics in the region, several of which have clear relationships to existing infrastructures and regional development. First, many key characteristics of the regional population have not been explicitly considered here, such as its age distribution, ethnic mix or economic prosperity, many of which may influence the population's susceptibility to weather and climate, and many of which are likely to change over the simulated one hundred years. Clinical studies and regional statistical analyses suggest, for example, that heat-related mortality varies with age and other demographic characteristics (Henschel, et al. 1969; Applegate, et al. 1981; Jones, et al. 1982; Greenberg, et al. 1983; Kunst, et al. 1993; Kilbourne 1997).

Second, a variety of behavioral and technological changes may likely occur as the region's climate changes. For example, an increase in the use of air conditioning will likely reduce susceptibility to heat waves for those individuals who have access to air conditioned space. One case-control study suggests that access to air conditioning may reduce rates of heat stroke by 400 per cent (Kilbourne, et al. 1982) while a large, household cohort study suggests that households with air conditioning may have a 42 per cent lower death rate than those without air conditioning (Rogot, et al. 1992) and a regional statistical analysis indicates that mortality rates in New York City declined 21 per cent due to air conditioning usage (Kalkstein 1993).

Similarly, improvements in health care, use of early warning systems for individuals most prone to changes in temperature and the often associated low outdoor air quality will likely reduce respiratory and cardiovascular stress, and thus also likely reduce heat-related morbidity and mortality (Goldman and Cook 1984; Seretakis, et al. 1997). Other adaptations to extreme temperatures include changing the extent to which individuals remain outdoors. Already, people in climates with extreme heat or cold periods have found ways to reduce exposure by moving from one cooled or heated space to another (for example, from the home to the car to the store and back) with little time spent outside.

Increases in access to air conditioned space, many improvements in health care and a multitude of behavioral changes have been observed in the past two decades on which the statistical analysis of this paper is based. These improvements largely determine the sign and magnitude of the trend variable discussed above. For that variable to continue its relevance over the simulated future 100 years requires that the factors contributing to it remain, in aggregate, comparable to the past. However, rates of expansion of air conditioning, for example, may likely be lower in the future than they have been in the past because continued proliferation tends to be more difficult as near 100 per cent saturation is reached. Also, expansion of air conditioning itself is not without problems as it increases regional energy consumption, contributes to urban heat island effects and potentially exacerbates health risks associated with low outdoor air quality.

Improvements in health care have likewise been quite significant over the last two decades. Not only are there now regular weather and health warning systems in place–from forecasts in daily news media of heat indices and chill factors to pollen counts and ground level ozone concentrations–but also the population and its health care system have found numerous ways to deal with cold spells or heat waves. Whether a continued high rate of improvements in warning and health care systems can possibly be maintained over the next 100 years is open to debate.

As any one of the factors that influence the trend variable reduces its impact on lowering cold- or heat-related mortality rates, the other factors need to make up for it, so that the results continue to hold. Alternatively, additional adaptations to climate change may be needed. For example, the region has seen only a few efforts to increase the use of shade trees to decrease albedo, increase moisture retention and thus contribute to local cooling. Similarly, little new construction uses materials or designs that reduce a building's albedo, its heating and cooling needs, and thus energy consumption and impacts on local air quality. Such engineering approaches to prepare the local building stock to a changing climate, together with appropriate zoning and transportation planning, could go a long way in reducing, for example, urban heat island effects, which may be exacerbated by climate change. The roles of urban planners and architects in providing summer relief from heat stress– through creative building designs and adjustments of the urban morphology– will become pivotal in reducing the potential impacts of climate change on temperature-related mortalities in urban areas.

The results presented above suggest that future reductions in heat-related mortality are likely under a wide range of climate scenarios. For these results to be achievable requires aggressive investments in all areas ranging from health care to space cooling to smart land use, as well as potentially drastic behavioral adjustments of the local population. On the one hand, such adjustments will need to be large, yet given past experience seem doable. On the other hand, they will quite likely entail major changes in lifestyles and infrastructure in the region. The analysis presented above calls for public debate on these tradeoffs and necessary investments in climate change mitigation and adaptation strategies. Since building stock and urban structure change only slowly, a window of opportunity exists to start this debate now and come to resolutions that can be implemented before the rates of decline in temperature-related mortality–caused by the fact that improvements in health care, warning systems and air conditioning are still possible–peter out.

NOTE

1.   Charlene Zion, Massachusetts Department of Public Health, 150 Mount Vernon St, Dorchester, MA 02125

REFERENCES

Applegate, W.B., J.W. Runyan, Jr., L. Brasfield, M.L.M.Williams, C. Konigsberg and C. Fouche (1981), 'Analysis of the 1980 heat wave in Memphis', *Journal of American Geriatric Society*, **29**: 337–342.

Baker-Blocker, A. (1982), 'Winter weather and cardiovascular mortality in Minneapolis-St Paul', *American Journal of Public Health*, **72**(3): 261–265.

Blum, L.N., L.B. Bresolin, et al. (1998), 'Heat-related illness during extreme emergencies', *Journal of the American Medical Association*, **279**(19): 1514.

Bridger, C.A., F.P. Ellis and H.L. Taylor (1976), 'Mortality in St Louis, Missouri, during heat waves in 1936, 1953, 1954, 1955 and 1966', *Environmental Research*, **12**: 38–48.

Bull, G.M. (1973), 'Meteorological correlates with myocardial and cerebral infarction and respiratory disease', *British Journal of Preventative and Social Medicine*, **27**: 108–113.

Bull, G.M. and J. Morton (1978), 'Environment, temperature and death rates', *Age and Ageing*, **7**: 210–224.

CDC (1995), 'Heat-Related Mortality–Chicago, July 1995', *Morbidity and Mortality Weekly Report*, **44**(31): 577–579.

CDC (2002), *Extreme Heat*, Atlanta, GA: Centers for Disease Control and Prevention.

Changnon, S.A. (2000), 'Human factors explain the increased losses from weather and climate extremes', *Bulletin of the American Meteorological Society* **81**(3): 437–442.

Changnon, S.A., K.E. Kunkel and B.C. Reinke (1996), 'Impacts and responses to the 1995 heat wave: a call to action', *Bulletin of the American Meteorological Society*, **77**: 1497–1506.

Chestnut, L.G., W.S. Breffle, J.B. Smith and L.S. Kalkstein (1998), 'Analysis of differences in hot weather-related mortality across 44 US metropolitan areas', *Environmental Science Policy*, **1**: 59–70.

Climate Change Impacts Review Group (1991), *The Potential Effects of Climate Change in the United Kingdom*, London, UK: HMSO, p. 124.

Colombo, A.F., D. Etkin, et al. (1999), 'Climate variability and the frequency of extreme temperature events for nine sites across Canada: Implications for power usage', *Journal of Climate*, **12**(8): 2490–2502.

Curriero, F.C., K.S. Heiner, et al. (2002), 'Temperature and mortality in 11 cities of the eastern United States', *American Journal of Epidemiology*, **155**(1): 80–87.

Curwen, M. (1991), 'Excess winter mortality: A British phenomenon?', *Health Trends, 1990*, **22**: 169–175.

Davis, R.E., P.C. Knappenberger, W.M. Novicoff and P.J. Michaels (2002), 'Decadal changes in heat-related human mortality in the eastern United States', *Climate Research*, **22**(2): 175–184.

Davis, R.E., P.C. Knappenberger, W.M. Novicoff and P.J. Michaels (2003), 'Decadal changes in heat-related human mortality in the eastern United States', *International Journal of Biometeorology*, **47**: 166–175.

Davis, R.E., P.C. Knappenberger and P.J. Michaels (2004), 'Seasonality of climate-human mortality relationships in US cities and impacts of climate change', *Climate Research*, **26**(1): 61–76.

Donaldson, G.C., S.P. Ermakov, et al. (1998), 'Cold related mortalities and protection against cold in Yakutsk, eastern Siberia: Observation and interview study', *British Medical Journal*, **317**: 978–982.

Donaldson, G.C. and W.R. Keatinge (1997), 'Early increases in ischaemic heart disease mortality dissociated from, and later changes associated with, respiratory mortality, after cold weather in Southeast England', *Journal of Epidemiology and Community Health*, **51**(6).

Donaldson, G.C. and W.R. Keatinge (2002), 'Excess winter mortality: influenza or cold stress? Observational study', *British Medical Journal*, **324**: 89–90.

Donaldson, G.C., V.E. Tchernjavskii, et al. (1998), 'Winter mortality and cold stress in Yekaterinburg, Russia: Interview study', *British Medical Journal*, **316**: 514–518.

Donaldson, G.C., W.R. Keatinge and S. Näyhä (2003), 'Changes in summer temperature and heat-related mortality since 1971 in North Carolina, South Finland, and Southeast England', *Environmenat Research*, **91**: 1–7.

Eurowinter Group (1997), 'Cold exposure and winter mortality from ischaemic heart disease, cerebrovascular disease, respiratory disease, and all causes, in warm and cold regions of Europe', *Lancet*, **349**: 1341–1346.

Gaffen, D.J. and R.J. Ross (1998), 'Increased summertime heat stress in the US', *Nature*, **396**(6711): 529–530.

Glass, R.I. and M. Zack (1979), 'Increase in deaths from ischemic heart-disease after blizzards', *Lancet*, **1**: 485–487.

Goldman, L. and E.F. Cook (1984), 'The decline in ischaemic heart disease mortality rates: An analysis of the comparative effects of medical interventions and changes in lifestyle', *Annals of International Medicine*, **101**: 825–836.

Gorjanc, M.L., W.D. Flanders, J. VanDerslice, J. Hersh and J. Malilay (1999), 'Effects of temperature and snowfall on mortality in Pennsylvania', *American Journal of Epidemiology*, **149**(12): 1152–1160.

Greenberg, J.H., J. Bromberg, C.M. Reed, T.L. Gustafson and R.A. Beauchamp (1983), 'The epidemiology of heat-related deaths Texas–1950, 1970–79 and 1980', *American Journal of Public Health*, **30**: 130–136.

Harmel, R.D., C.W. Richardson, et al. (2002), 'Evaluating the adequacy of simulating maximum and minimum daily air temperature with the normal distribution', *Journal of Applied Meteorology*, **41**(7): 744–753.

Henschel, A., L.L. Burton, L. Margolies and J.E. Smith (1969), 'An analysis of the heat deaths in St Louis during July 1966', *American Journal of Public Health*, **59**: 2232–2242.

Huynen, M., P. Martens, et al. (2001), 'The impacts of heat waves and cold spells on mortality in the Dutch Population', *Environmental Health Perspectives*, **109**: 463–470.

IPCC (2001a), *Climate Change 2001: The Scientific Basis*, Geneva, Switzerland: Intergovernmental Panel on Climate Change.

Jones, T.S., A.P. Liang, E.M. Kilbourne, M.R. Griffin, P.A. Patriarca, S.G. Wassilak, et al. (1982), 'Morbidity and mortality associated with the July 1980 heat wave in St Louis and Kansas City, Missouri', *Journal of the American Medical Association*, **247**: 3327–3331.

Kalkstein, L.S. and R.E. Davis (1989), 'Weather and human mortality: An evaluation of demographic and interregional responses in the United States', *Annals of the Association of American Geographers*, **79**(1): 44–64.

Kalkstein, L.S. (1993), 'Health and climate change–direct impacts in cities', *Lancet*, **342**: 1397–1399.

Kalkstein, L.S. and J.S. Greene (1997), 'An evaluation of climate/mortality relationships in large U.S. Cities and the possible impacts of a climate change', *Environmental Health Perspectives*, **105**: 84–93.

Katz, R.W. and B.G. Brown (1992), 'Extreme events in a changing climate: Variability is more important than averages', *Climatic Change*, **21**: 289–302.

Keatinge,W.R., S.R.K. Coleshaw and J.C. Easton (1986), 'Increased platelet and red cell counts, blood viscosity and plasma cholesterol levels during heat stress, and mortality from coronary and cerebral thrombosis', *American Journal of Medicine*, **81**: 795–800.

Keatinge, W.R. (1997), 'Cold exposure and winter mortality from ischaemic heart disease, cerebrovascular disease, respiratory disease, and all causes in warm and cold regions of Europe', *Lancet*, **349**(9062): 1341–1346.

Keatinge,W.R., C.G. Donaldson, E. Cordioli, M. Martinelli, A.E. Kunst and J.P. Mackenbach (2000), 'Heat related mortality in warm and cold regions of Europe: Observational study', *British Medical Journal*, **321**(7262): 670.

Kilbourne, E.M. (1997), 'Heat waves and hot environments', in *The Public Health Consequences of Disasters*, E.K. Noji (ed.), Oxford, UK: Oxford University Press.

Kilbourne, E.M., K. Choi, T.S. Jones, S.B. Thacker and Field Investigation
    Team (1982), 'Risk factors for heatstroke: A case-control study', *Journal
    of the American Medical Association*, **247**: 3332–3336.
Kirshen, P.H., M. Ruth, W. Anderson, T.R. Lakshmana, S. Chapra, C. Wayne,
    E. Edgers, D. Gute, S. Masoud and R. Vogel (2004), *'Infrastructure
    Systems, Services and Climate Change: Integrated Impacts and Response
    Strategies for the Boston Metropolitan Area'*, Report to the US
    Environmental Protection Agency, Office of Research and Development,
    Grant Number: R.827450-01, Washington, DC.
Kovats, R.S., A. Haines, et al. (1999), 'Climate change and human health in
    Europe', *British Medical Journal*, **318**: 1682–1685.
Kunst, A.E., C.W. Looman, et al. (1993), 'Outdoor air temperature and
    mortality in The Netherlands: A time-series analysis', *American Journal
    of Epidemiology*, **137**(3): 331–341.
Landsberg, H.E. (1981), *The Urban Climate*, New York: Academic Press.
Langford, I. H. and G. Bentham (1995), 'The potential effects of climate
    change on winter mortality in England and Wales', *International Journal
    of Biometeorology*, **38**(3): 141–147.
Laschewski, G. and G. Jendritzky (2002), 'Effects of the thermal environment
    on human health: an investigation of 30 years of daily mortality data from
    SW Germany', *Climate Research*, **21**: 91–103.
Lanska, D.J. and R.G. Hoffmann (1999), 'Seasonal variation in stroke
    mortality rates', *Neurology*, **52**: 984.
Larsen, U. (1990), 'The effects of monthly temperature fluctuations on
    mortality in the United States from 1921 to 1985', *International Journal
    of Biometeorology*, **34**: 136–145.
Lerchl, A. (1998), 'Changes in the seasonality of mortality in Germany from
    1946 to 1995: The role of temperature', *International Journal of
    Biometeorology*, **42**: 84–88.
Longstreth, J. (1991), 'Anticipated public health consequences of global
    climate change', *Environmental Health Perspectives*, **96**: 139–144.
Martens, W.J.M. (1998), 'Climate change, thermal stress and mortality
    changes', *Social Science and Medicine*, **46**(3): 331–344.
McGeehin, M.A. and M. Mirabelli (2001), 'The potential impacts of climate
    variability and change on temperature-related morbidity and mortality in
    the United States', *Environmental Health Perspectives*, **109**: 185–198.
National Weather Service (2002), *Heat Wave*, 2002.
NOAA (2002), *Daily Temperature in Boston*, National Oceanic and
    Atmospheric Administration, http://www.nws.noaa.gov.
Oberg, A.L., J.A. Ferguson, et al. (2000), 'Incidence of stroke and season of
    the year: Evidence of an association', *American Journal of Epidemiology*,
    152(6): 558–564.

Patz, J.A., D. Engelberg, et al. (2000), 'The effects of changing weather on public health', *Annual Review of Public Health*, **21**: 271–307.

Patz, J.A., M. McGeehin, et al. (2000), 'The potential health impacts of climate variability and change for the United States: Executive summary of the report of the health sector of the U.S. National Assessment', *Environmental Health Perspectives*, **108**: 367–376.

Pell, J.P. and S.M. Cobbe (1999), 'Seasonal variations in coronary heart disease', *Quarterly Journal of Medicine*, **92**: 689–696.

Rock, B. and B. Moore (2001), *The New England Regional Assessment of the Potential Consequences of Climate Variability and Change*, prepared for the US National Assessment.

Rogot, E., P.D. Sorlie and E. Backlund (1992), 'Air-conditioning and mortality in hot weather', *American Journal of Public Health*, **136**(1): 106–116.

Rogot, E. and S.J. Padgett (1976), 'Associations of coronary and stroke mortality in with temperature and snowfall in selected areas of the United States, 1962–1966', *American Journal of Epidemiology*, **103**(6): 565–575.

Ruth, M. and P. Kirshen (2001), 'Integrated impacts of climate change upon infrastructure systems and services in the Boston metropolitan area', *World Resources Review*, **13**(1): 106–122.

Semenza, J.C., C.H. Rubin, et al. (1996), 'Heat-related deaths during the July 1995 heat wave in Chicago', *The New England Journal of Medicine*, **335**(2): 84–90.

Seretakis, D., P. Lagiou, L. Lipworth, L.B. Signorello, K.J. Rothman, and D. Trichopoulos (1997), 'Changing seasonality of mortality from coronary heart disease', *Journal of the American Medical Association*, **278**(12): 1012–1014.

Smoyer, K.E. (1998), 'Putting risk in its place: Methodological considerations for investigating extreme event health risks', *Social Science and Medicine*, **47**(11): 1809–1924.

Smoyer, K.E., D.G.C. Rainham, et al. (2000), 'Heat-stress-related mortality in five cities in Southern Ontario: 1980–1996', *International Journal of Biometeorology*, **44**: 190–197.

Steadman, R.G. (1979), 'The assessment of sultriness. Part I: a temperature-humidity index based on human physiology and clothing science', *Journal of Applied Meteorology*, **18**: 861–873.

Steadman, R.G. (1984), 'A universal scale of apparent temperature', *Journal of Climate and Applied Meteorology*, **23**: 1674–1687.

Steward, S., M.B. McIntyre, et al. (2002), 'Heart failure in a cold climate: Seasonal variation in heart failure-related morbidity and mortality', *Journal of the American College of Cardiology*, **39**(5): 760–766.

Stone, R. (1995), 'If the mercury soars, so may health hazards', *Science*, **267**(5200): 957–958.

Tromp, S.W. (1980), *Biometeorology: The Impact of the Weather and Climate on Humans and Their Environment (Animals and Plants)*, Philadelphia, PA: Heyden and Sons Ltd.

van Rossum, C.T.M., M.J. Shipley, et al. (2001), 'Seasonal variation in cause-specific mortality: Are there high-risk groups? 25-year follow-up of civil servants from the first Whitehall study', *International Journal of Epidemiology*, **30**: 1109–1116.

Vogel, R.M. and A.L. Shallcross (1996), 'The moving blocks bootstrap versus parametric time series models', *Water Resources Research*, **32**(6): 1875–1882.

Watson, R.T. and A.J. McMicheal (2001), 'Global Climate Change–the latest assessment: Does global warming warrent a health warning?', *Global Change and Human Health*, **2**(1): 64–75.

Whetton, P.H., R. Siuppiah, et al. (2002), *Climate Change in Victoria: High Resolution Regional Assessment of Climate Change Impacts*, CSIRO and Department of Natural Resources and Environment.

WHO (2000), *Climate Change and Human Health: Impact and Adaptation*, Geneva, Switzerland: World Health Organization.

Yan, Y.Y. (2000), 'The influence of weather on human mortality in Hong Kong', *Social Science and Medicine*, **50**: 419–427.

16   A Summary of Lessons and Options

Matthias Ruth

LAND USE, REGIONAL DEVELOPMENT AND ENVIRONMENTAL QUALITY

Land use decisions, regional development and environmental quality are tightly interrelated. The chapters of this book clearly show the multi-dimensionality of those interrelationships. For example, water institutions shape water rights and allocation, which must collectively evolve to effectively address changes in socioeconomic, technological and environmental opportunities and constraints, and which drive land use and development (see, for example Chapter 10). Changes in urban form and the level of urban economic activity influence regional rainfall patterns, demand for energy and the infrastructure to generate and deliver it, as well as urban heat islands. Exacerbated by changes in atmospheric temperatures and precipitation patterns, any and all of those interrelationships are altered as humans impact the global climate (see, for example Chapter 13).

While the interrelationships among land use decisions, regional development and environmental quality have long been recognized, traditionally, investment and policy making have concentrated on individual systems–water, energy, transport, health and so on–in efforts to improve the economic base and quality of life in cities and surrounding areas. The multi-dimensionality of the interrelationships that influence the performance of regional economies and the infrastructures needed for their functioning poses formidable challenges for research and decision making. Finding appropriate investment and policy strategies requires an ability to answer at least the following key questions:

1. How do complexities of the interactions among land use, regional development and environmental quality manifest themselves through time and across space–from the short to the long run, and from local to regional and global scales?

2. What are the ripple effects by which changes in one system component and at one level of system hierarchy influence the behavior of other system components in space and time?
3. What roles can mitigation of root causes of undesirable system change, and adaptation to ongoing and anticipated change, play in reducing vulnerabilities?
4. What roles can science and society play in guiding investment and policy making?
5. How can the patterns and trends that describe change of individual system components be summarized to adequately portray their interdependencies?

To various extents, these questions have guided the research presented in this book. In this closing chapter, I will return to them and draw on the answers suggested by the various contributors to this volume.

The first two questions above point to the insights that can be gained from choosing a systems perspective rather than analyses that focus on individual aspects of the issues. The third question addresses challenges surrounding optimal response strategies in the short, medium and long run, again taking a systems perspective. The role of stakeholder guided science and stakeholder-based decision making lie at the heart of the fourth question, while question five addresses in more detail the requirements for effective treatment and communication of complexities and risks in the context of investment and policy making. All five questions are thus as interrelated as the land use, regional development and environmental quality issues to which they pertain.

UNDERSTANDING AND MANAGING THE REACH AND COMPLEXITY OF INVESTMENT AND POLICY DECISIONS

Regional economic activity and quality of life depend on a myriad of factors that can be influenced within a region, but many of which are imposed by the larger context within which regions operate (see, for example Chapter 2). Analysts and decision makers are often overwhelmed when trying to choose among alternative investment and policy options to accommodate, let alone actively shape, the trends that affect a region.

In efforts to address and deal with anticipated regional socioeconomic and environmental change, decision makers frequently ask: Should new areas be opened up and zoned for suburban or urban development? How should the region's transportation, water and energy needs be met? What design criteria and standards are needed to ensure adequate and safe provision of infrastructure-related services for the local population, as well as healthy local environments? Such high-level questions are quickly followed by more detailed ones relating to location, finance and management of activities.

Finding politically acceptable answers to these questions is no small feat. Even seemingly minor issues can have wide-ranging financial, social and environmental ramifications. Not knowing what those ramifications may be or when and where to expect them, analysts and decision makers are frequently tempted–in efforts to keep issues tractable–to narrow their scope rather than opening themselves up to the possibilities that actions will have unforeseen, often undesirable, side-effects that themselves require actions later on.

Urban and regional planning and development are replete with examples of 'solutions' to problems that in themselves grow into ever larger problems– such as expansions of roads to accommodate growing traffic volumes, thus stimulating development that requires further expansion of roads, or increased proliferation of air conditioning that increases energy consumption and emissions and thus contributes to heat island effects that in turn are addressed with the expansion of air conditioning (see the discussions in Chapters 12 and 13).

Conceptually, we may separate planning and development challenges by their reach and complexity (Figure 16.1). Reach refers to the number of people affected and/or the time frame over which effects are felt. Complexity refers to the number of system components, interactions, non-linearities and time lags involved. The larger the reach and complexity, the greater the uncertainties and risks associated with individual actions. For example, development of a local site for residential dwellings is technically, legally and economically fairly straightforward and will directly impact the local environment and the inhabitants in that area. In contrast, development of alternative transportation or energy systems is technically challenging, can raise fundamentally new legal issues, and can affect the local, regional and global environment in unforeseen (and unforeseeable) ways. Obviously, the boundaries between the categories are frequently fluid, but generally, the shorter the reach and complexity the more appropriate it is to leave decisions in the hands of local authorities and stakeholders. Conversely, the larger the reach and complexity, the more important a systems view will be for finding solutions and the larger the scientific expertise and pool of stakeholders needs to be from which to draw expertise when trying to identify those solutions.

Historically, smart growth initiatives have addressed issues of relatively short reach and low complexity. Many of them have been faulted for their lack of attention to larger societal, technological or environmental trends that significantly influenced their success. In contrast, the global climate change debate has focused on issues of long reach and high complexity, often neglecting unique and relevant local conditions that may foster or impede a solution. Complicated international negotiations and institutional mechanisms have been put in place to find and implement acceptable climate change policies and promote investments that help reduce greenhouse gas emissions.

		Complexity	
		Low	High

Reach	Short	Examples:
		Development of
		  vacant lots
		Expansion of
		  combined sewer
		  overflows
			Examples:
			Restoration of local
			  wetland
			Reclamation and
			  development of
			  local landfill

	Long	Examples:
		Expansion of
		  local
		  transportation
		  network, water
		  supply
			Examples:
			Development of
			  alternative
			  transportation and
			  energy supply
			  infrastructure

Figure 16.1   Reach and complexity in environmental investment and policy making

As land use, regional development and global environmental quality are increasingly seen to be related, the role of stakeholders in finding solutions needs to be expanded, the diversity of institutions involved in investment and policy making needs to be enlarged, and impacts of decisions for the performance on one part of the system need to be traced–and anticipated–for other parts of the larger system (see the discussion in Chapter 3). For example, development of an alternative energy infrastructure needs to be assessed with respect to its impact on water demand and public health as well as local and global environmental quality, not just with respect to its ability to meet demand for energy-related services. Changes in urban morphology, including urban use of green spaces and water ways, will need to be assessed not only with respect to aesthetics or ease of movement of people and goods, but also with regard to the microclimates those changes create, which in turn will affect local air quality, habitat for native and exotic species, and thus public health (see, for example Chapter 14).

LOCAL MANAGEMENT AND PLANNING FOR LOCAL AND GLOBAL GOALS

The interrelationships among land use, development and environmental change are highly complex. These complexities can result in surprising system behaviors where previously unnoticed thresholds may irreversibly be surpassed. Slowly changing the radiative profile of urban areas may impact the frequency and severity of regional precipitation events. Gradually increasing the amount of impervious surfaces in urban areas may suddenly result in flash floods that overwhelm local flood control and sewer systems. In combination, both changes may impact downstream ecosystems in unprecedented ways, irreversibly altering their structure and function. Similarly, the climate system itself may rapidly and fundamentally change, as critical concentrations of greenhouse gases are reached and atmospheric and oceanic processes are disrupted (see, for example Chapter 2). Reversing those changes and the impacts they have may be impossible, or at a minimum require significant resources and lead times, and the interventions that are chosen may themselves have adverse social, economic, environmental and public health impacts.

Being able to develop scenarios of possible future land use, development and environmental quality under a wide range of socioeconomic, technological and environmental scenarios becomes critical in finding sustainable investment and policy choices. For example, modeling landscape dynamics in close collaboration with planners and other stakeholders can provide a basis to explore the ramifications of a wide range of alternative actions and assumptions about the future. Inputs from stakeholders may be used to shape model assumptions and model design, while outputs from stakeholder deliberations and stakeholder-guided modeling may be fed back to promote individual and institutional learning about complex systems and to help identify robust strategies, such as policy and investment decisions that yield desirable outcomes for a range of possible scenarios.

Advances in modeling and decision support, such as those laid out in Chapter 8, can play a central role in the identification of robust strategies. However, they are usually only one of several mechanisms that guide local management and planning. They can be repositories of data and information, tools to explore potential futures and focal points for the generation of consensus. But making and implementing decisions will require flexible institutional arrangements and information sharing, effective communication across the hierarchies within institutions as well as among institutions and between institutions and the broader public. The society that can make changes in its institutions and built infrastructures most easily is likely also the one able to successfully adapt to climate change, mitigate its causes and implement truly 'smart' growth policies.

To be able to address new and emerging challenges requires institutions to have in place incentive mechanisms to reward actions that create benefits outside their purview. For example, energy systems managers may opt to promote increased use of renewable energy sources even if renewable energy seems more costly when viewed from a narrow, energy supply perspective. From a broader perspective, they may help improve regional air quality and public health, and reduce demand for cooling water and thus improve local water quality and environmental health. Those benefits may well surpass the extra short-term cost associated with expansion of renewable energy sources. Yet, if insufficient incentives are provided to energy systems managers to recognize and act with regard to the larger system performance, those benefits may never be realized, and decisions may be made that perpetuate seemingly economic cost efficient solutions at the expense of more sustainable practices. Similar arguments can be made for the management of any of the infrastructures in a region.

Striking the right balance between stakeholder-involved science and stakeholder-informed science, without compromising the science itself, or using science to support agendas of select stakeholder groups, will be key to the success of smart growth and climate change adaptation and mitigation strategies. Much is known in the physical, engineering and social sciences, in business management and planning on which stakeholder-informed science can, and must, build. Consensus is slowly emerging that taking actions sooner rather than later will help avoid lock-in of inefficient technologies, infrastructures and practices, that adaptation to climate change is necessary to avoid major socioeconomic vulnerabilities, and that–if done right–adaptation strategies can play a vital role in the transition to a low-greenhouse gas emission society. Yet, many of the details need to be worked out in specific regional, social, economic, legal and environmental contexts. Drawing on a single metric–such as cost efficiency–will clearly be insufficient when trying to devise land use plans, manage regional development and improve environmental quality.

Adaptation strategies may be chosen to ward off or to prepare for climate change as it occurs. Mitigation strategies may be chosen to address the root causes of anthropogenic greenhouse gas emissions. Some adaptation strategies may be found to oppose smart growth goals while also helping to meet mitigation goals. Others may promote smart growth while locking into place technologies and practices that are inconsistent with the goal of reducing human impacts on climate change. For example, an increasingly decentralized energy supply system may be less vulnerable to large-scale disruption from severe weather events and at the same time have lower greenhouse gas emissions because of more efficient use of local resources and lower losses in transmission and distribution. However, decentralization may also make development more footloose, enabling households and firms to be off the energy grid. Conversely, effective use of district heating often requires high densities of residencies and businesses whose energy demand is met by large-scale power, steam and heat generation.

A new kind of science will be needed to reconcile conflicting strategies and promote sustainable practices. This new kind of science will likely be guided by a high degree of social motivation, must meet the highest scientific standards, and will require a different organization, management and financial structure than is common in traditional environmental science. The managerial and leadership skills necessary to achieve success in such projects is neither taught to the next generation of scientists or decision makers in the institutions that govern land use change and regional development, nor is it well-documented. The chapters in this volume attend to the scientific insights both on the climate change impacts and adaptation front as well as opportunities and challenges for smart growth. The chapters also highlight opportunities for the scientific, modeling, planning and other stakeholder communities to rally around issues that affect all–from the local to the global scale. The next wave of analysis and decision making will need to expand beyond the topics and regions covered in this volume and add case studies from which more general lessons and insights may be extracted. A first step has been made here, but many more will be necessary.

Index